European Policy Research Unit Series

Series Editors: *Simon Bulmer and Michael Moran*

The European Policy Research Unit Series aims to provide advanced text-books and thematic studies of key public policy issues in contemporary Europe. They concentrate, in particular, on comparing patterns of national policy processes and policy content, but pay due attention to the European Union dimension. The thematic studies are guided by the character of the policy issue under examination.

The European Policy Research Unit (EPRU) was set up in 1989 within the University of Manchester's Department of Government to promote research on European politics and public policy. The Series is part of EPRU's effort to facilitate intellectual exchange and substantive debate on the key policy issues confronting the European states and the European Union.

Mass media and media policy in Western Europe

Peter J. Humphreys

Manchester University Press

Manchester and New York

distributed exclusively in the USA and Canada by St Martin's Press

84974

Published by Manchester University Press
Oxford Road, Manchester M13 9NR, UK
and Room 400, 175 Fifth Avenue, New York, NY 10010, USA

Distributed exclusively in the USA and Canada
by St Martin's Press, Inc., 175 Fifth Avenue, New York, NY 10010, USA

British Library Cataloguing-in-Publication Data
A catalogue record for this book is available from the British Library

Library of Congress Cataloging-in-Publication Data
Humphreys, Peter.
    Mass media and media policy in Western Europe / Peter J. Humphreys.
        p.   cm.
    ISBN 0–7190–3196–6.—ISBN 0–7190–3197–4 (pbk.)
    1. Mass media policy—Europe, Western.   2. Mass media—Economic
aspects—Europe, Western.   3. Mass media and technology—Europe,
Western.   I. Title.
P95.82.E85H86   1996
302.23'094—dc20   95-36975
                                                                              CIP

ISBN 0 7190 3196 6 *hardback*
     0 7190 3197 4 *paperback*

First published 1996

00 99 98 97 96   10 9 8 7 6 5 4 3 2 1

Typeset in Great Britain
by Northern Phototypesetting Co Ltd, Bolton
Printed in Great Britain
by Biddles Ltd, Guildford and King's Lynn

Contents

Tables

Preface and acknowledgements

This book provides a comparative study of television and press systems in Western Europe up to the 1990s. It looks at how mass media *systems* have been shaped by technology, economics and politics. It explains how the goals of media freedom and pluralism are constrained by states and markets, and how these goals can be promoted by public policy. It examines patterns and issues of regulation and state intervention, and of public and private control and ownership of the mass media, paying attention to any threats to pluralism that may arise from political and economic pressures. It considers the policies and issues surrounding cable and satellite television and, generally, the commercialisation of national broadcasting systems. It concludes by examining the media policies of the European Union in the age of transfrontier media operations.

My work on European mass media policies began on an ESRC financed research project (grant no. E00232099) directed by Kenneth Dyson, Professor of European Studies at Bradford University, between 1984 and 86. This collaboration produced some joint publications which help to inform Chapters 5 and 6. These are notably: *Broadcasting and New Media Policies in Western Europe: A Comparative Analysis of Technological Change and Public Policy*, Routledge, 1988; and 'Deregulating Broadcasting: the West European Experience', *European Journal of Political Research*, Vol. 17, No. 2, 1989, pp. 137–154. The sections about Germany draw on my book *Media and Media Policy in Germany: The Press and Broadcasting since 1945*, Berg, 1990 and 1994. Part of Chapter 8 is based on P. Humphreys, 'The European Community and Pan–European Broadcasting', *Journal of Area Studies*, Vol. 1, No. 1, 1992, pp. 97–114. Parts of the

Conclusion were presented at the Political Studies Association annual conference, York, 18–20 April 1995, and appear in the published proceedings, J. Lovenduski and J. Stanyer (eds.), *Contemporary Political Studies 1995*, Vol. 3, pp. 1403–1411.

I would like to express my special thanks to the European Institute for the Media in Düsseldorf (and until 1992 at Manchester University), to its past and present directors and to its staff, especially its splendid librarians, for their friendly helpfulness. I consider myself honoured and fortunate to have been an honorary Fellow of the Institute since 1988. The EIM's library, publications and *Bulletin*, edited by Philip Crookes, have all been extremely useful research resources over the years of preparing this book. Thanks are due to the EIM specifically for permission to reproduce Table 6.1 on p. 200–201 which appeared in the *Bulletin*, Vol. 10, No. 4., 1993. At the same time I must make very clear indeed that any errors in this book are mine and mine alone.

I would like to thank Professors Simon Bulmer and Michael Moran for their editorial guidance and also Graeme Leonard for his meticulous copy editing. Finally, most importantly, I thank my wife Sarah, my seven year old daughter Kate and my five year old son James for their support and patience.

Peter J. Humphreys, Government Dept, Manchester, April 1995.

Introduction

The scope, aims and method of the work

The subject of this work is mass media *systems*. It explores the relationship between the economic, technological and political factors that have given them shape. The focus is on macro-structures rather than micro-behaviour. What do Europe's media structures look like? What are their distinctive organisational and regulatory features? How have they developed historically? What are the traditional rationales underpinning Western European media systems? How are these values being challenged? What have been the salient media policy issues past and present? What policy alternatives have existed and exist now? How have policies been made, by whom, and in whose interests? What is the influence of economic lobbies, politicians, the public, etc.? In particular, the book examines the contemporary media policy agenda and highlights the scope for and constraints on public policy making in the rapidly changing field. Throughout, it is concerned with concepts like control, influence and accountability. The core theme is that of pluralism. How pluralistic are media systems? How can public policy contribute to media pluralism?

The study is limited to the press and television sectors. Apart from the historical references to the early days of broadcasting, radio is only mentioned incidentally. This decision is simply determined by the constraint of space. It is justified by the fact that the press and television are the main instruments of the mass media and the main agents of political communication in the modern world. The question of who controls these particular mass media is far more controversial than it is in other fields of the media like cinema, books, records, and even of advertising. Disputes about the ownership of newspapers and commercial television stations, about political influence within public broadcasting corporations, about the independence of journalists and broadcasters, and so on, are both commonplace and serious enough to merit special attention. In answering the kind of questions listed above, it is a central aim of the book to explain the similarities and the differences between Western Europe's media systems. It is a premise of the work that while economic laws and technological developments point generally towards historically convergent outcomes, nationally specific political and cultural factors will explain much of the divergence (Kleinsteuber, 1993, p. 324). Put simply, media systems can be expected to vary significantly across countries because politics and policy have made a difference. Clearly, the definition of 'politics' is broad, encompassing political histories, state traditions, party ideologies, variation in politico-institutional structures and policy orientations.

The systems studied are all highly 'comparable' cases. We shall be looking at the media systems of modern capitalist liberal democracies with many common historical and cultural attributes. Their media systems too have shared many core features. As will be explained, their press systems all evolved largely according to a 'free market' model. The forces of economics and technology tended to produce quite convergent patterns of press development, though policy and culture (and market size) still produced some interesting variation. European broadcasting systems came to share a core attachment to a model of 'public-service'. Given the rather greater role of politics, national broadcasting models varied more than in the case of the press. Nonetheless, national distinctiveness could be measured against a shared core model of 'public-service' broadcasting. Accordingly, the comparative method of the book is essentially a simple one. The salient core features of media systems – the 'free press' and 'public-service broadcasting' – are described and analysed. Their historical development, the major policy issues they raise, and the contemporary challenges they face, will all be addressed in a general way. Special attention will be given to cases of interesting national distinctiveness. These may occur because of departure from the norm. Equally they may arise because certain countries display special mechanisms or structures for fulfilling common normative goals. An attempt will be made to abstract lessons from the empirical evidence, to establish causal relationships, to weigh up the balance of factors making for certain developments and – not least of all – to point out the main policy issues, policy alternatives and policy problems.

The lay-out and central theme of the book

The book opens with questions concerning press freedom: how it historically came to be achieved, how it was defined as market freedom, how the market's operations affected the political press and the principal sources of news, and some of the economic constraints on the operation of the press (Chapter 1). Moving on, the book explores how much constraint, in the post-war period, has been placed on the free press by state action, law, and self-regulation (Chapter 2). The study proceeds (in Chapter 3) to examine how free markets and self-regulation have produced only limited press pluralism, and to discuss the contribution that public policy has made and might make to promote press pluralism. The book then turns to the broadcasting sector, looking first at the various rationales – technical, economic and political – for Western Europe's 'public-service' broadcasting monopolies. The various ways pluralism was promoted, and also abbreviated, by this traditional model of broadcasting are examined (Chapter 4). The book then moves on to examine how much plural isation of broadcasting has followed from the abolition of the public monopoly model and from the technical diversification of the broadcasting sector with the spread of cable television and satellite channels (Chapters 5, 6 and 7). The book concludes by examining the role assumed already by the European Community in media policy making and discusses the contemporary nature and future scope of European Union action to promote pluralism and competitive European markets on the threshold of the age of digital multi-channel broadcasting and multi-media communication (Chapter 8).

Throughout, a central aim of the work is to examine the extent to which those in positions to exert media power have been able to circumscribe the freedom of the media. Vulnerability to state interference is clearly the Achilles heel of publicly owned media. Yet, it will be argued, the press is no more free from market-based power holders. Certainly no less important than interference with, or even the downright politicisation of, broadcasting corporations is the question of the concentration of private proprietorial control of influential newspapers, magazines, and broadcasting stations. When media power becomes concentrated in a few hands pluralism is obviously threatened. Therefore, much of the study examines the extent to which there have been monopolistic or oligopolistic developments in the private commercial sectors of the media. In this regard, it is necessary to address the question of the extent to which, in the cause of pluralism, mass media, especially press and broadcasting, have been – and should still be – kept apart from each other in matters of ownership and control. Recent multi-media diversification strategies of companies have made this question of the 'separation of media powers' a very controversial issue. In sum, the work is much concerned with how public policy has been, and might further be, enlisted to safeguard pluralism – at the national and European levels.

The 'pluralist' versus 'dominance' perspectives on the mass media

Media theory provides two ideal-type polar views of how the power of the mass media might be exercised: the 'pluralist' and the 'dominance' perspectives. Following McQuail (1987, pp. 85–88), the 'dominance' perspective stresses the following features. Media power resides in the control of a dominant elite or ruling class. Ownership and/or control of the media organisations is highly centralised and concentrated in the hands of a relatively small number of very powerful interests. Media production is 'standardized, routinized, and controlled' by these interests. The media, thus organised, present a 'selective' view of the world, decided 'from above'. They reinforce the hold of the dominant interests over society. They present a very limited range of largely 'undifferentiated' viewpoints. They filter out alternatives and reduce the critical capacity of the public. The audience is a dependent, passive, mass public. The media therefore 'confirm' the established social order (McQuail, 1987, pp. 85–86).

By contrast, the 'pluralist' perspective stresses the more or less exact opposite. Media power is constrained within a social and institutional framework which is not dominated by any unified elite. Control is open to 'competing political, social and cultural interests and groups'. Power in the media system is balanced between a significant number of independent sources. The media system is 'open to change and democratic control'. Media output is 'creative, free, and original'. It is seen as a cultural good. Media production is free of coercion, censorship and editorial dominance. The media, therefore, present a range of 'diverse and competing views'. They respond to public demand rather than *vice versa*. They provide an avenue of expression of minority and alternative viewpoints. The audience is a 'differentiated' and independent public. It is 'fragmented, selective, reactive and active'. The media have a particularly important role as a 'Fourth Estate' of liberal pluralism. Rather than confirm the social power of a dominant elite, they criticise, circumscribe and exert an important measure of control over the actions of elites (McQuail, 1987, pp. 86–88; also Negrine, 1994, pp. 15–19).

These models are, of course, pure or 'ideal' types. The simple dichotomy between 'dominance' and 'pluralism' is a useful starting-point, but in reality media systems contain a complex mixture of these features. Media systems of West European liberal democracies may aspire to the 'pluralist' model. Yet, elite theorists have pointed to the tendency of all societies to produce a 'power elite' or 'Establishment' exercising power through bureaucratic regulatory structures and socio-economic networks. Marxists, of course, have always judged capitalist society, and therefore capitalist media systems, to exhibit class domination (for a classic exposition of the role of media in capitalist society, see Miliband, 1969, pp. 197–214). Marxists stress how market forces work within the media system *inevitably* to produce market 'dominance'; monopolies and oligopolies that con centrate economic and social power – and here media power – in the hands of a few. However, it is certainly not necessary to be an elite-theorist or a marxist to see how liberal–democratic media systems may contain at least certain elements of 'dominance'. Non-marxist industrial economists have always been concerned about the kind of public policies that may be required to keep markets competitive (ie. to counteract market dominance). Similarly, pluralist political scientists accept that between the diverse interests in society perfect competition simply does not exist. Quite evidently some interests predominate: imperfect competition is the rule. 'Neo-pluralists', in particular, have emphasised that business interests have a very privileged position within capitalist systems and, accordingly, business interests and values are highly influential within their commercial media (for a classic exposition of this viewpoint, see Lindblom, 1977). All pluralists, though, reject the marxist view of state, society and media, being dominated by an identifiable 'ruling class'. Also, pluralists allow that scope exists – by means of all manner of institutional, constitutional and legal constraints, and through regulation and public policy – to countervail traits of 'dominance' in politics and markets.

All the same, the media still occupy a vulnerable space of relative and conditional freedom between the market and the state. Ownership and control of the mass media is not necessarily always diffuse, democratically accountable, and responsive to public demands. To a marked extent the press is in the hands of large business interests while the public broadcasters are exposed – to a greater or lesser degree – to government or party pressures. Media production is, very often, not simply free and creative. Nor is media output necessarily seen as primarily a cultural good. The commercial media have been industrialised along capitalistic lines. This implies a degree of standardisation, routinisation and managerial control. It also implies a 'commodification' of media outputs. Nor is this media output invariably diverse and pluralistic. The dictates of commercialism may have a homogenising effect. The media may be geared, for instance, towards entertainment at the cost of other values. On the ideological front, powerful proprietors, with economic interests and particular political convictions and social views, will be in a position to use their media outlets to promote and to proselytise. Equally, politicians may try to press their causes through exerting influence on the publicly controlled broadcasters. As for the idea that the media have to be responsive to consumer demands, this is only the case in competitive markets. Wherever choice is limited – or where numerical choice simply means choosing between similar products – consumers will actually have rather little 'sovereignty'. Bureaucratic regulation may be no better at ensuring public accountability and responsiveness, and may be worse. Moreover, journalists and other production workers may have little control over their own creative or investigative activity. Proprietorial power, editorial disciplines, state secrecy, political interference, may all seriously restrict journalistic freedom to pursue this kind of activity. Against all this, regulatory frameworks and media policies geared towards promoting pluralism and diversity, openness and accountability, investigation and free creativity, are certainly conceivable. It is, of course, a hallmark of liberal democracies that they aspire to pursue the ideal of pluralism. Even imperfect pluralism is held to be far better than its authoritarian or monopolistic alternatives. This book inclines towards certain views, this will be clear. Yet, it aims to allow the reader enough scope, on the basis of evidence from a range of sources, to decide for herself

or himself the extent to which West European media systems are pluralist, and how much they exhibit traits of dominance.

Four historically derived ideal types of media system

The concepts of 'pluralism' and 'dominance' are the benchmarks by
which we can judge media systems, but we also need a workable
theoretical framework of analysis. Siebert, Peterson and Schramm
produced a useful framework for classifying media systems in their
1956 classic, *Four Theories of the Press*. (By 'press' they meant all
mass communications although more attention was given to the
press because television was still young at the time of writing.)
Negrine (1994, p. 25) suggests that 'there has been no significant
advance on the theories of the press as set out by Siebert *et al*.*
McQuail (1987, pp. 111–123) also gives their model considerable
attention, suggesting that it 'remains the major source and point of
reference' for comparative press theory (p. 111). Siebert *et al*. provide
a historical exploration of the four philosophical and political 'rationales' that have been relevant for Europe's mass media systems.
These are coupled into the 'authoritarian' and its modern outgrowth,
the 'Soviet-totalitarian' rationales; and the 'libertarian' and its
modified 'social-responsibility' rationales. The former two clearly fell
at the 'dominance' end of the above mentioned continuum. The
latter two took the 'pluralist' pole as their lodestar. As Negrine goes
on to note, this framework could be criticised for being too optimistic about the virtues and achievements of the Western pluralist
rationales. (They were writing at the height of the Cold War). It was
also over-informed by the US experience of 'social responsibility'.
Consequently, as Negrine notes, it failed to address adequately the
European contribution to the panoply of media rationales, namely
that of public-service broadcasting. Nevertheless, *Four Theories of
the Press* does provide a useful theoretical starting point for our
inquiry. What then did they say?

The authoritarian rationale was the dominant feature of the media
systems of Europe's *ancien régime*, before liberal democratisation. It

---

* It should be noted that Negrine sees the need to re-think media theory to take
account of the impact of new developments, notably internationalisation. The theme
is developed in this book.

came into being in the 'authoritarian climate' of the late Renaissance, following the invention of printing. It reflected the dominant ideology of absolutism. The press functioned 'from the top down'. Its main goals were to uphold established authority and social order. Truth was 'the property of power'. This was the justification for widespread and extensive licensing and regulation, libel and sedition laws, and censorship. In practice, there was some tolerance of elite political discussion and politico-philosophical debate. Enlightenment thinking did find its way into print. However, open and direct criticism of public authority and officialdom was strictly proscribed. The press certainly did not act as a check on government. It mattered little if media were privately or publicly owned, they remained subservient to the state. But they were not mobilised massively by the state as they were under totalitarianism.

A twentieth-century phenomenon, the totalitarian rationale based itself on powerful ideologies. Totalitarian media structures were 'in and of' the state, directed nominally on behalf of the interests of nation or class. Siebert *et al.* focused on the Soviet variant, suggesting that Nazi media control had been a complex mix of old authoritarianism and modern totalitarianism. A key difference was certainly that the Nazis tolerated private press ownership. All the same, the degree of media control was awesome. Both Nazi and Stalinist systems were far more repressive than the old authoritarianism. They disposed of modern technologies and mass distribution systems that made the media's reach all-pervasive. Nazis and Soviet Communists alike 'instrumentalised' the media for propaganda and social control. Western Europe's experience of both the authoritarian and the totalitarian rationales served to strengthen the commitment of liberal elites to the 'libertarian' rationale.

Liberal ideas (of Locke, Mill, the Enlightenment, etc.) provided the foundation of the 'libertarian' rationale. The latter's displacement of the authoritarian rationale occurred gradually over several centuries, but was mainly achieved by the nineteenth-century progress of liberalism in Western Europe. As just suggested, the experience of twentieth-century collapse into Fascism or Fascist occupation, together with the Cold War ideological confrontation with Communism, served to reinforce the 'libertarian' underpinnings of the free press in post-World War II Western Europe. In this model licensing and (most) peace-time censorship were abolished. State interference was deemed illegitimate save for the protection of state security and individual freedoms such as privacy. Press infractions like libel and defamation, were now the business of the courts. The main purposes of the media, from the libertarian perspective, were to inform objectively, to entertain and to sell copy. It was also held to be important that the media should serve to discover truth and to act as a check on government. At the core of this rationale was the notion that 'a free market of ideas' was both possible and highly desirable. The libertarian rationale had a key economic component: media activity was considered to be capitalistic, commercial and open to anyone. In essence, press freedom was analogous to a property right. This obviously placed a practical limitation on the 'free market of ideas'. The privately owned press was, in an important sense, the servant of a restricted number of owners.

This leads us, finally, to consider the 'social responsibility' rationale of Siebert *et al.*. A modification of the libertarian model, the doctrine gained ground during the early post-war period because of growing recognition of the pure libertarian model's shortfalls: notably, the limited public access it had granted; the way that industrialisation and commercialism of the free press was constricting other media values; and perhaps above all because of the concentration of media ownership in the hands of a powerful few. The power and monopoly position of the media in terms of providing information to the public, it was now felt, placed a special obligation on media owners and managers to be 'socially responsible'. The arrival of television and the growth of broadcasting as a mass medium too posed problems for the libertarian model: the air-waves were in limited supply. This necessitated some public control even if only to allocate frequencies. The libertarian model's stress on the media's role in establishing truth and checking government was now developed further to emphasise the need for informed public debate. Freedom of the press was no longer deemed to be sufficient; the citizenry required *adequate* information. The media had to reflect social diversity and minority viewpoints, to respond to community opinion and to respect professional ethics. The informational, educative and cultural purposes of the media were strongly emphasised. The marketplace should not be allowed to obstruct these aims. Public regulation and even ownership might be required. In fact, the latter was the case for nearly all of Europe's broadcasting institutions. In the field of the press or privately owned broadcasters, these 'social responsibility' duties might be safeguarded by such means as: specific media laws and regulatory codes; self-regulation by press councils or, for private broadcasters, by independent regulatory authorities; professional codes of ethics and advertising standards authorities; anti-monopoly legislation and direct market intervention (eg. subsidies to promote press pluralism); and so on (see McQuail, 1987, p. 117). Whatever the mechanism, it was held desirable that the media should serve society.

This book will be very much concerned with the relationship, and tension, between what are in effect the libertarian and social responsibility rationales advanced by Siebert *et al.* However, the term free market is generally preferred to indicate what Siebert *et al.* mean by 'libertarian' which is essentially the *laissez-faire* free market operation of the media. As we shall see, the West European press has functioned largely in a free market context overlain with certain 'social responsibility' features. Moreover, as suggested, we need to extend the understanding of the 'social responsibility' rationale (Siebert *et al.*) to include a 'public service' dimension relevant to West European public-service broadcasting. Their 'social responsibility' theory, elaborated with the US situation very much in mind, did not explore the possibilities of public ownership and strict regulation. Indeed, Siebert *et al.* had a distinctly market-orientated understanding of 'social responsibility'. Broadcasting in the USA remained very close to the libertarian/free market model. In Western Europe, by contrast, broadcasting was conducted as a 'public-service' monopoly (or duopoly) and it was strictly regulated. It was also far closer to politics and the state than intended by the American model which favoured privately owned media, a limited role for regulation, and 'hands off' government.

Moreover, the West European experience of public-service media stimulated yet another normative theory of the media of considerable relevance to our concerns: the 'democratic-participant' rationale (McQuail, 1987, pp. 121–123). The principal achievement of the public-service model was that it ensured a more diverse range of programming than the commercial US broadcasters, yet it was also open to criticism for being elitist/paternalist, bureaucratic and too close to the state and political elites. There arose, therefore, a radical theory of democratic participation which called for the democratisation of the media, and in particular the granting of far more opportunity for grass-roots and minority expression. This rationale had what we might call a 'Left-libertarian' ethos in that it sought freedom from the 'dominance' supplied both by the operations of the free market (eg. media concentration) and by the bureaucratic and politicised public-service models of media organisation. This 'democratic-participant' rationale informed the development of new ideas for democratising the public-service model and providing scope for a decentralised and publicly accessible range of non-market, non-state communications systems (Keane, 1991 and 1992). However, as we shall see, the shortfalls of the traditional public-service model also stimulated a radical 'Right-libertarian', neo-liberal critique that argued that the public-service principle had had its day and that there should be a return to *laissez-faire* media policy. Libertarians of both the Left and the Right pointed to how features of authoritarian dominance might still be detected in modern liberal-democratic media systems. However, they disagreed profoundly about the kind of reforms that were required. Some modest concessions were made to the 'democratic-participant' critique by the public-service broadcasters themselves from the 1960s onwards. However, as will be seen, the 1980s and 1990s saw the Right-libertarians in the ascendant. Most on the Left therefore now felt compelled to rally to the defence of an increasingly beleaguered traditional public-service model.

Political systems and the media

Liberal-democracies assume manifold forms. It is interesting to examine how these different forms impact on the question of media pluralism. A central hypothesis here is that, all things being equal, in the relations between state and the mass media, the ideal of pluralism in the latter will probably best be served by political systems that exhibit diffused and weak rather than concentrated and strong state power. One very useful distinction, therefore, is that between 'consensual' and 'majoritarian' democracies. In the former, the executive is constrained by various checks and balances and power is shared between political forces and levels of government. The latter allow for the largely unconstrained exercise of majority power by highly centralised governments. In these 'majoritarian' systems, we might expect the publicly owned media to be more vulnerable to capture by the dominant political tendency. By contrast, in consensual – 'power-sharing' – systems, we might reasonably expect influence over the media to be shared (on 'majoritarian' and 'consensus' democracy, see Lijphart, 1984).

As we shall see, these distinctions are worthwhile. Media power is shared in a number of Western European systems which, in their political structures, are 'consensual' in various ways and to different degrees. The Netherlands provides the best example of a very consensual, 'power-sharing' media system. But Germany, too, provides an example of a system where power is divided by federalism and the strong role of the country's Constitutional Court. A power-sharing tradition is reflected in a culture of 'negotiation government'. This is manifest in the relations between the *Länder* (i.e. the states in the sense of sub-national units of government) which are mainly responsible for media policy. It is manifest in the relations between the parties as well. Power-sharing is also reflected in the tradition of *Proporz* (influence in proportion to party strength). It is also evident in the corporatism that gives special 'voice' to the 'socially significant groups' and organised interests. Germany and many of Europe's small countries are consensual in this corporatist sense to greater or lesser extents (see below). By contrast, Britain and France are countries that have been characterised by strong and centralised executives that have been comparatively unconstrained in the exercise of their authority. One-party government in Britain and presidentialism in Fifth Republic France, plus the fact it had one of the weakest legislatures among liberal democracies, has conferred on governments in both of these countries tremendous potential for majoritarian rule.* In theory, this has presented more opportunity for media control and greater scope for executive voluntarism in media policy-making. As we shall see, France certainly testified to this possibility. In Britain, other factors worked against it.

In this connection, it is important not to ignore the importance of political traditions. Political convention and state tradition go a long way towards explaining why majoritarianism has not greatly affected the British media system, at least until under Prime Minister Thatcher (Humphreys, 1991). In great contrast to Britain and the United States, France had a long tradition of a 'strong state' (on state traditions see Dyson, 1980). This tradition went back as far as the monarchical system and owed much to Louis X1V and his chief minister Jean Baptiste Colbert (1619–83). Indeed, 'Colbertism' is the term often given to the French tradition of industrial interventionism

---

* Surprisingly Lijphart did not see France as 'majoritarian'. Here it is argued that France is!

or *dirigisme*. The triumph of the Jacobins in the French revolution and subsequent Napoleonic innovations meant that this statism – or *étatisme* – endured and flourished in the nineteenth and twentieth centuries. In particular, the Liberation of France after the Second World War saw a massive increase in state *dirigisme*. Finally, the Fifth Republic (1958–) greatly strengthened central political authority and confirmed the state's already overweening bureaucratic power and dominance. As we shall see, this statism (*étatisme*) has been a constant constraint on the media. Indeed, Kuhn (1995, p. 10) has noted that the 'key political actor ... whose role must be central to any analysis of the media in France, is the state'. Britain, by contrast, has usually been seen as having had a comparatively 'weak state' tradition. Britain's industrial and social modernisation was conducted in a culture imbued with doctrines of economic liberalism and of distinctly arm's length government. This British 'weak state' tradition was mirrored in the development of a non-political civil service and also of correspondingly strong institutions of civil society; among which towered key public institutions like the BBC and later the IBA. However, British 'liberalism', it should be pointed out, always had a strong economic ingredient which reasserted itself in the shape of 1980s 'neo-liberalism'. Public-service institutions like the BBC and the IBA have been profoundly shaken up in the name of the free market doctrine. Britain's 'weak state' tradition may have contributed to the rise of comparatively independent public institutions; as we shall see, it also served the free market well. Also, the British state does not appear to be so weak when it comes to looking to state's own interests (e.g. security) – hence the glaring paradox of a 'weak state' tradition but a highly centralised, secretive and occasionally very 'strong' state.

Though useful, the strong state/weak state distinction is rather limiting. Katzenstein (1985) has carried it further by adding a category to 'liberal' states like Britain (and the United States) and 'statist' states like France. In this new category were the northern European 'democratic corporatist' ones where organised social interests played a stronger and much more formalised role within the policy-making process than in either of the other two cases. In fact, many writers have pointed to the 'social partnership' – the politics of consensus – that has characterised Scandinavia and Austria, the Benelux countries, Switzerland and post-war (West) Germany. Katzenstein explains how important was the economic vulnerability of small countries as a factor for their characteristic politics of consensus (Germany was an exception to this 'small state' rule but there social consensus was similarly given a high premium for obvious historical reasons). Indeed, this theme has been picked up by experts on these small countries' media systems and policies. For most of the post-war period, corporatism was the very foundation of these countries' media policies; the 'social partners' were involved in making all important media policy decisions and the political parties, too, shared in this consensual approach. Corporatism, and its politics of compromise and consensus, was a particularly efficient way of managing the problems of preserving cultural autonomy and social harmony in economically vulnerable small states. During the 1980s, however, far-reaching processes of marketisation and internationalisation – to be explored in the latter half of this book – threatened to undermine this model of social partnership and to empower instead increasingly internationalised commercial interests (Trappel, 1991; Meier and Trappel, 1992).

Finally, an interesting concept, with potential relevance to understanding the relations between media and politics, has been developed by Katz and Mair (1995). Focusing on the historical evolution of the West European political party, Katz and Mair have come up with the concept of the 'cartel party'. Their theory holds that in much of post-war (North) Western Europe the mainstream parties have tended in effect to 'collude' with each other in that they have accepted to compete in only a rather limited sense and instead they have sought to share in government (we might add, either in central coalitions or through the 'power-sharing' implicit in federal systems). For these 'cartel parties', interested in controlling state resources, control of the media has been one of the principal attractions of office (access to party subsidies being another). It is interesting to note that Katz and Mair (1995, p. 17) consider this pattern to be most developed in – more or less consensual – 'countries such as Austria, Denmark, Germany, Finland, Norway and Sweden, where a tradition of inter-party cooperation combines with a … privileging of party in relation to patronage appointments'. Most pertinently for our purposes, Katz and Mair continue: 'it is likely to be least developed in a country such as the United Kingdom', with a 'tradition of adversary politics' and 'where the possibilities for patronage, while growing, also remain relatively limited'. As we shall see in Chapter 4, this concept would appear to have considerable purchase – at least for explaining the power relations between parties and the publicly owned media.

The new media revolution: back towards the 'libertarian' – free market – model?

In an important sense, developments in the media have always been driven by new technologies. The invention of the movable letter-press by Johannes Gutenberg ushered in a media revolution in the mid-fifteenth century; the application of rotary printing from the latter decades of the nineteenth century onwards industrialised the press; the introduction of computerised systems in the 1970s and 1980s was not without a major impact on the economics of newspapers as well as on the conditions and practices of media workers. In the modern era, first telegraphy and later advanced telecommunications revolutionised news-gathering. The invention of radio in the early twentieth century and the later invention of television constituted another communications revolution. The 1980s has seen another leap: with the convergence of information technology and the mass media, yet another 'communications revolution' has been under way for some time now. Much of the second part of this book is concerned with the attendant policy issues and in particular with the new technologies' impact on traditional broadcasting structures and regulatory policies. It will be argued that technological change has been instrumental in bringing about a 'paradigmatic change' from a model of public-service broadcasting towards a newly marketised model of electronic media.

At first sight this might imply the triumph of the libertarian/free market model, in key respects, over the social responsibility/public service model. Certainly, modern-day neo-liberal advocates of the former model see the latter as an anachronism in the age of multichannel broadcasting systems that is being brought about by cable and satellite broadcasting. Indeed, visionaries now predict the fairly imminent demise of 'broadcasting' as we know it. In its place, they announce, we will soon see 'electronic publishing'. Broadcasting, they suggest, is becoming analogous to the press sector. The regulators, they argue, should retreat with dignity because the broadcast media will escape from the state in any case. Moreover, new digital techniques (see the Conclusion) will mean mass broadcasting to pas-

audiences is replaced by hundreds of 'interactive' channels owing the consumers (though only subscribers) to call up the information and entertainment services of their choice from a vastly expanded menu. Even advertisers are said to be worried that there will be little place left for traditional commercials. Instead, they will soon have to find new ways of reaching audiences that are no longer held captive for them. From this perspective, the public-service broadcasting model, so much a special feature of Western Europe's media scene, is now written off merely as a temporary expedient for an age of limited hertzian air-space (broadcasting frequencies).

However, critics of this viewpoint point out that it reeks of technical adventurism and economic sophistry as well as, of course, 'social irresponsibility'. Certainly, one weakness of the above argument is that it derives too many conclusions from the diversification of possibilities for broadcasting distribution (including 'interactivity'). What has been missing in the debate, is an understanding that media economics is essentially about funding diverse programmes, sustaining an adequate choice of newspapers and magazines, affording networks of foreign correspondents, access to different news sources and so forth. Without public policies to meet these challenges, the counter-argument goes, large sections of the media industry will be unlikely to withstand the effects of fragmenting markets. Moreover, those that do will be the giant corporations. Media concentration, not media pluralism, will ensue. And all this is not to mention the harmful consequences of allowing market values to swamp the social responsibility/public-service functions of the media. Following this latter line of argument, the state should not abdicate its regulatory responsibilities. Instead, new market and technological developments should be seen as opportunities for policy innovation. Within the marketised paradigm, new rules and regulations, possibly new regulatory institutions, certainly new regulatory practices, are required to tackle the dangers of emerging oligopolistic structures of unaccountable market-based media power. They are needed to ensure that the new media do not have a harmful homogenising impact ('wall to wall' commercialism). They are needed to protect journalistic independence (not served at all well by the 'free' market's preference for 'flexible' employment contracts and a 'casualised' media workforce). They are needed more than ever to protect the cultural function of the media and to promote the cultural values of localities, small countries, and so on. Certainly, a new note of urgency can be detected in the calls for regulatory initiatives to counter media-concentration; to do more to secure journalists' independence (for instance by underpinning their employment and co-determination rights); to act more strenuously to limit media cross-ownership, and so forth. Given that satellite broadcasting has made for increasingly internationalised markets, some look hopefully to the European Union as an appropriate source of this kind of regulatory inspiration and policy initiative (see Chapter 8). For the advocates of continued social responsibility and public service, the press is no model for broadcasting. Rather, they see a new need to look afresh at the shortfalls of the 'free press' model as it has been practised. Whatever the viewpoint, the problem nowadays is how to ensure that the mass media perform in the best public interest – in the interests of pluralism – under the new technological and international market constraints.

1

Press freedom: the free market and the development of the modern press

The obligatory starting point, in studying the European press, is to mention the invention by Gutenberg in the mid-fifteenth century in the small German city of Mainz, of the movable letter press. Thereupon, printing companies proliferated across Europe. Thus began the 'first age of printing' (McQuail, 1992b, p. 5). At the same time the growth of a class of merchants, with its own special communication needs, led to the establishment of early postal systems. Printing became an industry serving commerce. This age was accompanied by the first stirrings of the demand for press freedom. However, these developments provoked a reactionary response from traditional authorities. Worried by the political consequences of a free flow of information, state and church – the *ancien régime* – developed strict systems for the censorship and licensing of printed matter. To publish political comment was to risk confiscation of printing presses, imprisonment of journalists and so on. Enlightenment thinking gradually undermined authoritarianism, but the freeing of the press had to await the overthrow or passing of the *ancien régime*. The American and French revolutions produced classic statements of press freedom: the 1791 First Amendment of US Constitution and the 1789 Declaration of the Rights of Man and Citizens. Whether won by revolution or not, press freedom was very much a product of the decline of pre-democratic elites and the rise to social and political power in their stead of the 'bourgeois' or liberal capitalist middle classes in the 'early industrial age' (McQuail, 1992b, pp. 6–7; Hardt, 1983, pp. 291–308).

The historical origins of freedom of the press: the granting of political freedom

The detailed picture is rather more complicated. Industrial capitalism was certainly crucially important for the growth of the modern press. It provided an abundance of print materials, communications infrastructure, modern technical facilities, and so forth. It also created a huge demand for news and information, primarily for commercial purposes. It contributed to the financial independence of the press, seen by many as no less than the midwife to press freedom. But the purely legal emancipation of the press depended, mainly, on the decline of traditional power structures. In Scandinavia, press freedom was actually granted long before the region industrialised. Famously, Sweden's parliament adopted a Freedom of Press Act as early as 1766 as part of its first constitution. Similarly, press freedom was granted by Norway's 1814 constitution. Both of these countries had a relatively weak experience of feudalism; the power of the aristocracy was much constrained by the existence of a strong peasant middle class that was a crucial outrider of the egalitarianism that came to distinguish modern Scandinavian society. Holland too – which granted press freedom as early as 1815 – had a fairly weak feudal experience and a long-established mercantile bourgeoisie (Katzenstein, 1985, pp. 158–159). The British case was also exceptional. Not only was Britain the first industrial nation in Europe, it also developed a strong orientation to *laissez-faire*. Britain developed a 'weak state' tradition in which the market was empowered and largely safeguarded from the interference of officialdom. Britain actually dispensed with state licensing of the press as early as 1694, following the Glorious Revolution (1688) which put an end once and for all to absolutism. All the same, Britain's early 'bourgeois' state successfully kept newspaper circulations restricted to a social elite by subjecting the press to stringent taxation. The 'taxes on knowledge' were only repealed in the period 1853 to 1861. Since newspapers were rendered expensive, their readership remained the bourgeoisie.

In France, where absolutism and feudalism were more strongly implanted, the first surge towards liberal democratisation – and press freedom – occurred violently, with the French Revolution. Thereupon, press freedom was boldly announced by Article 11 of the 1789 Declaration of the Rights of Man and Citizens. Briefly, a free press flourished before it was once again repressed successively by the

Directory, the Consulate, Napoleon I and the monarchist Restoration. Nevertheless, the growth of a liberal press, backed by business interests, with a circulation fast out-growing that of the royalists, was a major factor in the collapse of the Bourbon monarchy in 1830. However, the repressive 1835 press laws of its Orleanist successor regime immediately took revenge. The 1848 Revolution introduced another brief period of general press freedom before it too was replaced by the repression of the Napoleonic Second Empire (1851–70). Only with consolidation of the Third Republic, were sweeping bourgeois freedoms such as freedom of assembly and press freedom at last introduced in 1881. It was no coincidence that this was the very year that the Republicans gained their first large parliamentary majority. At the time this law was widely seen as being the most liberal in Europe. 'Crimes of opinion' were now abolished save only for the offence of insulting the President and defamation of the public authorities. Nominally at least, this law specifically protected the press from all *a priori* administrative action and stipulated that all *a posteriori* action against supposed abuses by the press be the subject of due legal process. Although the infamous *lois scélérates*, enacted by the Right in 1894, briefly re-imposed strict penalties on 'press offences', the Third Republic (1875–1940) was a period of marked *laissez-faire*. Therefore, the year 1881, shortly after the adoption of liberal democracy, was when France definitively gained press freedom.

Meanwhile, the 1848 revolutions had seen press freedom introduced in two more northern European small states. Denmark's constitution of 1849 enshrined press freedom. In Switzerland the 1848 revolution saw the culmination of decades of struggle between liberals and conservatives and the extension of press freedom to every canton. Both of these countries had long since seen the erosion of what were anyway comparatively weak feudal traditions. In Denmark the 'Age of the Nobles' had ended in the mid-seventeenth century. Like the Netherlands, Switzerland had a tradition of municipal (and cantonal) freedom. Also very like the Netherlands, both Denmark and Switzerland had a markedly strong mercantile bourgeois class (Katzenstein, 1985, pp. 159–160). Thereafter, the period from about 1850 to the turn of century could be described as the 'high bourgeois' phase of press history (McQuail, 1987, p. 12). In Britain, Scandinavia, Switzerland and the Low Countries – and from 1881 onwards in France – the extension of press freedom reflected the triumph of bourgeois liberalism. It followed from the rise of commercial and/or industrial middle classes, and their successful challenge to the established political power of traditional, authoritarian, pre-democratic elites. Moreover, as the bourgeoisie grew stronger during the latter half of the century, press laws were liberalised to a significant extent even in countries that remained essentially authoritarian and pre-democratic, where the forces of bourgeois liberalism remained blocked or diverted into national–conservative directions.

In Habsburg Austria the practice of pre-publication censorship was formally abolished by a law of 1862. In Bismarckian Germany, too, the first national press law of 1874 abolished pre-publication censorship and the state-licensing of most newspapers. Post-publication censorship was certainly not dispensed with in either of these cases, yet these important measures of liberalisation, by what remained highly conservative, regimes (especially Germany), were important steps towards press freedom. They reflected the rising socio-economic influence of the industrial and commercial middle classes. In Germany, by now undergoing rapid and intense socio-economic modernisation, the free expression of bourgeois political opinion was already widespread. Germany's tremendous industrialisation also produced Europe's strongest labour movement; the labour movement lent its considerable weight to the demand for a greater extension of democracy and press freedom. Bismarck's infamous Anti-Socialist Law of 1878, outlawing the publication of socialist opinions until lifted ten years later, served only to encourage the growth of Europe's most vigorous socialist press, albeit one that had to remain underground for the period in question. *Vorwärts*, the famous organ of the German SPD (Social Democrats), was founded in 1876.

What precisely was meant by press freedom?

The achievement of a free press, then, was a function of the transition to 'bourgeois' liberal democracy. What, though, exactly was meant by press freedom? In the first instance, of course, it implied abolition of practices like licensing and censorship. More generally, press freedom meant acceptance of the principle of the legitimate freedom of the press to become a Fourth Estate in the political realm. Newspapers became freer to engage in political debate, to publish social and political comment, and even to criticise state authority without fear of punishment or imprisonment. The 'bourgeois' press reflected new liberal values like independence from the state and antipathy to pre-democratic interests. Newspapers aligned themselves with the new social and economic elites and in particular with the bourgeois political parties that emerged during the nineteenth century to contest politics democratically. Indeed the press played a key role in the development of democratic politics. Negrine (1994, p. 42) notes that by the mid-point of the nineteenth century all the English metropolitan dailies, and four-fifths of the provincial press, reflected a commitment to either the Conservatives or the Liberals. The free press also brought a growing sense of 'social responsibility' and introduced an important measure of political reformism. It created a new journalistic professional class, dedicated increasingly to social criticism and an ethic of objective reporting. In Britain, where press freedom was never explicitly enshrined in statute, Negrine notes that by the mid-nineteenth century the press had emerged from its 'pre-Victorian shackles'.

By stark contrast, in Germany during the period of the Imperial *Obrigkeitsstaat* (the Bismarckian and Wilhelmine 'authoritarian' state), the press remained for the most part politically acquiescent. In Germany, it required defeat in World War I to bring about the full instauration of liberal freedoms. Thereupon, the liberal democratic Weimar Republic (1918–33) duly saw the majority of newspapers develop easily identifiable political allegiances and give free expression to political views. In fact, during the Weimar Republic's short lifespan, there flowered a rich diversity of free political reporting. Therefore, by the early part of the twentieth century the concept of press freedom had widely taken root across Western Europe. Moreover, by now a distinctly socialist press had appeared on the scene. Indeed, the first half of the twentieth century was the heyday of an overtly political press as a sub-section of the press.

The heyday of the political press

Political press freedom meant that the press became intimately involved in the political realm. Newspapers adopted political postures, reported a variety of political views, and developed partisan political identifications and alignments. There also quickly developed a thriving 'party press'. (For a highly interesting political-science discussion of press/party system 'parallelism', see Seymour-Ure, 1974, pp. 156–201). Alongside the general commercial press, characterised by mass-readership newspapers, there typically grew up a large number of smaller overtly political papers. These might have political paymasters, they might be owned outright by the parties themselves, often they were privately owned but still maintained very close political links. The inter-war period was a golden age for the political press. This was altogether unsurprising. It was a period of mobilisation in a new era of mass politics. Political cleavages were deep. Economic crises, immediately after World War I and again in the 1930s, contributed to the politicisation. Liberal democratic stability was precarious, national and social integration equally so. In this context, the political press was highly ideological.

In many countries, the labour movement remained 'negatively integrated'. Religion too served to 'negatively integrate' whole communities. During this period, for example, Dutch society was 'pillarised' into distinct socio-political segments. About two-thirds of the press became linked to the Calvinist, Catholic, Liberal (secular middle-class) and Labour pillars. Austria was similarly divided, but far more bitterly, into mutually antagonistic 'black' and 'red' subcultural 'camps' (*Lager*). The 'black' camp was Catholic, bourgeois and very strongly implanted in rural Austria. The 'red' camp was anti-clerical, working-class and concentrated in urban districts. Each *Lager* had an extensive network of political newspapers. Similarly, in Germany around a third of the press sector was accounted for by 'party papers': the Catholics had over 400, the Social Democrats around 200, and the Communists around fifty. In the early 1930s the number of Nazi papers grew from a handful to over a hundred. In France, too, a multiplicity of newspapers reflected conservative and centrist positions. The Radicals – the backbone of the Third Republic – had a number of papers, so too did the Left. One of these was *Humanité*. This newspaper still has a loyal readership today. Founded in 1904 by Jean Jaurès, it became the renowned organ of the Communist party (PCF) when it broke away from the Socialists in 1920. There were also a number of combatively conservative Catholic papers, one of which *La Croix*, founded in 1883, also still has a large circulation today. The period saw a number of fascistic papers flourish as well, the best-known being *L'Action française* launched by Charles Maurras and Léon Daudet. Generally speaking,

the politicisation of the press was a symptom of the political polarisation that these countries exhibited during this period; the press
stoking the fires of the political struggles being waged at the time.

Not everywhere, though, was this kind of 'political press' so vigorous. The British press had by this time already assumed its modern
form, dominated by mass-circulation commercial papers, alongside a
more limited 'quality' press, with the narrow political press increasingly marginalised. Negrine (1994, pp. 45–47) describes how by the
turn of the century explicitly political papers had been largely
replaced by the mainstream commercial press. The latter certainly
had strong political sympathies, but the press did not display the rich
variety of specialised papers with politics as their very *raison d'être*.
In the first place, Britain's political development was not marked by
the same intensity of doctrinal polarisation of society as was evident
across much of continental Europe. Accordingly, the 'political
market' for such papers was more limited. Britain's newspaper proprietors, whose principal motive was pursuit of profit, were averse
to maintaining newspapers for political reasons alone. They were
still partisan, usually towards the Right, but their papers adopted a
modern format that interlaced political bias with 'objective' reporting. Secondly, the industrialisation and commercialisation of the
press sector left little place for the narrow political press. On the
Left, as Curran and Seaton (1991, pp. 48 ff.) tell, the 'radical press'
went into terminal decline as early as the latter half of the nineteenth
century. The huge rise in publishing costs, they suggest, was the
major constraint: 'the committed Left press in the late nineteenth
century existed only as undercapitalised, low budget, high-price specialist periodicals and as community papers'. Curran and Seaton
(1991, p. 38) observe, poignantly, that 'market forces thus accom-
plished more than the most repressive measures of the aristocratic
state'.

Freedom of the press: market freedom

The principle of the 'free market' was an essential ingredient of the
nineteenth-century 'bourgeois' understanding of how a free press
should operate in capitalist democracies. That this should have been
so is hardly surprising. The 'high bourgeois' phase of press history
in the latter half of the nineteenth century was, above all, the result

of the proliferation of new middle-class elites in the public sector, the professions, business, commerce and industry. This was, after all, the age when mass capitalism began to take off across Western Europe: its most powerful doctrine was that of the 'free market'. Since newspaper markets were purely national (or regional and local) the free market creed encountered little obstruction from the protectionism that, in practice, characterised many other economic sectors (though news agencies were a different matter – see later). Above all, the free flow of business information was a vital precondition for capitalistic economic development. Ironically, it was in one of the politically most backward countries – Germany – that the process of capitalist economic modernisation proceeded fastest and most intensely. National unification in 1871 combined with rapid technological progress and socio-economic modernisation, to create a mass market for the German press industry by the beginning of the twentieth century. The main constraint on the take-off of press markets was not political, it was structural.

For much of the nineteenth century, newspaper readership remained confined to an educated elite, albeit a fast expanding one. The liberal 'quality' press largely catered to the bourgeoisie and the intelligentsia. Much of its content reflected the socio-economic and political aspirations and concerns of the business and propertied classes. However, as the century drew onwards, newspaper readership increasingly extended to the working classes as well. As suggested, there began to appear a distinctly working class political press. But there also appeared a mass market for 'popular' commercial newspapers. A major reason for the appearance of the mass press was, of course, the spread of basic literacy. Another crucially important factor was technological progress. The application from the 1870s onwards of rotary printing greatly reduced the costs of newspapers and made their mass production and distribution both feasible and economic. Other factors – like improved transportation (better roads, the arrival of railways), urbanisation, and the creation of nationally unified markets (in Germany or Italy) – contributed to the creation of mass commercial markets in Europe. With mass markets came new sources of income for newspapers. Firstly, advertisers were now attracted by the newspapers' fast growing circulations. Secondly, more and more popular newspapers could be sold on the street directly to a mass public. Suddenly, the press sector was big business and proprietors became principally concerned with profitability.The process of mass commercialisation of the press, taking off towards the end of the last century, both 'commodified' newspapers and increased the scale of publishers' operations.

However, the inter-war years presented the press with a combination of rising costs and financial insecurity. In the first place, newspaper proprietors were faced by rising costs of labour, transport and newsprint (paper). Secondly, the press sector suffered a slump as a result of the First World War. Thirdly, it experienced another trough after the Great Crash of 1929; the 1930s were years of general economic crisis. Many smaller newspapers were compelled to close down. In France, according to Albert (1990, p. 32) between 1914 and 1939 the number of Parisian papers declined from 80 to 31, and provincial papers from 242 to 175, while circulation remained stable in the Paris region and actually grew in the provinces. Even in Britain, where the press sector remained in better economic condition and did not experience such a dramatic hecatomb of titles, Curran and Seaton (1991, p. 63) note that 'no new national daily or Sunday newspaper was successfully established between 1919 and 1939'. Moreover, under largely unregulated and competitive market conditions, press concentration quickly became pronounced. Those concerns with powerful backers were the best placed both to prosper from rapid expansion and to survive periodic adversity. In Weimar Germany (1918–33) the dominant position of the giant right-wing Hugenberg press empire was a very good case in point. Backed by the industrial barons of the Ruhr, the Hugenberg concern was able to acquire the world's first 'multi-media' empire with effective control of hundreds of newspapers, its own advertising agency and news agency, as well as (untypically at that time) interests in the nascent German film industry. The Hugenberg media empire was aligned with the radical nationalist Right and its propaganda contributed much to undermine Weimar democracy. (In 1928 Hugenberg was elected leader of the very Right-wing German National People's Party which allied itself to the National Socialists in the infamous 'Harzburger Front').

Press concentration was by no means simply a German phenomenon: all over Europe the industrialisation of the press brought similar concentration tendencies in its wake. In France, where the economic crisis of World War I killed off a large number of titles, the development of press concentration was given a further stimulus by the deflationary policies of the period 1926 to 1932. As ever, the smaller newspaper concerns were the main victims. During this period, the Parisian press became dominated by five major titles. The situation in provincial France was less competitive still: this was the era when the famous *grands régionaux* established their provincial fiefdoms (see pp. 83–85). France's most famous press baron of the inter-war period, Jean Prouvost, had originally made his fortune in the textile business. His best known title was *Le Paris Soir*, bought in 1930; by 1939 it had a circulation of one and a half million. The success of this particular paper's 'new journalism' – mass-appeal, modern techniques – had a great impact on the French press (Albert, 1990, p. 165; Kuhn, 1995, p. 21). In Britain, too, the inter-war period has been described as the 'era of the press barons' (Curran and Seaton, 1991, pp. 49–69). This was, after all, the era of Lords Beaverbrook, Rothermere, Camrose and Kemsley (and Northcliffe, too, though he died in 1922). Curran and Seaton (p. 52) illustrate the scale of their press oligopoly by reference to the fact that by 1937 'they owned nearly one in every two national and local daily papers sold in Britain'. Their combined circulation was 13 million. One reason they were so successful was that they too understood the laws of a commercial press. They encouraged modern journalistic methods, downgrading political analysis, upgrading entertainment (a development already quite noticeable by the turn of the century). At the same time, though, they were certainly closely interested in the politics of their time, and highly partisan towards the Right. Very rich individuals, they were very much in charge of their papers; exercising strict, and often idiosyncratic, proprietorial control. The 'free market', it was already clear, was also characterised by oligopolistic press ownership structures.

The free market, the 'end of ideology', and the decline of the party press

Following World War II, market forces confirmed a trend already seen in the British case: the decline of the overtly political press. Party and radical papers were increasingly squeezed by commercialism. Since the mainstream commercial press mostly had a conservative orientation, albeit a moderate one in the post-war period, the Left was affected adversely – and the radical Left very adversely – by this development. The high costs of publishing and distribution were a major constraint. By the 1960s, the remnants of the 'radical press' in Britain had collapsed with the trade unions selling their share in the hitherto pro-Labour *Daily Herald* and Cadburys withdrawing their support from the Liberal *News Chronicle*, which finished off the publication. Under new direction, the *Daily Herald* went on to become the mass-tabloid *Sun*. The demands of profitability and audience-maximisation left little prospect for papers that continued to prioritise political proselytism over the information and entertainment function (Hollstein, 1983, p. 243). As Curran and Seaton (1991, pp. 107–109) explain, the failure to attract as much advertising as the conservative mainstream press was another factor for the 'death of radical papers' in Britain. Their mainly working class readership was not large enough to compensate for the difficulty that they had in attracting advertising. Some advertisers were prejudiced against Left papers.

In continental Europe, which had directly experienced Fascist dictatorship or occupation, a popular aversion to an overtly political press bore testimony to a widespread ideological fatigue. This was nowhere more so than in Germany where in the post-war period very little was to remain of the once-proud German tradition of a party press. During the post-war occupation, political expression in the press was strictly controlled. Many pre-war political linkages were broken. In the vacuum a new press system emerged. It was heavily influenced by Anglo-American ideas, especially the principle that news and comment be clearly distinguished. It was also fiercely competitive commercially. The only thing that now kept a tiny party press going was the relative wealth of the state-funded German political parties (Humphreys, 1994, esp. p. 91).

Similarly, in France the party press fell into marked decline. This reflected, Williams (1972, pp. 60–62) suggests, 'the reader's distaste for polemical politics'. After a brief post-war interlude when under the Left's brief ascendancy many papers passed into the hands of former Resisters sympathetic to it, there soon followed a dramatic collapse of all but a small handful of party papers. Furthermore, as Williams (p. 62) notes, most of France's great regional papers now desisted from re-engaging in old-style political battles; they became 'reluctant to offend potential readers by violent polemics'. The decline of the party press was most dramatic of all in Austria where historically it had been stronger than anywhere else in Western Europe, outside Scandinavia. Newspapers owned by or with close links to the parties actually dominated the Austrian press scene in the immediate post-war years. In 1953 they accounted for almost 50 per cent of the daily press. By 1971 this share had sunk to barely 20 per cent – still a very respectable figure in international comparison. However, by 1990 it had fallen as low as 5 per cent (Wimmer, 1992, pp. 479–490).

A factor for the possible survival of the party press has been the channeling of specific state support to 'papers of opinion' with a view to promoting political pluralism. As will be seen in Chapter 3, this policy explains the post-war survival of a noteworthy party press in Scandinavia and, until the 1980s, in Austria as well. It helps to explain its partial survival in France and Italy where there continues to exist a Communist press (or, strictly speaking, in Italy's case a post-Communist Left-wing press). Yet, the combination of market forces and a post-war popular ennui with ideological politics, accounts by and large for a marginalisation of the political press. This has not meant, of course, that the mainstream press was no longer partisan. As Chapter 3 also describes, in all countries the commercial press has leaned towards the conservative side of the political spectrum in its overall editorial orientation; in some cases, imbalance has been conspicuous. Nonetheless, commercialisation entailed a political secularisation process. Papers pitching for wide readerships had to take care not to alienate their customers.

News agencies and press freedom

The state did not relinquish its hold over national news agencies in most cases until much later than it did in the case of the press. These news agencies were important providers of information to the press. However, for reasons that will now be explored, the state played a key role in their establishment and subsequent progress. A brief survey of the development of Europe's great news agencies reveals a history of distinct vulnerability to state power. In continental Europe, news agencies were instruments for plying the free press with an official version of the news.

Like newspapers, news agencies' development was originally driven by a combination of technological and market imperatives. The last century saw a massive increase in demand for information as the result of industrialism and the expansion of world trade. Their rapid success was facilitated by the development of cable telegraphy and later radio telegraphy. However, the use of telegraphy required enormous capital investment and at first it was mainly restricted to the financial and commercial trade sectors. As Gross (1982, p. 16) has noted, it was hardly surprising that the founders of the great European news agencies – Charles Havas, Julius Reuters, and Bernhard Wolff – were all individuals with close links spanning the financial and commercial world and the press. The special success of Reuters owed (and has continued to owe) much to the prominence of the City of London (Tunstall and Palmer, 1991, p. 52). Until the post-war period, European news supply was dominated by the French Havas agency, founded in 1835, the British Reuters agency (1851), and the German Wolff's Telegraph Bureau (1849). These three great European news agencies formed an 'agency cartel or alliance which underpinned the international news flow between 1859–1940' (Tunstall and Palmer, 1991, p. 49). Together with the American Associated Press agency (AP), they divided the world into four zones within which they granted themselves exclusive rights to news gathering and distribution. Reuters had a monopoly in the British empire and parts of the Middle and Far East. Havas had a monopoly in the French empire, southern Europe and Switzerland. WTB had a monopoly in Germany and Austria, the Netherlands, Scandinavia, Russia and the Balkans. AP had a North American monopoly (Schenk, 1985, p. 54).

From the start, the press sector was highly dependent upon these rapidly growing commercial giants, whose clear priority was the supply of financial and commercial information. Even great newspapers like the *Times* of London, which had started up its own embryonic news and information networks, soon submitted to their superior resources. However, World War I played havoc with world trade, the commercial news agencies immediately found themselves reliant on the press as their principal source of custom. At the same time, developments in radio technology expanded dramatically the scope of their news gathering operations beyond the narrow commercial sphere. The quality and extent of their news and information services for the press sector expanded commensurately and the balance of influence in their relationship began to change in the favour of the press.

The Anglo-Saxon news agencies enjoyed a large degree of political independence. Reuters' independence – and press freedom – was confirmed when, from 1925 onwards, it passed progressively into the direct ownership of the press sector itself, as had been the case right from the start in the United States. The British Press Association held a majority stake in Reuters until 1941 when the Newspaper Proprietors Association became its joint owner. Now Reuters became an independent trust owned and managed by the newspapers of Australia and New Zealand and those of Britain which held over three-quarters of the shares. The founding articles of this trust contained the specific guarantee that the agency should never fall under the influence of an interest group or political party. Reuters remained a largely non-profit-making trust until the decision was taken in the 1980s to transform it into a private company, quoted on the London stock market. Nevertheless, even then, special steps were taken to assure the prized editorial independence of the company (for a detailed and very interesting history of Reuters, see Read, 1992).

By contrast, the continental European news agencies had always been very closely linked to the state. In return, they were granted quasi-monopoly status. This state of affairs reflected France's and Germany's 'strong state' traditions. In both countries the technical apparatus of telegraphy and later of radio was very closely supervised by governments (see Chapter 4). Inevitably, this meant that the news agencies were tied from the outset into an intimate relationship with the state. Another factor was the degree of state aid poured into these news agencies, particularly during the financial crisis that followed World War I. In return for state aid, they acquiesced in being instruments of officialdom. The period immediately after World War I saw the establishment by national governments of official news agencies all over Europe. This was largely prompted by *raison d'état*: a reluctance to remain dependent on foreign news agencies. As Smith (1978, p. 161) has eloquently described the situation: 'the establishment of a news agency, like the acquisition of a parliament, a flag or a currency, became one of the *sine qua non* of modern European nationhood'. Invariably these news agencies were heavily subsidised by their respective states. As Smith goes on to say, 'by this means Government in those countries has been able to develop a major role in providing the input, the basic content of the papers circulating within their boundaries' (p. 161). Therefore, the inter-war period saw the progressive loosening and finally the abolition of the great agencies' news gathering and distributing cartel. They were now faced by the proliferation of 'lesser' national news agencies. Moreover, the great agencies began poaching in each others' markets. By the mid-1930s the cartel was rendered well and truly a thing of the past by an international treaty declaring all markets for news-gathering and distribution to be open. Inevitably, this market-opening diluted the hold of 'official' news and weakened individual governments' traditional ability so effectively to manage the information sources of their domestic press (Schenk, 1985, pp. 55–56).

The Fascist episode saw the media subjected to a wholly new degree of totalitarian information control and misuse. In Germany, even before the Nazi accession to power, during the 1920s, the Rightwing Hugenberg press empire had established its own news agency, the *Telegraphen-Union* (TU). Like the hundreds of Hugenberg newspapers, this news agency had been little more than the mouthpiece of radical nationalist circles. After the National Socialist seizure of power in 1933, both the 'official' WTB and Hugenberg's TU agencies were rationalised into the notorious *Deutscher Nachrichten Büro* (DNB) under the direct tutelage of the Josef Goebbels' propaganda ministry (Gross, 1982, pp. 23–24). Yet this experience provided another stimulus to liberalisation. After the defeat of the Nazis, the *Deutsche-Presse-Agentur* (DPA), West Germany's new post-war agency, was deliberately constituted as a cooperative owned by a wide range of newspapers together with the new public-service broadcasting corporations. From now on, these media clients of the agency, not the state, between them wholly financed the agency's operations. In order further to safeguard pluralism, the maximum share taken by any single publisher in the agency was limited to a meagre 1 per cent (a figure subsequently raised to 1.5 per cent in 1975); the share given to the public-service broadcasters was 15 per cent. By these means, the state's influence was banished once and for all; nor could another Hugenberg gain control (Humphreys, 1994, pp. 60–65).

The French story was more nuanced. During the Occupation the entire press sector, including all information services, had fallen under Nazi information control. Havas was transformed into an advertising agency and Vichy France was equipped by Pierre Laval with a new state-controlled news agency, called the French Information Office which followed the line of the collaborationist regime. Despite this experience, after the war the French were slower than the Germans, who had been heavily influenced by their Anglo-Saxon occupiers, to draw the obvious lesson. The Liberation saw the establishment, by former Havas journalists with resistance credentials, of the *Agence France Presse* (AFP) as the country's central news agency. The AFP remained a 'provisional' state institution for the next thirteen years. However, in the new post-war climate of opinion, it soon became clear that state control was very detrimental to the agency's international image and to its commercial prospects. Therefore, in 1957, legislation was enacted to free the AFP from government. This reform specified that the agency should 'under no circumstances, pass into the control of any ideological, political or economic group'. The decision secured AFP's place as one of the world's four leading news agencies (Albert, 1990, p. 53). The AFP has since been governed by a board of fifteen members, of whom eight have given a majority representation to the press. In addition, two places have been reserved to representatives of the AFP staff. The state's direct and indirect numerical influence has been limited to three representatives of the public, these being actually ministerial nominees, and two representatives of the state-controlled broadcasting services. The board chose its own director-general. However, a source of continued influence was the contribution the state continued to make to AFP's budget both as a major client of the AFP and as a large-scale provider of subsidies. For some, AFP remained a rather ambiguous case of liberation from the state (Dunnet, 1988, p. 150; Eisendrath, 1982, p. 77).

In Britain, as mentioned, Reuters remained until the 1980s in the hands of the press interests it served. This had long ensured it an enviable measure of political independence. However, during much of this period, the organisation wallowed in relative decline, a state of affairs that reflected Britain's diminishing world role and the post-war expansion of American news services into Europe. In the 1980s, Reuters' fortunes were transformed. In 1984 it reverted to being a private commercial company, quoted on the London stock exchange. In order to protect the agency's famous editorial independence, a veto was given to the previous owners – ie. the British, Australian and New Zealand press interests. They retained a 25 per cent block shareholding with a special voting status giving them an effective veto; individual commercial interests were prevented from acquiring more than 15 per cent of the remaining shares. The Newspaper Publishers Association and the Press Association retained an important stake in the company. This too assured the British press a continued important voice in the company. The company now became much more commercially orientated again; and with it, exceedingly successful. While remaining one of the world's leading press agencies, the principal part of its activity came to focus squarely once again on the world of commerce and finance. The organisation had come full circle (Schenk, 1985, pp. 39–41; and Read, 1992, p. 1).

The 1980s witnessed an 'information revolution'. This confirmed the trend away from state power over news. This 'revolution' was the product of spectacular advances in technical communications systems arising from the convergence of telecoms with computing and the growth of satellite transmission. Reuters now joined the exclusive club of media giants that were embarked upon an international strategy of multi-media diversification to exploit this global information revolution (see Chapter 6). Just as the company had capitalised upon telegraphy and radio in the past, now it was foremost among companies to join the information revolution. Under its new more commercial direction, during the 1980s Reuters' operations in the world of finance and commerce leapt in magnitude. It became 'the indispensable tool of the foreign exchange or currency market' (Tunstall and Palmer, 1991, p. 46). It was now the world's leading provider to media and business customers of news, real-time price information, computerised trading facilities, and interface equipment for dealing rooms. Beyond the press, it branched out into other media, notably television. In 1992 it took over *Visnews*, the well-known international television news supplier. In 1993 it acquired a stake in ITN, released from ITV ownership by the 1990 Broadcasting Act. Reuters also supplied news to BSkyB, the commercial satellite channel. In 1994, Reuters bought into commercial radio in London as well. The company had become the world's leading electronic supplier of news and information to the press and broadcast media (Peak, 1993, p. 129). Reuters was not alone, merely the most dynamic, in pursuing this multi-media strategy. In 1988 the American agency UPI (which had been struggling throughout the 1980s) was taken over by Infotechnology. As Cayrol (1991, p. 78) has put it, it too transformed itself from a 'classic' supplier of news and information to the media, into a 'polyvalent' agency catering to the worlds of industry, commerce and finance. Similarly, the other major US agency, Associated Press, had a joint venture called 'AP–Dow Jones' serving the world of finance. AP also had branches catering to a wide range of sectors in commerce and industry, and also the fields of medicine, academia, and not least of all, television. Agence

France-Presse, too, diversified, albeit more modestly (despite state aid), into multi-media operations (Cayrol, 1991, pp. 76–78).

In conclusion, modern European news agencies had come a long way from being simple instruments of state control. Modern internationalised news markets were open to an extent unknown in the last century or in the first half of this one. Even though a select number of giant Western agencies still dominated the international information business, they found themselves in competition with many more national and international companies each with their own correspondent networks (eg. companies like ITN, and more recently CNN and its various imitators). As for domestic news, there was an abundance of specialist agencies and manifold other sources of news and information. The news agencies of the post-World War II period scarcely resembled their pre-war characters. They were now dedicated to the supply of objective factual information and were no longer the servants of officialdom that they once were. Their news values came quickly to reflect the more stable and less ideological context of post-war society and politics in Europe. They had rediscovered their original commercial identity, becoming again a key link between media and big business in a liberal capitalist international order.

The economics of the contemporary West European press: some general remarks

In the post-war period, the economics of the press sector has varied considerably across Europe. The industry has been stronger in northern Europe and weaker in southern Europe (see Table 1.1). This mainly reflects consumption patterns. Most northern Europeans are high consumers of newspapers; southern Europeans are low consumers. As a consequence, the northern European markets have supported a greater number of newspapers per head of population; interestingly, this has been especially the case in Scandinavia. At first sight this might be considered to be a surprising finding given the small size of these latter countries' markets in absolute terms (and the smaller scope they have presented for economies of scale). As Chapter 3 will explain, a crucial factor for the existence of so many papers in Scandinavia has been the selective state support directed to smaller papers in order to promote overall press pluralism. Britain and Germany, highly populous countries, have had the largest industries by far; this was altogether unsurprising. Surprisingly, France and Italy, despite having large populations, have had conspicuously weak press industries.

Table 1.1   Newspaper industry statistics in Western Europe, 1989/90

Country	Daily newspaper circulation (millions)	Daily newspaper circulation per thousand inhabitants	Dailies per million inhabitants
Austria	2.7	350.1	2.2
Belgium	2.1	211.4	2.8
Denmark	3.2	622.6	8.5
Finland	2.8	564.3	13.3
France	8.6	152.1	1.3
Germany	20.3	321.0	5.6[a]
Greece	0.8	79.8	1.9
Ireland	0.8	227.6	2.3
Italy	6.4	111.3	1.4
Netherlands	4.6	307.8	5.4
Norway	2.5	589.3	18.4
Portugal	0.5	47.5	2.3
Spain	2.9	74.4	3.3
Sweden	4.9	572.0	18.2
Switzerland	2.7	404.6	17.1
UK	22.3	389.6	1.7

Note:

[a] This refers to main titles only and does not count 'side-editions'. However, this figure still exaggerates the degree of genuine editorial pluralism. If 'independent editorial units' only were counted then the above figure would be around 1.9. See Chapter 3, pp. 79–80.

Source: Data from A. Sánchez-Tabernero *et al.*, *Media Concentration in Europe*, Dusseldorf: European Institute for the Media, 1993, Media Monograph No. 16, pp. 40–43.

A related factor for the comparative strength of the northern European press industries and the weakness of the southern ones has been the share of advertising expenditure received by the press. The lion's share of media advertising in the northern European countries has tended to be reserved to the press. This has certainly been the case in Scandinavia where the broadcasters were long prohibited from carrying any advertising whatsoever. It was also the case in the Netherlands and Switzerland where the broadcasters were restricted to very little advertising. As seen above, these cases accounted for all those smaller countries which sustained press industries that, comparatively speaking, were apparently characterised by reasonable or strong diversity in terms of the number of publications per head of population.

Table 1.2 Percentage shares of advertising expenditure by media

Country	Press		Broadcasters	
	1980	1990	1980	1990
Austria	49.5	52.3	42.4	40.0
Belgium	75.1	54.0	8.3	32.9
Denmark	96.2	85.0	0.0	12.1
Finland	82.0	79.1	15.1	18.1
France	60.0	55.9	24.6	31.8
Germany	81.5	77.2	13.7	18.4
Greece	44.5	44.5	55.5	47.4
Ireland	56.3	54.0	37.9	39.0
Italy	59.0	44.0	32.2	50.7
Netherlands	85.8	78.9	8.0	16.7
Norway	97.7	91.2	0.0	4.4
Portugal	26.7	30.5	66.6	49.2
Spain	46.8	54.7	45.1	41.6
Sweden	95.5	95.5	0.0	0.0
Switzerland	85.0	78.9	8.0	8.2
UK	66.0	63.6	29.3	32.4

Note:
The remainder is accounted for by cinema, posters, etc.
Source: Adapted from A. Sánchez-Tabernero *et al.*, *Media Concentration in Europe*, Dusseldorf: European Institute for the Media, 1993, Media Monograph No. 16, p. 129.

As will be seen (in Chapter 4) in most countries the press has had to face some competition from the late 1950s onwards from the broadcasters. Nevertheless, until the 1980s, this competition was kept within generally strict limits – in some cases, as noted, very strict limits indeed. However, as Table 1.2 shows, during the 1980s the press in many countries saw its share of the advertising cake diminish further as the result of the abolition of public-service broad-casting monopolies (or duopolies) and increased competition from new commercial broadcasters (a development to be explored in Chapters 5, 6 and 7). Belgium and Italy were most affected. Bucking this trend were countries which still had domestic (terrestrial) public broadcasting monopolies or where private broadcasting had only just commenced. Among these, the other Mediterranean countries' public broadcasters already accounted for high shares of advertising expenditure in any case. By 1993 only Austria had yet to abolish its public-service television monopoly (see pp. 187–190). In recent years the mainstream press has had to face up to the challenge of cable and satellite television, direct mail advertising and the proliferation of 'free-sheets'. Franklin and Murphy (1991, p. 10) estimate that there are, across Western Europe, around 4,000 free papers distributing 200 million copies; these are totally dependent upon generating advertising business.

Competition for what is ultimately a finite source of revenue has become very fierce. As we shall, however, this has advantaged those with market power. The strong players have been able to expand across the press sector and diversify their operations into other media. As we shall see in Chapter 3, the free market has been a very 'imperfect' one.

The industrial relations of the European press

Another factor that has had some bearing on the comparative eco-nomic health of press sectors across Europe has been the balance of industrial relations. As Hollstein (1983, p. 251) has remarked, 'news-paper unions throughout Europe have been among the best paid, most organised, and most left-inclined in the world'. Historically, print unions long tended to see themselves as being in the aristocracy of the labour movement. The leading French print union, the *Fédéra-tion du Livre*, was affiliated to the Communist-dominated trade union confederation, the *Confédération Général du Travail* (CGT) (Kuhn, 1995, p. 43). The German print workers had been the first workers to organise themselves in a union; in post-war West Ger-many, the *IG Druck und Papier* remained in the vanguard of the labour movement. In Britain, too, the print unions were strongly organised and powerful. The 'closed shop' was commonplace in Europe. Generally, employers were reluctant to confront their strongly organised workforces.

As a result of union power in the sector, the industry long suffered from overmanning; there was widespread aversion to replacing traditional processes of production with those involving new computerised technologies. Kuhn (1995, p. 43) characterises the French case as a 'conspiracy of inefficiency at the expense of the consumer'. Minc (1993, pp. 59–70), too, points out how for years French publishers preferred to cover the costs of inefficiency in the prices they charged for newspapers, rather than confront the unions. This helped to explain France's comparatively low newspaper circulation figures; in turn, this deterred advertisers. It was a key factor for the weakness of the French industry. Similarly, in Britain labour difficulties long afflicted an industry that remained, for all its strengths, especially vulnerable to periodic increases in the price of newsprint and slumps in advertising revenue (these being general problems across Europe). Both failure to rationalise production methods and disrupted production could do untold damage. Across post-war Europe, newspapers succumbed to takeovers in part because they were damaged by poor industrial relations; or because they failed to modernise production. Strikes afflicting the *Times* in the late 1970s and early 1980s were a direct contributory factor for the Thomson group's sale of the paper to Rupert Murdoch in 1981 (see pp. 100–101).

One reason for the comparative strength of the northern European small countries' industries was their relatively good industrial relations. In Scandinavia and the Netherlands corporatist relations between employers and workforces were a factor for a smooth transition to new printing methods; but occasional industrial action in Denmark proved that even here there could be problems. Elsewhere, the problems of modernisation were worse (Hollstein, 1983, p. 251–252). In West Germany, a series of grave industrial conflicts wracked the newspaper sector in 1976 (over wages), in 1978 (over the introduction of new technologies) and in 1984 (over the 35-hour week). The 1978 confrontation brought much of the industry to a halt and was met with widespread lockouts by the employers. In the end, German corporatism prevailed. A settlement was produced that secured some generous compensation for the workers for their cooperation in the introduction of computerised typesetting and photocomposition. The resultant collective agreement provided the model for similar agreements in Austria, Denmark, Italy and Switzerland (Humphreys, 1994, pp. 111–116).

In Britain and France, both countries with more combative unions, there were far worse conflicts. In France, a strike over the introduction of the rationalisation of production of *Le Parisien Libéré*, a large popular paper serving the Paris region, lasted for twenty-nine months. It was accompanied by demonstrations and 'solidarity strikes' that brought much of the industry to a halt. The action was only curtailed when the government intervened to compensate the workers. Very much a Pyrrhic victory for the employers, the conflict inflicted huge damage on the Amaury group that owned the paper. While the struggle did serve to 'blaze' a trail for other newspapers seeking to rationalise production processes, the modernisation hardly improved the economics of the sector (Kuhn, 1995, p. 43–44: Hollstein, 1983, p. 252). The main reason, as Minc (1993, pp. 62–70) has commented, was that French employers were generally afraid of provoking such destructive conflicts. They preferred instead to pass the costs of modernisation on to the consumer; consequently, in 1991 French newspaper prices remained much higher than those in Britain or Germany. High prices kept circulations low, which deterred the advertisers, and so the vicious circle was maintained. The French employers' situation was not helped by their comparatively weak financial standing. They had to finance the costs of modernisation by borrowing. Further, they simply could not afford to risk sustained conflict with the print unions.

In Britain, decades of union power were reversed, it seemed, almost overnight. The assault on union power was actually led by a relatively small-time regional publisher, Eddie Shah, who first defied the unions and introduced new technologies into his northern English newspaper chain and then followed his success up by launching a new national daily called *Today* (subsequently taken over by Rupert Murdoch). He was promptly followed by better known national newspaper proprietors, Robert Maxwell, Rupert Murdoch and Conrad Black. Most dramatically, when confronted by the unions, Murdoch simply moved his newspapers – literally overnight – away from Fleet Street, hitherto the famed home of the British national press, to a fortified complex in London's docklands, at Wapping. The fact that Murdoch won the resultant conflict could be explained by two factors: he did have the financial resources and staying power to withstand the union counterattack; and he benefited from new industrial relations legislation introduced by the Thatcher government that outlawed both the 'closed shop' and secondary picketing. Indeed, as Negrine (1994, pp. 77–78) notes, this legislation might have been cast with the print unions in mind. As the result of this victory, British proprietors were able to rapidly modernise production, rationalise their workforces and reap large profits. Lorimer (1994, p. 121) cites the case of Conrad Black who bought the *Daily Telegraph* for £30 million in 1986 and by 1992 was turning a pre-tax profit of £40.5 million. By the 1990s the publishers of the press in Britain had gained a new supremacy over their work-forces. Their market freedom was unmatched in Western Europe.

Summary

To conclude, the European press had travelled far in the course of a century and a half. Under the impact of new print technologies and tremendous socio-economic changes, it had been thoroughly indus-trialised. It had played an important part in the mobilisation of mass politics. Yet commercial pressures and the de-ideologisation of post-World War II politics, brought about a later 'depoliticisation' of the press. The party press became marginalised: this disadvantaged most the European Left. Importantly, the industrialisation and commer-cialisation of the European press had been achieved through a large measure of *laissez-faire* economics. Exceptions to this rule were rare. A French ordinance of 1944 that attempted to structure press mar-kets – notably by restricting ownership – was remarkably short lived in its effect (as will be seen in Chapter 3). Very quickly, the princi-ple of the economic freedom of the press re-asserted itself. National news agencies – historically closely linked to the state – were delib-erately freed from political supervision. In any case, their former quasi-monopolistic control of international news was progressively swept away by market developments. These national news agencies' trajectory from state organs to internationally competitive providers of economic information symbolised, as clearly as anything else in the world of the media, the primacy of markets and the com-modification of 'information'. However, the conventional wisdom that press freedom was fully achieved as the forces of liberalism tri-umphed over those of repression, is too simplistic. As Curran and Seaton (1991) remind us, economic pressures and market forces, leading to the marginalisation of the radical press and the concentration of the mainstream press into relatively few hands, constrained the diversity of viewpoints presented to the citizenry. We will return to this theme of press concentration and its effects in Chapter 3. In the meantime, we need to examine more closely the quality of the press freedom established by liberal democratisation.

Guide to further reading

On the history of the press

P. Albert, *La Presse Française*, Paris: Documentation Française, 1990.

J. Curran and J. Seaton, *Power Without Responsibility: The Press and Broadcasting in Britain*, London: Routledge, 1991, Chapter 1.

P. Humphreys, *Media and Media Policy in Germany: The Press and Broadcasting Since 1945*, Oxford/Providence, RI: Berg, 1994, Chapter 1.

R. Kuhn, *The Media in France*, London/New York: Routledge, 1995, Chapters 1 and 2.

R. Negrine, *Politics and the Mass Media in Britain*, London/New York: Routledge, 1994, Chapter 3.

J. Sandford, *The Mass Media of the German-Speaking Countries*, London: Oswald Wolff, 1976, Chapter 1.

On news agencies

R.W. Desmond, *The Information Process: World News Reporting to the Twentieth Century*, Iowa City: University of Iowa Press, 1978.

H.-W. Gross, *Die Deutsche Presse-Agentur*, Frankfurt/Main: Haag & Herchen Verlag, 1982.

D. Read, *The Power of News: The History of Reuters*, Oxford: OUP, 1992.

U. Schenk, *Nachrichtenagenturen*, Berlin: Vistas Verlag, 1985.

J. Tunstall and M. Palmer, *Media Moguls*, London/New York: Routledge, 1991, Chapter 3 (pp. 45–84).

2

Press freedom and its limits: the state, the law and the private individual

How much political freedom has the post-war press enjoyed in Western Europe? This might at first strike the reader as a rather surprising question. After all, had not censorship and state licensing, the hallmarks of a pre-democratic press system, been abolished? Following the experience of Nazi dictatorship and occupation, there occurred a powerful reaffirmation of the principle of the free press (Franco's Spain and Salazar's Portugal aside). This invigorated post-war commitment to press freedom was symbolised, as seen, by the freeing of state-controlled news agencies. Where there continued to exist a press registration requirement (eg. France and the UK), it was now merely a formality; registration was no longer a mechanism for censorship (Lorimer, 1994, p. 57; Article 19, 1993, p. 262). While there certainly was an expectation that comment would be clearly distinguished from information, in editorial matters the press was free to practise self-regulation. It was universally accepted that the press was a very different medium to broadcasting. There was no 'scarcity of frequencies' that called for public allocation of licences or that necessitated strict regulation of the medium. Whereas broadcasters were subject to requirements of balance and impartiality, the journalists of the press were expected to give free voice to their opinions (Lorimer, 1994, p. 58). Above all, the principle of media freedom was now enshrined in the Council of Europe's *European Convention on Human Rights*. Its article 10 stated explicitly:

> everyone has the right to freedom of expression. This freedom shall include the right to hold opinions and to receive and impart information and ideas without interference by public authority.

This key provision gave concrete expression, in international law, to the principle of the inviolability of press freedom.

State censorship

In fact, John Keane (1991, pp. 94–114) has suggested that we are entering a 'new era of political censorship'. In his view, the modern state, a 'democratic Leviathan', continues to hinder the free flow of information through five 'interlocking types of political censorship'. Firstly, the state still resorts to 'emergency powers' of censorship. These are typically exercised during times of war or national crisis; the French state's 'muzzling' of the media during the Algerian war of independence (1954–62) was a prime example. Secondly, he points to the 'armed secrecy' of modern states by which he is referring to the classification of information as secret, the covering up of 'dirty tricks', the 'weeding' of public documents, and so forth. He cites as a good example the British 'D-notice' system for the official vetting of newspaper articles that bear on national security. Thirdly, Keane suggests, political 'lying' is a common feature of the official public relations process; it is conducted through practices such as the selective priming of the media through the issue of government statements, the official accreditation of certain reporters, the exercise of subtle pressures on journalists, and the like. Fourthly, Keane points to how 'state advertising' is used by governments for self-promotion; again he cites Britain where the state is the second largest individual advertiser and deploys an annual budget of nearly £200 million to advance 'any conceivable policy matter' (the French case, too, might have been adduced – see below). In Keane's words, the use of advertising budgets gives government 'enormous powers of blackmail'. Finally, Keane refers to the 'corporatistic' performance, in modern states, by private sector organisations of governmental functions. In Keane's negative view, corporatism blurs the boundaries between the state and civil society, incorporating important parts of the latter into the web of the state apparatus at the cost of 'openness'. By all these means, the media's investigative and watchdog powers are circumscribed. Press freedom is reduced.

Keane's perspective is a radical one. He presents a picture of enduring and overweening state interventionism in the press sector. In so doing, he overestimates the bureacratic unity of the state and underplays its essential 'leakiness'. He also ignores the way that investigative media – including the 'alternative' press, a radical press that re-appeared in the post-1960s decades – can influence the modern news agenda. Once a secret is leaked, whether by an investigative news journal like Germany's *Spiegel*, an 'alternative' paper like the *taz*, a satirical news magazine like France's *Le Canard enchaîné*, or a mainstream quality paper like the *Guardian*, then it is invariably picked up by the rest of the media. In the competitive world of selling copy and attracting audiences, investigative media exert a crucial influence on the agenda of the rest of the media (see Mathes and Pfetsch, 1991). Also, in the media agenda-building process, the modern state is but one player among many. Yet, handled with care, Keane's perspective is still very instructive.

Surprisingly, there has been little empirical study of media censorship in Western Europe by political scientists. A major problem has been a shortage of systematic data, particularly of comparative data. A cross-national study has made an important contribution towards redressing this state of affairs. By researching *Index of Censorship* – a publication of an independent body based in London – Newton and Artingstall (1994), examined the incidence of censorship in nine liberal democracies, six of which were West European. They covered two decades – 1970–1990 – and discovered significant cross-national variation. They found Britain's censorship record to be the worst over the whole period, which seemed to confirm the country's reputation as a 'secret state'. The study showed, too, that British media censorship had increased markedly during the 1980s, the period of Thatcherism. In searching for an explanation, Newton and Artingstall concluded that the British system created 'the opportunity to censor'. This, they suggested, resulted from its 'rather special constitutional and political features'. Among these features, they noted especially the absence of a written constitution with a bill of rights, and the country's 'majoritarian' political system. Other obvious factors were its 'weak' freedom of information legislation and the 'draconian' nature of official secrets legislation. Thatcher's leadership style, they suggested, was an important factor; she was evidently more willing than her predecessors to use the powers of censorship that this system placed at her disposal. The increase in censorship was evident in the increased the use of D-notices (Britain's name for official secrecy restraints), restrictions on news reporting on Northern Ireland and a revision of the Official Secrets

Act that actually increased the state's powers of censorship (Newton and Artingstall, 1994. For a study of the methods, see Franklin, 1994, Chapter 4).

France's censorship rate, which Newton and Artingstall found to be much lower than Britain's, was still high compared to the other West European countries, whose record appeared to be rather good. Both Italy's and West Germany's censorship rate was a fraction of that pertaining in Britain and France. One obvious explanation for this was the possibility that Italian and German governments were restricted in their exercise of censorship by the folk memory of a recent experience of dictatorship, censorship and propaganda; as a result of history, their populations were more wary of government. Above all, Newton and Artingstall's empirical survey found that the two Scandinavian countries studied testified to a remarkable respect for freedom of information. Both Sweden and Denmark had truly derisory censorship rates during the 1970s and 1980s. Of course, it deserves pointing out that Britain and France were nuclear powers with large military–industrial complexes; the Nordic states were either neutral (Sweden) or a minor partner (Denmark) in NATO. In fairness, as Newton and Artingstall point out, a country's place in the international system and its geopolitical importance are factors that help to account for the patterns of incidence of media censorship. Indeed their study found that the United States, normally viewed as an 'open' society, also had a censorship rate that approached Britain's. More might have been made of this line of enquiry: it would have been interesting to know just how much of the comparatively high levels of censorship in Britain and the USA, and indeed France, could be put down to Keane's 'armed secrecy' of leading (nuclear-armed) states in the international system. Moreover, quite unlike the states with which they were being compared, these three had all experienced significant military conflicts during the post-war period. Much of Britain's censorship could be accounted for by the Northern Ireland conflict; much of France's could be put down to the Algerian war. All the same, Newton and Artingstall's point that Thatcher was presented – by the configuration of Britain's political and legal system – with the 'opportunity to censor', must also carry some of the burden of explanation. The same might have been observed of de Gaulle's France.

It is important to note, however, that there is a great difference between coercive censorship and the weakness of freedom of information. Moreover, to simply look at censorship rates may be very misleading. They may actually be – in part – an indicator of the health of a country's investigative media. Seymour-Ure (1991, p. 224) points out that in the heyday of British investigative journalism, in his view the period between 1967 and 1979, there was a rash of attempts both by officialdom using the Official Secrets Act and by well resourced corporate actors with clever lawyers, to prevent publication. Moreover, Seymour-Ure (1991, pp. 230–236) tells how British censorship has actually declined in its *effectiveness* since the 1960s, leaving the libel laws as the main inhibitor of the British press's freedom. Indeed, Britain is often held up as a paradigm both of governmental secrecy and of independent and investigative quality media.

The point about the quality of the censorship is an important one. If the British state was renowned for its secrecy, the French state had a reputation for coercive interference. Despite the experience of Vichy, the post-war period did not get off to an altogether auspicious start when the Socialist Minister of Information exploited the *purification* of collaborationist publishers to try to re-balance the press towards the Left (Williams, 1972, p. 392). Later, during the Algerian war, papers providing a forum for Left-wing critics of the war were subject to repeated censorship and seizure (Keane, 1991, p. 97; Kuhn, 1995, pp. 62–63). This practice was continued by the Gaullists. Hayward (1983, p. 160) notes that, as the new Gaullist Fifth Republic was consolidating, selected fringe papers were subjected repeatedly to seizures. The aim was 'simply to drive them out of existence'. He notes the contrast between the Third Republic, 'amazingly tolerant' towards the anti-system extreme-Right press, and the Fifth Republic and the Gaullists' treatment of the extreme-Left press. Safran, too, (1985, p. 240) points to the Gaullists' 'revival' of that part of the 1881 law on press freedom making it a felony to publish statements damaging to the President of the Republic and the public authorities in general (see Chapter 1). Since the President was not just Head of State, but also the head of the executive in the French Fifth Republic, this was a potentially powerful limitation on the press's watchdog function. Eisendrath (1982, p. 69–70) suggests that this law was invoked by President de Gaulle 350 times! (Safran suggests it was applied about 100 times). Eisendrath goes so far as to suggest that in France 'all reporting on Watergate would [have [constitute]d] "outrage" to the chief of state'. However, if this might have been the case under de Gaulle, it is important to note that the law practically fell into desuetude under Presidents Giscard d'Estaing and Mitterrand (Cayrol, 1991, p. 128). Even so, on one famous occasion, the politically moderate quality paper, *Le Monde*, found itself the object of criminal proceedings, during the last days of the Giscard d'Estaing presidency, for alleged defamation of the judiciary. The paper had committed the crime of criticising a court decision concerning President Giscard d'Estaing's acceptance of the 'Bokassa diamonds'. This lawsuit 'silenced *Le Monde* on a sensitive subject and, with it, the rest of the French press' (Eisendrath, 1982, pp. 63–64; also see Hayward, 1983, p. 161; Safran, 1985, pp. 240–241). As suggested, direct state interference was associated with the Fifth Republic consolidation phase. Nonetheless, during the presidency of Georges Pompidou (a Gaullist), in 1970, the Maoist journal *La Cause du Peuple* was seized and its editor arrested. This was followed, in 1974, by a state raid and the wiretapping of the offices of *Le Canard enchaîné*, a popular journal of political satire. *Le Canard enchaîné* had been (and still is) an unceremonious critic of the government and the political establishment (Safran, 1985, pp. 240–241).

In Britain, by contrast, government may have been 'shrouded in secrecy' but its censorship activity was far more discreet. 'Despite the breadth of the language of the Official Secrets Acts, prosecutions are rare' and 'it is rarer still for the media to be charged' (Nicol and Bowman, 1993, p. 179). From the 1960s onwards journalists became 'more reluctant to keep the government's secrets' and by the 1980s the legislation's 'inhibiting effect' had greatly diminished (Seymour-Ure, 1991, pp. 230–235). Nevertheless, the Thatcher government's 1984 Police and Criminal Evidence Act did grant the police new powers of seizure. By obtaining a court order, the police were now empowered to compel newspapers, freelance photographers and broadcasters alike, to hand over confidential material, both published and unpublished. Subsequently, these powers were exercised on occasion, most notably in the 'Zircon affair' though here the BBC Radio Scotland offices were raided and the press was not the target. Moreover, during the Thatcher era Britain's Contempt of Court legislation was employed, on one occasion to identify a 'whistleblower' in the public service (on the Sarah Tisdall case – see below). Even Germany – inhibited by its Nazi past – had its own great post-war scandal: namely the '*Spiegel* affair' of 1962. Because of an article highly critical of government defence policy, the investigative magazine's offices were raided, its press embargoed and its owner-editor and the responsible journalist arrested by the security services. These acts were widely seen as a naked attack on press freedom and the West German press rallied to the *Spiegel*'s defence and loaned the magazine printing facilities allowing it to continue to publish. As a result of the public outcry the government's actions had caused, the prisoners were released and the minister responsible felt it necessary to resign. Several years later, the journalists were exonerated by the West German Federal Constitutional Court. In fact, the whole affair acted as an early kind of constitutional 'Magna Carta' for safeguarding the press freedom enshrined in the country's written constitution and in its various press laws (Humphreys, 1994, pp. 72–74; also Schoenbaum, 1968). Interestingly, the court upheld the legality of the police raid on the *Spiegel*'s offices. However, the affair led to an amendment to the law of disclosure to provide a limited public interest defence for the disclosure of secrets (Karpen, 1993, p. 93). It is also noteworthy that, exceptionally, in its campaign against terrorism, the German state has resorted to raids and confiscation of material and equipment (Humphreys, 1994, pp. 120–121).

Official news management

What about Keane's reservations about the political management of news more generally? Keane actually refers specifically to the developed public relations activities of American government, the accreditation of certain reporters, the provision of special services to the media, and so on. In Britain, the 'lobby' system has amounted to an effective instrument of official news management. Introduced as long ago as 1884, the 'lobby' is a shorthand description of a system of political journalism whereby a special coterie of selected journalists have been granted privileged access to government; today they number around two hundred and two hundred and fifty. These journalists are granted special access to non-attributable governmental news briefings going up to the highest level (the PM's Office). Understandably, the lobby system has long provoked the criticism that the relationship between the British press and government is an excessively manipulative one. There is an obvious danger of bias towards the 'reproduction of ready-made political statements disguised as fact'. It has been suggested that it amounts to an 'endemically secretive system', reform of which would require no less than 'changes in the "nanny state" philosophy that runs through most of Britain's administrative machinery' (Negrine, 1994, pp, 134–138). In the 1980s, the *Independent* and the *Guardian* both briefly withdrew from the lobby to protest how this had become precisely so, at the height of Thatcherism. Against this, it should be added, the fact that they soon returned seemed to testify to the fact that journalists still felt that the system allowed 'much sensitive information to flow out of government' (Negrine, 1994, p. 138). It deserves mention, in this context, that there was considerable evidence of a general increase in government news management during the Thatcher period; the key role of the Prime Minister's press secretary, Bernard Ingham, is usually highlighted (Harris, 1990; Franklin, 1994, Chapter 4). Moreover, a pronounced feature of the Thatcher era was a marked increase in the government's use of official advertising to promote its policies (Jones, 1991, p. 206).

The lobby system might be characteristically 'British' in its character and style, but it is by no means unique in its function. All governments have operated systems of official news management: France, for example, had a special ministry performing this function; no doubt for the sake of public relations France's sinister-sounding Minister of Information was renamed in 1971 *secrétaire d'état de la fonction publique et des services de l'information*. Kuhn (1995, p. 122) notes how, especially with broadcast journalists, this ministry 'came to be associated ... with the authoritarian face of Gaullism' (see Chapter 4). In fact, Kuhn's (1995) study shows that the French state was much more directly interventionist than the British state. He speaks about the French state having an 'authoritative status as a primary definer of issues on the media agenda'. In some contrast to the British case, the French state's role was 'institutionalised' in the shape of its historically heavy, and to some extent enduring, influence on the national news agency, a prime source of news for the media (see Chapter 1). Eisendrath (1982, p. 70) notes that the French state also 'showers benefits on those ... who play by the rules'. This is a reference to the very generous state assistance granted to the French press in the shape of indirect and even direct subsidies to newspapers. Further, Eisendrath (1982, pp. 76–77) points out that French publishers could not afford to forget that the state determined the allocation of advertising by the country's nationalised companies, these 'ranking among the nation's largest ... accounts'.

In fact, exactly the same point is made by Kuhn (1995, p. 11) and Dunnett (1988, p. 148), both of whom also point to the state's role in the banking sector as yet another potent source of indirect state influence on the press. Hayward (1983, p. 161), too, has commented upon what he describes as the 'occult influence' of the state banks on press concerns that have relied on them 'to finance their takeover bids or help them through periods of financial difficulty'. According to Eisendrath, this feather bed of state aid discouraged any challenging of the system. An essentially similar picture is painted by Dunnett (1988, pp. 147–150).

Finally, as Kuhn (p. 67) notes, 'to help ensure that the official version of events dominates press coverage the political executive is assisted by a range of support staff and official bodies, including public relations personnel and media advisers, presidential and government spokespersons, press offices and governmental information agencies'. In fact, this latter situation is common to all liberal democracies. Britain had a Central Office of Information and West Germany established a special governmental press and information office. As seen, in contrast to France, in Germany's case state influence on the national news agency was quickly abolished after the Nazi dictatorship. All the same, one empirical study (Baerns, 1987 – reported in McQuail, 1992, pp. 128–129) examined political affairs coverage in one German *Land* (state – in the sense of sub-federal unit). The study found that approximately two-thirds of the items covered by the media, with little variation between press, radio and television, came from public relations sources – in other words from official handouts, press releases or news conferences – rather than from journalistic activity (investigation, etc.). It is also important to note that press services were provided by many departments and branches of government. The parties had their press services, so too did numerous public and semi-public organisations. Indeed, the unions, employers' organisations, the churches, and many social and political minority groups, making up the 'pluralistic fabric of German society', all provided the media with information services (Humphreys, 1994, p. 57). It is as well to remember that in all liberal democracies the state is neither monolithic nor is it the only news-manager.

Pluralism and the press

Qualification is now required lest the reader be tempted to conclude, unreservedly, from the foregoing discussion that the state has indeed exercised the powers *vis-à-vis* the press of Keane's Leviathan. In the first place, it should be stressed that direct state interference with the press has been the exception rather than the norm. Largely, infringement on media freedom in France under de Gaulle (also see p. 147) could be explained by reference to the peculiar circumstances surrounding the Algerian war and his ending of it. As mentioned the press controls actually pre-dated his arrival in power. Further, the period surrounding the regime change from Fourth to Fifth Republic, was a dangerously unstable period in French political history. In de Gaulle's view, any activity that undermined the initially insecure legitimacy of the new regime had to be discouraged (it might be recalled that Winston Churchill wanted to take over the BBC during the 1926 General Strike!). Moreover, in France, as elsewhere in post-World War II Western Europe, infringements of the principle of political independence of the press typically provoked fierce public opprobrium and political controversy. Indeed, they have usually had the effect, unintended by their instigators, of confirming the power of the Fourth Estate. Germany's '*Spiegel* affair' was a classic example of how direct interference could backfire on government. Yet the targeting of *Canard enchaîné* produced a similarly counterproductive public furore in France. Right across post-war Western Europe publics have positively expected the press to be critical of their governments. Attacks on press freedom were a very dangerous expedient for those wishing to remain in office.

Secondly, important though official powers of news management were, the state was not a unified entity. Again, this was true even in *étatiste* France, where presidentialism during the Fifth Republic endowed the central executive with concentrated powers. As Kuhn (1995, pp. 68–69) comments, in a pluralist society, the media's agenda is determined by competing interests. A 'primary definer' it may have been, but the state was not the only definer of the agenda, nor was it a monolithic entity. In France, the media exploited internal divisions within the executive 'in the interest of public information'. Moreover, especially the quality press – reinforced by those with an 'alternative' status, like the *Canard enchaîné* – managed to rely on 'non-primary' news sources. Kuhn concludes that 'even with the odds stacked in its favour, the state cannot always rely on the official perspective dominating press coverage all the time'. He mentions the Bokassa diamonds and the *Rainbow Warrior* affairs. Equally, the press attention to scandals over HIV-infected blood and alleged financial wrong-doing by politicians shows that, the French press has generally performed its watchdog function seriously and kept the citizenry informed about important matters of public interest (Errera, 1993, p. 76).

Thirdly, in post-war Western Europe the media have enjoyed protections and prerogatives granted by the law. These have varied among countries but they might include: laws prescribing free access to information; laws granting to journalists and to their sources the right, and even the duty, to maintain confidentiality; laws granting protection against seizure of journalistic material; and laws proscribing, or at least seriously circumscribing, the state's ability to arrest, harass or otherwise control, journalists. Here France might be seen as exemplary. It has a law granting its journalists a *clause de conscience*, a 'freedom of conscience' clause, which assures them very generous compensation if they feel compelled to leave a paper's employ because of a change in its orientation likely to compromise their integrity (Albert, 1990, pp. 54–57). Across Western Europe, the press has been allowed considerable scope for professional self-regulation. As the following survey illustrates, the extent to which the law prescribes freedom of information varies considerably; some states have been far more open with official information than others. Similarly, some states have gone further than others in granting journalistic confidentiality. Instances of seizure and/or arrest by the state have, in practice, been rare. An important reason for their rarity has been the existence of legal safeguards.

Freedom of information and protection of rights of disclosure

In all countries government has the right to withhold official information that is sensitive for national security and defence. This has undoubtedly been the pretext for much of the censorship that has been mentioned. In addition, normally laws have existed to limit the free flow of information in order to protect individual privacy, commercial secrecy and law enforcement. Beyond such restrictions, there is a fairly wide commitment to freedom of information in Europe (see Table 2.1). In fact, Britain is exceptional in not having produced general freedom of information legislation. Coliver (1993, p. 275) notes pointedly that in Britain 'there is a presumption in favour of government secrecy'. There is, of course, a difference between having freedom of information legislation and practising it. Even in Sweden, commonly regarded as a model of open government, Axberger (1993, p. 161) notes that 'as in every other country, efforts are made to bury sensitive matters to prevent public scrutiny'. Axberger cites the infamous 1980s 'Bofors affair' as a case where the Swedish government attempted to withhold extracts of an official report into a controversial deal made by the country's largest arms manufacturer. Under pressure, though, the full report was released, this outcome actually serving to underscore Sweden's good overall record. In Sweden, freedom of information is supervised by a Justice Ombudsman appointed by parliament who has often taken up arms in defence of the principle.

In Germany and the Netherlands the matter is normally dealt with by general administrative review. In most countries, appeal against refusal to disclose information can be made to the courts. In *étatiste* France there even exists a special commission, the *Commission d'accès aux documents administratifs* (CADA), whose purpose is to safeguard public access to official information (Errera, 1993, p. 69).

As regards disclosure of restricted information, Sweden ranks alongside the United States in providing the press with protection against prosecution – unless national security is at stake. In Sweden journalists cannot be compelled to name 'whistleblowers'. In a number of other countries, including Germany and Norway, a public interest defence can be mounted in such cases. In Norway there is no law saying that the government is owed confidentiality (Coliver, 1993, pp. 275–276). In Britain, civil servants are bound by a duty of confidentiality and 'whistleblowers' enjoy no legal protection (Nicol and Bowman, 1993, p. 179). The media could be required by the courts to disclose their sources when national security was deemed at stake, as the notable case of Sarah Tisdall illustrated in 1985. (However, arguably Tisdall's crime had been to embarrass the government rather than imperil national security – Curran and Seaton, 1991, p. 362.) Further, in Britain national security was just one of several grounds on which journalists could be required to disclose their sources. In fact, Britain's protection of journalistic confidentiality has been judged to be wanting by a 1994 opinion of the

Table 2.1 Freedom of information in a number of West European states

Country	
Austria	Express constitutional right. All documents are public unless deemed otherwise by statute. There is a public interest defence for disclosure (unless related to national security).
France	A 1978 Act provided for general access to public documents but enumerated certain exceptions.
Germany	Right of access to government information is prescribed in *Land* press laws. This right is protected by Article 5 of the constitution. Public authorities have a 'duty to inform'. There is a public interest defence for disclosure (though not for top secret information).
Netherlands	Express constitutional right.
Norway	All administrative documents are in principle public unless deemed otherwise by statute.
Spain	Access to government documents is implicitly recognised as a right in the constitution. Classified matters are defined by statute.
Sweden	Express constitutional right. All documents are public unless deemed otherwise by statute. There is a public interest defence for disclosure (unless national security is at risk). Journalists can protect confidentiality of 'whistle-blowers' in public service.
UK	No freedom of information. Disclosure requires official authorisation. There exists a 'presumption in favour of government secrecy'.

Note:
In all countries, national security and defence are grounds for secrecy. Other common grounds for exception are personal privacy, commercial secrecy, law enforcement and public safety.
Source: Article 19, *Press Law and Practice*, 1993, especially pp. 274–276.

European Commission of Human Rights at Strasbourg (now pending a definitive Court ruling). The case in question was a private sector dispute touching 'interests of justice' rather than national security. However, the important point is that the Commission argued that Britain's laws on contempt of court (the instrument requiring journalists to disclose their sources) failed to meet the requirements of Article 10 of the European Convention on Human

Rights, which stipulates the requirement of freedom of expression. The Commission argued that protection of journalists' sources was vital if the press was to perform its function as a public watchdog in a democratic society (*Guardian*, 26 May 1994, p. 5).

Protection of sources

Nevertheless, aside from issues of national security and extreme criminality, legal protection of confidentiality of sources is regarded as a norm of journalistic conduct. It is respected, usually. Without it, investigative journalism would be ineffective and the press's watchdog function would be harmed. However, the legal situation varies across Europe (see Table 2.2).

Table 2.2   Protection of confidentiality of sources in a number of West European states

Country	
Austria	Media Act provides for confidentiality of sources.
France	The 1993 Criminal Code has been amended to grant journalists right not to disclose sources.
Germany	*Land* press laws contain right to refuse testimony. Moreover, there is protection against search and seizure except under very limited circumstances.
Netherlands	Confidentiality is not legally underpinned but is defended by the Dutch Press Council.
Norway	The courts can order disclosure, but such cases are rare. In 1992 the Norwegian Supreme Court defended the principle of confidentiality.
Spain	Confidentiality is not legally underpinned.
Sweden	Freedom of Press Act prohibits either the investigation (by public authority) or the disclosure (by journalists) of sources.
UK	The 1981 Contempt of Court Act gives several grounds for compelling disclosure; these include national security and the 'interests of justice'.

Source: Article 19, *Press Law and Practice*, 1993.

In Sweden, journalists are even positively required to observe professional secrecy. Austria, Germany and since 1993 also France, all provide strong legal protection of confidentiality of sources. In Norway, too, confidentiality would appear to have been widely practised though it is not legally prescribed. Norway's Supreme Court has ruled that the right to confidentiality increases in line with the public interest value of the information revealed. By contrast, in Britain the courts have actually compelled journalists to reveal sources in matters beyond those relating to national security (Coliver, 1993, pp. 282–283). Sweden is once again a very special case. As Axberger (1993, pp. 164–165) describes, 'the protection of news sources under the Swedish Constitution is very strong'. The country's 1949 Freedom of the Press Act prohibits official investigation as well as the disclosure of sources. The government is not allowed even to try to trace the sources of journalists' information; and for their part, journalists are legally required to protect the identity of their sources (also see Stenholm, 1993, pp. 63–64; Gustaffson, 1992, p. 211; Allaun, 1988, p. 79). In Germany, too, journalists enjoy a special Right to Refuse Testimony and journalistic premises are protected from search and seizure. These protections can only be waived under the most exceptional circumstances (Karpen, 1993, p. 93).

Privacy and the right of reply

Within the distinct bounds set by the law, the post-war West European press generally has had large discretion to publish what it has wanted to. Journalistic freedom to hold politicians, public officials and other powerful interests to account, has been highly valued by the public. After the continental experience of Fascism, elite attitudes altered profoundly; no longer did politicians expect to be able to control the information flow as they had in past. News management required a new professionalism; the old-style crude approach was simply not viable in a more open market situation. The main trend has been away from state dominance towards political marketing, the 'packaging' of politics (Franklin, 1994). Further, as noted already, an important post-war development, evident right across Europe, was a *de-politicisation* of the commercial press. Albeit to varying degrees according to the *genre* of publication and the country in question's press traditions, newspapers now embraced an entertainment function. Certainly, information had become a commodity and, increasingly, the information market demanded unfettered freedom of expression. Indeed, since the 1960s the frontiers of freedom of expression have been pushed back a very long way. In these matters the European press has been liable to all the normal legal disciplines regarding decency, incitement to violence and criminal acts, and so forth. But what has bounded the press's behaviour *vis-à-vis* social mores and respect for the private individual? After all, freedom also brought new responsibilities.

One of the most important issues of all regarding the regulation of the press, has been the safeguarding of respect for the individual's privacy against unwarranted incursions. All countries have provided a defence for individuals against press intrusion through having routine defamation and libel laws. In theory at least, the free press has been constrained by a dense thicket of such laws. For ordinary individuals, however, the legal costs normally involved in taking action of this kind have amounted to a real deterrent against actually doing so. Therefore a number of European countries have adopted special legislation providing for privacy and the right of reply specifically with a view to constraining the media. France's 1881 press law, granting freedom of the press, long ago introduced a right of reply. Privacy legislation came much later. During the 1960s it was developed through case law and later adopted under Article 9 of the Civil Code. The law allowed for seizure of publications that offended in this regard. French privacy law, it has been suggested, has even 'acquired constitutional status' (Errera, 1993, p. 67). France's privacy legislation helps to explain the comparative weakness of French investigative journalism. Very much on the credit side, it should also be emphasised, is the marked absence of a French 'gutter press'.

As Table 2.3 shows, France is by no means alone in having such laws. Sweden, however, is an interesting exception; both privacy infractions and right of reply are matters left to the Swedish Press Council to regulate according to its Code of Ethics. A Press Ombudsman also provides some protection (see below). This voluntary system has been judged to have worked well (Axberger, 1993, pp. 158–159). In Britain, by contrast, self-regulation has appeared to have had many shortcomings. By 1990 the Conservative government had become so concerned about tabloid excesses that it established the Calcutt inquiry into the matter. Following the 1990 Calcutt report's recommendation, a Press Complaints Commission (PCC) was established (replacing the Press Council – see below) which incorporated respect for privacy into its new Code of Practice. However, the PCC had no sanctions. When a second Calcutt report (1993) found the PCC to have been an ineffective regulator and recommended statutory intervention the National Heritage Secretary (the minister responsible for the media) set about preparing a white paper on the press. Nevertheless, in 1995 (at the time of writing) there were indications that privacy legislation was unlikely to result although there would be recommendations to improve self-regulation and provision for compensation to be made to victims of unwarranted press intrusion (*Guardian*, 15 March 1995, p. 1). The rather free-and-easy situation in Britain contrasts sharply with those countries where privacy infractions are matters of criminal law. In France, privacy law, unlike defamation, is a tort only. This is also the case in the Netherlands and generally in Austria. In Germany, though, protection is offered by several criminal laws. Norway, too, protects privacy under its Penal Code. Privacy infractions can be punished by imprisonment, fines and the confiscation of publications. In Norway, the right of reply is similarly enforceable in criminal law under the threat of unlimited fines, though recourse to this sanction has not been made since the 1950s (Wolland, 1993, pp. 122–123; generally, see Article 19, 1993).

Table 2.3 Privacy laws and right of reply

Country	Privacy laws	Legal right of Reply
Austria	+	+
France	+	+
Germany	+	+
Netherlands	+	+
Norway	+	+
Spain	+	+
Sweden	–	–
UK	–	–

Source: Article 19, *Press Law and Practice*, 1993.

Self-regulation by Press Councils

Professional self-regulation has been a general privilege of the European press. A number of West European countries have operated a system of voluntary self-regulation in the shape of national press councils. These were originally established precisely with a view to promoting press freedom, usually by the joint initiative of publishers and journalists. They were financed by the national press associations. They commonly elaborated press codes that dealt with press standards; these codes typically included commitments to honesty and fairness, objectivity, a duty to distinguish between facts and opinion, respect for privacy, general standards of decency and taste, confidentiality of sources and so forth. They also handled complaints about press conduct. Those of the Netherlands, Norway and Sweden have been judged to have been the most effective (Coliver, 1993, pp. 263–266; Lorimer, 1994, p. 120).

Britain's Press Council was among the less effective. It was established in 1947 on the recommendation of the first Royal Commission on the press (the Ross Commission). The main reason was rising public and parliamentary concern about declining standards and also about press concentration. It was, however, a weak and lop-sided regulatory body: 'deriving its authority from the press itself and not from statute' (Calcutt, 1990, p. 58). Its membership was entirely drawn from the press, and 'it had no weapons beyond publicity and wounding criticism' (Seymour-Ure, 1991, p. 236). The second Royal Commission on the press (the Shawcross Commission) criticised the Council's lack of any lay representatives (ie. from the public) and as a result the body's membership was extended. Still, the Council was 'publicly perceived more as a champion of the press than as a watchdog for the public' (Calcutt, 1990, p. 59). Following a third Royal Commission in 1974 (the McGregor Commission), lay representation was increased to half its membership. Yet it continued to lack authority. One reason was that these lay representatives were actually chosen by an Appointments Commission made up of the Council's members: unsurprisingly, therefore, the Press Council never came to be regarded as independent from the press. Another reason was its non-statutory status and its complete lack of effective sanctions. Yet another was its self-limitation to dealing with individual complaints; it did not see its role as being widely to monitor press behaviour (unlike the regulators of broadcasting – see Chapter 4). In 1980 the National Union of Journalists, which had helped call the council into existence in 1947, withdrew from it pronouncing it 'incapable of reform' (Calcutt, 1990, p. 60).

In the 1980s the tabloid press in Britain plumbed new depths of intrusion into citizens' privacy. The third Royal Commission on the press had expressed concern about this issue in particular. By the end of the decade the issue was taken up by a private members' Bill in parliament (politicians being especially sensitive to press intrusions into their own privacy). Under rising public pressure as well, the government established the Calcutt committee to look into the matter. However, the Calcutt committee's report (1990) recommended improving self-regulation. The tabloid press was given a last chance to mend its ways. As seen, the Press Council was replaced by the Press Complaints Commission, colloquially described by the government as the press's 'last chance saloon'. Failure to perform, would result in legislation to establish a statutory complaints body. The new commission's composition was, however, illustrative of the strength of the enduring British commitment to 'hands-off' self-regulation: it was composed of newspaper editors and 'Establishment' figures. In the view of the second Calcutt report (1993, p. xi) the PCC 'was a body set up by the industry, financed by the industry, dominated by the industry, and operating a code of practice devised by the industry and which [was] over-favourable to the industry'. The report criticised the PCC for not being 'truly independent body which it should be' and recommended a statutory regime.

Modelled originally on the British Press Council Germany's Press Council was introduced in 1956 at a time when the publishers feared that, in the absence of such an initiative, the federal government might introduce stricter measures. The composition of the council relected Germany's traditions of corporatism and *Proporz* (proportionality). That is, it gave representation to both sides of the industry – publishers and journalists – in equal numbers. It worked through providing a code of ethics and following up complaints against the press. It issues reprimands which it may require newspapers to publish. The German Press Council relies entirely on moral pressure and evaluations of its effectiveness vary (Sandford, 1976, p. 59; Humphreys, 1994, p. 60; Karpen, 1993, p. 84). Austria's Press Council, too, reflected that country's political tradition of corporatism. Founded in 1961, by the joint initiative of the Association of Austrian Newspaper Publishers and the Austrian Journalists Union, it consisted of ten representatives of each organisation. As well as practising self-regulation, it represented the interests of the press before parliament, the administration and the public. However, it had no legal sanctions. Moreover, its authority was seriously weakened by the fact that the country's most powerful newspaper, the *Neue Kronen-Zeitung*, consistently refused to recognise the many negative judgements levelled at it. The Council has also been criticised for not giving representation to impartial experts or members of the public. With little public support, it has been widely viewed as lacking authority (Berka, 1993, pp. 28–29).

By contrast, Sweden's Press Council has been publicly respected and, by all accounts, very effective. It was established as early as 1916, the first in Europe. Its code of ethics was adopted in 1923. Reflective of the country's 'group orientated' corporatist political culture the Swedish Press Council was originally instituted by the Association of Newspaper Publishers, the Union of Journalists and the Publicists' Club; the latter was a professional organisation committed to press freedom. In the 1960s membership of the council was opened up to lay representation and a Press Ombudsman was instituted to ensure even more public accountability. The first three holders of the post of Press Ombudsman were judges, the fourth a journalist. Since 1969 the Swedish Press Council has consisted of one representative of each of the three named press organisations, plus three representatives of the general public (these being respected public figures), and a chairperson who is a judge (usually a member of the country's Supreme Court). The representatives of the public interest, therefore, have formed a majority in it; by themselves, the publishers are a minority. Thus the more representative corporatist Swedish Press Council stands in stark contrast to the comparatively weak British model in which the publishers and editors effectively have held sway. It also contrasts with the more 'closed' German and Austrian variants of the corporatist model in which representation has been restricted to publishers and journalists. The Swedish Press Council also has teeth: it has the power to fine newspapers and magazines that offend against its code; further, member newspapers are bound to respond to its criticisms. Between them the Press Council and the Ombudsman have acted as an important channel for holding the press accountable to the public. They have offered opportunity for the redress of complaints, enforced the press's code of conduct, and provided the public with a preferable alternative to the courts. By all accounts, these two institutions have provided for an effective and publicly accountable system of self-regulation (Axberger, 1993, pp. 155–156; Stenholm, 1993, pp. 65–67; Curran and Seaton, 1991, p. 363).

Different Press Traditions

Britain, clearly, has not been notable for the enactment of specific press legislation. As Seymour-Ure (1991, p. 205) has put it, governments 'seemed to have had ... a traditional policy of no policy'. This, he makes clear, was not literally the case; the press were subject to all sorts of indirect policies, for instance, affecting their finance (eg. VAT exemption – see Chapter 3) or trade union rights (Thatcher's ban on 'secondary picketing' – see Chapter 1). Moreover, British governments have been as concerned as they have anywhere else to manage news, and arguably more concerned than most to guard the privilege of state secrecy. But Britain's tradition of *laissez-faire* was certainly reflected in the absence of specific press laws. Also absent was general freedom of information legislation. Censorship in Britain was usually discreet and security related, symptomatic of a 'secretive' rather than a *dirigiste* state. The British press was, in fact, largely free in its private sector operations. During the 1970s, the quality press developed a reputation for incisive investigative journalism. By the same token, the tabloid press was unconstrained by right of reply and privacy laws – and deference to authority – to indulge in its own characteristic brand of human interest journalism and muck-raking.

France, by contrast, has had a body of press law dating back to the famous law of 1881 originally granting press freedom. The Third Republic was a period of relative *laissez-faire*, but in post-war France the boundaries of press freedom have clearly been circumscribed more closely. This reflects France's strong civil law and *étatiste* traditions. It contrasts with the British preference for 'hands-off' self-regulation. French press regulation has invited some negative comment particularly with regard to the constraints it has placed in the way of investigative journalism which is poorly implanted in the professional journalistic culture (Kuhn, 1995, p. 69). Also, the French state has been – on occasion – very interventionist *vis-à-vis* the press. Yet, much of the coercion directed at the press in the post-war period could be explained by the siege mentality that prevailed in government during the early years of the Fifth Republic. Against this, French law has provided for some notable positive rights and freedoms: the principle of right of access to official information, a right of reply, strict privacy laws protecting individuals against unwarranted press intrusion, and, not least, the recent protections afforded to journalists and their sources.

In between Britain's *laissez-faire* approach and France's interventionist *étatisme*, stands the *decentralised* German model. Like the French model, it was rule-bound. Germany like France had a long established civil law tradition. On the other hand, German statism had been dealt a blow by the experience of the Third Reich. Media freedom was immediately enshrined in the constitution (Basic Law) of 1949. Article 5 of the Basic Law made very explicit indeed the fundamental guarantee of freedom of the press and the banning of censorship. Evidence suggests that overt state censorship has indeed been minimal. The press system was also decentralised, though the numerous *Land* press laws were all fairly similar in their content. Like the French model, the *decentralised* German one subjected the press to some comparatively strict laws and obligations. However, unlike in France, or in pre-war Germany itself, the central state's role in the post-war German press sector was conspicuously weak.

Plainly, Sweden's *corporatist* model provided yet another highly distinctive approach. Sweden offers the best example of a self-regulated system that actually does regulate. This system laid great stress on freedom of information and journalistic freedom of inquiry. At the same time, it provided accountability through the balanced representation within its regulatory institutions of both sides of the press industry and also lay representatives. The existence of a Press Ombudsman was an additional safeguard of the public interest. The Swedish version of self-regulation, it has been suggested, has a certain model character. It would appear to have safeguarded generally high journalistic standards and provided for a very open system of access to information. The other Scandinavian countries share some attributes of the Swedish model; in particular, they would appear to have been comparatively open in the provision of freedom of information.

All cases, however, share one overriding characteristic: the publishers have been empowered to determine the ideological, philosophical, social and political orientations of the publications they own or control; and they have been granted a conspicuous degree of freedom from restrictive regulation of the markets in which they operate. In fact, German law went so far as to rule explicitly in favour of the positive right of proprietors of newspapers and magazines to prescribe the general political, economic and cultural line of their publications. Accordingly, journalists can be legally bound to observe this line in their contracts of employment. The legal specification of this 'protection of the (publishers') right to determine editorial orientation' (the *Tendenzschutz*) reflected the strong position of the publishers' lobby, and the weakness of the journalists' associations, during the immediate post-war period (Humphreys, 1994, p. 67). However, German law merely confirmed what had long been an essential part of the universal understanding of press freedom in Europe as in the United States. In matters of ownership and control of newspapers and magazines, the West European press was virtually entirely free from regulation.

Guide to further reading

Especially

Article 19, *Press Law and Practice*, London: Article 19, 1993.

But also

P. Albert, *La Presse Française*, Paris: Documentation Française, 1990.
P. Humphreys, *Media and Media Policy in Germany*, Oxford/Providence, RI: Berg, 1994.
R. Kuhn, *The Media in France*, London/New York: Routledge, 1995.
R. Negrine, *Politics and the Mass Media in Britain*, London/New York: Routledge, 1989.
C. Seymour-Ure, *The British Press and Broadcasting since 1945*, Oxford: Basil Blackwell, 1991.

3

Press concentration in Western Europe

What is press concentration?

Press concentration signifies the state of affairs that exists when the sector is dominated by a relatively few large publishers and publishing groups. It arises as the sector becomes increasingly 'horizontally' integrated; that is, when large concerns gain ownership of multiple titles and the sector becomes dominated by newspaper chains. The press sector would appear to be very prone to precisely this kind of oligopolistic development. As seen already, the inter-war period had produced its powerful press barons. The post-war era saw press ownership continue to concentrate into relatively few hands. Proprietors may have come and gone, but ownership structures became if anything, even more concentrated. Large concerns continued to flourish – through merger and acquisition and as the result of business failures among their generally smaller competitors – and the number of independent titles diminished progressively.

Kepplinger (1982, p. 64) has usefully identified several different manifestations of concentration: (1) a significant trend towards concentration of publishers, generally referred to as 'industrial concentration'; (2) a significant trend towards concentration of circulation, leading towards 'market dominance' by one or several publishers; and (3) an additional trend towards 'editorial concentration'. The latter needs a further word of explanation. Editorial pluralism is not just reflected in the number of titles available, it ultimately depends upon the number of independent 'editorial units' in the sector. When this number diminishes, for instance, as the result of the growth of newspaper chains, there may still appear superficially to exist an impressive array of titles, but in reality many papers are no longer any more than generally local or regional editions of a 'mother' paper. This was a characteristic of the German press, in particular.

The schema described so far refers only to what is known as the 'horizontal' integration of the sector. In other words, it refers only to the scale of concentration of ownership and editorial control, and market dominance in the various markets for newspapers and magazines. Another manifestation of industrial concentration is 'vertical' integration: where the same company controls the various stages of the production process: editorial, printing, distribution, etc. This too is obviously of major economic importance. However, it is horizontal integration of the press sector that raises the most important questions concerning the pluralism – and political balance – of media content.

Press concentration in Europe is pronounced at a number of different levels: local; regional; national. An abundance of evidence suggests that it is very widespread indeed at the first two levels; local and regional monopolies abound. The national situation is nowhere characterised by outright monopoly, but this does not mean that there is little press concentration at this level: oligopolistic competition is the rule. Moreover, a situation of near monopoly definitely does characterise some national-level press markets: for example, both the market for Sunday papers and the tabloid market in Germany are dominated by the giant *Springer* newspaper concern. In certain instances, press concentration has even extended beyond national frontiers. The Austrian press is in the hands of a few giant German concerns, including *Springer*. What, then, has caused this phenomenon of press concentration?

Economic causes of press concentration

From a purely commercial perspective, it is entirely rational for publishers to seek profit via the achievement of the largest possible market share for their publications. It is therefore rational for them to adopt expansionist strategies. Whether an enterprise is actually able to marshal the resources required to expand varies according to several factors: most obviously the company's size, its credit-worthiness, related to the latter its profitability, and so on. It is a fairly simple rule of thumb that the larger and more profitable the firm at the outset, the more easy it is to expand at the expense of smaller, less profitable competitors.

Hardly surprisingly, many of the earliest European press barons were entrepreneurs that already had considerable standing or important financial backers in the world of industry and commerce. Alfred Hugenberg, the extreme nationalist politician who established a massive press empire in Weimar Germany, was backed by the intensely nationalistic and conservative industrial magnates of the Ruhr. In Britain, Lords Beaverbrook and Rothermere both had extensive industrial interests. In France, Jean Prouvost built his inter-war press empire on the back of resources acquired in his textile factories. It is true, some post-war press barons constructed empires from humble beginnings, starting with a small number of successful publications in niche markets and, borrowing heavily, they expanded from these. Opportunities snatched amidst the upheavals of the early post-war period (Springer; Bertelsmann; Maxwell) help to explain most of these cases. The main point, however, is that press concentration has its own dynamic effect; the strong grow at the expense of weaker competitors. They do so because they enjoy competitive advantages: economies of scale, higher profitability and, by virtue of this, increased borrowing power.

Papers that establish a circulation lead over their competitors can expect to enjoy lower unit costs. As circulation increases, the cost of typesetting and printing diminishes as a share of expenditure; profits increase accordingly. Not only do high circulations mean higher sales, but they also make newspapers more attractive to advertisers. Because their business volume and profitability levels are higher, the stronger concerns find it easier to negotiate loans from financial institutions. All these benefits allow them to invest more than their competitors in production, distribution and marketing. Further, their strength provides the opportunity to undercut competitors' prices. Their expansion – through takeovers and chain ownership – leads to further cost savings and increased income from sales and advertising. Mergers and acquisitions permit the large press concerns to rationalise their workforces, to pool their editorial and journalistic resources, and to share their administrative, production and distribution facilities. Large press concerns can also negotiate the most favourable terms of business with their advertising customers. Press concerns with a large share of the national press market, and large regional newspaper chains, present obvious attractions to the advertising business: they deliver very large circulations.

In one sense, of course, concentration implies a decrease in 'competition': in the sense that the number of market players decreases. It does not follow, however, that competition between those that are left becomes any less fierce. In fact, during the post-war period increasingly cut-throat competition has been a factor making for press concentration: small and weak papers have fallen victim to these competitive pressures. Often expansion has been achieved by means of destructive price-wars, heavy borrowing and cost-cutting rationalisation, all of which are beyond the capacities of weaker concerns. Also, newspapers have had to face a challenge from other media. The post-war decline in the number of newspapers could partly be explained by a drop in readership caused by competition from radio and television, and more recently, the appearance of 'free papers', all of which have escalated competition for the advertising cake (ultimately a finite quantity). The advertising industry, too, has been prone to periodic recessions to which weaker newspapers have fallen victim. Press concentration, as has widely been remarked, has therefore tended to come in waves following the general economic cycle. Concentration has leaped in times of recession, a fall in advertising revenue ruining many papers. Newspapers in financial crisis obviously become easy pickings for stronger rivals. Both Rupert Murdoch in Britain and Robert Hersant in France, drawing heavily on their credit with the banks, established their dominant positions in their respective countries' press markets by coming to the 'rescue' of papers facing bankruptcy. Taken together, all the above noted factors mean that newspapers have had to struggle ever more fiercely to avoid becoming uneconomic. Smaller companies confronted with steadily rising costs of manufacture and distribution, have faced limited choices: for many, the choice has been between folding, being directly taken over, or becoming an off-shoot of a large concern (for a concise discussion of the causes of concentration, see Lorimer, 1994, pp. 88–93; for a lengthier discussion of concentration and its causes, see Sánchez-Tabernero *et al.*, 1993).

Technological developments and deconcentration?

Optimistically, many expected that the introduction of new production technologies would promote de-concentration of the sector. Photocomposition and computerised text systems certainly presented new scope for cost cutting. Many hoped that this fact would help small and medium-sized publishers survive; these were precisely the sections of the press that were most vulnerable to takeover by large press groups. Moreover, the reduction of costs should theoretically lower barriers to market entry and make the survival of new ventures more likely thereafter. This should open the way for an expansion of the number of newspapers and newspaper groups.

However, the reality has been disappointing. The launch in 1986 and subsequent survival of the *Independent* in Britain may have owed much to the embrace of new technologies and the decline of old Fleet Street practices (see Chapter 1). It was the first new national quality daily to be successfully launched in over a century (Negrine, 1994, p. 50). But there have also been dramatic failures, notably the *Correspondent* and Robert Maxwell's abortive *London Daily News*. Moreover, no new tabloids were launched independently – or long remained independent – of established publishing groups. Eddie Shah's *Today* was soon swallowed up by Rupert Murdoch's News International. There may have occurred a proliferation of specialist publications, mainly magazines; the technologies may have helped the free sheet sub-sector flourish. However, it is fair to say that the new technologies have not produced a flowering of new mainstream newspaper titles. In the case of the British press, Curran and Seaton (1991, p. 92) note: 'the introduction of the new print technology has not had the salutary consequences that were predicted. Between 1985 and 1988, the big three publishers' proportion of total daily and Sunday circulation declined by only one percentage point'. They immediately add that 'the leading publishers of regional newspapers also consolidated their position'. Realistically, new technology could not be expected of itself to de-concentrate the sector. In the first place, the initial costs of technological modernisation had to be borne. This investment amounted to a high financial hurdle and a burden to be amortised for new market entrants. This was particularly the case for small- and medium-sized enterprises and for entrepreneurs without strong financial backers. Secondly, new technology did not banish the intense competition that was the underlying cause of newspaper failures and takeovers. New papers could not match the promotion and prices of the established press. Indeed, in the fierce struggle for finite revenue, newspapers were compelled to introduce the technologies simply in order to remain competitive. Many could not carry the cost of remaining in the game. As Kuhn (1995, p. 44) notes about the French situation, 'overall, new technology has not had a major influence in reducing the costs of entry into the newspaper market.' Nor had it 'reversed the decline of the daily newspaper sector as measured by the number of titles and their circulation figures'.

Why worry about press concentration?

Among economists, interpretations about how markets actually work vary. The mainstream neo-classical view assumes that the market process is basically a competitive one. Some distortion is seen as unavoidable and acceptable but if it should prove to be unacceptable, then it can be safely overcome by competition policy. Neo-liberals stress the importance of entrepreneurial rivalry; by implication the actual number of market players matters rather less so long as competition (or potential competition) exists. On the other hand, many economists (and not only marxists) see monopoly or oligopolistic competition as the natural tendency of capitalistic competition. The key question, though, is whether or not it threatens pluralism.

There are a number of reasons why press concentration *per se* might not be considered harmful. One common argument is that the economies of scale that large companies enjoy, provide the consumer with positive benefits. These economies of scale, it is suggested, allow large organisations to provide a range of different publications and enable them actually to sustain a number of sub-sectoral markets. Further, small independent newspapers cannot afford to hire very many columnists and correspondents. For their news supply they are heavily dependent upon the wire services of news agencies; there arises an obvious danger of uniformity of news agendas and values. By contrast, giant press concerns, through their economies of scale, can supply a better quality of information to consumers at a significantly lower cost. They can certainly employ more journalists and maintain their own correspondent networks. Therefore they can supply a wide-ranging and independent information service on a scale that smaller businesses are unable to match. The strength of press conglomerates may even be better at protecting editorial independence, from political as well as influential economic interests like the advertisers. It is even suggested that independent newspapers present more scope for proprietorial interference; whereas the sheer size of increasingly huge and impersonal press companies compel proprietors to cede more and more control to a more 'neutral' class of managers and editors (Sánchez-Tabernero *et al.*, 1993, pp. 158 and 183).

For all this, there remains widespread concern that press concentration does entail some negative effects. Most obviously, it erects market entry barriers and distorts the operation of the 'free' press markets themselves. As mentioned, giant groups find it relatively easy either to take over, or to drive out, smaller companies. Their resources of increased editorial power and financial muscle can be disposed progressively to engrandise their scope of operation. Large companies can, for example, deploy inter-organisational cross-subsidies strategically to undercut the price of weaker competitors in target markets. Nor does the story end here. As Chapter 6 will describe, the large companies' editorial power has recently been deployed to promote their multi-media strategies. By using their newspapers to attack, sometimes very fiercely, the public-service broadcasting monopolies in Western Europe the European publishing giants revealed from the 1980s onwards (earlier in Germany) their ambitions to diversify into broadcasting operations. There seems, then, to exist an inexorable law: press concentration breeds further concentration, both in the press sector itself and, lately, in the wider media field. This distortion of media markets may be taken as undesirable in itself, but there are further reasons for possible concern.

Arguably, there has occurred a certain loss of diversity of the press. It is often suggested that there used to exist a 'golden age' of diversity. In the United States, for instance, this is said to have occurred roughly between 1880 and 1930. In France it is supposed to have characterised the period 1870 to 1914. This diversity had several components: intellectual and ideological diversity, regional diversity, cultural diversity and diversity of format. As explained in Chapter 1, an undoubted ideological diversity suffered a marked decline in the post-war period. Although this loss of diversity only partly reflected the industrial concentration process, the latter was unquestionably an important factor. The rise of regional and local monopolies, often linked together in an oligopoly of national press chains, can very obviously reduce regional and cultural diversity. But surely in market systems the existence of local tastes and manifold cultural constituencies within society will still make for diversity of content in publications plying for their custom? The fact remains that press concentration would appear to have been accompanied by an increased standardisation of both the cultural content and the format of modern newspapers. Concentrated markets, it would appear, are highly conducive to product imitation. In oligopolistic markets there is little incentive towards product differentiation. Rather, players constantly seek to accommodate a competitor's successful style. Changes in the production process may have allowed for an increase in specialist publications (magazines catering to sports enthusiasts, computer buffs, etc.). However, the mainstream publications have increasingly sought to imitate each other. The proliferation of specialist publications appears to be the exception that proves the rule, their very success suggesting a need that is largely unfulfilled by the restricted range of mainstream mass media. It seems to be a general rule that 'within oligopolies, competition to satisfy the customer is carried on in a relatively limited way and products become more and more similar' (Lorimer, 1994, p. 77).

Yet another concern is the danger of political bias arising when media ownership is concentrated in a relatively few private hands. Marxist analysts in particular have been criticised for taking too much for granted that a direct relationship always exists between ownership, control and ideological content. It is true, often such comment is not empirically grounded. Yet, there can be little question but that proprietors (and their chosen chief editors) can and do exert a number of irresistible direct and indirect pressures by which they can set the general editorial tone of their publications. Proprietors typically appoint editors, and chief editors appoint sub-editors, managers and journalists. Proprietors also 'decide budgets and manning levels' and 'put their imprint on the total organisations', the consequence of which is that 'editors and journalists work within already defined structures and processes' (Negrine, 1994, p. 64). It would only seem reasonable to believe that this bears on the manner in which editors and journalists perform their functions. If only by reducing the scope for their professional mobility and narrowing their career opportunities, press concentration can be said to exert a hidden discipline on the editors of news and information and on the producers of social and political comment. Under such conditions, it is hardly surprising if editorial independence and journalistic integrity fall by the wayside (for an account of aims and methods of proprietorial intervention, see Curran and Seaton, 1991, Chapter 7).

Although their primary motivation is to seek commercial profit within a competitive marketplace it is beyond question that powerful press barons and chief editors have exerted pressure on politicians and the political process, quite directly at times. In the first place, it is commonly accepted that press bias can affect the outcome of elections, although quite to what extent is a matter of fierce debate. The conventional wisdom that the media merely reinforce political views has come under increasing question, the suspicion being that their influence may often be more decisive. Secondly, media power can be deployed quite overtly to influence the direction of public policy on issues of public concern. Thirdly, media proprietors and top editors have exerted more subtle kinds of influence, playing upon the natural sensitivities of politicians about how they are represented in the media. Fourthly, they certainly act as 'gatekeepers' of media access. Fifthly, powerful media proprietors and leading editors may gain an influential voice in the innermost policy sanctums of individual political parties and governments. Their political connections may be very explicit. Robert Hersant was a Gaullist Member of Parliament. Silvio Berlusconi became Prime Minister of Italy!

Of course, not all press corporations are dominated by individual proprietors or newspaper dynasties. As noted, the other striking characteristic of the modern press is the degree to which press companies have become parts of much larger impersonal communications groups (though sometimes these are owned by single proprietors). All the same, it might be argued, in capitalist press systems where the main outlets of opinion are in restricted private commercial ownership or control there inevitably arises the danger of an overall bias towards corporate business values. In this vein, the American political scientist Charles Lindblom (1977, p. 202) has suggested rather colourfully that the commercial media are likely to carry 'a heavy freight of business ideology'. In Lindblom's 'neo-pluralist' view the commercial media are part of the overall systemic bias towards corporate business in capitalist societies which, due to business's 'privileged position', can only be expected to be imperfectly pluralist. Certainly, it does not seem too polemical to suggest that the commercially organised press as a whole is naturally more likely to favour conservative political interests. It is true that there may well be scope for a limited pluralism with a measure of support accorded to the Centre-Left. Market considerations are very likely to make for a limited pluralism of this kind. After all, there is plainly a large Centre-Left readership to cater to. As will be seen shortly, the moderate Left in Europe definitely does have its own sympathetic press outlets. Yet, only a small number of newspapers (like the *Guardian* or *Libération*) are owned by independent trusts or part-owned by the newspaper staff and there are relatively few Left-wing press barons. Press concentration, as we shall see, has tended to reduce the ideological pluralism of the press.

An overview of post-war press concentration in Western Europe

Ample evidence can be mustered, from a wide range of sources, to show that over the course of the post-war period large press groups have achieved a commanding position in the press markets of most West European countries. In the first place, Table 3.1 shows that in nearly all cases, in 1990, two publishers shared between one-third and two-thirds, in some cases over two-thirds, of national press markets in Europe. The table indicates that, the UK apart, this market dominance was most extensive in a number of countries that shared a language with a larger neighbour; their own press markets were therefore more vulnerable to unwelcome competition and even foreign domination. This was spectacularly the case in Austria, as we shall see. Among Europe's larger countries, Britain appeared to present the most striking example of oligopoly.

Press concentration in Britain

During the inter-war period the British public had already come to rely largely on a fairly restricted number of national newspapers for news and political analysis and comment (there was, of course, a distinctive Scottish press; see Kellas, 1989, pp. 197–204). The British press was distinguished by a striking dichotomy between 'quality' and 'popular' markets. This distinction, too, had already become evident before World War II but it became much more marked after it. Also, Britain had a large Sunday newspaper market. As we shall see, none of these characteristics were nearly so evident in a number of other European countries. Indeed France did not really have a mass market 'popular' press. When considering press concentration these national-specific characteristics have to be borne in mind.

Table 3.1 Concentration of European newspaper markets: % market shares of top two newspaper publishers in a number of West European countries, 1990

Country	According to European Inst. for Media Study[a]	According to EC report by Booz.Allen & Hamilton[b]
Austria	68	–
Belgium (fr)	68	71
Belgium (fl)	59	58
Denmark	48	46
France	35	33
Germany[c]	29	33
Greece	36	–
Ireland	75	76
Italy	32	34
Netherlands	35	35
Norway	45	–
Portugal	30	–
Spain	29	26
Sweden	31	–
Switzerland	21	–
UK	58	58

Notes:

[a] A. Sánchez-Tabernero *et al.*, *Media Concentration in Europe*, Media Monograph No. 16. Dusseldorf: European Institute for the Media, 1993, p. 102. Data from reports by national consultants.

[b] Commission of the European Communities DG III/F-5, *Final Report. Study on Pluralism and Concentration in Media. Economic Evaluation*, Brussels, 6 February 1992; Booz.Allen & Hamilton; Data from Carat International 1990.

[c] Old *Länder* only (i.e. not incl. the new *Länder* of former GDR).

At first sight the structure of the British national press would seem to have changed rather little over the course of the post-war period; the number of national dailies hardly changed. However, much else did. In 1945 most people read a broadsheet newspaper, whether 'quality' or 'middle-brow popular'; by the 1980s the latter tradition had been well and truly 'tabloidised' (Seymour-Ure, 1991, pp. 32–33). Another transformation occurred in the ownership structure of the press sector. In 1945, national papers were in the hands of individual family concerns with a connection to the pre-war barons. Multiple ownership of national dailies was not the rule; twelve companies controlled between them nine dailies and eleven Sundays. This ownership pattern was revolutionised from the 1960s onwards (Seymour-Ure, 1991, pp. 33–43). The British press – national and local – now fell under the ownership of a number of multinational conglomerates such as Tiny Rowland's Lonrho group (no longer his), Trafalgar House, Reed, Pearson, Conrad Black's Hollinger group (Conrad Black is the Right-wing owner of the *Daily Telegraph* and *Sunday Telegraph*), Robert Maxwell's Pergamon Holding Foundation (owner of Mirror Group Newspapers until the collapse of the Maxwell empire after his 1991 death) and of course Rupert Murdoch's News International (Curran and Seaton, 1991, p. 94). The 1980s was a particularly turbulent period of takeovers. In an increasingly cut-throat market, weak papers – crippled by battles with the unions over the introduction of new technologies – came close to closure and were acquired by new players. The most famous case was the sale of *The Times* by the Thomson organisation to Rupert Murdoch (see later, pp. 100–101). By the close of the 1980s Rupert Murdoch's News International (the British branch of his global News Corporation) had gained a commanding, and some would say a dominant, market position in the British national press markets. News International owned two daily tabloids, the *Sun* and *Today*; it owned the *Times*, one of the country's leading quality papers; and it owned the popular Sunday, *News of the World*, together with the quality Sunday paper, the *Sunday Times* (see Table 3.2).

The post-war period also saw a loss of political diversity. In 1945 four pro-Conservative national dailies faced two pro-Labour ones, the *Daily Herald* and the *Daily Mirror*, and two pro-Liberal ones, the *News Chronicle* and the *Manchester Guardian*. However, in 1960 the *News Chronicle* closed and this was soon followed by the TUC's withdrawal from the *Daily Herald* (which opened the way for its tranformation into the mass tabloid, the *Sun*). All the same, the mass circulation of the pro-Labour biased *Daily Mirror* helped to ensure that in 1964 just under 50 per cent of the British adult population still read a Labour paper. Yet, by 1983 only 24 per cent did so (Negrine, 1994, p. 54), a marked imbalance that endured throughout the 1980s. In the 1987 general election seven of the eleven national dailies supported a Conservative victory; only the *Mirror* and the *Guardian* – still accounting for a mere one-fifth of the total circulation – favoured Labour (Jones, 1991, pp. 201–203). In 1993 70 per cent of national daily readers and 62 per cent of Sunday readers were advised to vote Conservative (Marsh, 1993, p. 337). A major reason for this increase in Conservative orientation of the British press since the 1970s, was a loss of market share by the *Daily Mirror* to the pro-Conservative tabloid, the *Sun* (which ironically was the successor to the pro-Labour *Daily Herald*). The *Sun* had been purchased in 1969 by Rupert Murdoch, who became a strong sympathiser of Thatcherism.

Table 3.2 Market share of press groups in Britain 1992: by % of circulation, disaggregated into markets for dailies and Sundays, popular and quality papers

	Dailies		Sundays	
Press group	*Popular*	*Qualities*	*Popular*	*Qualities*
News Corp./Int.	37.3	15.4	34.7	44.1
Mirror Group	25.9	–	35.7	–
United Newspapers	21.1	–	12.7	–
Associated Newspapers	15.6	–	14.6	–
Telegraph Plc.	–	41.6	–	21.1
Pearson (*FT*)	–	11.5	–	–
Newspaper Publishing (*Independent*)	–	14.9	–	14.6
Guardian Group	–	16.6	–	20
Sunday Sport	–	–	2.3	–

Source: R. Negrine, *Politics and the Mass Media in Britain*, London/New York: Routledge, 1994, p. 62.

As for the local and regional press, a large number of titles varied widely in circulation, balance of national and local news, catchment area, and many other respects. However, according to Franklin and Murphy (1991, p. 11) 'more than half of the daily morning and evening newspapers published outside London [were] controlled by eight groups, while nine (mostly the same) groups control [ed] 35 per cent of the paid-for weekly press'. Similarly, Veljanovski (1990, pp. 28–29) found that 'the four largest regional publishers accounted for over one-third of total regional newspaper circulation'; and also that 'of the ten largest regional proprietors, four [were] Associated Newspapers, United Newspapers, Pearson and the Guardian and Manchester Evening News group. Moreover, unlike the national papers, a large proportion of local newspapers enjoyed a complete monopoly or near-complete local monopoly; and they were organised into chains generally concentrated in particular regions. As Seymour-Ure (1991, p. 55) reminds us, 'the implications of concentration of provincial press ownership are greater when its geographical variation is taken into account.' Clearly, ownership of the British press sector was conspicuously highly concentrated.

Press concentration in Germany

An abundance of meticulous research conducted in post-war Germany (West Germany until 1990) demonstrates that the German press has experienced considerable post-war growth but also very marked concentration.* Table 3.3 illustrates this pattern of concentration very clearly. Despite a healthy and growing circulation, the German press has seen a steady decline both in the number of newspaper titles and in the number of independent editorial units. Unification in 1990 increased the overall size of the market, but did not see a reversal of these trends.

Most West Germans read a local daily newspaper and/or the country's principal national tabloid, the *Bild* (see below); only a minority read one of the 'supra-regional' quality dailies. This fact explains the surprisingly large number of titles the country could boast of. However, the great majority of these local papers are not editorially independent. They are merely side editions of a 'mother paper' usually based in the nearest large town. They differ from the main edition only in the few pages of local news and adverts they carry. For their 'jacket' sections providing the main news and comment, these 'papers' draw upon the central editorial unit. Therefore, to the uninformed visitor, the multiplicity of titles is suggestive of a diversity that is really very much more modest (Sandford, 1976, pp. 38–42; Humphreys, 1994, pp. 74–78). Moreover, there also abound confusing and intricate webs of co-operation and capital integration

---

* Media concentration has been thoroughly researched by a number of experts. Their work has been regularly reported in the journal *Media Perspektiven* and in its annual compendium of media statistics.

(*Verflechtung*) between papers. The number of publishers – which gives a far more realistic idea of the number of genuinely different papers – also exceeds the number of independent editorial units. It is common for a number of publishers to cooperate within these central editorial units, many of which are dominated by the larger concerns. This further qualifies the picture of diversity. Finally, national reunification saw East Germany's titles fall into the grip of mainly the larger West German concerns (Humphreys, 1994, pp. 304–311).

Table 3.3 Trends in the German daily press, 1954–93

Year	Independent editorial unit	Publishers	Titles/ editions	Circulation (millions)
1954	225	624	1,500	13.4
1964	183	573	1,495	17.3
1976	121	403	1,229	19.5
1983	125	385	1,255	21.2
1989 (West)	119	358	1,344	20.3
1989 (East)	37	38	291	9.8
1991 (United)	158	410	1,673	27.3
1993 (United)	137	385	1,599	25.5

Source: W. Schutz in *Media Perspektiven. Basisdaten 1993*, Frankfurt am Main: *MP*, 1993, p. 45.

Over the course of time, competition in the German press sector has greatly diminished. In the mid-1950s local newspaper monopolies were the exception not the rule; in 1954 only 8 per cent of the population lived in 'single newspaper districts'. However, by the mid-1970s it was a third of the population and by 1993, it was nearly 40 per cent! (Schütz, 1985, p. 20; Schütz, 1994, p. 172). More often than not a monopoly publisher in a German town or city dominates the outlying and neighbouring districts; the country is covered by regional or sub-regional monopolies. The post-war German press system has seen the progressive and disproportionate growth of the larger concerns. The largest of these by far is the politically conservative Springer group (established immediately after the war by Axel Springer who died in 1985) with a 1993 market share of 23 per cent of the circulation of the daily press. Before unification diluted its dominance a little, the Springer press had come to account for between 28 and 30 per cent of this market. Moreover, the Springer press produces Germany's main tabloid, the *Bild*, which has a strong Right wing populist orientation. The only tabloid with a national circulation, it has dominated the German market for street sales: it accounted for no less than 79 per cent of the so-called 'Boulevard press' market in 1991 (Humphreys, 1994, p. 337). The Springer press also produces both of Germany's main national Sunday newspapers, the *Bild am Sonntag* and the *Welt am Sonntag*. In addition, it produces one of Germany's best-known and most widely distributed 'national' quality dailies, the highly conservative *Die Welt*, and its largest evening newspaper, the Hamburger *Abendblatt*. With holdings in many papers and publishing houses, the Springer group ranks among the largest press empires in Western Europe.

Germany's second largest newspaper concern, the *Westdeutsche Allgemeine Zeitung* (WAZ) group, has established a virtual regional monopoly in North-Rhine Westphalia, which is the most densely populated area in the Federal Republic, taking in the major industrial conurbations of the north Rhineland and the Ruhr. This state of affairs actually puts the *WAZ* next to the *Bild-Zeitung* in circulation, although it is 'only' a regional newspaper concern (Humphreys, 1990, p. 87). The popular magazine market is similarly dominated by a few large concerns. Together four large groups – the Springer concern among them – dominate the market, accounting for no less than 62.5 per cent of the market in 1992. In this market, the Springer group's major rival, Bertelsmann, one of the largest (according to some estimates, the second largest) multi-media concerns in the world, is very prominent. Its 75 per cent owned major subsiduary, Gruner and Jahr, markets a number of popular illustrated periodicals, the best-known of which is the Left-of-Centre *Stern* magazine. It also has a holding in the liberal and investigative *Spiegel* magazine and owns several major eastern newspapers.

The political spectrum of the mainstream West German mass press extends from Centre-Left to staunch conservative Right. Kleinsteuber and Wilke (1992, p. 81) note that a large number of papers, while claiming to be independent, are in fact 'highly sympathetic' to the Christian Democrats. The Springer newpapers have a definite Right-wing political orientation. The *Frankfurter Allgemeine Zeitung*, Germany's leading quality daily with a circulation of nearly four hundred thousand, is also very conservative; it occupies a comparable position in Germany's press scenario to Britain's *Daily Telegraph*. The *FAZ* group was Germany's seventh largest daily press group in 1993. Apart from the *Tageszeitung (taz)*, which started off as an 'alternative' (ie. counter-culture) paper and now reflects the green Left, there are no daily newspapers of a distinctly Left-wing nature. However, there are a couple of Left liberal 'quality' newspapers which are regional papers with a considerable national readership: namely, the *Frankfurter Rundschau* and the *Süddeutsche Zeitung*, the latter being the flagship paper of Germany's sixth largest daily press group. The *WAZ* Group of newspapers, which as seen has a virtual monopoly in the Ruhr area and extends into much of the rest of North-Rhine Westphalia, is not unfriendly to the SPD; this could partly be explained by its industrial and pro-SPD catchment area. Finally, *Die Zeit*, a highly prestigious and serious weekly, deserves mention; its political orientation is best described as liberal independent (Kleinsteuber and Wilke, 1992, p. 81; see also Table 3.4).

Table 3.4 Germany's national (supra-regional) newspapers

Title (1993)	Type of publication	Ownership	Circulation
Bild	Tabloid	Springer	4,299,687
Die Zeit	Broadsheet	Die Zeit	500,000
Frankfurter Allgemeine Zeitung	Broadsheet	FAZ	391,013
Süddeutsche Zeitung	Broadsheet	Suddeutscher Verlag	304,499
Die Welt	Broadsheet	Springer	209,677
Frankfurter Rundschau	Broadsheet	FR	189,000

Note:
All these papers are dailies except Die Zeit which is a weekly paper.
Source: Data from H. Röper in *Media Perspektiven. Basisdaten 1993*, Frankfurt/Main: MP, 1993, pp. 47–56. The figure for *Die Zeit*'s circulation is an estimate.

Press concentration in France

At first sight France, like Germany, has presented a picture of considerable diversity in the press sector. Traditionally, the French press market has been far less dominated by powerful national press concerns than has been the case in Britain (though national press groups have become important in France – see below). The principal reason for the apparent diversity of the French press is the continuing importance of the provincial press. During the post-war period, the total circulation of regional papers has far exceeded that of Parisian national dailies (see Table 3.5). More French people have relied for their news and current affairs on provincial papers. These have provided national and international, as well as regional and local, news. The French provincial press is, in this respect, similar to its German counterpart. Another similarity is the fact that these papers produce numerous local editions. In 1988, 67 provincial papers produced around 400 editions (Albert, 1990, p. 117). An important difference with Germany, however, is that no provincial paper could be considered to have a national readership. The paper that has come closest to doing this is *Ouest France*, which has been able to boast a circulation nearly double of that of the largest Parisian daily, *Le Figaro*. Yet it still cannot be compared with German 'supra-regional' papers like the *Frankfurter Allegemeine*, the *Frankfurter Rundschau* or the *Süddeutsche Zeitung*. The national dailies – read by the country's elites – have been Parisian quality papers like the liberal-Left *Le Monde* and *Libération* and the conservative *Le Figaro*.

The relative importance of the French regional press is perhaps surprising, in view of the capital's traditional political and administrative dominance (in great contrast with Germany, France is highly centralised). Partly, it reflects the country's pronounced cultural heterogeneity, partly its political tradition of localism (it took the Fifth Republic to truly 'nationalise' French politics), and partly an enduring and marked provincial hostility towards the overmighty capital. Also, it long reflected a certain lack of modernity of the industry. Like large swathes of French industry in the 1930s, many regional press concerns were unambitious and investment-shy family businesses. Fiercely jealous of their independence, they were loath to raise external funds in order either to modernise or to expand. The print unions, too, were an obstacle to change. Consequently, the development of the French press long remained stunted. Characterised by under-capitalisation, high debt and weak profitability, it remained trapped in a vicious circle of relatively low circulations, comparative unattractiveness to advertisers, and high sales prices, which in turn kept circulations low, and so the circle went round. In 1991, French newspaper prices remained significantly higher than those in Germany or Britain (Minc, 1993, pp. 59–70).

Table 3.5   Some data on the Parisian and provincial press in France, 1945–90

	Paris		Provinces	
Year	No. of papers	Print run	No. of papers	Print run
1945	26	4,606,000	153	7,532,000
1955	13	3,779,000	116	6,823,000
1965	13	4,211,000	92	7,857,000
1975	12	3,195,000	71	7,411,000
1985	12	2,777,000	70	7,109,000
1990	11	2,741,000	62	7,010,000

Source: Data from table in R. Kuhn, *The Media in France*, London/New York, Routledge, 1995, pp. 26–27.

These fiercely independent provincial press firms were also resistant to takeover. This fact, coupled with a 1944 press ordinance preventing chain ownership (see later, p. 96), helped to keep the brakes on press concentration for a while. Nevertheless, Table 3.5 shows how the number of titles – of both the Parisian and provincial press – has more than halved over the course of the whole post-war period. Some famous papers fell victim to the conspicuous decline in readership of the Parisian press; the most recent case of collapse, in 1988, was the (Socialist orientated) daily, *Le Matin*. Table 3.5 shows, however, that the readership of the provincial press remained stable (though it did not grow with population increase as might have been expected). In fact, what has happened is that a number of '*grands régionaux*' (larger provincial papers) have progressively swallowed, or reduced to local editions, their weaker competitors. The figures themselves are testimony to a clear concentration process (for elaborate detail, see Albert, 1990).

As a result of newspaper failures and some takeovers (despite the

1944 ordinance), regional and local monopolies soon appeared. Kuhn (1995, pp. 34–35) points out that, strictly speaking, these were often 'quasi-monopolies' in that dominant regional papers continued to face 'pockets of resistance' within their regions from 'strongly rooted' competitors. Nevertheless, large regional concerns still gained a 'strategic position'. All in all, the French press landscape presented the image of a relatively large number of regional fiefdoms which occasionally engaged in 'frontier wars', concluding generally with 'cease-fires' and 'non-aggression treaties'. By the 1980s this picture of regional monopolies had stabilised. The reason was quite simple: even quite powerful and famous belligerents had so exhausted themselves in their 'feudal' struggles, that they had fallen easy victim to a third party (*Les dossiers du Canard*, 1984, p. 74).

Beset by economic weaknesses, and poorly placed to face the costs of modernisation and competition from other media (notably television), for many French newspapers the only salvation from collapse was to be absorbed by a press group. By the end of the 1980s, the five leading groups had come to account for 55 per cent of the sector's turnover (see Cayrol, 1991, pp. 144–146). One of the two largest press groups was Hachette which controlled 9 per cent of the regional press and 20 per cent of the magazine sector; among Hachette's best known titles were *France-Dimanche, Journal de Dimanche*, and *Le Nouvel Economiste*. Hachette also had important interests in two other large press concerns, Editions Amaury and Filipachi. As will be seen, Hachette attempted to venture into television in the 1980s (for detail on France's principal press groups see Cayrol, 1991, pp. 148–153; also Albert, 1990, pp. 87–94). The other leading press group, Socpresse, was owned by France's principal press baron – a right-wing Gaullist, Robert Hersant. In quick succession during the 1970s Hersant, already proprietor of a number of provincial papers, acquired three Parisian dailies: *Le Figaro* in 1975, *Le France-Soir* in 1976 and *L'Aurore* in 1978 (which merged with *Le Figaro* in 1980).

Hersant's Socpresse continued to acquire provincial papers. By the late 1980s it owned around thirty newspapers (Cayrol, 1991, pp. 150–151). By now Hersant controlled around 22 per cent of the circulation of provincial dailies and almost one-third of that of Parisian dailies (Albert, 1990, p. 91). In addition, the Hersant group controlled a large share of the periodicals market. The Hersant group possessed a large printing concern and, exceptionally for the French press, also its own distribution network, spanning Paris and the provinces. The group also had its own major advertising agency, Publiprint (Albert, 1990, p. 91; also see *les dossiers du Canard*, 1984, pp. 7–19). With an annual 1988 turnover of Ffr. 7.2 billion (Cayrol, 1991, p. 149) the Hersant concern ranked among Europe's leading media concerns (see Table 6.4) and was venturing into foreign press markets (notably Belgium) and diversifying into broadcasting (see Chapter 6). Hersant's press empire was the nearest equivalent that France had to Britain's News International or Germany's Springer press.

Table 3.6   French national (i.e. Parisian) dailies, 1989

Title	Ownership	Orientation	1989 circation (thousands)	Market share (%)
Le Figaro[a]	Hersant	Gaullist	424	18.9
Le Parisien	Amaury[b]	Populist[c]	405	18.1
Le Monde	Le Monde	Left of Centre	386	17.2
L'Equipe	Amaury	Sports	301	13.4
France Soir	Hersant	Gaullist	257	11.5
Liberation	Liberation	Left of Centre	182	8.1
La Croix	Hachette	Catholic	103	4.6
L'Humanité	PCF[d]	Communist	84	3.7
La Tribune de l'Expansion	Hersant	Gaullist	61	2.7
Le Quotidien de Paris	Q de P	Mainstream Right	40[e]	1.8

Notes:
The Socialist *Le Matin* went out of business in 1988. Also the table excludes the specialist economic paper, 'Les Echos'.
[a] *Figaro Magazine* has a circulation of around 665,000.
[b] Amaury is 36% owned by Hachette.
[c] *Le Parisien* is a downmarket tabloid, rare in France.
[d] The *Parti Communiste Français*, the Communist Party.
[e] This single figure is for 1988 (taken from M. Hirsch, 'Die Franzosische Presselandschaft – Expansion trotz Krise', *Media Perspektiven*, 6/88, pp. 329–337, p. 330.
Sources: 1989 figures from EC Commission, *Final Report. Study on Pluralism and Concentration in the Media*, Brussels, 6 February 1992; Booz.Allen & Hamilton, 1992 p. 3.11.; R. Kuhn, *The Media in France*, London/New York, Routledge: 1995, pp. 69–76, for orientation.

In Paris, the marked conservative influence of Hersant's national dailies has been counterbalanced by a number of papers. The heavily serious *Le Monde* is Centre-Left in overall orientation. Originally inspired by the New Left, *Libération* retained a liberal-Left orientation, was open to the new 'post-materialist' radicalisms of the 1980s and 1990s, and displayed a distinctly more investigative edge than most French papers. Balance has also been provided by the venerable Catholic daily, *Le Croix*; once fiercely conservative, this paper moved in a more reformist direction during the post-war period. In addition, a Communist readership has been catered to by *L'Humanité*. It should be noted, however, that the pro-Socialist *Le Matin* folded in 1988 and *L'Humanité* suffered a serious readership crisis that paralleled the flagging influence of the Parti Communiste Français (PCF) itself. All in all, the circulation figures still speak for themselves (see Table 3.6). The Hersant press empire has undoubtedly swung the political balance of the provincial press towards the Right. Against this, concerned to maximise their readership, many provincial papers have tended to be apartisan, in marked contrast with the partisanship of the pre-war French press. Some provincial papers, like *Ouest-France*, actually France's largest circulation daily (dominant in Brittany, the Loire and Lower Normandy), most emphatically rejected any particular political identification. A few provincial papers have remained sympathetic to the Socialists and there continues to exist a struggling Communist provincial press (kept alive by state aids for papers that have a low ability to attract advertisers – see later). However, on the whole, the French provincial press has tended to be 'socially conservative and politically circumspect' (Kuhn, 1995, p. 70).

Finally, as any visitor knows from having seen Parisian newsstands, France can boast an impressive number of news weeklies (see Table 3.7). Given the relative absence of French quality Sunday newspapers (aside from Hachette's *Journal de Dimanche* with a circulation of around 360,000), these have been a key source of political analysis and commentary. Diversely owned and orientated, with fairly impressive circulations, they have helped to provide France with an important measure of political press pluralism, partly compensating for the decline of the party press (Kuhn, 1995, p. 75; also see Albert, 1990, pp. 131–133). Among these, *Le Canard enchaîné* deserves special mention. A Parisian news weekly, with a mass circulation, it has provided a steady diet of fierce political satire,

making an art of its persistent exposure of scandals affecting the
French political establishment, regardless of who is in power.

Table 3.7   French news weeklies

Title	Ownership/ control	Orientation (thousands)	1988 circulation	Market share
Paris-Match	Filipachi	Independent	875	23.6
L'Express	Goldsmith	Right	554	14.9
Le Canard enchaîné	Journalists' cooperative	Critical satire	423[a]	11.4
Le Nouvel Observateur	Perdriel	Socialist	370	10.0
Le Pelèrin magazine	Bayard	Catholic	364	9.8
Le Point	Gaumont[b]	Centrist	320	8.6
La Vie	La Vie Cath.	Catholic	270	7.3
L'évenément du jeudi	J-F Kahn and its readers	Independent	177	4.8
Valeurs actuelles	R. Bourgine	Right	90[a]	2.4

Notes:
[a]   Estimate.
[b]   The cinema chain.
Sources: P. Albert, *La Presse Française*, Paris: Documentation Française,
1990, pp. 131–133; and R. Kuhn, *The Media in France*, London/New York:
Routledge, 1995, p. 75. The market share is my calculation. The 'market' is
defined quite broadly since the magazines vary in style and content. The
table is intended to be illustrative only.

Press concentration in Italy

In Italy, large-scale press concentration during the 1950s and 1960s
occurred not so much because of the expansion of large newspaper
publishers at the expense of their smaller brethren (ie. the main pattern in Germany and France), but because of the extensive buying up
of daily newspapers by the country's leading industrialists, businessmen and financiers. First, during the 1970s, a number of successful
companies in book and magazine publishing, dubbed 'pure publish-

ers', entered the sector; the most notable were the Milan-based Mondadori and Rizzoli groups. Soon these groups fell into the orbit of so-called 'impure publishers', namely non-media big business interests led by prominent industrialists or financiers. Thus, financial problems led to Rizzoli being rescued in 1984 by a financial deal involving Gianni Agnelli's Fiat conglomerate. As for the Mondadori group, it merged in 1988 with another major magazine publisher, *Editoriale L'Expresso*, which was controlled by De Benedetti, a leading financier. Then during the 1990s, control of this group passed to the most controversial of all of Italy's media magnates, Silvio Berlusconi. In 1987 the Montedison publishing group, which owned the leading Roman newspaper *Il Messagero*, also fell into the arms of an industrialist, Raul Gardini, whose fortune was based in chemicals and agribusiness (Gardini committed suicide in 1993). Other examples of 'impure publishers' were a state company (ENI), owner of *Il Giorno*, and the largest industrial association Cofindustria, owner of the country's premier financial paper, *Il Sole 24-ore*. Other newspapers were in the hands of banks. Nearly all these papers were identified with what was until the 1990s Italy's ruling Establishment, namely the Christian Democrats or the smaller parties of the Centre and the Socialists (the Christian Democrats' coalition partners). However, it is noteworthy that one of Italy's mass circulation daily papers, *L'Unita*, stood out as the organ of the erstwhile Communist party – now a reformed Left party called the Party of the Democratic Left (Sassoon, 1986, pp. 154–5).

Fiat, owned by the Agnelli family, presided over the largest single concentration of press power in Italy; this empire included two of the country's three most influential newspapers (see Table 3.8). Fiat was also the country's biggest multinational corporation. As the largest spender of advertising in the country, the Agnelli industrial empire also exercised an influence on newspapers beyond its direct control. Fiat also owned Publikompass, one of the country's largest advertising agencies. In 1984 the Fiat group gained indirect control – through a financial branch – of *Rizzoli/Corriere della Sera* (RCS). This development caused considerable political controversy. Critics argued that it flouted Italy's anti-concentration laws prescribing a 20 per cent limit to the share of the press owned by any single person or company. The 'rescue' of RCS arguably gave the Agnelli group effective control of almost a quarter of the national daily newspaper circulation. This drew criticism from the Guarantor, Italy's parliament-appointed media regulator, as well as from the non-Agnelli media and the Italian parliament. However, the Supreme Court ruled in Agnelli's favour maintaining that formally a 'Fiat trust' did not exist (Mazzoleni, 1992b, p. 128). In 1987 further concern was provoked by Rizzoli's rumoured interest in acquiring a stake in Telemontecarlo, an Italian language news television channel based in Monaco beyond Italian legal jurisdiction. Although Gianni Agnelli, Fiat's chairman and major shareholder, tended to remain aloof from politics, many felt that his media power, and the political influence that it gave him, served his economic interests (Friedman, 1988, esp. pp. 111–119). Indeed, the principal motivation for so many of Italy's leading industrialists, businessmen and financiers to become directly involved in the press, which historically had not been a lucrative business at all (far from it), was the political influence it brought them. In no other Western European country, were big business, the political Establishment and the media, so intimately and brazenly enmeshed. In Italy, it has been observed, 'the media moguls support[ed] – sometimes financially – the politicians and the latter favour[ed] the expansionist strategies of the moguls' (Mazzoleni in Tunstall and Palmer, 1991, p. 169).

Table 3.8   Ownership of Italy's top ten national dailies, 1988

Title (base)	Ownership	Circulation
La Repubblica (Rome)	Mondadori/L'Expresso	730,000
Corriere della Sera (Milan)	Rizzoli/Fiat	715,000
La Stampa (Turin)	Fiat	560,000
Il Messagero (Rome)	Montedison	370,000
Il Sole-24 Ore (Milan)	Cofindustria[a]	320,000
Il Resto de Carlino (Bologna)	Monti	310,000
L'Unita (Milan)	PCI[b]	300,000
Il Giorno (Milan)	ENI	290,000
La Nazione (Florence)	Monti	288,000
Il Giornale/Nuovo (Milan)	Berlusconi	275,000

Notes:
[a] This was Italy's confederation of industrialists.
[b] The Communist Party, renamed the PDS – Party of the Democratic Left in 1990.
Source: Adapted from a table in Roland Cayrol, *Les Médias: presse écrite; radio; television*, Paris: Presses Universitaires de France, 1991, p. 368.

The small countries of Europe

The smaller countries of Europe faced special problems with regard to press concentration. Media diversity was constrained by the amount of capital available, the smallness of the domestic market and, related to this, the more limited economies of scale that these small markets offered (Trappel, 1991; Meier and Trappel, 1992). In some cases, notably the Scandinavian democracies, very high readership rates coupled with a virtual monopoly of media advertising helped to counter these disadvantages and these countries sustained an impressive number of newspaper titles (see Chapter 1, pp. 35–37). Moreover, as we shall see, most small states responded to the vulnerability of their press markets by implementing special interventionist policies. However, small states that shared a common language with much larger neighbours and where the press faced considerable competition for advertising from television – unlike the Scandinavian states – could hold neither their readers nor their advertising markets captive. Their newspaper markets were consequently more prone to fail and they were even vulnerable to takeover by a larger neighbour's press groups (cultural and linguistic affinity making them attractive targets). This vulnerability was starkly illustrated by Austria whose press sector presented an extreme case of combined concentration and capital penetration by the press giants of a large neighbour, Germany.

In a comparative study of the media in some of Europe's small countries, Trappel (1991, pp. 136–137) notes that between 1946 and 1957 Austria experienced a steady decline in both the number of newspapers and their overall circulation. Between 1958 and 1973 a first wave of very intense concentration occurred even though circulation doubled. This was the period when the press had to face up to the challenge of television advertising, beyond Scandinavia a Europe-wide phenomenon during this period. The concentration process seemed to be under control between 1973 and 1987 as overall circulation continued to grow while the number of newspapers remained fairly stable. One reason for this period of stability was the state aid introduced to support the newspaper sector (see p. 106). After 1987, however, a second wave of concentration coupled with German capital penetration – notably by the politically conservative Springer and the centrist WAZ groups, respectively Germany's largest and second largest newspaper concerns – rendered the Austrian press sector the most monopolised in Western Europe. In 1988 the last important party publishing company – the Socialist *Vorwärts-Verlag* founded in 1900 – succumbed to financial pressures and was bought up for a Schilling by the German WAZ-controlled Mediaprint company, an unceremonious end to the longevity of the once remarkably dominant Austrian party press (Trappel, 1991; Trappel, 1992; and Wimmer, 1992).

Trappel's small-country comparative study revealed a serious, though not quite so dramatic, process of concentration in Belgium (Trappel, 1991, p. 135. Also see De Bens, 1992; and Servaes, 1988). In Dutch-speaking Flanders the press market became entirely dominated by five indigenous publishing groups. None of these was orientated towards the Left, though one of them was Centrist-liberal. In French-speaking Wallonia the market was shared between three groups, the largest of which, the *Rossel* group, accounting for half of the francophone readership, had substantially fallen into the hands of the Right-wing French press baron, Robert Hersant. Hersant had acquired 40 per cent of the shares in Wallonia's most popular newspaper, *Le Soir*. Between 1945 and 1992 not only had the number of Belgian titles fallen from around 40 to 28 but of these only 9 were 'truly autonomous; the remaining 19 papers [were] parallel editions of the main papers' (De Bens, 1992, p. 20). The role of the banks and finance houses had increased, that of the independent family firm had waned. The section of the press historically sympathetic to the Socialists was now 'as good as dead'. Whilst around a quarter of the Flemish voted for the Socialists, only 4 per cent read a Left-leaning paper. In Wallonia, where well over a quarter voted Socialist, only 6 per cent read a Left-leaning paper. Overall, the highly concentrated Belgian press had become sympathetic to the Christian Democrat and Liberals way out of proportion to the political balance of the electorate (Servaes, 1988, pp. 338–346).

Sweden presented a very different picture. The country did not share a language with a large neighbour and this appeared to have afforded its press markets a crucial measure of protection from penetration by foreign press groups. In Sweden – as in Norway and Denmark – the press enjoyed comparatively high newspaper readership rates and a virtual monopoly of media advertising. As will soon be described, extensive public support had also been channelled towards financially weaker papers in order to safeguard pluralism in the press sector. As a result of all these factors, the number of newspapers remained very high relative to the size of the population (Trappel, 1991, p. 140; See also Table 1.1). All the same, there occurred a steady decline in the number of newspapers over the post-war period as a whole and a limited number of large indigenous press groups still dominated the national market. The largest, the Bonnier group, owned the country's two most successful daily papers and, taking all its papers into consideration, had an overall share of a quarter of the market in 1989. It was also the country's principal magazine publisher and produced its main business journal. The Bonnier publications had a pro-liberal political orientation. Against this, the second largest group, the A-Pressen, with actually the largest number of titles and the second largest share of the readership, was pro-social democrat and jointly owned by the Social Democratic party (SAP) and the Swedish trade union federation (the LO). More-over, the country's third and fifth most successful daily papers, respectively the *Aftonbladet* and the *Arbetet*, were both pro-social democrat (Gustafsson, 1992, p. 213). In Norway the situation was very similar. Again partly thanks to public support for the financially weaker newspapers, there was a relatively high number of newspa-pers per head of population and there was strong competition in most localities. Three companies still dominated the national market but one of these – called A-pressen – was a newspaper group owned by the labour movement (Wolland, 1993, pp. 118–119). In Norway the labour press accounted for around 20 per cent of the total circu-lation (Østbye, 1992, p. 172). In both of these Scandinavian democ-racies, the survival of an overtly Left press, commanding a significant readership, combined with the strength of the centrist-orientated press, was quite exceptional in Western Europe. Moreover, both countries could boast an exceptionally high number of dailies per head of population (see Table 1.1). An important reason for this plu-ralism was the support of Social Democratic governments and Cen-trist 'bourgeois' parties for interventionist policies to subsidise the press.

Regulation of ownership

Clearly, patterns of concentration varied in Western Europe; in some countries the impact on press pluralism was worse than in others. Yet it was everywhere perceived to be a problem. Unsurprisingly, therefore, policy makers came under considerable pressure to take countervailing action. Most of this pressure came from European parties of the Left and Centre, from trade unions and journalists' associations, and from consumer associations. To counter press concentration, policy makers disposed of two principal instruments. Firstly, they might subsidise the press in order to maintain its diversity; as we shall see, a number of states have done precisely this. Secondly, they could regulate the ownership structure of the press sector, an approach that had the attraction of being without cost to the state exchequer. All European governments have some form of general competition legislation. However, few West European countries have enacted anti-concentration measures catering specifically for the special character of the press despite the compelling argument that the press should not be treated simply as an economic activity and despite the fact that generic anti-trust laws are usually concerned with much larger concerns than newspapers. Moreover, in those cases that have done so, the provisions and the mode of implementation vary considerably from country to country. It is fair to say that in no cases have these measures been very restrictive in practice.

The countries that do have such legislation break down into two groups. Some, like Britain and Germany, rely on modified anti-trust laws. These treat the press as a special case within the general framework of existing competition laws. This approach is relatively flexible and allows considerable discretion to the minister responsible (as in Britain) or to the independent anti-trust authority (as in Germany). Thus, in Britain, employment of the only regulatory instrument against press concentration – namely referral to the Monopolies and Merger Commission under the terms of the Fair Trading Act of 1973 – is at the discretion of the Minister for Trade and Industry. Any merger that would give a proprietor control of newspaper circulation amounting to more than 500,000 copies per day requires a Commission report unless the minister deems the newspaper not to be 'economic as a going concern'. In most cases, the minister has chosen to refer press mergers to the Monopolies and Mergers Commission. However, the latter body possesses only advisory powers. Nicol and Bowman (1993, p. 171) note that 'there is no presumption against the concentration of ownership'; the Commission merely advises the minister as to whether proposed mergers might be expected to operate against the 'public interest'. The minister has the last word in deciding whether to prevent a merger of not. In practice, Nicol and Bowman suggest, the legislation has been 'ineffectual' largely because of the 'passive attitude' of ministers. Ministerial decisions are open to legal challenge but the costs involved have deterred journalists, and other parties, from taking this course of action (Nicol and Bowman, 1993, p. 171). The Labour politician and media reformer Frank Allaun (1988, pp. 67–68) observed that since 1965 around forty mergers had been referred on to the Monopolies and Mergers Commission, and only one refused (at the time of writing in the late 1980s).

In Germany, by contrast, the Federal Cartel Office is an independent para-state authority equipped with autonomous powers of intervention. General anti-trust legislation was first introduced by a 1958 Law Against Restrictions on Competition (normally referred to as the Cartel Law). The problem, with regard to press concentration, was that this law only covered mergers and amalgamations of companies reaching a gross turnover of DM 500 million: press companies typically fell way below this threshold. In fact, the legislation had been aimed at the country's industrial giants; press concentration had not even been a consideration. However, from the late 1960s onwards considerable pressure built up on the German Left, and also from the trade unions and journalist associations, for the enactment of specific measures against press concentration. The German Social Democrats, finding themselves in power during the 1970s, were compelled to act. Therefore they introduced a 1976 amendment to the Cartel Law specifically lowering the threshold at which press mergers became notifiable to the Federal Cartel Office to DM 25 million, a far more relevant figure for the press sector. In making its rulings on press takeovers and mergers the Federal Cartel Office was guided by the earlier recommendations of a special government commission into press concentration. The report of the Günther commission, published in 1968, had suggested that when a press concern achieved 20 per cent of a particular market it should be taken as a sign of at least growing danger that 'press freedom' might be impaired. However, the report had gone on to state, leniently, that press freedom could only be said to have been infringed when a single press concern had accumulated no less than a 40 per cent share of all dailies and Sunday papers (Humphreys, 1994, p. 100).

In practice, the Federal Cartel Office has not been at all interventionist. On one notable occasion, in 1981, it did act to prevent the very large Burda publishing group from acquiring a 25 per cent participation in the giant Springer concern; it deemed such a merger of two of Germany's largest press concerns to be excessive. It also acted to block the giant Springer concern's expansion into Bavaria by taking over that region's main regional publishing group. Generally, though, the Federal Cartel Office has achieved rather little against press concentration. As seen, the Springer concern has long enjoyed a share of around 28 per cent of the daily newspaper market, with a virtual monopoly of the Sunday paper and the tabloid markets (the ubiquitous *Bild-Zeitung*). Moreover, the Cartel Office has generally tolerated the dominance by large concerns of local and regional markets (see Humphreys, 1994, esp. p. 103).

France and Italy constitute the second group of countries with rules against press concentration; in these cases the mechanisms are more specific and, nominally at least, far more rigid (Todorov, 1990, p. 28). In France, the groundwork was laid by the interventionist 1944 Tripartite government of Socialists, Communists and Christian Democrats. The Liberation presented a unique window of opportunity for a radical reshaping of the French press. At the time there existed much support for a major reform that would settle scores with the pre-war press barons. Therefore the main provisions of the famous 1944 press ordinance were to 'guarantee pluralism, prevent concentration of ownership and to introduce transparency into the financial dealings of the press'. The ordinance amounted to a break with the *laissez-faire* (free market) paradigm of the pre-war years. It aimed deliberately to counter the perceived *'economic* threats to press freedom from capitalist entrepreneurs' (Kuhn, 1995, pp. 53–55; Albert, 1990, p. 42). The ordinance's principal regulatory instrument for dealing with concentration of ownership was a measure restricting control by the same individual or company to a single daily newspaper. For a while, this measure did at least put the brakes on the concentration process (Albert, 1990, p. 42). All the same, as seen earlier in this chapter, this law soon came to be widely ignored; a number of press chains appeared. In particular, the Right-wing publisher and Gaullist deputy (between 1956–78), Robert Hersant, built up an extensive personal press empire from the 1970s onwards.

A radical attempt to counter press concentration was made nearly forty years later by the French Left, following François Mitterrand's ascendancy to the presidency in 1981. The French Left had an obvious ulterior motive; they were most concerned about Hersant. Palmer and Tunstall (1990, p. 173) note that 'reform of the press was to

Table 3.9 Specific legal restrictions on concentration of the press, 1992

Country/ies	Nature of restriction, if any
Austria	None (but an amendment to anti-trust law, making all media mergers subject to inquiry by the Anti-Trust Authority, is under discussion).
Belgium	None.
France	Comparatively restrictive. A 1986 law prohibits control in excess of 30% of daily newspaper market.
Germany	A 1976 amendment to general anti-cartel legislation introduced a merger threshold for notification to the Federal Cartel Office: namely, DM 25 million of combined turnover.[a]
Greece	None.
Ireland	1987 law allows industry minister to refer any press merger to Fair Trade Commission.
Italy	Nominally strong. A 1981 law prevents a company controlling more than 20% of national press market or 50% in any given region.[b]
Netherlands	None.
Portugal	None (though general competition law restricts press companies to 30% of any particular market).
Scandinavia	None.
Spain	A 1989 law provides for referral to Tribunal of Fair Competition of mergers leading to control of 25% of national press market
Switzerland	None.
UK	Since 1965 the Home Secretary's consent has been required for any acquisition leading to a combined daily circulation of over half a million. He may refer to Monopolies and Merger Commission.

Notes:

[a]   The German Federal Cartel Office has considerable discretion and has not been notably interventionist. The rule of thumb for its intervention appears to be that one major press company should be limited to taking less than 25% stake in another major company.

[b]   Companies can get around this through subsidiaries. A 1987 amendment sought to help the courts prevent this happening.

Sources: notably, Sánchez-Tabernero *et al.*, *Media Concentration in Europe*, Media Monograph, No. 16., Dusseldorf: European Institute for the Media, 1993, pp. 208–217; and Commission of the European Communities, *Pluralism and Media Concentration in the Internal Market*, COM (92) 480 final, Brussels, 23 December 1992, pp. 40–52; Article 19, *Press Law and Practice*, London: Article 19, 1993; and Pierre Todorov, *La Presse Française a l'heure de l'Europe*, Paris: Documentation Française, 1990, pp. 28–30.

many Socialist and Communist Party supporters an article of faith to which they were as attached as were Luther's followers to the 95 theses'. Shortly after its accession to power in 1981, the Socialist government (it had four Communist ministers at the time) produced a draft bill which aimed, with unashamed and single-minded purpose, to curtail Hersant's media power drastically. Colloquially referred to as the 'anti-Hersant law' (Cayrol, 1991, p. 113), the bill's passage through parliament was vigorously contested by the conservative opposition. The Right argued that the bill amounted to a politically motivated coup against press freedom. The newspaper publisher associations fought a fierce publicity campaign against it and Hersant's own newspapers lent their weight to the struggle. The controversy produced the longest recorded parliamentary debate in the Fifth Republic, a colossal number of amendments were proposed, and in the end, the Socialists had to invoke the quintessentially majoritarian instrument of Article 49 of the constitution, making the bill a vote of confidence in the government, in order to eventually push it through parliament (Keeler and Stone, 1987, p. 172).

However, the RPR/UDF opposition had also resorted to judicial review: they had referred the law to the Constitutional Council, a body whose political composition still reflected long years of conservative patronage. The Council found in favour of the law's constitutionality but, as Kuhn (1995, p. 57) notes, it 'so altered its provisions as to make it virtually useless as a weapon against Hersant'. Stringently, the 1984 statute stipulated that no single person or press group could control more than 15 per cent of the total circulation of national dailies, more than 15 per cent of that of regional dailies, or more than 10 per cent of their combined circulation. These comparatively severe restrictions were to be policed by a Commission for the Transparency and Pluralism of the Press (CTPP). However, the Constitutional Council ruled that the restrictions could not be applied retrospectively. Existing concentrations of press power were untouchable so long as they had been acquired legally. The Hersant press empire was not deemed to have offended against this latter stipulation (Cayrol, 1991, pp. 113–114). The result was that 'no group, not even the Hersant group, had to divest itself of newspaper titles'; the press commission proved to be a 'moral', rather than an 'inquisitorial and regulatory' body (Palmer and Tunstall, 1990, pp. 176–177). In any case the Commission was abolished, and the law replaced, when the Right returned to power, briefly, in 1986.*

The Right immediately replaced the 1984 statute with a law of their own making. At first they attempted to dispense altogether with restrictions on press holdings, but they too were forced to take account of the Constitutional Council's opinion. As a result, their 1986 law on media concentration (it contained provisions for other media too) restricted any press group from controlling more than 30 per cent of the national market for dailies regardless of whether they were 'national' or 'regional' papers. Kuhn (1995, p. 58) remarks pointedly: 'curiously, the Hersant group's [total] market share at the time fell somewhere between 28 and 29 per cent'. The law did not take into consideration Hersant's share of around 38 per cent of national newspaper circulation; nor did it place any restriction on local or regional monopolies. As seen, the latter abounded in France. In this connection, Minc (1993, p. 68) notes, sharply, that the regional press constituted a powerful lobby that the new government was averse to offend. The law did allow for stricter limits for press groups that had significant interests in other media; however, these provisions did not appear to restrict Hersant either (see Chapter 6, p. 221). Nevertheless, it should be emphasised, the 1986 French law was still one of the strictest in Europe. It could be argued that, in placing press pluralism on the 1980s legislative agenda, the Socialists had achieved a policy success which may have been modest in terms of their own aims but which was far less so in international comparison.

Italy actually adopted the strictest model of anti-trust legislation specific to the press – at least on paper. After years of bitter controversy over press concentration, a law was finally enacted in 1981. Unlike the French Right's 1986 law, the Italian one did distinguish between different press markets. It prohibited any company from controlling more than a 20 per cent share of the national market or

---

* The new government, led by Gaullist Prime Minister Jacques Chirac, now 'cohabited' with a lame-duck President Mitterrand whose power was in effect limited to the reserved presidential domains of defence and foreign policy. This first period of 'cohabitation' ended in 1988 when presidential elections renewed Mitterrand's tenureship of the presidency and subsequent legislative elections gave him back sufficient support in the Parliament to allow him to govern quasi-presidentially. A second period of 'cohabitation' ensued in 1993 when, once again, legislative elections robbed Mitterrand of his parliamentary power-base. This second period of 'cohabitation' ended with the victory of Jacques Chirac in the 1995 presidential election.

more than 50 per cent of a regional one. The law also invested a magistrate with the supervisory powers of 'Guarantor-ship' to ensure that the press complied with its stipulations. In Italy, however, there appeared to be problems of implementation and compliance (Todorov, 1990, p. 29; Sánchez-Tabernero *et al.*, 1993, p. 216; and Mazzoleni, 1992b, pp. 125–128).

Anti-concentration legislation: pros and cons

The above survey suggests that there has long existed a Europe-wide regulatory deficit with regard to press concentration. A number of countries have made no specific provisions for the press. Those states that have done so, present the picture of having achieved rather little. A case might be made for more rigorously crafted anti-concentration rules, as well as for the more vigorous implementation of existing policies. The French Socialists' policy might be held to point the way forward. However, the French Socialists' experience also illustrates one of the major problems with governmental anti-monopoly legislation. Rightly or wrongly, it may be widely seen as primarily politically motivated, and, as such, an unwarranted abridgement of the liberal democratic principle of press freedom. Also, the law of unintended consequences can be invoked to justify non-intervention. Restrictions on corporate activity, aimed at preventing concentration, may well run the risk of creating a net loss of newspapers. The perverse result of preventing mergers and takeovers of papers in financial difficulties, it is frequently argued, would be even greater press concentration.

There may well be something in both of these arguments. However, the 'unintended consequences' line might itself give lie to a political motivation. On two occasions in Britain, during the 1980s, Conservative Ministers of Trade and Industry used it to justify several major acquisitions in the already highly concentrated British national daily press sector. First, in 1981 Rupert Murdoch, proprietor of the mass-circulation tabloids the *Sun* and the popular Sunday paper *News of the World*, was allowed to take over not only the *Times* but also the *Sunday Times*. On this occasion, the Times was indeed in serious financial difficulties, but the *Sunday Times* was arguably quite profitable. In all probability, both papers could have been found another buyer or, as some have advocated, floated successfully on the stock exchange. Secondly, within a short space of time, in 1987 Rupert Murdoch was again allowed to extend his grip to no less than 35 per cent of the national press market by acquiring the tabloid *Today* when the paper fell into dire financial straits. In none of these takeovers did the minister responsible make a referral to the Monopolies and Mergers Commission. In the case of the *Sunday Times* the journalists prepared a legal objection to the takeover but subsequently withdrew it, deterred by the legal costs of such an action. The circumstances of all three takeovers unsurprisingly gave rise to the suspicion that ministerial discretion might have been exercised in a politically self-serving manner. This suspicion arose because, during the 1980s, Rupert Murdoch's newspapers had been conspicuously partisan to the Thatcherite Conservative cause.

The main problem of anti-monopoly legislation as an instrument of press-pluralism has been summed up by Smith (1978, p. 165): 'at the point of merger it [is] generally too late for intervention'. It may be that structural policy intervention in the press sector is also required, in the shape of various kinds of state aid to the press and especially to companies threatened with financial collapse. We will shortly turn to an examination of the achievements and problems of this particular policy. Nevertheless, across the economy competition law is widely regarded as a useful instrument of public policy. An argument can certainly be made for deploying it to greater effect in the cause of press pluralism. Indeed, more rigorous resort to it might be regarded as being especially apposite in the media field. After all, newspaper markets are not simply commodity markets; that is, unless press freedom is viewed purely as little more than 'market freedom' and as analogous to a property right. At the same time, it must be acknowledged that there are manifold difficulties involved in regulating press ownership. State interventionism is bound to smack of political gamesmanship unless regulatory authority is vested in a genuinely independent public body with teeth. The short-lived French Commission for the Transparency and Pluralism of the Press might have provided an example. On the other hand, there was a French tradition of state influence over such bodies.

There are also practical difficulties in defining market dominance. Should local press monopolies be considered to infringe media pluralism when citizens can choose to read a national newspaper instead? In answering this question, the kind of press system surely requires taking into account. Local or regional press monopolies in countries with a decentralised press system, like Germany or France, clearly have a greater significance than do local press monopolies in Britain where local papers are very secondary sources of information about current affairs. By the same token, power in markets for national newspapers will matter more in Britain than in Germany or France. Some might even question whether we should worry at all about the limited choice between newspapers when other media providing alternative sources of information are available – notably the broadcast media? In this regard, it has at least been an axiom of media policy in countries with commercial broadcasters – including the United States – that cross-media ownership between the press and broadcasting should be kept at minimal levels. In most of Western Europe, until the recent period, there long existed a strict 'separation of powers' in the media – between the private commercial press and the public-service broadcasters. However, as later chapters will explain, this state of affairs is currently being relegated to the pages of history by a technologically triggered expansion of media markets and an international trend towards the integration of media operations. Policy makers have, as a result, come under increased pressure to give more serious consideration to the question of how to regulate media ownership (see Chapter 6).

State aid to the press sector

As already averred, another way press pluralism might be promoted is through the granting of state aid. In fact, indirect support to the press sector, of one kind or another, is given by all West European states. For instance, all states have granted the press sector preferential rates of VAT. Reduced rates of VAT, or even outright exemption as in Britain, could amount to an important saving and has been a very jealously guarded privilege. The suggestion in Britain that the 1993 budget might remove this particular concession provoked quite cataclysmic prophesies about its impact on the industry's economics. There were dire predictions of newspaper bankruptcies and of investment flight, designed to worry the government. An intense lobbying campaign by the publishers was, unsurprisingly, successful in protecting the exemption.

Another indirect aid, this time not very relevant to Britain or Ireland but important in a large number of other European countries, took the shape of preferential postal rates for the distribution of newspapers and magazines. Also, most countries have set favourable telecommunications tariffs, a good number special rail transport rates. Other measures have included tax breaks for investment and other kinds of tax alleviations. A number of states have subsidised the price of newsprint (paper) partly motivated by the concern to support the latter industry, partly out of recognition that newsprint amounts to a significant part of the costs of newspaper production. France and Italy had central offices performing this function; newsprint subsidies were generous. Journalists in some countries even benefited from state aid; in Italy, Belgium and Portugal they were provided with cheap public transport. In Latin Europe it was customary for national news agencies to be state supported (for a quite detailed overview of state supports across Europe, see Todorov, 1990, pp. 32–40). By and large, these various kinds of indirect aid have been uncontroversial, yet they could amount to very impressive sums. In France, for example, by the end of the 1980s the value of total indirect support approached half a billion francs; far more than was spent by the state on direct subsidies. Under the Socialists these subsidies registered strong growth (for detailed break-down of French subsidies, see Albert, 1990, p. 72). Direct aid was not granted by every European country and it tended to be far more selective than indirect aid in that it was directed towards financially weak papers or papers handicapped by their non-commercial character. Indirect aid tended to be indiscriminate.

The extent of overall state aid has varied very considerably between countries. Britain, Germany, Ireland and Switzerland made no direct transfers of resources to the press and the indirect aid they granted was limited (though, as suggested, VAT alleviation was a significant saving for the industry). By contrast, Italy followed by France and Spain would appear to have been by far the most generous in terms of absolute expenditure (Todorov, 1990, p. 37; Kuhn, 1995, p. 41). Undoubtedly a significant factor was the weaker economic state of the press in these Latin countries. This was especially the case in Spain where subsidies were introduced in 1984 to combat a crisis in the press industry and later withdrawn in 1990 once the crisis had been weathered (de Mateo and Corbella, 1992, p. 195). By contrast, Britain and Germany had the strongest press companies in Europe. The difference could also partially be explained by reference to different traditions of political economy; Britain and post-war

Germany being 'liberal' and the Latin countries historically more 'state interventionist'. Certainly, in France's case the introduction of state subsidies to the press could be traced back to the tremendous expansion of state economic intervention introduced by the Tripartite government of 1944. Yet, as suggested, French interventionism in the press sector could be explained by more than simple French 'Colbertisme' (the traditional political economy of state economic intervention). The view had been influential at the time, that inter-war *laissez-faire* had led the press to become dominated by 'capitalist financiers'. The main aim of state aid was to 'foster pluralism among newspaper titles' (Kuhn, 1995, p. 40). In fact, this concern to ensure that the readers were presented with access to diverse sources of information was an aim of (direct and indirect) state press subsidies across Europe.

But there were important differences in the method of allocation. In France, the emphasis was on 'political neutrality'; as a result, aid flowed largely 'indiscriminately' (Kuhn, 1995, p. 42; Albert, pp 71–73). There were special allocations to publications that drew little advertising revenue; these helped publications like the Communist newspaper *L'Humanité*, the Catholic *La Croix* and the liberal-Left *Libération* to survive. However, this selective aid accounted for a fraction of the total state support which, as noted above, was largely of the indiscriminate indirect kind. Indeed, critics pointed out that prosperous papers accounted for most of the state's aid, no start-up help was provided to encourage the foundation of new papers and, overall, the system worked to support the status quo (Albert, 1990, pp.72–73; Kuhn, 1995, p. 42). In Italy, by the 1970s, the press, financially always a precarious business, had fallen largely into the hands of external big business interests (the so-called 'impure publishers'). Therefore in 1975 the government – dominated by the Christian Democrats – enacted a law that provided for very generous direct subsidisation of the press to promote pluralism by strengthening the industry's own resource base. However, these subsidies were calculated in direct proportion to the size of newspapers' circulations. As a result, large press concerns were overwhelmingly the principal beneficiaries of the state's bounty, though party-affiliated papers also benefited (Bockelmann, 1984, pp. 144–145). Portugal was another country that allocated aid in proportion to newspaper distribution; in Spain as well large papers seemed to benefit the most. Sánchez-Tabernero *et al*.. (1993, p. 229) remarked that in Italy, Spain and Portugal 'the type of aid seem[ed] to contradict the *raison d'être* of the subsidies'. However, Todorov (1990, p. 96) shows that during the 1980s Italy moved to a system that limited direct grants of aid to newspaper cooperatives, cultural publications and party papers. Nevertheless, fairly indiscriminate indirect aid continued to flow to the Italian press industry at large.

Table 3.10   *State aid to the press (not counting VAT alleviation)*

Country	Largely indiscriminate	Targeted on weaker papers
Austria	+	+
Belgium	+	Flanders only
Denmark	+	
Finland	+[a]	
France	+	+
Germany		
Greece		
Ireland[b]		
Italy	+[c]	+[c]
Netherlands	+	
Norway		+
Portugal	+	
Spain	+[d]	
Sweden		+
Switzerland		
UK		

Notes:
[a] To party papers, as well as other financially weak ones.
[b] Apart from subsidies to Irish-language publications.
[c] During the 1980s direct aid was limited to party papers and those owned by journalist cooperatives. Large indirect subsidies continued to flow indiscriminately.
[d] Only between 1984–1990 to surmount an industrial crisis.
Sources: Various. See references in the text.

Other countries, less munificent in absolute terms, were also more discriminatory. In the Netherlands, for example, since the 1960s, state aid flowed to 'papers with a special character'; in 1974 the Press

Fund was established precisely to help those in financial difficulty and also to help new papers get off the ground (van Lenthe and Boerefijn, 1993, pp. 101–102). Similarly, in Norway direct government subsidies were targeted on newspapers facing adverse market conditions. These were not to be the largest in their respective markets. The aim was to 'ensure a wide variety of editorial viewpoints' (Wolland, 1993, p. 119). In Denmark too, since 1970, a direct subsidy has been targeted on 'needy' papers through the Finance Institute of the Press. In 1984 the subsidy was increased nearly fourfold. One of its purposes was to help new papers get started (Petersen and Siune, 1992, p. 37). In Austria, where in 1975 direct subsidies had been introduced for all newspapers, a 'special subsidy for the maintenance of variety' was added in 1984; the latter support was targeted exclusively at the smaller, financially weaker papers with limited circulations (Trappel, 1992).

Sweden has been widely seen as a model system. Among the more generous in the levels of its direct state support to the press, it introduced a scheme of support for so-called 'second newspapers', these being the second in circulation in their relevant markets. This was designed explicitly to promote pluralism; two large dailies, the Social Democratic *Arbetet* and the conservative *Svenska Dagbladet* received huge sums without which they would not have been able to survive (Axberger, 1993, p. 154). In Sweden, state support has been granted to help firms that were unable to obtain capital in the private loan markets. Help has also been given to low-circulation newspapers and papers with infrequent editions (ie. only two or three issues a week, or less), the scale of the subsidy depending upon the amount of editorial content (Hultén, 1984, pp. 15–16). Finland also had certain interesting model features. Firstly, generous state support has been directed towards the economically weaker papers. Secondly, the committee that disbursed this state support was composed in strict accordance to the proportionality principle (ie. reflecting directly the political composition of the Finnish parliament). Thirdly, a special subsidy was explicitly earmarked for the party press; the allocations were strictly proportional to party strength (Trappel, 1991, pp. 151–152).

Finally, advertising on radio and television was customarily limited at least partly out of consideration of the interests of the press. In many countries, press lobbies were instrumental in having broadcast advertising restricted to very low levels. In the Netherlands, when very limited television advertising was initiated in 1967, the government introduced a highly complex system for transferring a proportion of this revenue to the press. Similarly, in Belgium, the allocation of state subsidies to the press has been seen mainly in terms of legitimate compensation for the competition it faced from the broadcasters.

State aid: pros and cons

An undoubted advantage of state support for the press is the contribution it *may* make to the economic viability of diverse and pluralistic press sectors in the face of market forces predisposing them towards concentration. It is an important and potentially effective public policy instrument by which the state can intervene to safeguard the principle of freedom of opinion, defined more broadly than in the narrow terms of proprietorial 'freedom of opinion'. Moreover, state intervention of this kind can promote democratic pluralism; by helping to ensure that the press sector reflects a more healthy range of different political orientations than would likely be the case if the press were left to market forces alone. Thus in Scandinavia – where the weaker concerns received special support – there survived a Social Democratic press which was the envy of Labour parties the world over.

But he who pays the piper can often call the tune. State support for the press, it has been pointed out, can result in an unwelcome dependency by the press on state beneficence. Newspapers which feed from the hand of the state might not always be disposed optimally to perform their watchdog function. They may not hold the political executive to the same degree of account that genuine financial independence might allow for. As seen, some have suggested this to be the case in France (see Chapter 2). This was a reason cited against introducing such subsidies, when the matter was discussed in Germany. There may or may not be much substance to this concern. It should be pointed out that special provision can be made against any potentially negative effect on journalism. State subsidies in the Netherlands and Norway are conditional on the recipient paper's granting editorial independence to its journalists (Coliver, 1993, p. 261).

Other kinds of action to safeguard pluralism of the press

This latter observation points to another way in which public policies might be produced to counter the negative effects of press concentration. Coliver (1993, p. 261) has suggested that 'in the light of the fact that concentration of ownership is a reality of press life, mechanisms for protecting independence *vis-à-vis* publishers may be at least as important as controls on ownership concentration'. One very important measure that has seldom been enacted, but that has been more widely discussed, is specific legislation to codify a degree of special protection from their employers (i.e. beyond normal employee rights) for journalists and editors. In this regard French media law might be taken as exemplary; a law dating back to 1935 grants journalists a *clause de conscience*, including provision for full severance benefits to journalists who resign or who are sacked when a change occurs in the publication's ownership. As Eisendrath (1982, p. 75) notes, 'being fired or even quitting can be … a highly remunerative affair in France … Journalists fleeing papers taken over by press baron Robert Hersant to escape his strident, Right-wing politics have made legendary claims'. Offering journalists this kind of protection can safeguard their profession's independence. In Austria, too, press law explicitly states that journalists should enjoy 'freedom of opinion' which includes their right to refuse to collaborate on a piece of work that does not reflect their private opinion. Moreover, they enjoy rights to severance pay if they feel compelled to leave the employ of a newspaper because of a 'shift in its general orientation' (Trappel, 1992, p. 4). In the 1970s, the German Social Democratic government of that period discussed legislating for extensive journalistic co-determination rights. However, in the face of stiff resistance from the publishers' association the government backed down. In Germany, the publishers were successful in defending their valued *Tendenzschutz* (see p. 65) against such legislation (Humphreys, 1994, pp. 104–110).

In a number of countries journalists themselves have managed to achieve mechanisms to protect their editorial independence *vis-à-vis* publishers by collective negotiation with their employers. It hardly seems to be coincidental that this has been the case in some of Europe's more corporatist countries: Germany, the Netherlands, Norway and Sweden. Many of Germany's more liberal papers have introduced company statutes giving journalists some say in editorial policy. In the Netherlands these statutes are included in their collective labour agreements. In Norway editors are protected by an Editors' Code granting them the sole right to decide what is published; this is recognised as a custom in common law by the courts. In Sweden, it is common for papers to have two editors-in-chief, one of whom is responsible for the editorial page (Coliver, 1993, p. 261). Further, Swedish journalists can refuse to write a story that offends against a code of conduct negotiated between the publishers' organisation and their union, although this right is not underpinned in statute as in Austria.

Such limited achievements aside, the legal norm in Europe still grants the proprietors of the press an overwhelming right to establish the general political and editorial content of their publications. It is a general rule of thumb that the only European newspapers where the journalists are *guaranteed* a significant degree of editorial control are those relatively few newspapers: (1) with special voluntarily negotiated editorial statutes; (2) owned, to a meaningful extent, by the workforce; (3) owned by independent trusts; and (4) where the company's statute deliberately prescribes that shareholdings should be spread widely and editorial independence guaranteed thereby. The leading French newspapers, *Le Monde* and *Libération*, are both good examples of newspapers part-owned and controlled by those who actually write for them. Journalists working for the British *Guardian*, owned by a trust, also enjoy freedom from proprietorial intervention and considerable editorial autonomy. However, such newspapers are the exception rather than the rule in Western Europe. The fate of the British *Independent* provided a good illustration of how difficult it is for papers to exist without strong proprietorial backing. Originally supported by a large spread of investors in the City, the prospects for its independence initially seemed strong. However, within only a few years, in the face of determined opposition from its journalists, in 1994 it fell into the joint hands of two very powerful press groups. By 1995 Mirror Group Newspapers and Ireland's main press baron Tony O'Reilly had 44 per cent apiece of the paper, which could no longer boast to be quite so independent.

Concern among journalists about protection of editorial and journalistic independence has mounted considerably during the 1980s and early 1990s. The main reason has been the tendency towards cross-media ownership and the use of new technologies to create large integrated transnational media businesses. Quite naturally the journalists' unions have attempted to coordinate their own response at the international level. At a conference in Milan in March 1993, they adopted a declaration calling for the enactment of common minimum standards of editorial independence across Europe. Among their demands was the right of internal editorial councils to be consulted about decisions affecting the appointment and dismissal of chief editors and the definition of editorial policy. They also demanded the right to refuse assignments that violated their professional ethics and the right to prevent interference in editorial content by the management or third parties (Mayer, 1993, p. 59).

Guide to further reading

P. Albert, *La Presse Française*, Paris: Documentation Française, 1990.

R. Cayrol, *Les médias. Presse écrite, radio, télévision*, Paris: Presses Universitaires de France, 1991.

J. Curran and J. Seaton, *Power Without Responsibility: The Press and Broadcasting in Britain*, London: Routledge, 1991.

Article 19, *Press Law and Practice*, London: Article XIX, 1993.

Commission of the European Communities, *Pluralism and Media Concentration in the Internal Market*, COM (92) 480 final, Brussels, 23 December 1992.

P. Humphreys, *Media and Media Policy in Germany: The Press and Broadcasting since 1945*, Oxford/Providence, RI: Berg, 1994.

R. Kuhn, *The Media in France*, London: Routledge, 1995.

B. S. Østergaard (ed.), *The Media in Western Europe: The Euromedia Handbook*, London: Sage.

R. Negrine, *Politics and Mass Media in Britain*, London/New York: Routledge, 1994.

A. Sánchez-Tabernero *et al.*, *Media Concentration in Europe*, Media Monograph No. 16. Dusseldorf: European Institute for the Media, 1993.

C. Seymour-Ure, *The British Press and Broadcasting since 1945*, Oxford: Basil Blackwell, 1991.

P. Todorov, *La Presse Française à l'Heure de l'Europe*, Paris: Documentation Française, 1990, pp. 28–30.

J. Tunstall and M. Palmer, *Media Moguls*, London/New York: Routledge, 1991.

4

European public-service broadcasting systems

Until recently a public-service monopoly, or duopoly in Britain's case, has characterised nearly all the broadcasting systems in Western Europe (Luxembourg being the significant exception). Within this public-service paradigm, however, there long existed important national differences in the way broadcasting systems were traditionally organised and controlled. This chapter looks first at the 'universal' principles of public-service broadcasting developed in Western Europe, then more closely at distinctive national variations. It will show that the different national models can be explained, to an important degree, by reference to the different political contexts – historical, cultural and institutional – in which they have been embedded. A marked congruence can be demonstrated between structures of broadcasting and the particular character of the respective political systems. In the past at least, politics has played a key role in defining the shape of national broadcasting systems and, not infrequently, in intruding upon the broadcasters' freedom. The next chapter will examine how this primacy of 'politics', in the shape of different patterns of public regulation and state intervention, is giving way to the primacy of markets. For reasons of space, the focus will be on television; it should be pointed out, though, that the more historical content of this particular chapter refers to radio.

The three rationales for public regulation

Radio broadcasting developed during the early part of this century; television became a mass medium after World War II. The main difference, from a public policy perspective, between the broadcast media and the press has been that both radio and television have been subjected – more or less from the beginning – to comprehensive and strict regulation. The broadcasters have been controlled and licenced by the public authorities. Moreover, from the very start, broadcasting has been regarded as an entirely legitimate field of public policy intervention. There are essentially three sets of reason for this: one is technical, another economic, and the third is political.

The technical rationale for regulation

Radio broadcasting in Europe commenced as a mass-medium during the 1920s following the huge stimulus that the radio industry had received from the use of radio during the Great War. In some countries – such as Britain, Belgium, Norway and Denmark – radio broadcasting was started by the private sector as in the United States (where it has remained a private sector activity ever since). In Switzerland, on the other hand, it was launched by a number of smallish public corporations serving distinct localities and based in the larger cities. In Sweden too, radio broadcasting began as an exclusive public service monopoly of the Swedish Broadcasting Corporation. In some cases, most notably Germany, radio developed under the auspices of very tight state control. This was also true of the state radio service in France, although in that country an unofficial private radio sector was tolerated alongside it until the post-war period. Whatever the case, though, there was one common denominator. Since radio as a technology grew out of telephony and telegraphy, it remained very much under the influence of state postal, telegraph and telephone authorities (PTTs). Moreover, the state (through the PTTs) 'owned' and administered the airwaves.

European PTTs were quick to draw the lesson from the United States experience where, so rapid and uncontrolled was the growth of private radio stations there soon resulted a chaotic overcrowding of the airwaves. Accordingly, European PTTs commonly took steps to control access to the medium through the power they retained to award broadcasting licences if they did not control the broadcasters outright. In Britain, for example, the Post Office took the decision in 1922 to establish the British Broadcasting Company as a cooperative venture owned by the radio industry. By this means, it was hoped at first to permit the continuance of commercial enterprise and at the same time to avert the free for all that characterised the United States. The Post Office successfully obtained the compliance of the private radio concerns by employing carrot and stick tactics. The stick was its power to withhold broadcasting licences; the carrot was its ability to grant monopoly rights to this private commercial 'cooperative' that was the BBC in its early days. Moreover, as elsewhere in Europe, it offered the blandishment of generous and assured funding from the broadcasting licence fee payable by all citizens who owned radio sets. The main point, however, is that, whether the state immediately established a public monopoly or not, one important rationale for closely regulating broadcasting was technical: the need to ration access to the medium because of the relative 'scarcity of frequencies'.

The monopoly rationale for regulation

Clearly, once a monopoly is granted or market access is rationed there arises a powerful economic rationale for public regulation. It was necessary to ensure universality of service provision and to avoid a situation where only densely populated areas were provided for. Further, the press could be granted its exceptional freedom from regulation precisely because it was characterised, at least in principle, by a free and competitive market. The situation with broadcasting was obviously very different. The listeners, and later the viewers, were captive audiences. Public intervention was therefore required to guard against all the familiar abuses of market dominance, most notably monopoly pricing and the retailing of 'inferior products'. Clearly, the broadcast media established a relationship of dependency on the part of the consumers. The latter could not pick and choose among a wide range of products to the same extent that they could with regard to their newspapers and magazines. There was therefore a powerful public interest rationale for public regulation of media content in order to ensure the quality and diversity of programmes. In the 1930s, and for some time after the war as well, regulation held the broadcasters accountable to what the authorities and traditional elites deemed to be suitable public taste. From the 1960s onwards, the broadcasters obtained more freedom and it was considered crucial that a wide range of social groups and categories would be catered for.

Finally, the media obviously had the ability powerfully to influence people's behaviour. One very important aspect of broadcasting's behavioural impact was its evident ability to influence consumer buying habits; it was a marvellous medium for advertising. In a monopolistic or quasi-monopolistic context there was clearly an economic rationale for an important measure of regulation, and not merely to govern advertising standards and practices. Since broadcast advertising represented a potentially serious threat to the publishers' main source of revenue, the public authorities soon faced a militant demand from the press sector – typically a very influential lobby indeed in view of its commercial size and its customary political connections – for a very strict regulation of the broadcasters. In Austria, Sweden and Switzerland, for instance, the press lobby has even been a key insider actor in the broadcasting policy community, granted very privileged rights to co-determine official policy. Indeed, not least for this reason, European broadcasters have long had to content themselves with strict limits – sometimes even a complete ban – on carrying advertising. As will be seen later, this situation is changing dramatically now.

The political rationale for regulation

The behavioural impact of broadcasting was obviously not limited to consumer buying habits. It quickly became clear to those who wielded, or contended for, political power that the broadcast media had a very effective capacity to focus public attention, to contribute to the creation of public opinion, to legitimise (or de-legitimise) public policy, and even directly to influence voting behaviour. Politicians and public administrators soon became aware that, unchecked or unconstrained, the medium presented a potential threat to their public authority. Enlightened elites were equally alert to the medium's vulnerability to political misuse (not least since the state rationed the air-waves). Indeed, the Nazis' misuse of the medium for the purposes of almost 'total' social control, led those who reconstructed West German broadcasting to stress the need to safeguard the medium's independence from politicians, from overbearing state officials or indeed from any holder of social power. Whether before or after the war, because of its political saliency and extraordinary powers of persuasion, European broadcasting came typically to be subjected to strict regulation according to principles of impartiality and political pluralism. It became a fundamental ideal of public broadcasting that democratic pluralism should be upheld: that the public-service broadcasters should reflect a range of democratic viewpoints. Yet, the public broadcasters would still have to be held democratically accountable and this requirement was bound to constrain their political independence. Therefore, in practice, as we shall see, European broadcasting exhibited a questionable closeness to the political power holders; in some cases executive dominance was striking, in others politicisation of broadcasters was more balanced. In fact, during the early days of broadcasting, there emerged clearly different national patterns with regard to this key relationship between the medium and the political realm. In this brief historical section, it is useful to examine two contrasting cases: those of Germany and Britain.

In Germany, endowed with Prussia's 'strong state' tradition and its legacy of nineteenth-century authoritarianism, the degree of control of radio broadcasting enjoyed by the political executive was striking from the start. During the liberal–democratic Weimar Republic (1918–33), the *Reichpost* (PTT) not only allocated broadcasting licences but also owned and controlled all the country's transmission facilities. In 1925 this state control was increased even further by the establishment of a centralised Imperial Broadcasting Company in which the *Reichpost* held a majority share of the capital. In these early days of the medium, there were none of the carefully crafted public-service broadcasting laws that have come to be associated with that country in the post-World War II period. Instead, there existed a complex web of regulations and franchises that ensured that the state remained overweeningly in control of the medium. The Interior Ministry also exercised a large degree of influence over the medium, not least of all because of its tutelage of the government's central information office upon which the broadcasters were compelled to rely for their news and information. Therefore, the definition of public service that developed in Germany during this early period of the century was one that stressed the role of broadcasting as a function of public administration rather than as an independent self-regulating social activity. The state's grip on the medium had become almost absolute even before Hitler came to power and misused it for Nazi propaganda purposes (Humphreys, 1994, pp. 124–125).

By contrast, in Britain, with its 'weak state' and strong liberal traditions, a very different understanding of public service regulation emerged during exactly the same period. In 1926 the Crawford Committee – an official government inquiry into the future structure of broadcasting – recommended that the BBC should be run as a public monopoly free from governmental interference. In 1927 the private monopoly of radio concerns mentioned above was duly transformed into the public corporation that we know today. Significantly, the British Broadcasting Corporation was granted a Royal Charter rather than set up by Act of Parliament, precisely in order to establish the principle of its freedom from political dependence. Although the 1926 General Strike showed that the BBC was ultimately compliant to government, the Corporation still 'emerged from the crisis with an ethic of political neutrality ... that was to have profound consequences for politics' (Curran and Seaton, 1991, p. 143). During the inter-war years, under John Reith's leadership, the BBC was a rather autocratic institution that certainly presented a one-sided, Establishment-biased view of politics and society. All the same, through its status as an independent public corporation the BBC was protected from becoming simply a submissive instrument of the political power-holders and public administrators in the German mould. The BBC's war-time role, ironically as purveyor of propaganda and upholder of public morale, served only to heighten its institutional status which, in turn, underpinned its post-war relative autonomy.

Thus, clearly, there was considerable scope for variation among the political rationales for regulating broadcasting. That broadcasting actually required much stricter regulation than the press, both on high moral political grounds and for the sake of political expediency, was beyond serious question. In addition to technical and economic necessity, squarely political determination played an important role.

Is there a model of public service broadcasting in Europe?

Some mixed public/private systems endured until the end of World War II. This was the case, for instance, in France and Belgium. Mixed systems re-emerged fairly early on in the post-war period too in Britain and Finland, but now their commercial elements were constrained within a developed public-service paradigm. The negative experience of the media under Fascism or Fascist occupation had served only to reinforce the need for principled public-service regulation. What, then, constituted this 'public-service' mould? Already we have gained a brief insight into how interpretations of the concept could vary considerably: according to different patterns of institutional development and political tradition. As with the press sector, European countries' broadcasting systems have been shaped by other factors too, such as (market) size, language community, socio-political cleavage structure, and the lessons of history (eg. in the German case). In what ways these various factors produced distinctive features among the national systems will be examined in the course of this chapter. First it is necessary to consider commonly shared public-service features.

Two conceptual models provide helpful guidance (see Table 4.1). Blumler (1992, pp. 7–21) has suggested that a European public-service model can be defined, in contradistinction to the market-oriented American model, by six shared features. Blumler's six features are a very clear statement of the existence, at least at a general level, of a distinctive European public-service model. Another helpful, and much cited, guide to understanding the public service model has been provided by the Broadcasting Research Unit (1986). This latter study refers specifically to the British broadcasting system. Nevertheless, it is still useful to apply it to other European broadcasting systems. According to the Broadcasting Research Unit there are eight principles of public-service broadcasting. It is, of course, important to emphasise that different systems may fulfil these criteria rather differently. Indeed, it is interesting to note that the BRU's 'British' model stresses the broadcasters' independence from government while Blumler's more general model points to their closeness to the political realm.

Blumler's first criterion is what he calls an 'ethic of comprehensiveness', meaning omnibus services supplying educational and informational as well as entertainment programmes (as is well known, the latter predominate in the United States). The BRU's model extends this notion to the idea of geographic universality. This is important. It excludes the notion of 'pay-TV' where services are limited to those who pay a subscription. Public-service broadcasting aims to deliver a wide ranging quality service to the whole population. The monopoly character of the services explains Blumler's second criterion: the requirement that the broadcasters adhere to what he calls 'generalised mandates'. These may assume various forms – for instance, a charter or an act of parliament, a licence or a concession,

Table 4.1 Characteristics of public-service broadcasting: two similar models

Blumler's criteria	The Broadcasting Research Unit's criteria
Ethic of comprehensiveness	Geographic universality – equal access to same services
Generalised mandates	Catering for all interests and tastes
Diversity, pluralism and range	Catering for minorities
Cultural vocation	Catering for national identity and community
Non-commercialism	Universality of payment: system funded by users (i.e. licence fee)
	Competition to produce good programming rather than audience size
	Guidelines to 'liberate' programme makers, rather than restrict them
Place in politics	Independence from vested interests and government

Note:
Here, the criteria are not reproduced in the original order.
Sources: Jay Blumler 'Public Service Broadcasting before the Commercial Deluge', Chapter 2 in J. Blumler (ed.), *Television and the Public Interest*, London: Sage, 1992, pp. 7 21; BRU, *The Public Service Idea in British Broadcasting – Main Principles*, BRU, 1986.

– but whatever the case, European broadcasting systems are commonly bound by general statements of their public service mission. Moreover, the broadcasters' compliance with their 'generalised mandates' is policed by special regulatory bodies, either within the broadcasting organisation itself (as in the case of the BBC) or placed above them (like the IBA, which regulated ITV). Blumler suggests that in most European countries these bodies are composed of political appointees. However, as we will see, there may well exist strict legal rules specifying the exact make up of their membership and providing for political pluralism within them. Blumler also notes that, inside the parameters defined by these 'generalised mandates', European broadcasters have had a 'considerable amount of freedom and authority': they have been 'allowed to plot their own courses, so long as they did not steer too closely toward dangerous political reefs and sensitivities' (1992, p. 9). The BRU's suggestion that the guidelines should 'liberate' programme makers, rather than restrict them, makes creative and innovative freedom a particular specification.

Typically, these 'generalised mandates' provide in one formulation or another the requirement to supply diverse programming, to respect cultural, religious and political beliefs, to cater to cultural variety, to be objective, impartial and balanced in their reporting, to respect principles of democratic pluralism, and so on. In fact, all this is covered by Blumler's third criterion, commitment to 'diversity, pluralism and range' and his fourth criterion, the 'cultural vocation' of European broadcasters. The BRU's model draws attention to essentially the same features: the requirement to cater to all interests and tastes, to cater for minorities, and to cater for national identity and community. These features do not refer only to the programmes. As suggested, a number of European broadcasting systems have elaborate rules providing for pluralistically composed membership of regulatory bodies. As we will see, some countries go to great lengths to ensure that their diverse cultural communities are fairly represented and that their communication needs are met.

Interestingly, Blumler (1992, p. 10) suggests that 'the pluralistic model contrasts with the more majoritarian model of television provision that is fostered by advertising'. Here Blumler is clearly not referring to political majoritarianism whereby election winners 'take all' in terms of state power (including whatever state influence may exist over broadcasters). He is, nonetheless, pointing towards an important way in which a broadcasting system may cater to a social 'majority' rather than a diversity of minorities. In the United States, for example, broadcasting was geared towards audience maximisation; broadcasters sought to deliver the largest possible audience to the advertisers. This state of affairs conflicted with the goals of pluralism, diversity and cultural provision that defined the European public-service model. So 'non-commercialism' was Blumler's fifth criterion. He cast this rather more broadly than the BRU's specification for direct public funding. This was because many European public channels came to carry advertising. However, here advertising was regarded as a supplement to the licence fee and confined to strict limits. These restrictions 'existed to ensure' that the public service broadcasters were 'not compromised in [their] ability to serve the public interest by [their] need to seek revenue' (Lorimer, 1994, p. 81). Luxembourg was the exception to this rule but, as already mentioned, Luxembourg did not conform to the European public service model. The main point is that, during the long period of public-service supremacy in Europe, reliance on supplementary advertising was not allowed to 'marketise' the broadcasting system. The British duopoly broadcasters, as the BRV noted, did not compete for the same revenue source; allowing them to compete for quality.

Blumler's final feature is concerned with the European broadcasters' 'place in politics'. He refers to the broadcasters as 'creatures ultimately of the state' rather than of the market as in the United States. He notes that the European public service broadcasters have tended to have a very close relationship with the political realm. There are some very positive aspects of this feature. Blumler acknowledges that broadcasters have contributed much to the 'health of the political process and the quality of discourse generated within it'. They have accorded a very important place to news, current affairs and political reporting generally; and they are bound by their generalised mandates to maintain a stance of strict impartiality and balance. Careful rules have been elaborated to govern party political broadcasts and the broadcasters' conduct during elections has typically been subject to strict supervision by theirregulatory bodies. More broadly, the concept of public-service includes the normative goal of contributing to the democratic process and providing an important check on the political system, for instance by exposing any abuses of political authority.

However, there has also certainly been a negative side to this feature: the tendency to politicisation of the European public-service broadcasters. They may be prone to direct state intervention. The composition of regulatory authorities may reflect a particular political bias; appointments within the broadcasting organisations, even down to the level of producers and journalists, may be politically determined. Blumler certainly characterises them as 'highly politicised organisations' (p. 12). As we will see, this evaluation is unquestionably generally true of European broadcasting systems. Indeed, in the Dutch case it might be said to have been a deliberate choice, even seen for a long time as a positive virtue of that country's system rather than an unwelcome intrusion of the politicians as in so many other cases. However, as Blumler notes it is important to realise that the patterns and extent of politicisation differed considerably across Europe. In this connection it is interesting that the BRU's model stresses instead the broadcasters' independence from vested interests and government. Here the distinction is partly explained by the fact that the British broadcasters have been generally much more independent of the politicians. Another explanation is that the BRU model is more normative, while Blumler's is more descriptive. Nevertheless, whatever the system, as Etzioni-Halevy (1987, p. 7) has explained in an interesting comparative study of political pressures on broadcasting, broadcasters were always likely to come under some pressure; this arose from the fact that they 'were expected to be both politically independent and politically accountable'. This fundamental tension reflected a 'deep-seated ambiguity ingrained in the role-definition of broadcasting in a democracy' (p. 37). Since we are mainly concerned with the relationship between politics and the media, much of this chapter will be concerned to examine this particular question.

These two lists are not exhaustive. We might add the public-service commitment to professionalism; this includes quality programming and the maintenance of high standards of journalism and artistic production. Indeed, commitment to quality and creativity are implied by the BRU's stress on competition to produce quality programming rather than audience size. This quality aspect is also implicit in Blumler's fourth criterion, the 'cultural vocation' of European broadcasters. Sepstrup (1989, pp. 30–31) adds that this includes obligations to 'produce a substantial part of the programmes nationally' and 'to support the national production of cultural products' (by supporting national artists, maintaining orchestras, etc.). For Western Europe's public broadcasters, to help sustain national and regional cultural production was a very important obligation.

We should also include the principle of accountability to the citizenry. Accountability here is intended in a more generous sense than the simple existence of mechanisms for researching audience-preferences and dealing with viewers' complaints. Such mechanisms are important but generally they leave power in the hands of the broadcasters. In addition, therefore, there should be scope for a public input into broadcasting decision-making: whether through the representation of diverse 'socially significant groups' within the broadcasters' governing bodies (as in Germany or Sweden, for example); by giving a regulatory role to a Council of Viewers and Listeners (as in Austria); or by regular efforts to consult the public and to invite comment from social organisations (as in Britain where this has been done by the broadcasters themselves and by special Committees of

Inquiry). Finally, it should be pointed out that from its earliest days public-service broadcasting has played an important role as an agent of national and societal integration and stabilisation. During the dangerous 1930s, under the Director Generalship of John Reith, later Lord Reith, the BBC pursued a deliberate paternalistic mission to maintain public confidence in the values of the liberal British Establishment (of which, under Reith, the BBC itself became very much a part). In the words of Tom Burns (1977, p.41), the BBC could be seen as 'a kind of domestic diplomatic service, representing the British or what he [Reith] saw as the best of British to the British'. President de Gaulle – who had once used the BBC to rally the war-time French – later used the state controlled broadcast media in France as a political instrument to spread support for the French Fifth Republic and to unify the country during a particularly turbulent period in its postwar history. His successor Georges Pompidou referred famously to the state broadcasters as the 'Voice of France'.

Bearing all these broad features and goals in mind, we can now turn our attention to an empirical examination of European broadcasting systems. As suggested already, there is considerable scope for national variation within the paradigm of public-service broadcasting. We will begin by looking at these systems' various structures of ownership and finance and the ways they achieved non-commercialism. Then we will examine some distinctive attempts to cater to diversity and fulfil the cultural vocation. Different kinds of institutional safeguards for pluralism will be explored. Finally, we will consider the important matter of their relationship with the political realm. In each respect, the focus will be on special cases. In other words, particular models will be examined wherever they depart from, or wherever they reflect in a particularly distinct manner, any of these general features.

Ownership and finance

With respect to ownership and finance, Western Europe has displayed a diversity of structures. Brants and Siune (1992, pp. 102–103) have usefully distinguished between what they refer to as: 'pure' public monopolies funded solely by the licence fee; 'mixed revenue' public monopolies drawing on licence fees and advertising; and 'dual' systems where a public sector coexists with a private commercial one. These were certainly the main structural alternatives for the public service model. Yet, within these parameters there existed some interesting variation. For instance, Sweden's 'pure' public monopoly was quite singular. In every other respect a thoroughly 'public' broadcaster, the Swedish Broadcasting Corporation was actually a joint-stock company, its shares divided between interests from the press (20 per cent), other business (20 per cent) and popular movements/voluntary groups (60 per cent). This mix of private commercial interest and social group ownership was very distinctive indeed (Hultén, 1984, p. 38; Gustafsson, 1992, p. 208). Among the 'mixed revenue' systems, Spain's model was unusual in that the public broadcasters were financed almost entirely by a mixture of advertising and direct state subsidy rather than by the usual licence fee. In fact, Spain was the only case of direct state subsidy (although this was reduced to next to nothing over the course of the 1980s). The Finnish 'dual system', too, was different to the familiar British understanding of this version of the public-service model. The monopoly of the Finnish Broadcasting Company (YLE) was relaxed in 1959, when a private commercial station (MTV) was allowed to operate alongside it. However, the private television service was delivered via air-time it still had to buy from YLE, the public broadcasting corporation (Tapper, 1992, p. 51; Lorimer, 1994, p. 82). The Italian 'dual system' was very different yet again. It is very important to note that Italy's model did not constitute a public-service duopoly like Britain's. Rather, the commercial pillar was very largely unregulated. It came about because of a sudden proliferation in the 1970s of local television stations exploiting a loophole in national regulations. Very much against the spirit of the law, these local stations then became organised into a number of national commercial networks. During the course of the 1980s the three main networks were then allowed to fall into the hands of a single entrepreneur, Silvio Berlusconi. Italy's system, therefore, was characterised by a regulated public sector and a largely unregulated private sector. Finally, yet another distinction deserves mention, which bears crucially on the question of 'closeness to the political realm' to be explored later. Although most broadcasting companies were publicly owned, there were very important differences between those that were unambiguously state organisations like the French broadcasters, those that were independent public corporations like the British BBC and the German ARD member stations and ZDF, and those in which social groups played a key role as in Sweden (see above) and especially as in the Netherlands (as we shall see soon).

There existed, of course, yet another alternative: that of exclusively private commercial broadcasting (see Table 4.2). As suggested, Luxembourg stood out conspicuously among Western European countries because it never developed a public-service model of broadcasting. A tiny country, with hardly more than a third of a million citizens, Luxembourg was strategically situated right at the heart of Western Europe. The 'reach' of its broadcasters extended, very widely for radio and not insignificantly for terrestrial television, into neighbouring countries. Luxembourg's policy makers very soon perceived the advantage of granting a concession to a private sector monopoly, the CLT (*Compagnie luxembourgeoise de télédiffusion*) so that it might 'collect advertising revenue from [these] neighbouring countries', as it has been bluntly put (Lange and Renaud, 1989, p. 30). Although the CLT remained subject to considerable state influence, particularly with regard to keeping it under national control (it was part-owned by Belgian and French interests), its public-service obligations were few and only 'loosely worded' (Hirsch, 1992, p. 147). The 'Luxembourg gambit' was also played by commercial interests using two tiny principalities on the borders of France – namely, Andorra (in the Pyrenees, population 5,000) and Monaco (near Nice, population 20,000) – as bases from which to provide francophone radio services from beyond French regulatory jurisdiction. As a result of competition from these so-called 'peripheral' radio stations as well as from Radio Luxembourg, the three official French state radio networks were never able to enjoy much more than half of the national listening audience. (In actual fact, the so-called 'peripheral' radio stations fell largely under the control of a French state holding company called Sofirad). As we shall see, this model of commercial media 'havens' using their strategic geographical position to provide commercial radio access to wider European markets, was destined to become far more significant in the age of transfrontier television broadcasts by cable and satellite (see Chapters 5 and 6).

Why some systems embraced advertising

Mixed revenue systems, some might be inclined to argue, are by definition not as 'non-commercial' as pure public-service systems

Table 4.2   Types of broadcasting system, 1980

Pure public	Belgium, Denmark, Norway, and Sweden
Mixed revenue	Austria, France, Germany, Greece, Ireland, Netherlands, Portugal, Spain, and Switzerland
Dual system	UK (private sector established in 1954); Finland (in 1959); and Italy (from 1976 onwards – see next chapter)
Pure commercial	Luxembourg, Monaco, Andorra

Source; Adapted from Kees Brants and Karen Siune, 'Public Broadcasting in a State of Flux', in K. Siune and W. Truetzschler (eds), *Dynamics of Media Politics: Broadcast and Electronic Media in Western Europe*, London: Sage, 1992, p. 104.

financed exclusively by public funding (i.e. via the licence fee). Thus, Sepstrup (1989) has distinguished between 'commercial public-service broadcasters' which ran adverts, and 'non-commercial public-service broadcasters', which did not. Neither of these, though, were profit-motivated and therefore Sepstrup stresses that they could still be easily distinguished from 'private commercial broadcasters' which drew profits from operating advertising-based or pay-TV services. The crucial point is that both kinds of public-service broadcaster faced no competition for the same sources of finance. Whether those public-service channels that depend to some extent on advertising revenue are more vulnerable to commercialisation when suddenly confronted with competition for this revenue is an interesting question that will be explored in Chapter 7. This was not the case during the period of public-service monopoly.

The 1950s and 1960s were a period of broadcasting expansion with first the arrival of television, then of colour television. As more and more people bought television sets, then colour sets, income from the licence fee increased measurably and steadily. However, this era of rapid growth ended just as that of inflation arrived in the 1970s. Also, broadcasting costs tended to outstrip the general rate of inflation. Therefore, governments were faced with a difficult choice. They could simply raise the licence fee on an 'inflation plus' basis. The problem was that the licence fee was widely perceived as a tax. Few citizens appreciated that it actually represented a very small price to pay for the range of service provided (compare with current rates for subscription television whose very attraction much depends on rights to programmes previously carried by the public broadcasters!). Ever wary of incurring popular displeasure, governments sometimes failed to raise the licence fee even enough to cover the ordinary rate of inflation. (In Britain there occurred a discussion about replacing the licence fee altogether). Through the 1970s into the 1980s, across Europe the real income from the licence fee was allowed to decline or at least to stagnate (Lange and Renaud, 1989, p.150 and p. 154; Blumler, 1992, p. 16; Booz.Allen and Hamilton, 1988, p. 6).

Advertising represented a particularly attractive supplementary source of income for the public broadcasters since it was an 'invisible' burden on the viewer. As a consumer the viewer still carried its costs, though unwittingly since they were covered by the retail prices of the products advertised. From the viewer's perspective advertising-based broadcasting appeared to be entirely 'free'. It was therefore politically speaking a very attractive policy option to cover the increasing costs of television. Some countries had introduced it during comparatively early days of the medium. Sepstrup (1989, p. 36) cites both the Netherlands and West Germany as cases of 'high quality public service broadcasters' which had long carried strictly regulated advertising. An important reason why they had been able to do so without suffering any appreciable adverse effects on programme quality was because the monopoly status of the public broadcasters precluded commercial competition for advertising funds. Moreover, within the public-service monopoly framework the demand for advertising far exceeded its supply; the broadcasters therefore had the whip hand and did not have to pander to the advertisers' interests in audience maximisation above other programming criteria. Advertising could be said to have had an additional attraction: the less the public broadcasters depended on income from the licence fee, the greater were their resources of independence from political pressure (since the politicians always decided the level of the licence fee). The view gained currency that the funding mechanism for public broadcasting mattered much less than that it should receive adequate resourcing. From the 1960s onwards, under pressure from the advertising lobby, a number of countries chose the path of introducing advertising as a supplementary source of funding for public-service broadcasting. By the mid-1980s, advertising revenue accounted for a significant percentage of the total income of many European broadcasters (see Table 4.3 below).

This broadcast advertising was commonly subject to strict control

Table 4.3 Advertising as a share of total income of European public broadcasters 1985/86

Country/broadcaster	%
Austria (ORF)	36.7
Finland (YLE)	23.0
France (A2)	62.0
(FR3)	18.0
Germany (ARD)	12.4
(ZDF)	37.0
Greece (ERT1)	21.2
(ERT2)	80.8
Italy (RAI)	32.7
Ireland (RTE)	33.0
Netherlands (NOS)	35.1
Portugal (RTP)	43.9
Spain (RTVE)	97.6
Switzerland (SSR)	26.2
UK (ITV)	97.0

Note:

Belgium's broadcasters were drawing negligible amounts by now too. Also note that France's TF1, privatised in 1986, became wholly dependent on advertising and cannot be here included as a public broadcaster – see next chapter.

Source: European Institute for the Media, *Europe 2000: What Kind of Television?*, Report of the European Television Task Force, Media Monograph No. 11. Manchester: EIM, 1988, p. 49.

regarding content and standards. There were other strictures too. Most of Europe's public-service corporations did not broadcast sponsored programmes. In Austria, where they did, the promoter was prevented from exercising American-style control over the programme (Sandford, 1976, p. 149). Most European countries set the amount of advertising air-time far below what was allowed in the United States (Luxembourg's and Italy's private channels were the exceptions to this rule). Moreover, some countries had very strict ideas about when and how television advertising should be scheduled. Thus, Germany's public broadcasters were limited to running only twenty minutes per day (averaged through the year) and they were banned from advertising on Sundays and national holidays.

Also, advertising was restricted to pre-announced blocks early in the evening; adverts could not break programmes. Similar rules applied in Austria: a maximum of twenty minutes of advertising per day, confined to early evening blocks, not to be broadcast on national or religious holidays. Switzerland, too, specified a daily limit of twenty minutes in four blocks. Almost as strict was the Netherlands with its advertising ceiling of thirty minutes per day, Sundays excluded. Dutch adverts were concentrated in blocks before and after the news. This approach contrasted with Britain's more relaxed regime where 'spot advertising' could interrupt programmes, albeit in 'natural breaks', every day of the year. ITV was allowed to run an average of seven minutes per hour and slightly more in peak periods. It is worthy of special note that Germany and Britain came to logger-heads within the Council of Europe and the European Community during the 1980s over the issue of 'block advertising' and the principle of non-interruption of programmes (see Chapter 8, pp. 274–275).

Britain's duopoly model

The British duopoly deserves special mention not least because with the passage of time it earned considerable acclaim and in so doing it helped to overcome considerable West European prejudice against privately owned television. During the 1980s its high quality was held up by European proponents of commercialisation to strengthen their case for deregulating broadcasting (see next chapter). In fact, this line of argument was specious. The British model showed that private ownership could be reconciled with public-service broadcast-ing by regulatory means. It is true that ITV actually came into being because a very successful commercial pressure group campaign pre-vailed upon a Conservative government to abridge the BBC's broad-casting monopoly (Wilson, 1961). However, in marked contrast to the Luxembourg model, the British commercial sector (ITV since 1955 and ILR since 1973) was subjected to statutory obligations and close hands-on regulation by the Independent Broadcasting Author-ity (IBA).* Indeed, the IBA drew its guiding principles from the very same public-service ethos and tradition that the BBC had developed

---

* At first this was called the Independent Television Authority [ITA]; the IBA has been now replaced by the lighter touch Independent Television Commission (ITC)

during its period of monopoly. The IBA presided over a 'federal system' of fifteen commercial independent television (ITV) companies serving fourteen regional areas (London had two companies, one broadcasting at the week-end, the other during weekdays) and since 1973 a much greater number of commercial independent local radio (ILR) stations. The IBA allocated their franchises. In performing this task, it was not simply concerned with commercial considerations. It selected franchise-holders according to strict criteria of programme standards and schedules, and the 'public interest'. The process itself involved prior public consultation, although the IBA conducted its actual business of decision-making behind closed doors in what critics have described as an atmosphere of impenetrable secretiveness (for an account see Briggs and Spicer, 1986). The IBA also had authority to withdraw or fail to renew the broadcasters' franchises. This latter power was exercised on occasion (notably in 1967) and it therefore exerted a powerful discipline over the ITV companies. Their programming policies had continuously to take account, not simply of commercial criteria, but also of the need to retain their franchises in the next franchise round. The IBA also had considerable interventionist powers: it co-determined and had the last say about programme scheduling, it could prohibit the transmission of programmes it did not like, and it regulated advertising (content, quality, amount, etc.).

In order to provide further protection for the public-service nature of the duopoly, the financial bases of the ITV/ILR and BBC were kept strictly separate. The BBC continued to be funded from the licence fee while the commercial ITV companies financed their operations and made their profits from limited spot-advertising, which was carefully regulated by the IBA to conform to strict codes of conduct. Although there certainly was competition for audiences (the ratings battle), the deliberate avoidance of structures of direct competition for the same source of revenue between the BBC and the ITV sector, limited the incentives for broadcasters to subordinate standards of public service to commercial demands. The same principle was also operative, albeit in a different guise, within the ITV sector itself. Direct commercial competition between the ITV companies, and the corresponding negative effect that this would have had on programming standards, was precluded by the fact that each ITV company held a franchise giving it a regional monopoly (until the 1980s there was no competition from cable or satellite). When the system was expanded by the addition of the 'minorities channel' Channel 4 in 1982, care was taken to prevent this development from entailing commercial competition. To this end, ownership of Channel 4 was conferred wholly upon the IBA. Moreover, Channel 4 was financed not by competitive advertising but instead by an annual subscription set by the IBA and paid by the ITV companies, who sold the advertising for the channel. Moreover, the ITV companies also sold their own advertising on Channel 4 and retained the profits therefrom. As a result of these carefully crafted structures, the duopoly functioned in a uniquely symbiotic fashion; its various channels competed to produce quality programmes as well as simply for audiences. As much as was possible in any system, standards were protected from open market competition; the duopoly was most decidedly not a 'free' market. The British case demonstrated how public-service regulation and in particular protection from commercial competition – the absence of competition for the same source of revenue – were more important than public monopoly ownership of the broadcasting services.

Organisational and regulatory arrangements providing for pluralism, diversity and accountability

As mentioned, it was also a fundamental axiom that public-service broadcasting systems should provide a universal service catering to democratic pluralism and social diversity. This aim was written into their 'generalised mandates' (see above) and practised within their programme schedules by all public service channels; the Germans called this 'internal pluralism'. From the 1960s onwards, with the expansion of television, quite often a special remit was given to particular channels as well. Thus in Britain, for instance, the more highbrow/BBC 2 was introduced in 1964 so that BBC 1 could become more popularly orientated and compete with ITV. Nearly twenty years later, in 1982, Channel 4 was established with the remit to cater specifically to a wide range of different cultural tastes and to serve social minority interests as well as to run quality entertainment programmes (its minority orientation went rather further than BBC2's). In Germany, the function of providing both highbrow and other kinds of minority programming was given to the so-called 'Third Channels', set up during the 1960s and operated by the country's regional broadcasting corporations (individually or jointly). Public-service radio stations tended to specialise more than television. The public broadcasters offered distinct classical music and pop, light entertainment and serious channels (e.g. devoted to current affairs). Increasingly in the 1970s and 1980s, minority and local services were introduced as well; for instance, in corporatist Sweden the public broadcasters' monopoly was relaxed when voluntary organisations were allowed to operate non-commercial neighbourhood radio. In general, the 1960s and 1970s were decades of great change in the content of West European broadcasting – all within the context of enduring monopoly (or duopoly) structures. The latter's broadcast services were now characterised by greater liberalism and permissiveness, and less deference to tradition and authority (clearly the degree of freedom varied according to the system – see later). The introduction of minority channels and greater concern to schedule for minorities helped to meet a growing demand – from the libertarian Left, from special interests, and from a whole range of single issue movements – for increased minority representation and for more 'media democracy'. (In the 1980s, however, this libertarian theme was hijacked by a libertarian Right arguing that media pluralism would be best served by abolishing public-service monopolies in favour of the 'free market' – see next chapter).

A commitment to provide equal services to all parts of the country governed the expansion of both television and radio. Indeed, catering to regional diversity was considered to be a vital ingredient of the public-service model. Both BBC and ITV were required to provide regional services; respect for regional diversity had been one of the principal rationales for ITV's decentralised construction from the outset in the 1950s (franchises for fourteen regional areas). Both the BBC and the IBA had broadcasting councils for Scotland, Wales and Northern Ireland; the BBC had set up ten regional councils as well. In France, regional diversity was the business of the third channel, *France Régions 3*, launched in 1972. This policy was not restricted to the larger, highly populous countries. Norway was very fragmented, cleaved by strong centre-periphery tensions as well as by many diverse dialects. To respond to these demands, NRK started transmitting regional broadcasts in the 1950s, devoting considerable resources to this end from the 1970s onwards. A number of other countries – notably Switzerland and Belgium – decentralised broadcasting to cater to linguistic and cultural fragmentation (see below).

Partly because of its history, Germany's commitment to decentralised public broadcasting was special. During the post-war occupation public broadcasting was deliberately (re)constituted upon an entirely regional basis. This reflected the concern of the Allied occupiers to protect broadcasting structures against any future recurrence of despotic central control. The decentralisation of broadcasting was also congruent with the federal construction of the Federal Republic (this too, of course, was a hedge against any return of centralised dictatorship). To this end, the 1949 constitution (actually called the 'Basic Law') consigned jurisdiction of cultural policy, which included broadcasting apart from its telecommunications aspects, to the republic's constituent regions or 'states' (the *Länder*). Over the period 1948 to 1956, these *Länder* enacted their own broadcasting laws (individually or in some cases jointly) providing for nine regionally decentralised public-service broadcasting corporations (unification in 1990 added two more). Legally autonomous corporations governed under public law, they were supposed to be independent from the state. Joining together in the Association of Public Broadcasting Corporations in Germany (the ARD) they operated a joint television network, the so-called 'first channel' (DFS), consisting of programmes they each provided according to their size and resources (both of which varied considerably). In the 1960s, a second channel, the ZDF (literally, the 'second German television' service), was set up alongside the ARD network. ZDF was a centralised national channel but it was not under central control. In accordance with the federal nature of broadcasting, ZDF was introduced by an inter-state treaty of all the *Länder* and it remained subject to their shared jurisdiction. As mentioned, the 'third channels' were a regional initiative (for detail, see Humphreys, 1994, pp. 132–169).

Linguistic diversity, too, was reflected in decentralised structures of public-service broadcasting. Thus, in Belgium there were separate radio and television services for each of the country's three linguistic groups, the French speakers, the Flemish (Dutch) speakers and even the small minority of German speakers. Similarly, the Swiss Broadcasting Corporation provided a full service for that country's French, German and Italian linguistic communities. In Spain, during the 1980s, a number of 'third channels' began operating to cater to the Basques, Catalans, and Galicians (as well as other regions). In Britain, a separate fourth television channel for Wales, called S4C, was launched alongside Channel 4 in the 1980s. Also, by the 1980s, public broadcasters were providing some air-time for ethnic minority and 'guest worker' communities (and the expansion of local community radio and also cable television was making a key contribution as well).

As already suggested, the need to respect the principles of pluralism and diversity was also reflected in the public broadcasters' regulatory structures and accountability mechanisms. In this matter, however, practice varied considerably across Europe. In Britain, the regulators could hardly be described as being socially representative. They were officially chosen, in an opaque manner, from the ranks of a social elite (they were often referred to as the 'Great and the Good'). These Establishment figures were served by advisory councils that were more socially representative, but authority clearly lay with the social elite. In liberal Britain, the regulators were at least independent of government in contrast to statist France (see later). Somewhat greater social representativeness and accountability were evident in Europe's corporatist countries. In these cases, unsurprisingly, certain organised interests gained an important say within the broadcasters' regulatory bodies. In Austria, for example, there existed a quasi-official Council of Viewers and Listeners. This body did not merely have an advisory or lobbying role like Britain's similarly named pressure group. It was actually accorded representation within the regulatory body – called the Board of Trustees – which supervised the Austrian public broadcasting corporation (the ORF). Moreover, in typical corporatist fashion, so too were the ORF's employees. In Austria, direct political appointees outnumbered these organised interests within the Board of Trustees, but the latter were appointed according to the *Proporz* principle – that is in proportion to the party balance both in the government coalition and in the parliament. This effectively gave authority in broadcasting regulation to a restricted party 'cartel' of Social Democrats and Christian Democrats. Nevertheless, as we shall see, this politicisation was fairly commonplace in Europe. Choosing the regulators in a way that reflected genuine social pluralism was far less so.

The German system resembled the corporatist Austrian case but ensured rather wider social representation and more open democratic accountability; the regulatory bodies were supposed to be politically independent. (Again, the German model of regulatory body was explicable by the country's history and the concern to learn from it). All of (West) Germany's broadcasting corporations were governed by independent broadcasting councils (*Rund-funkräte*)* These broadcasting councils were supposed to reflect what were referred to as the 'socially significant groups'. According to the various *Land* broadcasting laws, these bodies were largely composed of delegates nominated directly by the social groups concerned. This system gave representation to diverse social groups like the parties, business and labour organisations, churches, universities, teachers, women, and so on. Representation was also given to figures from the fields of journalism, culture, the arts and science (see Humphreys, 1994, p. 143). Formally much more democratic than the British model, the regulators still proved to be much closer to the realm of party politics than was true in the elitist British case (see later).

Yet another interesting kind of institutional arrangement – to safeguard media pluralism – was Italy's adoption of 'Guarantor' responsible for ensuring that media interests comply with the law and fulfil their special duties. Italy's adoption of this particular institution could be explained, in large measure, by the country's history of slack enforcement of media control and by the seemingly chronic failure of the parties ever to reach consensus themselves on media issues. A parliamentary commission that was supposedly responsible for supervising the broadcasters had amounted to little more than 'the parties' agency for political control' and had been 'rarely distinguished for its interventions in overt defence of viewers' rights and interests' (Mazzoleni, 1994, p. 129). Therefore a Broadcasting Act of 1990 extended to the 'Guarantor' ultimate authority over broadcasting regulation (this was ten years after the same provision had been applied to the press sector). A single individual, typically a magistrate, appointed by the chairmen of both houses of the Italian parliament, the Guarantor was a 'monocratic authority' with a wide range of regulatory duties. These included keeping ownership structures under review and making sure that the broadcasters respected the interests of the viewers as outlined in the Broadcasting Act. Attached to the Guarantor's office was a Viewers' Advisory Council staffed by members of the various viewers' associations and media experts.

---

* With national re-unification in 1990, West Germany effectively took over East Germany and its media system was reconstructed on West German lines – Humphreys, 1994, Chapter 7.

Despite this innovation, Mazzoleni (1994, p. 133), suggests that 'political rather than social accountability of the media seem[ed] more characteristic of the Italian case'.

Pluralism, elitism and broadcasting policy styles

Unsurprisingly, broadcasting policy reflected distinctive national policy styles and traditions. Italy's broadcasting policy style could best be described as 'immobilist', like the country's political system itself. In most Northern European countries policy-making was corporatist, consensual and incremental. In France it tended to be more majoritarian and prone to radical leaps. French policy-making could be termed *dirigiste*. In Germany it was highly legalistic. Britain's traditional broadcasting policy style, too, was distinctive.

In keeping with the British administrative tradition, important decisions about broadcasting were customarily made only after an 'institutionalised consensus' had been reached through widespread consultation of the relevant interests (Humphreys, 1991, p. 205). An important mechanism for achieving this consensus was the independent committee of inquiry. These were headed by an Establishment figure, but composed carefully along pluralistic and meritocratic lines. At regular intervals of about twelve years during the post-war period, British governments enjoined these ad hoc committee to seek ways of accommodating public broadcasting to changing social needs. These committees then invited submissions from interested individuals and groups, held public hearings, and on the basis of evidence and opinion gathered in this way, produced reports that were both weighty and highly influential, giving direction to subsequent reform. Thus, the Beveridge Report (1949) criticised the BBC's old fashioned paternalism and a minority report opened the way for the introduction of ITV. The Beveridge report also mooted the idea of decentralising broadcasting, an idea that was implemented both by the BBC and in the shape of the ITV system. The Pilkington Report (1962) was highly critical of the early experience of ITV and helped to ensure that the new commercial sector soon conformed to the public service model. Its recommendation that the powers of the IBA (then called the ITA) be increased, were accepted. (If anything the Pilkington report was too critical of ITV – see Seaton in Curran and Seaton, 1991, Chapter 12). Later, the Annan Report (1977), pointed to the need for more diversity, greater expression of minority concerns, and new ideas and experimentation. This prepared the ground for the introduction of Channel 4. (However, the Annan report rejected the view that the broadcasters' regulatory bodies should be made more socially representative.) Between these special commissions of inquiry, parliamentary committees – such as the Select Committee on the Department of National Heritage – provided another channel of accountability. Elite commissions and special committees concerned with broadcasting policy were not a uniquely British phenomenon. They played a key role at times in other countries too, particularly when the 'new media' of multi-channel cable and satellite television began to be seen as a matter of great public policy import in the 1980s (see next chapter). Nevertheless, the regularity and the authority of these major British inquiries – and not least their reports' character as classic documents of public service broadcasting principles and debates – marked them out for distinction. The reports were the product of a liberal elite that viewed broadcasting's public-service nature as a very serious business indeed; yet they were practically informed by the wider policy community. This balance helped to explain the capacity which British broadcasting policy makers displayed for pragmatic and adaptive, yet sometimes inspired innovative change (the duopoly's careful structures, Channel 4, etc.).

Statist France provided a great contrast. As Minc (1993) has described, crucial policy decisions were all too often taken upon executive whim without an effort to canvass public opinion and without allowing policy to be guided by the broadcasting community. All too often, the only voices that the executive seemed to listen to, were the technocrats and engineers. As a result, policy tended to reflect a narrow mix of political and technocratic criteria; it also tended to be highly voluntaristic. A classic example of this policy style was the manner in which de Gaulle decided that France should pursue its own SECAM colour television standard in the 1960s despite the fact that the German PAL standard became the West European norm. This decision burdened French industry with comparatively high costs, which translated into high prices for broadcast equipment, which adversely affected consumers, resulting in a slower diffusion of the equipment. Through isolating France, though, the standard consolidated the state's control of broadcasting. Again, in the 1980s, this *dirigiste* approach led to the adoption of a number of statist and technocratic projects – for the development of cable and satellite television – which similarly proved to be over-ambitious technically (cable) or largely superfluous to market demand (satellite). However, not all voluntaristic broadcasting policies were disappointments. A pay-TV channel called Canal Plus, launched in the mid-1980s, went on to become a market leader in Europe. The fact remains that French broadcasting policy was a rather closed technocratic business, beyond which it was dictated more by the comings and goings of governments than by anything else. Between 1959 and 1986 French broadcasting underwent no fewer than five organisational reforms, three of which were major ones as will be seen. As Sorbets and Palmer suggest (1986, p. 90) 'it [was] symptomatic that any new regime ... result[ed] in a more or less thorough reform of audiovisual law and regulations'.

In Germany, by contrast yet again, the main parameters of broadcasting policy were ultimately decided by – and pluralism underpinned by – constitutional–legal means. In Germany constitutional law played a very special role in broadcasting policy. There were several reasons for this particular characteristic feature of the post-war German system. In the first place, Germany had an old *Rechtstaat* tradition.* This tradition could be traced back to the nineteenth century. In the second place, the Nazi dictatorship had showed how necessary were constitutional underpinnings of democratic pluralism in the media field. During the post-war period, therefore, no lesser body than the Federal Constitutional Court quickly established the objective parameters of broadcasting policy-making. Policy in Germany was guided by what has been described as 'broadcasting constitutionalism' (Humphreys, 1991 and 1994). The court, which like the US Supreme Court was the highest authority in the land, was first called upon to defend the cultural sovereignty of the *Länder* in 1961. This intervention was prompted by a blatant attempt by the federal Chancellor Konrad Adenauer to launch a second channel which, though commercial, was clearly intended to be controlled by the federal government (i.e. Adenauer). The Court's famous 1961 ruling served as a kind of 'Magna Carta' for the public-service system, confirming unequivocally the independent cultural jurisdiction of the *Länder* and therefore their responsibilty for regulating broadcasting services. It also seemed to entrench the public monopoly, pointing

---

* The translation of this as 'a state within which law plays a very special role' conveys the sense rather better than the commonly encountered 'state ruled by law'.

explicitly to the distinction between broadcasting and the press. While the press provided pluralism and diversity through the market, broadcasting was restricted to a limited number of services by factors of a technical (scarcity of frequencies) and economic nature (the high costs of becoming involved in broadcasting operations). This, it was argued, provided the rationale for the public monopoly. Later, in the 1980s, it was the Constitutional Court that opened the way up for the introduction of private commercial broadcasting (the 'scarcity of frequencies' having meanwhile been overcome by technical change). At the same time, however, it stipulated that the very precondition for this should be the safeguarding of the basic public-service role of broadcasting. The Constitutional Court's deliberations always tended to range well beyond the narrow legal issue in dispute, to consider the broad questions of broadcasting as a social institution. In this regard, the court – a legal 'Establishment' – could be said to have played a quite similar role to the British commissions of inquiry just mentioned. Within the parameters decided by the court, the *Länder* enacted their own broadcasting legislation. Whenever national regulations were called for (eg. for satellite broadcasting), they had to come to collective agreements in the form of inter-state (inter-*Land*) treaties. This was another key feature of the German broadcasting policy process that made for consensual, or at least incremental and bargained, rather than majoritarian, policies.

To a point, the German policy style also shared a marked feature of Northern Europe's small states: namely, corporatism. In the Scandinavian countries, Austria and Switzerland, it was most uncommon for major media policy decisions to be taken without a determined attempt to arrive at a consensus between the relevant organised interests (in Sweden, Austria and Switzerland, this included the press). As will shortly be seen, in the Netherlands and Belgium, a very high premium indeed was placed on consensus. In all these countries, executive voluntarism was definitely not the norm. The networks, commissions, working groups and so forth, where policy was formulated, typically involved all the relevant 'social partners'. The media policy community would play an important role in influencing legislation. However, it is noteworthy that this corporatistic policy style has been eroded in the 1980s. In broadcasting policy-making, certainly, the new tendency has been towards direct – and successful – lobbying of government by powerful commercial interests (Trappel, 1991; Meier and Trappel, 1992).

Structures of broadcasting in culturally 'plural' societies: the Dutch and Belgian cases

Nowhere, perhaps, was *congruence* between the characteristics of the political system and those of the media system more striking than in the case of those culturally plural societies with 'consensual' political systems (Lijphart, 1984 – the term 'consociational' has also been used, but this concept proved to be controversial among political scientists). In different ways the Netherlands and Belgium illustrate this point neatly. In both cases, the structures of broadcasting, like the macro-political structures in which they were embedded, were designed specifically to cater to the countries' social and political heterogeneity. In such societies, majoritarian decision-making styles and institutional structures were wholly unsuitable. Instead, national integration was best served by mechanisms making for elite accommodation and consensus. Among these mechanisms were the principle of proportionality in electoral systems, appointments in the bureaucracy, distribution of resources, and so forth; and the granting of a crucial degree of autonomy for the different subcultures. These key features – proportionality and subcultural autonomy – were the main characteristics of the structures of broadcasting. As we shall now see, the Dutch case provided for years an excellent example of catering to marked social 'pluriformity' (McQuail, 1992a, p. 100) through a non-territorial kind of 'sociological federalism' (Lijphart, 1984, p. 185). In Belgium's case, the linguistic cleavage was catered for by a federalism that was mainly, but not entirely, territorial in view of the fact that the Brussels region of the country was a mixed community and also the fact the German-speakers were catered for by broadcasting structures even though they did not gain a political regional entity of their own. Usefully, Lijphart suggested that for the decentralisation of cultural affairs in Belgium – which includes broadcasting – the term 'corporate' federalism was more apt than territorial federalism (Lijphart, 1984, p. 184).

The Netherlands

The Netherlands was the largest of the small West European countries in terms of population size, with around fifteen million inhabitants. For much of the twentieth century, Dutch politics and society presented an image of 'segmented pluralism' or socio-political 'pillarisation' (*Verzuiling* in Dutch). From their earliest mobilisation in the last century, Dutch social movements, voluntary associations and political parties were all organised within the distinctive encapsulated 'pillars' that were formed by the religious and ideological cleavages that vertically segmented Dutch society and politics. Two religious groups – Calvinists and Catholics – had a cross-class appeal within their two pillars, while the secular 'pillar' was itself divided by class cleavage. With the extension of the mass suffrage, this pattern resulted in a multi-party system. No less than three religious parties (until they united in the Christian Democratic Appeal in 1974) faced on the Right a conservative Liberal party (the VVD), and on the Left a Socialist labour party (PvdA). Despite 'de-pillarisation' since the 1960s, there has still never been a majority party. Coalition government was the norm. During much of this century, large areas of Dutch public life reflected this pillarisation, including the public administration, the education system, and the media system. Indeed, hardly had radio broadcasting commenced in the Netherlands than the 'pillars' took over. By the 1930s the radio spectrum had been legally shared out exclusively between corporations closely tied to the different political pillars of Dutch political society: the Catholics, Protestants, Socialists and Liberals (ideologically conservative). In the post-war period, a 1969 Act served to make the rigidly pillarised system more flexible and open. There followed a limited expansion of the range of broadcasting organisations. The Act also allowed a number of smaller bodies to receive small amounts of air-time (eg. party political broadcasts for small parties, 'open access' type broadcasts, etc.).

The 1969 Act also established a new public service body, the Dutch Broadcasting Corporation (*Nederlandse Omroep Stichting*, NOS), to administer, regulate and coordinate these various broadcasters. The high premium placed on reaching consensus was faithfully reflected in the composition of the supervisory board of the NOS which was generally representative of the range of broadcasting organisations. NOS took over the provision of technical services and provided a balance of general consumption programme fare (eg. news, current affairs, sports, etc.) amounting to some 20 per cent of total air-time. Perhaps rather bizarrely to an outsider, the remainder of the air-time available, on three national television channels, was meticulously allocated on a ratio of 5:3:1, calculated according to the size of relevant social group membership (membership being conferred either through payment of a simple fee or by subscription to the broadcasting magazines that the groups each produced). Air time on *Nederland 1* was largely reserved to VARA (socialist), KRO (Catholic) and NCRV (Protestant), these all being deemed 'class A' broadcasters. The majority of air-time on *Nederland 2* went to three more 'class A' broadcasters: AVRO (conservative), TROS and VOO (ideologically neutral, popular, entertainment-orientated). There were two 'class B' broadcasters: VPRO (liberal–progressive) and EO (evangelical). No groups fell into the 'class C' category (see Tables 4.4 and 4.5).

Table 4.4   *Air time allocation in the Netherlands public broadcasting system, 1991*

Broadcaster	Group membership threshhold	Television (hours p.w.)	Radio (hours p.w.)
'A'	450,000	12	65
'B'	300,000	7	39
'C'	150,000	n/a	n/a

Source: Calculated from data in Kees Brants and Denis McQuail, 'The Netherlands', in Bernt Østergaard (ed.), *The Media in Western Europe: The Euromedia Handbook*, London/Newbury Park/New Delhi: Sage, 1992, pp. 152–166, pp. 158–159.

Table 4.5   *Broadcasting associations in the Netherlands*

Broadcaster	Established	Political identity	Status
AVRO	1928	Liberal/conservative[a]	A
EO	1967	Evangelical	B
KRO	1925	Catholic	A
NCRV	1924	Protestant	A
TROS	1964	Neutral	A
VARA	1925	Socialist	A
VOO	1973	Neutral	A
VPRO	1926	Liberal/progressive	B

Note:
[a] Nominally neutral.
Source: Kees Brants and Denis McQuail, 'The Netherlands' in Bernt Østergaard (ed.), *The Media in Western Europe: The Euromedia Handbook*, London/Newbury Park/New Delhi: Sage, 1992.

Though they were free to provide ideologically biased programming, all these 'corporations' were strictly speaking required by law to offer a balanced mix of information (25 per cent), culture (20 per cent), amusement (25 per cent) and education (5 per cent). *Nederland 3* was used for NOS's news, sports and cultural programmes, and to grant air-time to numerous smaller organisations (Brants and McQuail, 1992, pp. 158–159).

So we can see very clearly indeed, in the Dutch case, an example of more or less exact congruence of structures of the political and the media system. This congruence reflected the traditional 'pillarisation' of Dutch society into distinct political cultural communities and the consequent attempt to achieve a consensual political balance within the structures of broadcasting. Clearly, the shaping of these structures along the lines of social and political community meant that they were politicised. Historically, as Brants and Jankowski (1985, p. 74) have put it, 'the media, as the core propaganda organs of the pillars, constituted core elements in the politics of control'. McQuail (1992a, p. 99–100) has observed that some ideologically biased programming was 'even a positive expectation'. On the other hand, the system did provide for 'external pluralism': in other words, there was choice across the various services (as distinct from 'internal pluralism' within each programme service). Moreover, the Dutch system was not under the government's thumb. 'The various broadcasting organizations, to a certain extent, broadcast what they wished' (Nieuwenhhuis, 1992, pp. 204–205).

It should be noted, too, that from the 1960s onwards Dutch society became progressively fluid and decreasingly segmented; it became 'de-pillarised'. Viewers no longer felt tied to any particular broadcaster. Increasing numbers, particularly the young, now preferred instead to 'view around'. The secular loosening of religious and ideological ties led to a corresponding 'de-pillarisation' of the media system, if not in structure at least in consumer behaviour and programme content. A loosening of political/consumer loyalties, and increased competition within the media system for readers and viewers, had the *de facto* effect of secularising and commercialising media patterns, shifting the balance of media fare towards a more de-ideologised entertainment function. This has been referred to as a 'TROS-ification' process, as the traditional broadcasting organisations felt compelled to copy the popular entertainment programming style pioneered by TROS. By the close of the 1980s over half of the overall progamme fare of Dutch public broadcasting was of this kind. For VARA and VOO it was over two-thirds. Moreover, by now the Netherlands found itself in 'turmoil' as a result of competition from commercial channels introduced in neighbouring countries, most notably a Dutch language offspring of Luxembourg's CLT, called RTL 4. This latter development will be explored in the following chapters (Brants and Slaa, 1994, pp. 13–14; McQuail, 1992; Nieuwenhuis, 1992).

Belgium

In Belgium 'pluriformity' translated into federalism along the lines of linguistic community. The country's ten million population divided between Dutch-speaking Flemish (57 per cent), French-speaking Walloons (42 per cent) and a small German-speaking community. Historically there was also a milder version of the Dutch kind of pillarisation. Accordingly, in the earliest days of radio a number of stations were sponsored by ideological organisations reflecting the Catholic, secular Liberal (ie. conservative), Socialist and Flemish nationalist political communities. After World War II, a unified public service monopoly was established. However, in order to counter an intensification of the linguistic cleavage, from the 1960s onwards a series of reforms led eventually to the federalisation of the country. This was mirrored in new broadcasting structures. In 1960 the main language communities were granted their own autonomous broadcasting corporation, each responsible for the functions of transmission, administration and finance: the RTBF for the francophone Walloons and the BRT for the Dutch-speaking Flemish. These broadcasting organisations fell within the jurisdiction of the cultural communities. They were each governed by highly politicised boards that reflected the prevailing 'political arithmetic on the regional level' (Hirsch, 1986, p. 22) and that 'stifled the broadcast system' (de Bens, 1992, p. 19; for a detailed account, see Burgelman, 1989). Much later in 1977 an additional small broadcasting service, the BRF, was established for the country's German speaking minority.

Closeness to the state and the question of politicisation of the broadcasters

The politicisation of public broadcasting was by no means a feature of these systems alone. Far from it. From the 1950s expansion of mass television onwards, the broadcast media were increasingly perceived to be crucially important for politicians seeking both electoral support and popular legitimacy for their policies. In the interests of balanced pluralism, paid political advertising, as occurred in the United States, was disallowed (Italy's private channels were an exception). Undoubtedly, this reflected the much greater strength of the Left in Europe; it also followed from the European Left's comparatively weaker links to business sponsors. Instead, all of Western Europe's democracies developed rules governing electoral broadcasting. These rules were concerned with ensuring equality or at least 'equitability' of a limited amount of free access before and between elections. In Denmark, Finland, France and the Netherlands, this came to be allocated on an equal basis to all parties. In Britain, there was equality for the two major parties. Elsewhere, it was worked out in relation to party strength, on some kind of a proportional basis. For such broadcasts, the choices about content was left in the hands of the politicians alone. Important as they were, however, such formal rules had little bearing on the most controversial aspect of the relationship between broadcasting and politics: the extent to which politicians were able to exercise control over the broadcasters themselves and thereby continuously to influence the agenda of other political broadcasting, notably news and current affairs.

Western Europe's public-service broadcasters generally enjoyed certain safeguards designed to protect them from being creatures of the state and politicians. In the first place they were normally granted the legal identity of autonomous corporations. Secondly, they were regulated by special boards internal to the organisation (as in the case of the BBC and the German broadcasting councils) or by special bodies external to them (like the IBA) or sometimes by both (the case in Sweden). Thirdly, although the level of the licence fee was determined by government or parliament, broadcasters usually had a degree of autonomy over their finances. However, there were exceptions and weaknesses in all of these respects, as we shall see. In fact, the extent of politicisation of the public-service broadcasters varied very considerably. Different political systems presented varying opportunities for it to occur and encouraged different manifestations of it. The most obviously dominated broadcasting systems were those closest to the state. Indeed, in marked contrast to consensual and corporatist systems, statist systems presented the political executive, rather than a balance of social forces, with scope for direct media control. As will be described shortly, France's statist public broadcasting 'monolith' provided a good example. Where the broadcasters were at an important remove from the state, by dint of being self-regulating public corporations, like the BBC or the German corporations, the scope for state domination was much less.

However, there remained avenues for political influence. Firstly, politicians could exert pressure through their control over the user licence fee. Rarely was the business of setting the level of this mainstay of the broadcasters' income not directly in the hands of government, though the German Constitutional Court has recommended giving this authority over to a genuinely independent body. Moreover, governments could exert pressure through proposals to introduce advertising or subscription as in Britain under Thatcher (Franklin, 1994, p. 82; Etzioni-Halevy, 1987, p. 74; Jones, 1991, p. 217). The broadcasters' ultimate dependence on the state for finance, then, was an obvious weak link in the public-service model. Clearly, privately funded broadcasters could be more securely independent in this regard. However, even here governments might retain the right to grant franchises or else to exert such pressure through their influence on the franchising bodies (see next chapter). Secondly, governments determined media policy: this allowed them to change, or threaten to change, the rules of the game to the advantage or disadvantage of the broadcasters. This too could be a potent source of 'blackmail'. Thirdly, as with the 'free press', governments could invoke security requirements to censor the broadcasters. Constraints on the reporting of Northern Ireland by the British broadcasters were a good case in point (Franklin, 1994, pp. 79–81; Jones, 1991, p. 217). Fourthly, as with the press, governments could manage the news by various means (see Chapter 2). They could even use the media to advertise their policies under the guise of public information programmes. In Britain, for example, during the 1980s government advertising leapt from £35 million of expenditure to £200 million (Jones, 1991, p. 206). Finally, responsibility for appointing the regulators usually lay with the politicians. Even where law or convention provided for a pluralistic composition of such bodies, the fact that regulators were political appointees remained a weak link in the public-service model. Moreover, the politicians might be in a position to 'colonise' the broadcasting corporations by making strategic appointments to their management structures. This kind of politicisation – and its effects – would then percolate downwards in the organisation.

France: a highly politicised 'statist monolith'

In France political control of the broadcast media was the subject of intense controversy throughout the whole of the post-war period. French political culture was part of the explanation. Public broadcasting had always been seen as the official 'voice of France'. France also had a marked 'strong state' or *étatiste* tradition; centralised statism was the constant of French history, providing a bureaucratic antidote to the centrifugal social and political forces that historically had often seemed to threaten the country with instability. Finally, in the modern era, during the generally stable Fifth Republic, the political system usually functioned in a distinctly 'majoritarian' executive-centred fashion; periods of 'cohabitation' apart, the political power centre was the presidency. Whoever won the presidency disposed of extensive powers of patronage including in the field of broadcasting; the president's government held all the levers of power. Even cohabitation (the state of affairs when the president lost his parliamentary support base) merely transferred uncommonly strong executive powers in most policy fields – including broadcasting – to the prime minister and his cabinet. Parliamentary constraint was feeble; the Fifth Republic had one of the weakest legislatures among Western democracies. Quite simply, all this 'afforded opportunities for political propaganda which [were] consistently ... used and often abused by successive governments' (Vaughan, 1985, p. 20). As Kuhn (1985a, p. 47) puts it 'the two most salient features of broadcasting in France ... [were] first its legal status as a state monopoly and, secondly, its use for partisan political purposes by the government of the day'.

The Liberation government not only tightened up the state's formal monopoly of broadcasting, it transformed the broadcasters into state servants, thereby placing them under effective political control. Throughout the Fourth Republic *Radiodiffusion–Télévision de France* (RTF) remained a highly centralised organisation, its director-general being directly appointed by the government and the state exercising total control of its budget. An organisational reform was introduced with the change of regime to the Fifth Republic as the result of which the RTF gained a degree of nominal financial autonomy. However, the director-general, his deputy and the directors of the various broadcasting services, all remained government appointees. Change occurred again in 1964 when another administrative reorganisation saw the RTF transformed into the *Office de Radiodiffusion–Télévision Française* (ORTF). This reform created a 'pluralistic' board of management (*conseil d'adminstration*) but this body was allowed very little autonomous authority. As Minc (1993, pp. 15–17) has remarked, a kind of tacit agreement appeared to exist between the political power-holders and the broadcasters whereby the latter accorded to the former omnipotence over information in return for protection of their corporate interests. The broadcasting monopoly guaranteed the state's political control; the broadcasters' compensation was their virtual monopoly of broadcasting production. Information control was exerted through a complex network of official links so that through successive organisational reforms the medium remained under constant political tutelage. Minc even described French broadcasting executives as 'prefects responsible for information and entertainment' (analogous to the state *préfets* that, since Napoleonic times, had been the central state's principal regional agents). Kuhn (1995, p. 5) has employed the same analogy, suggesting that 'centralised state control of television by the Gaullists … was intended to reinforce the legitimacy of the one and indivisible (Fifth) Republic as the embodiment of the national will, just as the prefectoral system of 150 years previously had been used to bind the nation under the control of the Napoleonic Empire'.

With the arrival in power of president de Gaulle – and the establishment and consolidation of the majoritarian Fifth Republic – the state broadcasting monopoly was wielded for political purposes in a very blatant manner indeed. During the 1960s and early 1970s, the ORTF was literally packed with Gaullist appointees. One result, as Kuhn (1985b, p. 53) tells us, was that 'prior to 1965, opposition spokesmen, such as François Mitterrand, were kept off the screen or suffered from malicious editing'. Even after principles of political balance and impartiality were formally enshrined in the ORTF statute in 1964, the Ministry of Information continued to fix the agenda of radio and television news programmes and even to indulge in direct censorship. It is true that with de Gaulle's demise political control of information became more discreet. Following Giscard d'Estaing's assumption of the presidency in 1974, a new broadcasting law was enacted that confirmed the state monopoly but broke up the ORTF into seven separate, supposedly autonomous, public enterprises: three television channels, TF1, Antenne 2 and the regional service, FR3; the radio service, Radio France; the technical and transmission service, TDF; the production service, SFP; and finally the archival and research institute, INA. The organisational reform did little to reduce the statist grip. The state continued to own and to direct all seven services. The Giscardians claimed that, under them, the broadcasting system was now neutral. Certainly the 'excesses of the Gaullist period were now out of fashion'. Under the presidency of Giscard d'Estaing 'overt ministerial censorship became the exception rather than the rule'. However, 'controls were [now] largely internalised within the television companies' (Kuhn, 1995, pp. 158–159). As Minc (1993, p. 18) has explained, Giscard's presidency merely replaced overt hierarchical dominance with a more diffuse kind of influence, exerted through his powers of patronage. Vaughan (1985, p. 20) noted how 'the list of appointees ... showed a clear shift towards Giscard's retinue'. Similarly Flichy (1984, p. 232) concluded that 'the main change between the 1960s and the 1970s was that the government no longer controlled the release of daily information but instead, chose journalists sympathetic to its political beliefs'.

It is, then, hardly surprising that the Left came to power, following Mitterrand's victory in the presidential election of 1981, with a firm commitment to 'liberate' the broadcast media from a majoritarian spoils system which had patently worked to their disadvantage for over two decades in opposition. One of their first acts was to establish, by a particularly radical broadcasting law of 1982, a High Authority for Audiovisual Communication *(Haute Autorité de l'Audiovisuel* – see next chapter). Formally at least, the government's power to make political appointments in the broadcasting organisations was now removed and given over – for the first time – to an independent IBA-type authority. The body was also charged to ensure the right to reply to governmental statements; to watch over political broadcasting generally; and, more narrowly, to regulate programmes broadcast during election campaigns. Yet the Left too was soon accused of having conducted a customary witch hunt through the public service broadcasting organisations. Despite the Socialists' reform initiatives, which without any question significantly shifted the organisational framework of French broadcasting away from centralised state monopoly control (see next chapter), there remained distinct traces of surreptitious politicisation about the system. In particular, there were serious controversies surrounding the appointment of director generalships of the public-service television channels. The appointment of Socialist sympathisers to these key jobs seemed to illustrate 'the tenacity of certain long-standing traditions' (Kuhn 1985b, p. 54; Kuhn, 1995; Quatrepoint *et al.*, 1987, pp. 13–154).

Britain: a paradigm of broadcasting independence?

Britain's duopoly system has often been held up as a counter-model of comparative independence of the broadcasters; in Britain, government's influence has been of the 'arm's length' kind. Again political traditions can be adduced to explain this state of affairs; in particular, Britain's long-standing liberal, 'weak state' tradition. The corollary of this weak state tradition was Britain's development of strongly entrenched, autonomous institutions of civil society, like the BBC and later the IBA. To the extent that this model character of British broadcasting held true, political traditions must be considered to have been very important. Post-war British broadcasting certainly benefited from an uncommon willingness on the part of government to respect the principle of the broadcasters' independence even if this did not preclude all manner of subtle (and not always so subtle) manoeuvres to exert external pressure on them. All the same, the parties did exercise restraint; there existed a clear 'gentlemen's agreement' between the political parties to desist from any overt politicisation of the media. The British broadcasters' 'relative autonomy' also unquestionably reflected the uncommonly strong institutional authority and independence established over the years by the BBC itself which rubbed off later on the ITV/IBA sector. The most obvious point of contrast with the French case was that the broadcasters were not directly state organisations: the BBC was a public corporation and the ITV companies were privately owned. In neither case were the broadcasters state servants. Further, both parts of the duopoly were governed according to the 'trusteeship' mode of regulation. Both the BBC's Board of Governors and the IBA (supervising ITV) were formally autonomous and powerful regulatory bodies, charged with the task of ensuring that the broadcasters respect the principal of political impartiality and fulfil their many other public service obligations. The members of each supreme regulatory body may have been government appointees but they were regarded as trustees of the public interest. They were there to 'shield' the broadcasters from outside pressure and to 'protect' them from from politicians and pressure groups, 'more than the other way round' (Seymour-Ure, 1991, p. 63).

However, as Negrine (1985, p. 17) has suggested, the BBC's Board of Governors and the IBA could be seen either 'as a buffer between the state and the broadcasters or as an indirect mechanism by which the state [could] exert control over broadcasting'. The fact that both bodies were effectively composed of government nominees might lead sceptics to expect the latter. Nevertheless, the fact remains that even the most radical critics of the British model have accepted that (at least until the 1980s) the system was not at all party politicised. Thus, for Stuart Hood (1983, pp. 39–52) the regulators, appointed from the ranks of the Great and the Good, 'represent[ed] the ideas and values shared by some of the most important groups within the British ruling class'. Yet, Hood still acknowledged, the regulators were 'not appointed on a party basis'. Similarly, a respected British academic marxist, Ralph Miliband (1969, p. 200), conceded that the broadcasters 'preserve[d] a fair degree of impartiality between the Conservative, Liberal and Labour parties' though he went on to emphasise how undemocratic the system really was. Echoing Hood, Miliband noted that the trustees of British broadcasting were 'Establishment figures, whether Conservative, Liberal, Labour or "non political"' (p. 209).

Britain's trusteeship model was certainly elitist and socially unrepresentative. Further, the broadcasting independence that it upheld was excessively reliant on political cultural safeguards. There was an absence of the constitutional–legal guarantees that, for instance, the German broadcasters enjoyed (in fact, the legal status of the BBC's independence was quite ambiguous). As everyone knows, political culture can change; 'gentlemen's agreements' can go out of fashion. It has been suggested that the BBC's Board of Governors did become more politicised during the Thatcher era (Milne, 1988, p. 82; Franklin, 1984, pp. 78–79). An interesting academic study by Etzioni-

Halevy (1987) found that, although British broadcasting was not internally 'colonised' by parties or governments, it was far more vulnerable to external political pressures than expected. These pressures, Etzioni-Halevy noted, intensified during the 1980s. The 'casualisation' of working conditions within the corporation actually rendered BBC journalists more vulnerable to pressure than their counterparts in Germany where politicisation was the rule but where more broadcasting journalists also enjoyed job security. A strong argument could be made for democratising Britain's elitist version of 'trusteeship' regulation by increasing the representativeness and accountability of the regulatory bodies and underpinning this in law. Indeed the German variant of trusteeship does suggest itself as a potentially more pluralist model. The problem, as we will now see, was that in practice it was also effectively a party politicised one.

Germany: a more democratic model?

During the Third Reich, the Nazis had used the notorious 'People's radio' as a powerful instrument of propaganda and social control. Therefore, the post-war German elites were above all concerned to uphold principles of fairness and impartiality within the public broadcasting system. When liberal democracy was restored after World War II, under the watchful guardianship of the Western Allies the electronic media system was profoundly reorganised and democratised. The influence of politicians was supposed to be confined to public policy aspects of the media; editorial control was taken out of their hands. The country's post-war political system was far less majoritarian than Britain's or France's (under the Fifth Republic). West German government was decentralised and executive power was dispersed. Key constraints were placed on the central political executive by the federal nature of the political system and by the legalistic political culture. As emphasised already, a vital role in public policy was played by constitutional law.

These features were faithfully reproduced in the organisation and control of the broadcasting system. Each broadcasting service was supervised by an internal broadcasting council. As already described, these councils were composed according to the principle of regulatory power-sharing by the socially significant groups. In most cases, too, these councils chose the service's director-general (called the

Intendant). This system was supposed to ensure diversity, ideological balance, and so forth, within each service (rather than across a number of biased services as in the Dutch case). Germans referred to their system as one of 'internal pluralism' (as opposed to Dutch-style 'external pluralism'). However, despite its model character, the self-consciously pluralistic West German broadcasting system all too soon became wracked by bitter controversies about the extent to which it had become effectively party politicised (rather than state dominated). The main question, in the German case, was whether or not the politicisation worked to benefit one political party more than another. That the system was politicised was a matter of common agreement, among political parties, media researchers, academics and all concerned. Not only were regulatory authorities composed of party members and sympathisers, the politicisation extended to party card carriers being appointed to key jobs within the corporations, even down to middle management, producers and journalists (the links between broadcasting and party politics in Germany is explained by *inter alia*; Williams, 1976; Kleinsteuber, 1982; Etzioni–Halevy, 1987; Porter and Hasselbach, 1991; and Humphreys, 1994).

This party politicisation may seem paradoxical, in view of the aforementioned determination to safeguard the broadcasting corporations from the negative influence of the state. The explanation was in part historical/political cultural. In the immediate post-war context of the Cold War and the lost legitimacy of other elites, the democratic political parties in West Germany soon acquired an overweening presence in many areas of social life. German political scientists referred to the emergence of a 'party state' (*Parteienstaat*). Like the bureaucracy, the notionally independent broadcasting corporations quickly fell victim to this extensive reach of the democratic parties' influence (Dyson, 1977). The broadcasting system also had an institutional weakness. The regulatory bodies may have been composed more democratically than in the British version of the trusteeship model, with detailed laws carefully apportioning representation pluralistically to the 'socially significant groups'. The problem was that, on the one hand, seats in these bodies were also given to parliamentarians; and on the other hand, these 'socially significant groups' (eg. trade unions, business associations, etc.) usually had clear political allegiances. This notwithstanding, the German case contrasted with the French. Firstly, it is important to note that the 'socially significant groups' were not simply party instruments. Even if all too often they had close party identifications and links, they remained important agents of genuine public accountability and pluralism. They had their own views, made their own input, and did feel bound to respect the public interest. Secondly, an important measure of democratic pluralism was guaranteed by a factor which was both political, cultural and institutional in nature: namely, the German respect for 'proportionality' (*Proporz*). This principle was also characteristic of a number of other northern European democracies. As seen, it was to be found in the Netherlands, Belgium and in Austria; it contrasted directly with the strongly majoritarian ('winner takes all') model of France. In the latter case, after elections the new government reaped all the 'spoils' of victory, including control of broadcasting. In the West German case, by contrast, *Proporz* accorded a share of political influence within the regional broadcasting corporations to the loser of the relevant *Land* election. All the same, an important measure of political influence was gained in the regional broadcasting corporations by the winners of *Land* elections. However, this is where federalism provided another safeguard against majoritarian dominance of the entire system. Taking the country's broadcasting system as a whole, there were important regional counterbalances, reflecting the country's variable political geography. Since both main party parties had their heartlands, there were certainly some regional corporations where the Social Democrats tended to be in the ascendant, and others dominated by the Christian Democrats. Political bias was often quite clearly reflected in the regional 'third' channels. However, since the other programmes of the regional corporations were networked by the ARD there was still a systemic confrontation and counterbalance of political orientations in the first national channel. The second national channel, the ZDF, as a collective organisation of all the *Länder*, similarly displayed this systemic balance. All these factors meant that no single political party ever enjoyed undue influence over the entire public-service broadcasting system. In Germany, Left and Right each gained 'their share' of the broadcast media.

Italy: the 'partyocratic' model

Italy presented an interesting variant; its broadcasting system moved from a lengthy post-war period of majoritarian, one-party dominance to a state of multi-party politicisation lasting from the late 1970s through the 1980s. In the 1990s it then reverted to a brief state of executive dominance before this model too was thrown into question. That broadcasting was politicised reflected what the Italians themselves called *partitocrazia* or 'partyocracy'. This was a rather extreme version of the German 'party state' or *Parteienstaat*. Through patronage networks, positions of influence in all areas of Italian public life, including the public-service broadcasting channels, were allocated according to party loyalties. For a long period, this assured the predominant Christian Democrat party (the DCI) a large measure of control over the state broadcasting service, the RAI. However, as Mazzoleni (1992, p. 81) has described, in 1975 a reform of the system 'opened up control over RAI to a plurality of political forces, supplementing the Christian Democratic influence with lay and democratic socialist elements'. Control of RAI now became the responsibility of a parliamentary commission composed of forty representatives drawn from all the parties. However, consensus between them was very elusive. Under these circumstances, control was divided between the main political parties on a channel by channel basis. This produced a kind of 'external pluralism'. The Christian Democrats remained most influential within RAI I, but the Socialists dominated RAI 2, and the Communists the rather 'highbrow' RAI 3. In effect, (not unlike the Dutch case) the Italian viewer could choose the ideological flavour of the news and current affairs programmes that s/he watched (Barile and Rao, 1992, p. 262).

For years this remained the pattern. However, in 1994, briefly, a return to executive dominance seemed likely. The old parties of the Establishment, the Christian Democrats and Socialists, collapsed in the wake of grave corruption scandals. Into the vacuum now stepped the media baron Silvio Berlusconi who deployed his virtual monopoly of private commercial broadcasting – this having been steadily acquired during the 1980s – in order to set up a new 'party' of the Centre-Right. *Forza Italia* was far more a media-created social movement than a conventional party. It derived its strength from the support it gained from Berlusconi's three national commercial television networks rather than from any developed organisational base. Nevertheless, backed by a very partisan media campaign, it won the 1994 elections. Berlusconi was able to head a government in alliance with the 'post-fascist' National Alliance and the ideologically mixed northern Italian regionalists. Amid controversy, the RAI board resigned and was replaced with new political appointees. Managerial changes ensued within RAI. A controversial plan to run a series of information slots advertising the government's programme was blocked by the media Guarantor. All in all, the question of media control in Italy caused huge political rows. However, Berlusconi's premiership proved to be very short-lived. His coalition lacked ideological or programmatic cohesion and it collapsed in the last days of 1994. Thereupon, Italy's President Scalfaro was called upon to appoint a new 'technocratic' caretaker government which soon let it be known that it would attempt to curb Berlusconi's media power. Italy's constitutional court, too, ruled in favour of a popular referendum on whether Berlusconi should be divested of his private broadcasting monopoly. For a brief moment, in the early 1990s, the politicisation of Italian broadcasting had promised to emulate that of Gaullist France. Nonetheless, the Italian people voted in 1995 to allow Berlusconi to keep his channels.

Towards a classication of patterns of politicisation of public-service broadcasting

This survey clearly has not covered all countries in Western Europe. Yet it points to some interesting patterns. French public broadcasting stood out as being conspicuously prone to capture exclusively by the party or parties forming the presidential majority. This could be explained in large measure by the fact that the French broadcasters operated within a centralised, statist and majoritarian polity (in the sense that 'winners took all' after elections). Certainly, it might be pointed out, Britain's political system was no less majoritarian (and given the two-party system arguably more so). However, in France electoral majoritarianism was combined with an intense rivalry, an historic polarisation, between the countries' parties. As a result the parties had consistently proven themselves incapable of producing consensual 'rules of the game'. As Kuhn (1995, p. 9) has explained, 'the post-war British concept of a consensual middle ground cutting across the two-party division and underpinning a public service approach by broadcasters to political coverage has been an alien one in French party politics'. It is interesting that public broadcasting in 1980s Greece arguably much resembled the situation in France under de Gaulle. Following the end of military rule in 1975, Greece opted for a centralised quasi-presidential system along French lines. Moreover, the party system produced a distinctly majoritarian system of government. As historically was the case in France, polarisation between the political parties presented little scope for reaching a British-style 'gentlemen's agreement' over broadcasting. Given the *dirigiste* state tradition, the absence of a self-regulatory tradition, and the marked culture of patronage politics, it was unsurprising that Greece's public broadcasters were subjected to excessive executive domination (Katsoudas, 1985; Papathanassopoulos, 1990).

By contrast, countries with institutional mechanisms and political traditions geared more towards political 'power-sharing' provided pluralism, even if they were politicised. The Dutch model was even predicated on a degree of politicisation, yet it counterbalanced bias with an external pluralism of programmes. Majority domination was impossible. In different ways, a number of other of Europe's more consensual systems combined politicisation with political pluralism. The case of Germany has been highlighted. Austria and Belgium have also been mentioned; Meier and Trappel (1992, p. 135) refer to the 'massive political influence in personnel decisions' in these two cases (see also Trappel, 1990, p. 33). In both, however, there existed a tradition of inter-party cooperation and a respect for political proportionality (*Proporz*). The Scandinavian democracies also deserve a mention. They were countries with a distinctively consensual corporatist political culture. They had strong traditions of open government and parliamentary accountability as well. Among them, Denmark's broadcasters were the most vulnerable to party politicisation. Its broadcasting council (regulator) even became known as the country's 'mini-parliament', its politically appointed members as 'radio politicians'. Nevertheless, the council was composed largely to reflect the party balance in parliament; the executive's representation was weak. Sweden resembled Britain's model of broadcaster 'relative autonomy' or 'arm's length influence'. Controversy over political bias in programmes was fairly rare. In strongly corporatist Sweden, the 'popular movements' – voluntary organisations and socially relevant groups – actually owned a 60 per cent majority stake in the broadcaster's parent company. This acted as an important shield between state and the programme companies. Again, the regulators reflected broadly the party political balance in parliament.

The Italian case was highly idiosyncratic; it veered from one model to another. However, this could be explained by reference to

Table 4.6 A classification of some Western European public broadcasting systems according to patterns of politicisation

Executive or single party dominated	Arm's length influence	Multiparty/group dominated
France	Britain	Germany
Italy (until 1975)	Sweden	Austria
Italy (1994)		Italy (post-1975)
Greece		Denmark
		Netherlands
		Belgium

squarely political factors. In the first place, the political culture was very different to the northern European countries just mentioned. It shared with the other countries of Mediterranean Europe a culture of clientelism. This was rooted in historic patron–client networks but it clearly persisted throughout the post-war period of democracy in the shape of the 'partyocracy'. However, only two parties were strong: the Christian Democrats and the Communists. For a long period the system was polarised between them. The Christian Democrats dominated Italian government, while the Communists were effectively excluded from the system as pariahs. Under such conditions, as in Gaullist France, the spoils of power – including control of broadcasting – flowed exclusively to the Christian Democrats. Over time, though, the Italian system moved shakily towards a more consensual model; at least the polarisation diminished. In particular, the Christian Democrats became reliant on their main coalition partners, the Socialists; and the Communists became more or less fully legitimised within the system. This explained the shift from majoritarian-style dominance of public broadcasting towards a pattern of multi-party dominance. However, in Italy consensus was always fragile; stable compromises between the parties remained difficult to attain. Power was not easily shared. What then was more natural than to share out the channels between the main parties? This created a semblance of consensus. When finally the partyocratic model collapsed from its own corruption, briefly a media tycoon assumed office.

Berlusconi, it should be recalled, arguably owed his political career to the fact that since the mid-1970s he had acquired a quasi-monopoly of private commercial television. Elsewhere in Western Europe the public-service broadcasting monopoly (or duopoly) prevented this kind of political entrepreneurship by rich and powerful citizens. The broadcasters may have been subject to bureaucratic party pressures, but generally there existed a degree of political pluralism. This section of the chapter's focus on the 'closeness to the political realm' of public broadcasters should not overshadow the undoubted achievements of public-service broadcasting. Social minorities were provided for, at least more than in commercial systems. Cultural standards were also maintained. Localism, regionalism and linguistic communities were certainly catered for. Accountability mechanisms, although they were bureaucratic and aloof from the average viewer, marked the public service model out as distinct from the commercial media. All the same the price for these achievements seemed to be a vulnerability to political influences that ranged from the discreet power of an establishment in Britain to outright dominance by the political executive as in France. In between, lay the European norm of politicisation by 'party cartel' (Katz and Mair, 1995).

Guide to further reading

J. Blumler (ed.), *Television and the Public Interest: Vulnerable Values in West European Broadcasting*, London: Sage, 1992.

J. Curran and J. Seaton, *Power Without Responsibility: The Press and Broadcasting in Britain*, London/New York: Routledge, 1991, Part II.

P. Humphreys, *Media and Media Policy in Germany*, Oxford and Providence, R.I.: 1994, Chapters 3 and 4.

R. Kuhn, *The Media in France*, London/New York: Routledge, 1995, Chapters 3, 4, 5 and 6.

J. Mitchell and J. Blumler (eds), *Television and the Viewer Interest; Explorations in the Responsiveness of European Broadcasters*, London: John Libbey, 1994. European Institute for the Media, Media Monograph No. 18.

R. Negrine, *Politics and the Mass Media in Britain*, London/New York: Routledge, 1994, Chapters 5 and 6.

V. Porter and S. Hasselbach, *Pluralism, Politics and the Marketplace: The Regulation of German Broadcasting*, London/New York: Routledge, 1991, especially Chapters 1, 2 and 3.

C. Seymour-Ure, *The British Press and Broadcasting since 1945*, Oxford: Basil Blackwell, 1991.

5

The 'new media', and broadcasting deregulation in Western Europe

This chapter explores the Europe-wide adoption in recent years of national broadcasting policies leading away from the established public-service paradigm described in the last chapter towards a multi-channel, marketised broadcasting model which many anticipate will more and more resemble that of the United States. This particular prospect has engendered both enthusiasm and apprehension. Whatever the preference, though, it is increasingly generally recognised that the kind of 'hands-on' public policy control of broadcasting customarily exercised in Europe, is being eroded by the 'new media' revolution, part of the wider technology-induced 'information revolution'.

From broadcasting's earliest days, as seen already, policies have been shaped by a complex mixture of economic, technological and squarely political factors. However, the balance between these various factors has undergone a significant change. The last chapter described how, quite in contrast to the press sector, West European broadcasting had for most of its existence been extensively shaped by public policy and regulation. The cultural and political arguments in favour of public-service principles are still valid; indeed, there remain sources of considerable political support for these principles. However, observably, for some years now regulation has tended increasingly to follow technological and market developments. The trend of public policies has been deregulatory even when this was not the intention. Moreover, the scope for distinctive national regulatory structures is now measurably weakened by the homogenising impact of an internationalisation of media markets. All this has led to the development being described as a 'paradigmatic shift' (Hoffmann–Riem, 1986). This and the following chapters will describe how this paradigmatic shift has involved:

1 a trend towards the abolition of the public-service monopoly; the opening of the regulatory gates to new private commercial entrants to the sector (a key feature of deregulation);
2 the waiving of public-service obligations for the new commercial sector; or the imposition of minimal obligations that do not conflict with economic requirements (another key feature of deregulation);
3 a crisis of the effectiveness of regulation as a result of new opportunities to evade or circumvent national regulation (a third, in policy terms involuntary, feature of deregulation);
4 the rivalling of the public-service doctrine by notions of 'consumer sovereignty' – the viewer as consumer rather than as citizen – and the primacy of the 'free market';
5 following on from this, a 'commodification' of broadcasting (with programmes viewed increasingly as marketable products, programme libraries seen as commercial assets, etc.). In general, a tendency to see broadcasting as an economic sector like any other;
6 and finally, to an extent varying between countries, a questioning of the future of public-service broadcasting, its legitimacy, its future funding, its place and orientation within the new paradigm, etc.

Generally, broadcasting has come to be treated increasingly as an industry or a sphere of commercial enterprise. Confronted by new competition for advertising, compelled to justify continuance of their basic licence fee income, the public broadcasters have faced a harsh dilemma: to continue with their traditional practices or to vie with their private competitors in running 'popular' programming. Governments have not always been very supportive. Calling for efficiency gains, they have allowed licence fee income to stagnate or to diminish in real terms while pegging the amount, if any, that public broadcasters can draw from advertising. As will be seen, the public-service broadcasters have embraced, albeit to varying degrees, more commercial standards and practices. In France there has even occurred considerable privatisation of the public-service broadcasting system. On the other hand, the process and extent of deregulation has varied significantly between countries. Moreover, it has produced some unintended consequences. Policy makers are still climbing a learning curve. Before considering these important matters, it is important to consider those factors that have nevertheless given clear shape to this paradigatic shift. The main *imperatives* driving policy in this new direction have been threefold: ideological, technological and economic. The balance between them has varied from national case to case.

The ideological challenge to the public-service monopoly

As seen, the traditional view in Western Europe stressed the cultural function of broadcasting. This underpinned the argument that the broadcasting sector should be the preserve of public-service broadcasters. Strict public-service regulation was required to ensure that broadcasting performed its special social and cultural functions. However, the 1980s witnessed the arrival in positions of power, or at least the growing influence, of ideological radicals on the business orientated political Right in Europe. These were Thatcherite conservatives, the neo-liberal faction of Christian Democratic parties, Gaullist neo-liberals, and continental Europe's more right-wing Liberal parties ('Thatcherite' in their economic doctrine). Giving vocal support to the sectional interests of important industrial and commercial lobbies (see later, pp. 172–176), the free market radicals vigorously promoted an economistic counter-viewpoint to the public-service ethos. They argued in favour of treating broadcasting as a market that ideally should be freed of all but minimal regulation. These free marketeers protested the debilitating effects of public regulation and state intervention. Proponents of deregulation and economic liberalisation, they marshalled a number of coherent intellectual objections to the public-service paradigm (in particular see Veljanovski, 1989).

The marketisation of broadcasting, these Right-wing libertarians argued, would free the viewer from the old fashioned moral paternalism of 'nanny state' broadcasting and deliver genuine consumer sovereignty in its place. Consumer choice, expressed as audience preferences, should therefore replace the regulated media. The industry, free to pursue profits in a much more competitive market for audiences, would assuredly respond to popular preferences. Accordingly, the market itself was regarded as an adequate regulator in the public interest. It would provide a new external pluralism of channels, in the place of the old 'bureaucratically' manufactured internal pluralism. Indeed, the market was seen as a much more neutral and efficient regulator than any state or para-public agency. The latters' interventions were viewed, from this perspective, as being excessively prone to capture by partisan interests and not responsive enough to public demands. Political parties and organised interests were held to have exercised, all too often, an unhealthy degree of influence over public-service broadcasters and their regulatory bodies. As the preceding pages have described, there was some foundation to this particular criticism (Brittan, 1989).

According to this perspective, the communication needs of individual media consumers were inadequately served by the public broadcasters. Consumers were relatively incapable of voicing their preferences through bureaucratic channels. The free market, it was argued, would provide these consumers with a near perfect mechanism for signalling their preferences directly to the service providers. The latter, so long as they were market players, would respond immediately to these signals. The public-service model's other major inefficiency, so the argument went, was its alleged aversion to innovation. Once marketised, however, the broadcasting sector would become imbued with the entrepreneurial spirit which the public-service broadcasters were said to lack; further, new technologies would be more quickly diffused. Free enterprise would see to it that exciting new opportunities for providing consumer satisfaction were sufficiently exploited. Moreover, the disciplines of the market would compel broadcasters to reduce their alleged top-heavy bureaucracies and drop their restrictive practices (Thatcher's famous 'Spanish customs'). Broadcasters would be forced to become cost-effective. This, it was argued, would free up resources for the wide range of more innovative services and programmes that could be provided for by a proliferation of new media delivery systems that were becoming available (see next section). Moreover, small producers, unencumbered by the large bureaucracies of the broadcasting monopolies, would be given a fair crack of the whip. Media pluralism would be increased.

Against all this, the defenders of the public-service paradigm argued that the commercial principle was quite incapable of catering to the full diversity of public informational requirements. The free market was definitely not conducive to the supply of quality programming. In competitive markets, quality drama would be too 'cost-inefficient' to produce in significant measure any more. In the fierce struggle to maximise audiences, informational and educative programming would be both quantitatively reduced and qualitatively transformed into 'infotainment'. Public-service news values would be debased. The market would badly serve the need for the culturally diverse, 'social responsibility' kind of programming provided in the past. Many minorities would be ill catered for by the 'majoritarian' commercial imperative of audience maximisation. The regions, ethnic and religious communities, social and political minorities, and so on, would get short shrift from the market. The old and the poor would be positively disadvantaged when relatively expensive pay-television services attracted film and sports television rights away from the universally available mainstream public channels. All in all, this critical view deplored the neo-liberals' tendency to see the audience as as a collection of individual consumers rather than as citizens in society. Pointing to the press sector the advocates of retaining the public service model expressed disquiet, too, at the new scope for proprietorial influence on privately owned media operating within a commercial and unregulated framework. At risk were basic journalistic freedoms and citizens' genuine information requirements rather than simply their tastes. Threatened were the principles of universality, broad and balanced coverage of issues, independence from commercial influences, respect for diverse cultural needs, and so forth. These latter values could be said, reasonably, to underpin the humanistic principle of freedom of information no less than the individual proprietor's simple freedom to disseminate opinion. Such values lay at the core of broadcasting conceived as a profession and as a public service, rather than as a mere industry or arena of commercial exchange. These fundamental public-service values, the defenders of the public-service paradigm argued, would be at great risk of being swept away. Technological factors, however, seemed powerfully to strengthen the case of the deregulators and 'free market' liberalisers. In the age of new media technologies that provided for a considerable multiplication of programme delivery systems, the public-service monopoly (or duopoly) became exceedingly difficult to justify (though it did not follow that public-service regulation was now redundant). The main catalyst for change, giving practical force to the liberalisers' arguments, was undoubtedly the development of new technologies, especially the 'new media' of cable and satellite.

The technological challenge: 'new media'

In addition to the cultural argument, the public-service monopoly in
Europe had always been underpinned by the 'scarcity of frequencies'
rationale. Indeed putatively this had been its primary rationale
(though some point out that it was in fact more an excuse for politically motivated regulation). However, during the 1980s the expansion of new media – the proliferation of cable systems combined
with the arrival in a big way of transfrontier satellite broadcasting –
was progressively removing this particular foundation of the public-
service monopoly paradigm. It is important to note too that new
hertzian (terrestrial or 'off air') frequencies have been made available
as technological progress has allowed for a more efficient usage of
the airwaves. It is also worth a mention that a further expansion of
spectrum usage now beckons with the prospect of signal digitalisation and particularly digital compression (see the Conclusion, pp.
301–303). In the main, though, satellite broadcasting – including
direct-to-home (DTH) broadcasting, but beyond Britain so far
mainly satellite-to-cable relay – has already registered an important
impact, in that it has provided for transfrontier broadcasting and
therefore undermined the effectiveness of national regulation.

During the 1980s, the number of European cable television channels measurably increased. Most of northern Europe is now well
equipped (see Table 5.1). There are two reasons for this. Firstly,
some countries were already densely cabled. This was the legacy of
an earlier era when cable was deemed to be highly appropriate for
the relay of multiple public-service channels in densely populated
small but industrially advanced countries like the Benelux countries
and Switzerland. Secondly, often the state intervened energetically
during the 1980s, partly for reasons of industrial policy rather than
media policy, in order to provide new cable infrastructure. Cable
was seen as an essential component of the 'information age'; it was
widely viewed as vital to the development of a modern information
technology and telecommunications industrial sector. Another
reason was the desire of policy makers simply to promote a multi-
channel television revolution. In France policy was driven by a
tremendous technological and industrial ambition: the Socialists'
early programme (during the radical early years of office) was
described in humour as 'nationalisation plus fibre optic cable'.
Helmut Kohl's Christian Democrat-led coalition, by contrast, priori-

tised speed of cabling over the modernity of the chosen cable technology (for a full discussion of the technological issues, see Dyson
and Humphreys, 1988).

Table 5.1 The growth of cable penetration

Country	% of all TV homes 1987	Homes connected in 1987 (thousands)	% of all TV homes 1992	Homes connected in 1992 (thousands)
Austria	16.2	450	29.7	878
Belgium	84.3	2,950	92	3,450
Denmark	19.0	399	50.0	1,100
Finland	21.0	400	42.0	800
France	0.5[a]	100	4.5	927
Germany	13.7	3,520	32.5	10,844
Ireland	31.2	299	40	400
Lux'bourg	66.0	100	90.0	117
Netherl.	70.4	3,801	87.0	5,225
Norway	28.0	420	36.3	550
Sweden	13.3	438	50.2	1,800
Switzerl.	67.3	1,641	76.6	1,865
UK	1.2	260	2.5	552[b]

Note:
Southern Europe hardly had any cable systems at all.

[a] Lange and Renaud made a miscalculation of the % here. They give 100,000
cable homes of a total of 19.6 million TV homes, as 5%.

[b] This is 'new build', genuinely 'multi-channel' cable. As opposed to 'redif-
fusion' cable limited to a very small number of channels. Also the source
describes it as a 'minimum estimate'.

Sources: 1987 figures calculated from data in A. Lange and J.L. Renaud, *The
Future of the European Audiovisual Industry*, Manchester: European Institute
for the Media, 1989, p. 17. 1992 figures directly from *Cable & Satellite Yearbook '93*, London: 21st century Publishing, 1994, pp. 70–75.

Whatever the case, only a few countries were still hardly cabled at
all by the end of the decade; these were notably the more backward
countries of southern Europe though in France and Britain, as well,
cable laying proceeded far slower than planned (for an explanation
of the problems, see Dyson and Humphreys, 1988). France's state-led

French cable programme proved to be technologically too ambitious and was mismanaged; in Britain cable received no state funding and by the late 1980s cable companies faced serious competition from Rupert Murdoch's commercial satellite channels (broadcasting direct-to-home). Despite these qualifications, multi-channel cable television was a key factor for the remarkable expansion of commercial broadcasting in a large area of northern Europe, including the major German market. By the mid-1990s cable was taking off in Britain and France. Even countries that by the end of the 1980s still had not yet officially liberalised their broadcasting systems were tolerating the re-transmission of a large number of foreign services, including commercial ones, on their cable systems. By 1990 twelve were available on Austrian cable, between twelve and twenty on Swiss cable, and in Denmark cabled homes were served by between twenty-five and thirty (Brants and Siune, 1992, p. 103).

Satellite broadcasting

A key factor in the paradigm change towards a marketised broadcasting system in Europe has been the deployment for broadcasting purposes of three generations of satellite. The oldest are the so-called low-powered satellites – these being relatively simple telecommunications satellites – of Eutelsat and Intelsat (European and international satellite organisations respectively). These have been capable only of 'point-to-point' transmission, which means that their programmes have been up-linked from ground stations and then beamed down again for re-transmission into Europe's infrastructure of cable systems or else to earth stations for low-power terrestrial relay. Despite these satellites' originally rather limited technical capability, the rapid expansion of cable systems keen to relay their programmes, meant that they made an early contribution to a significant expansion of Europe's commercial broadcasting markets.

The broadcasting revolution already under way, a second type of high-powered satellite was developed during the 1980s specifically for direct broadcasting by satellite (DBS) (now usually referred to as 'direct to home' transmission – DTH), to small household dish antennae of the kind that have now become a very familiar sight in the United Kingdom. These satellites did not count as conventional telecommunications satellites and consequently their technical regulation fell under a rather special regime. Concerned to pre-empt the risk of anarchy and congestion of the air-waves that appeared to be promised by direct broadcasting from space, as early as 1977 the World Administrative Radio Conference (WARC) – organised by the International Telecommunications Union (ITU) based in Geneva – had assigned to each European country its own orbital position and frequencies for five channels per country. At the time, DBS had been expected to become a complementary means of providing broadcasting capacity to national territories. The latter point is an important one. WARC 77's intention was that DBS would provide services that would mainly be confined to specific national reception areas. This, it had been then expected, would enable the services to be regulated nationally in accordance with the traditional requirements and customs of national cultural sovereignty in broadcasting affairs. However, there were two problems with this, both of which illustrate graphically how technical progress has a habit of outrunning regulation.

Firstly, the elliptical shape of the 'footprints' of these DBS satellites created a *de facto* situation of considerable 'overspill'. Moreover, very soon, improved transmission and reception equipment meant that this overspill was very much greater than WARC 77 had anticipated. Like modern cable systems, construction of DBS satellites was perceived for a while during the early to mid-1980s to have high industrial and commercial promise. Ambitious DBS satellite construction plans were unveiled in a number of countries including France, West Germany and Luxembourg. For the former two, industrial policy was undoubtedly the main motive (there was expected to be a world market for such satellites). For Luxembourg the attraction was rather the opportunity to exploit the increased overspill potential of DBS satellites in order to offer private commercial media investors access to internationalised broadcasting markets in Europe.

Secondly, however, it soon became clear that the main challenge would come instead from a third category of satellite, namely medium-powered satellites. They were in essence simply more powerful telecommunications satellites. These medium-powered satellites could still be used to feed cable systems and for terrestrial relay, but they could also provide television direct-to-home (DTH). Thanks to related improvements in reception equipment, viewers would be able to receive these services with dish aerials no larger than those required to receive the signals from the 'custom-built' DBS satellites. WARC 77 had made no provision for these medium-powered satellites; consequently, they faced no special international restriction. (They still had to be coordinated with Eutelsat, so there was still scope for inter-governmental bickering – see below). Not only were they cheaper to develop and deploy than high-powered DBS satellites, they were actually capable of providing more channels. Therefore, they made it certain that a rapid proliferation of DTH broadcasting would occur. Such was their perceived promise that both the French and West German telecommunications authorities soon decided to sponsor their development alongside their high-powered DBS satellite construction programmes.

More significantly, the Luxembourg government decided to shelve earlier plans for development of a high-powered satellite. (Part of the reason was that massive French pressure had been exerted against this project through the French stake in the Compagnie Luxembourgeoise de Télédiffusion (CLT) which was originally to have developed the service). In the interests of stealing a march on competitors, a medium-powered satellite was bought 'off the shelf' from the Americans. Indicative of the high stakes attached to getting to the market first, there then followed a complex struggle as rival German and French interests sought through Eutelsat to obstruct the Luxembourg medium-powered satellite project. This battle won, the Luxembourg satellite, called 'Astra' immediately proceeded to revolutionise the European broadcasting landscape. The first Astra satellite had sixteen channels, a second quickly brought the number to thirty-two, and later a third increased it to fifty (two more were planned). Their shared footprint ranged widely over Western Europe, including the British isles. They soon attracted a full range of channels, some of them general entertainment services, others more specialist (see next chapter). Astra's operating company, the *Société Européenne de Satellites* (SES), was backed by an impressive line-up of German, Belgian and Luxembourg financial interests, and the Luxembourg authorities. The latter's policy always had been to attract media investment through a solicitous policy of liberal regulation. The Astra satellites, with their pan-European reach and multinational financial backing, complemented the impressive expansion of Luxembourg's indigenous broadcasting multinational, the CLT, to confirm the small country's new strategic centrality to European broadcasting' development in the 1980s and 1990s (Dyson, 1990, pp. 125–147).

The opportunities for circumvention of national regulation

Satellite broadcasting, combined with the expansion of cable outlets for the new services, ushered in a new age of transfrontier broadcasting in Europe. Of course, there had always existed some terrestrial overspill in Western Europe. Belgium, for instance, had always been exposed to television from France; Austrians had always received television from neighbouring Germany. However uncomfortable this was for these smaller countries' indigenous broadcasting and advertising interests, such incursions had been generally contained within the old paradigm of public-service broadcasting. For one thing, there had been very few private commercial channels around (only those from Luxembourg and Britain and the latter were public-service by regulation). Most overspill, and most pre-existing cable services, had been public-service fare from nearby countries. The rapid expansion of satellite channels had a tremendous impact. It removed, effectively, all practical constraints on the prompt development of private commercial channels. The Astra satellites attracted the lion's share of the distribution business; from their relatively unregulated centre of operation they could now access the whole of Western Europe. Commercial interest could not fail to be stimulated by this kind of access to wider international markets.

Europe's commercial broadcasting markets were, in fact, still largely dependent on the cable sector. Even by the early 1990s, the impact of direct-to-home satellite broadcasting was still very limited in most countries of Western Europe. The total number of homes equipped with a satellite receiving dish was well over eight million by 1992, and growing fast, but this was still a small fraction of Western Europe's population. Moreover, these DTH households were largely accounted for by Britain (14 per cent of television homes), Germany (11.5 per cent) and Austria (17 per cent). Elsewhere still only a low percentage of television homes were equipped (according to the *Cable and Satellite Yearbook 1992*). In Britain, the popularity of DTH could be explained by the slow growth of multi-channel cable television; and in turn it helped to retard the latter's growth. Elsewhere the availability of cable, and increasingly of new terrestrial services as well, was a distinct impediment to the diffusion of this means of receiving television. Nevertheless, this should most definitely not be taken to diminish the trans-national impact of satellite broadcasting. Quite simply, satellite broadcasting presented the

opportunity for circumvention of overstrict regulation. New commercial entrepreneurs could up-link from the least regulated countries in Europe (e.g. Luxembourg) and either beam into suitably
equipped DTH homes or else access a very much larger and fast
growing European cable market (Dyson and Humphreys, 1989).

Operating from the most favourable regulatory base, they could
access more strictly regulated markets. Thus, the West German
media conglomerate Bertelsmann joined up with Luxembourg's CLT
to launch the German-language RTL Plus satellite channel operating
out of the relatively unregulated Duchy. Later the international press
baron Rupert Murdoch launched his English-language Sky television
services on Luxembourg's Astra satellite, thereby escaping more
restrictive British broadcasting regulation that would have debarred
him from taking more than a 20 per cent stake in a domestic broadcasting operation. These cases of circumvention of national broadcasting regulations established a precedent which helped to
undermine the case for continuing to regulate national markets
according to strict criteria. To do so, it was now clear, carried the
danger of a flight of media investment to operational centres with
more favourably lax regulatory environments. (Significantly, once a
suitably deregulated environment was produced in Germany, RTL
Plus transferred 'home' to Bertelsmann's headquarters in Gutersloh,
Lower Saxony). Thus, cable and satellite broadcasting together rendered old notions of broadcasting sovereignty distinctly threadbare
for large and small states alike. This set in train a dynamic towards
what might be referred to as 'competitive deregulation' (Dyson and
Humphreys 1986 and 1989). Once certain countries started to go
down the road of deregulation and marketisation of their national
broadcasting systems – and as we shall see a number deliberately
pursued this option – their neighbours were unavoidably faced with
often unwelcome commercial pressures of a new quality and order
of magnitude to do exactly the same.

The economic stakes

Behind the decision by governments to pursue deregulation there had
also been a number of more immediate economic imperatives and
lobbies. Three factors were particularly important. Firstly, governments were concerned to promote the information technology

revolution. Secondly, they became increasingly aware of the media's importance for inward investment and equally aware of the threat of disinvestment. The media became an important consideration for what, in economic jargon, is called 'locational policy'. Thirdly, governments were lobbied hard by the advertising industry which argued persuasively that an expansion of advertising opportunities in the field of broadcasting, would lead to an increase in the latter industry's production base and improve its trade balance.

The information technology revolution

During the late 1970s and early 1980s, governments had become keenly aware of the information technology (IT) revolution. To explore the issues raised, in particular how IT policies might be developed to promote national economic goals, they had established official commissions of inquiry. Generally composed of technocrats and industry experts, these commissions had produced a number of landmark reports which commonly urged the quick adoption of the new communication technologies. The 'wired society', they made clear, promised to register a very extensive economic impact across the economy. There were some differences of emphasis, the French stressing the role for generous state support, the British favouring an industry-led policy. In Germany measures of technology assessment in the form of exploratory pilot projects were also recommended, to explore the social consequences of the new media. Generally, though, the recommendations reflected the industrial and commercial interests of the electronics and telecommunications industries. These latter interests had formed very influential policy networks with technocrats in the world of officialdom. Political decision-makers were thus led by technocratic hype, and a good measure of industrialist pressure, to embark upon plans to develop their quite ambitious cable and satellite programmes as part of a much wider package of IT policies. The most salient point here is, diffusion of these new technologies was to be 'entertainment led'. Logically, this required deregulation of the rules for the provision of new services (i.e. the 'broadcasting' aspect).

Locational policy

Technological and economic developments in the media sector

meanwhile served to increase awareness among public policy makers that the media themselves had acquired a wholly new economic significance. Industrial policy (e.g. the development of DBS satellites and cable systems) was only one aspect of the much broader economic stakes of new media development. The media embraced very important commercial interests; global developments were already beginning to see the rise of international conglomerates which straddled broadcasting, news and information services, publishing, film and video, and other communications forms. In modern 'service societies' the media *per se* had become a very important field of commercial economic activity. To promote a strong and dynamic commercial media sector was, therefore, a matter of growing economic concern to official policy makers. In the increasingly internationalised competition to attract media investment, national politicians disposed of a major instrument which might be deployed in the cause of locational policy: namely, regulatory policy. Unlike financial inducements to investors, this instrument was without economic cost. (Any costs were likely to be more of a cultural nature). Literally no financial burden fell upon state exchequers in matters such as the allocation of franchises to new commercial broadcasters and the loosening of rules governing their operations. Of course, all things being equal, the new investors were most likely to be attracted to locations where the regulatory constraints were suitably lax (Hoffmann-Riem, 1989).

The advertising lobby

A particularly important economic lobby attracted by the prospect of more commercialism was the advertising industry. Abolition of the public broadcasting monopoly situation would present much scope for growth of broadcast advertising in Western Europe. National restrictions had meant that there was much unfulfilled demand for television advertising. During the 1980s the advertising lobby became very proactive at both the national and European levels. In 1980 the advertising and commercial media interests together created the European Advertising Tripartite (EAT) as a joint pressure group to promote their case for a free market in advertising in Europe. The EAT was largely the joint initiative of the International Union of Advertisers Associations (IUAA) and the European Association of Advertising Agencies (EAAA). It also embraced the

Communauté des Associations des Editeurs de Journaux (CAEJ), a Eurolobby of national and provincial newspaper publishers' associations in the EC; and it included the European Group of Television Advertisers (EGTA). It operated alongside already very powerful national advertising lobbies – like the British Advertising Association (AA) and the Institute of Advertising Practitioners (IAP) or the German *Zentralausschuss der Werbewirtschaft* (ZAW). As we shall see, the advertisers were keenly supportive of an EC initiative to create a single market in broadcasting but equally fierce in their opposition to any EC imposition of restrictions (see Chapter 8). Advertisers welcomed the prospect of an abolition of the public-service monopoly paradigm. Hitherto the public service monopoly had precluded competition among broadcasters to attract advertisers. The abolition of this broadcaster monopoly would introduce this competition. The effect would be to reverse the balance of relations between advertisers and broadcasters. Competition between broadcasters for advertising revenue would bid down the prices they were able to charge the advertisers. In a marketised broadcasting system, the advertisers and advertising agencies could expect to gain the whip hand at last. (For an informative overview of the European-level mobilisation of the advertising lobby in the 1980s see Mattelart and Palmer, 1991.)

The advertising lobby was, therefore, formidably organised. It also disposed of a powerful resource: industry information. It was able to lobby so effectively because it could supply the data that policy makers needed (Mattelart and Palmer, 1991, p. 554–555). In order to support their case, the advertisers pointed to the benefits that broadcasters could expect to gain from the expansion of broadcast advertising that would follow upon marketisation. In particular, they pointed to the way marketisation would measurably increase overall the resources flowing to the broadcasting industry. (An increase could be anticipated, they argued, despite the lower rates that the broadcasters would henceforth be compelled to charge in a more competitive market.) This postulated infusion of resources would be able to fund expanded production both nationally and at the European level, helping thereby to boost the balance of trade in broadcast programmes. Naturally, the force of this argument was not lost on media policy makers who were bound to be interested in ways to fund expansion of production that did not require the unpopular raising of additional public funds.

The media policy actors: the coalitions for and against change

A whole host of economic actors were enticed by the prospect of a media revolution. Their conjunction gave them an uncommonly powerful weight. Along with the electronics and advertising industries, there were the publishers of the press, the cable television lobby, independent producers, broadcasting facilities companies and, of course, financial interests with an eye for new investment opportunities. They shared a common aim: the opening up of the public broadcasting monopoly and the establishment of a regulatory framework that would be favourable to commercial enterprise. Governments, concerned as ever to promote national economic success, were naturally receptive to their pleas for deregulation. At the same time, the EC Commission too became concerned about the future competitiveness of Europe's audiovisual and electronics industries *vis à vis* US and Japanese competition. As Chapter 8 describes, from the mid-1980s onwards the Commission lent its considerable weight to the argument for a liberalisation of Europe's internal market for broadcast services. Its prime motive was to render European broadcasting and ancillary interests, viewed as economic actors, more efficient and competitive in global markets. At the domestic level, the above-mentioned business lobbies combined with Europe's parties of the Right especially where these embraced neo-liberal ideas (this included continental Europe's business-orientated Liberals) to form a powerful coalition for change.

These parties of the Right were sometimes inspired by more than free market doctrine and economic logic, or their closeness to business and susceptibility to powerful lobbies. The marketising broadcasting policies of both Thatcher's Conservatives and Kohl's Christian Democratic-Liberal coalition, coming to power after a fairly lengthy period in opposition, were motivated as well by a concern to 'outflank' public-service broadcasters which they perceived as having been consistently biased against them (Humphreys, 1991, p. 203). Similarly, the Belgian Right-wing parties ran a 'major campaign' against public-service broadcasting accusing it of presenting a 'biased picture of the world.' This campaign of the Belgian Right undermined support for the public-service monopoly that had long been unquestioned in that small country (Burgelman, 1986, p. 187). In the French case, this kind of political motivation helped to explain why the French Socialists – rather out of step with their counterparts elsewhere – were most enthusiastic about abolishing the state's broadcasting monopoly. For years it had been biased against them and they wanted to ensure – through 'liberating' the sector – that this could not be repeated in the future (Dyson and Humphreys, 1988 and 1989). The fact that governments thus motivated came to power in Britain, Germany and France almost simultaneously at the beginning of the 1980s, was an important factor for the sudden reversal – across a large area of Western Europe – of policies that for decades had sustained the public-service monopoly; policies, it might be added, that had even obstructed new media development during the 1970s.

National Posts and Telecommunications authorities (PTTs) – and their interest in protecting their monopoly or dominant market position in telecommunications provision – played a key role too. In the past, PTTs, responsible or co-responsible with broadcasters for transmission, had been highly influential in technical matters but traditionally they had not trespassed into other spheres of media policy. However, during the 1980s the fact that the PTTs were keenly interested in the introduction of the new technologies – precisely in order to strengthen their dominant position in the telecommunications sector – meant that they too became objectively part of the coalition for change. In France the Direction Générale des Télécommunications (now called France Télécom) was at the head of the policy coalition pushing for the speedy introduction of the new media and the requisite relaxation of public-service regulations.

In Germany the Bundespost's (now Deutsche Telekom's) control of technical resources – cable, satellite, and terrestrial frequencies – was used by central government actually in order to by-pass *Länder* control of broadcasting, to launch a voluntaristic national 'broadcasting revolution'.

Facing this powerful coalition for change was a counterforce resisting radical change; or at the very least seeking to temper it with a strong commitment to public-service requirements (see Table 5.2). This latter coalition encompassed the public-service broadcasters themselves, the broadcasting and journalists associations and unions, and generally Europe's Social Democratic parties. In Germany, the SPD was divided between proponents of fundamental and 'constructive' opposition; the latter prevailing once it was recognised that powerful regional (*Land*) economic interests stood to lose out if the SPD persisted in adhering to overstrict regulation in the *Länder* it governed. (In other words, considerations of regional 'locational policy' swayed SPD policy). The French Socialists hoped to introduce a 'controlled deregulation'. Europe's Christian Democrats were often divided between their neo-liberal and their 'moral conservative' wings. In Germany, the former prevailed. In the Netherlands and Austria, on the other hand, Christian Democrats were sceptical about deregulation (Dyson and Humphreys, 1989, p. 147–148).

Table 5.2   The deregulation of broadcasting: the coalitions of actors

The pro-market actors	*Their interests*
The electronics industry	To exploit markets for new TV sets; pay-TV decoders; satellite reception equipment, etc.
The cable and satellite television lobbies	Freedom to provide commercial services
PTTs	To develop and diffuse new media technologies; to maintain monopoly or dominant market position in telecoms provision
Newspaper publishers	To diversify media operations; to pre-empt further competition for advertising revenue[a]
Advertisers	To gain outlets and strengthen market position
Governments	To promote the economy; to attract media investors
Parties of the Right	Pursuit of neo-liberal agenda; promotion of business interests
European Commission	To liberalise European markets
Public-service supporters	*Their interests*
Public-service broadcasters	Self-defence; continuance of public resourcing, etc.
Unions	Protection of employment and conditions of employment
Parties of the left	Promotion of public-service ethos and communitarian values; promotion of labour interests

Note:

[a] Not universally the case. In some countries the press remained a force resisting commercial broadcasting.

Technological determinism? What scope for 'politics'?

The coalitions of actors and their logics pro or contra change were fairly predictable across Europe, but what about the policy process? Deregulation did not follow a uniform path across Europe, far from it! Just as the traditional characteristics of broadcasting systems varied considerably across Europe, so too did the policy processes by which marketisation was introduced in the 1980s. Technology and economic factors were factors for policy convergence – towards deregulation and marketisation. Differences could be explained by political factors: different political and regulatory traditions, different ideological predispositions of governments, different patterns of institutional constraint on governments, and so forth. The enduring weight of different media traditions was reflected in the German concern to ensure continued respect for 'safe' traditions of public service. In France, the ideology of *indépendance nationale* made cultural 'sovereignty' a key theme. Differences could be explained, further, by the different distribution of power resources in national media policy communities. In Britain, for instance, the IBA – later the ITC – was able to draw on reserves of independence and high social status in order to tone down the implementation of certain Thatcherite policies. Finally, implementation problems meant that policy outcomes did not always turn out as planned. In France, for instance, media policy was afflicted by inter-ministerial disputes and administrative rivalries resulting in a proliferation of initiatives, each backed by different administrative and political sponsors – the cable plan, duplicate satellite projects, new off-air channels, privatisation. Resources were squandered, competition between rival projects became destructively fierce, and certain technological initiatives were disappointing failures (Minc, 1993, pp. 40–54; Dyson and Humphreys, 1986, 1988 and 1989).

Above all, it is important to realise that the technological factor was not even a necessary condition for deregulation. In Britain and France – because of policy implementation problems – the new media were not diffused nearly as fast as had been expected in the early 1980s, yet governments still introduced some radical marketising policies. In both cases the technological factor helped set the new agenda of broadcasting policy, but in the Italian case – and in other Southern European countries – the new media played virtually no role at all. Yet marketisation occurred all the same through the use of local frequencies for commercial television services (linked up to form national networks). In Germany, by contrast again, the new media were adopted and diffused very rapidly and extensively, yet here deregulation was moderated significantly by public policy. Clearly, technology does not of itself determine the direction of its social application and of the public regulation of its consequences. Still less does technology compel governments to treat broadcasting franchises as something to be auctioned to the highest bidder (as occurred in Britain) or to privatise public service corporations (as occurred in France). Technology does not dictate that governments allow the concentration of private broadcasting interests overwhelmingly in the hands of one individual's concern (as occurred in Italy). These specific policies will now be examined.

The private sector ascendent: Luxembourg, Italy and France

Luxembourg

With respect to the patterns of broadcasting marketisation Europe can be broken down into distinct groups of countries. Luxembourg was already 'deregulated'. As early as 1931 its government had decided to encourage the growth of a commercial broadcasting industry by adopting a liberal regulatory approach that contrasted with the public service monopolies established elsewhere in Western Europe. By the 1990s, *Compagnie Luxembourgeoise de Télévision* (CLT), a long-time beneficiary of this liberal environment, had become one of Europe's leading media companies with stakes in production companies, radio and television channels (under the emblem of CLT's *RTL* subsidiary) in a number of European countries. Another beneficiary was *Société Européenne de Satellites* (SES), the private commercial company established in 1985 that already operated three Astra broadcasting satellites (and aimed to launch two more); these satellites made available to over fifty million European households no fewer than fifty television channels. Luxembourg was widely seen as a model of commercial freedom. Notably, advertising rules were lax.

Italy

Since the mid-1970s Italy also had come to present the picture of a dramatically marketised system. The Italian case was widely referred to as a 'wild deregulation'. Very much a market driven affair from the outset, it was allowed to happen largely due to the characteristic immobilism of the country's politics. The actual trigger was a surprise 1976 ruling of Italy's Constitutional Court, declaring that while a public-service monopoly was necessary at the national level to ensure pluralism and impartiality, a monopoly was not called for at the local level. In the period leading up to this court ruling, RAI's monopoly had been increasingly challenged by a number of small local pirate stations. These had quickly become popular. In the words of Barile and Rao (1992, p. 263), the court appeared to have been 'influenced by developments in the broadcasting market'. The immediate consequence of the court's 1976 ruling was a very rapid proliferation of new private commercial radio and television stations. Several leading publishing groups – Rizzoli, Mondadori and Rusconi – diversified into television and, in disregard of the court's restriction, organised many of these local stations into national broadcasting networks. Once again the court intervened; again it appeared to follow the market, now ruling in 1981 that pluralism could be ensured at the local level even if private commercial networks were allowed to operate nationally. The court qualified this, however, by making the first of many calls for national parliamentary legislation to prevent media concentration. In fact, from 1975 onwards the Italian parliament had debated broadcasting bills but party dissension meant that no rules were produced (Mazzoleni, 1991, p. 166). By 1984 Silvio Berlusconi's Fininvest company had taken over the networks owned by the major publishing groups and thereby acquired a virtual monopoly of Italy's private broadcasting sector. His Fininvest conglomerate now owned the three principal commercial networks, Rette 4, Canale 5 and Italia 1. By this time, these networks had between them achieved audience shares the size of the public sector RAI's, around 40–45 per cent. They were drawing well over three quarters of the advertising revenue going to the private sector. The rest, and about 10 per cent of the audience, was shared among hundreds of other local stations, and a few smaller networks. While the policy makers had been immobilised by their inability to reach compromises, the field of action had been left more or less entirely free for the economic actors – in particular, Berlusconi – to establish their own rules of the game. As will be seen (Chapter 6) Berlusconi's private commercial television empire amounted to a case of concentration of media ownership unparalleled elsewhere in Europe, even in the press sector. Programme schedules were geared to commercial goals. Reliance on cheap entertainment programming imports and home grown imitations thereof increased strikingly. The amount of advertising breaks on television, too, had increased very alarmingly. According to one source, advertising sometimes accounted for 20 per cent of the length of a feature film (Mattelart and Palmer, 1991, p. 549). When in 1990 the politicians were finally able to produce a Broadcasting Act commanding majority support, the parameters of the new broadcasting system had already been established by the market. The Act essentially legitimised market *faits accomplis* and was dubbed the 'Lex Berlusconi' (Wagner, 1994, p. 71). In Italy, therefore, the private sector had been unconstrained by default of public policy. In turn, the policy deficit resulted from the country's characteristically immobilist politics.

France

During the 1980s France, too, moved rapidly from a state monopoly to a predominantly marketised system. The Socialists, coming to power in 1981, actually made the first strides in this direction by legalising France's mushrooming pirate commercial radio sector, launching an ambitious cable plan and licensing two new national commercial channels (one of which did not long survive) as well as a highly successful pay-TV service. The Socialists had various motivations. An important aim was to free broadcasting once and for all from the state's iron grip. They themselves had long suffered from the way state television had been manipulated by Gaullists and Giscardians. Rather than imitate the Right's abuse of the medium they announced their intention to 'liberate' it. Another of the Socialists' aims was the desire to promote the development of the new technologies. Yet another was the ambition to stimulate the French audiovisual industry. Within the Socialist camp there was great concern to to control the process of liberalisation by all manner of regulatory means, including the imposition of 'made-in-France' programme quotas and provisions against the appearance of American-style networks of the kind that had appeared in Italy. However, broadcasting policy was all too soon hijacked by a presidential inner circle and driven by political expediency.

Operating on frequencies originally intended for a French 'Channel 4', a new pay-television channel called Canal Plus was launched in 1984 by the state-backed media and advertising company Havas. Against many Socialists' idealistic wishes, Canal Plus emerged from the drawing board as a highly commercial project masterminded and managed by a close presidential aide, André Rousselet. It was funded by subscription, granted a monopoly of advertising by sponsorship, and freed from all but minimal programme requirements – that is, apart from measures to protect the French cinema and to promote the French film industry. Next, in 1985, President Mitterrand stunned most Socialists by awarding a franchise for a national commercial entertainment channel, called La Cinq, again relatively free from public-service obligations, to a consortium of businessmen widely presumed to be friendly to the Socialists. This consortium included Italy's private television magnate, Silvio Berlusconi. Both of these high-handed acts by the powerful central executive seemed to fly in the face of the Socialists' avowed aim to control deregulation and to avoid the 'Italian scenario'. These decisions seemed motivated, far more, by a combination of presidential populism and the concern to award new channels to presidential allies in the run up to an election that the polls suggested would leave Mitterrand facing a parliament dominated by the Right. Indeed, briefly returned to power between 1986 and 1988, the Right dramatically escalated the process of marketisation by privatising France's principal public-service channel, TF1 – a most radical step that has not since been imitated anywhere else in Western Europe. Also privatised were SFP (the state programme production company), Agence Havas (owner of Canal Plus) and SOFIRAD (the state holding company that controlled the so-called 'peripheral' radio stations – see p. 124 above). Further, the Right turned the cable plan over to the private sector. The Socialists, back in office between 1988 and 1993, did not reverse any of these privatisations. By the end of the decade, therefore, France had one the most marketised broadcasting systems in Europe.

Policy-making had been characteristically *dirigiste* and voluntaristic. This feature reflected the central executive's comparatively unconstrained ability to act. That is not to suggest that policy encountered no implementation problems or produced no unintended outcomes. The cable plan encountered grave implementation problems. France's television satellite projects, too, were beaten to the market by Luxembourg's Astra satellite series. These were costly disappointments. The state had poured enormous sums into both its cable and satellite projects (Minc, 1993, pp. 40–54; Kuhn, 1995, Chapter 8). The more efficient use of the terrestrial frequency spectrum to launch several new commercial channels hardly amounted to the great technological leap forward that the Socialists had promised. The new channels' reliance on foreign programme imports, mainly American, seemed to run counter to the Socialists' promise to protect French culture against 'Coca Cola' television (Kuhn, 1995, p. 184). Further, the Right's privatisation of TFI in 1986 produced the most unintended of consequences; it strangled at birth La Cinq, France's other main commercial channel, and therefore produced a result that was contrary to the Right's aim of opening up the market even more than the Socialists had already achieved (see Chapter 7). For all this, the pattern of policy-making was a familiar one. The executive was able to exert its will to an extent unmatched elsewhere in Western Europe. That 'heroic' policy outcomes were not always as intended, was not at all unusual.

Marketisation of duopoly: Britain

Britain, of course, already had private broadcasters but the unique feature of the ITV/IBA system was its combination of commercial profit-seeking with very strict regulation by an external authority – the IBA – in the public interest. Indeed, the ITV companies had been more rule-bound than the self-regulating BBC. Moreover, British broadcasting policy had always been highly evolutionary and pragmatic. Changes – such as the introduction of ITV and later of Channel 4 – had typically emerged from 12-year policy cycles, punctuated by lengthy and exhaustive committees of inquiry (Tunstall, 1984, p. 315; also see Chapter 4). An abrupt change of policy style occurred with the arrival in office of Margaret Thatcher. Now a series of deregulatory steps followed in comparatively swift succession. The policy cycles were rather shorter than had been customary, consultation seemed to be less serious, policy appeared to be guided by a combination of Thatcherite doctrine and commercial interests. Prime Minister Thatcher herself made very clear in a number of famous pronouncements that she had very little time for the traditional British broadcasting 'Establishment'. She regarded the duopoly as the 'last bastion of restrictive practices'. Thatcherites generally were averse to the absence of competition in British broadcasting, disliking equally the BBC's monopoly of licence fee funding and the ITV companies' regional advertising monopolies. Thatcherites were also consumed by the belief that the broadcasters, in particular the BBC, were hostile to their political philosophy. At the same time, the duopoly came under attack from another quarter. During the 1980s Rupert Murdoch's papers conducted a press campaign against it, arguing for a more 'open less monolithic system' (*Times* leader of 15 January 1985).

First of all, the new media were deregulated by the Cable and Broadcasting Act of 1984 which created a new type of regulatory body, the Cable Authority. The latter's task was to supervise programmes only reactively and with a 'light touch'. Cable franchises were awarded in a rather informal manner. The Authority's explicit role of promoting the cable industry seemed to eclipse its regulatory function. Cable's subsequent failure to take off in Britain until the 1990s could not be explained by any over-strict regulation, far from it. Rather it resulted from the absence of the kind of state support to the cable sector that was available on the continent (this too reflected Thatcherite doctrine) and also from the competition provided by direct-to-home (DTH) satellite broadcasting in the shape of Rupert Murdoch's Sky TV (later BSkyB). Only when in 1990 the rules were further relaxed to allow British cable companies to provide telephone services did the purely market-driven industry start to attract major investment (mainly North American) and begin to register dynamic growth. All manner of implementation problems also dogged plans for a market-driven British broadcasting satellite. Again, no state support had been forthcoming. Therefore, the British DTH market was quickly dominated by Rupert Murdoch's 'off-shore' Sky TV operation (for details of failures of British new media policies see Negrine in Dyson and Humphreys, 1988).

Nothing symbolised the doctrinaire nature of Thatcherite broadcasting policy better than the ITV franchise 'auction'. This was the most radical component of the Broadcasting Act of 1990 which was largely designed to introduce more competition into the ITV/IBA sector. In the past, ITV franchises had been allocated by the IBA through a discretionary process that, though rather secretive, had prioritised quality programming. Proven quality performance had been an important factor for ITV companies' retention of franchises in successive rounds. The 1990 Act now ruled that these franchises should be 'auctioned' to whomsoever bid the most money in a 'blind' auction, a feature of the legislation that bore the unmistakeable imprint of the Treasury's overweening influence in British policy making as well as pure Thatcherite free market doctrine. However, the franchise auction aside, the 1990 Broadcasting Act turned out to be a more moderate piece of legislation than Thatcherites had originally intended. Rather than lift public-service obligations from the ITV companies, the Act included a quality threshold which the regulator – renamed the Independent Television Commission – had to take into account when choosing among the bidders in the franchise auction. Moreover, although commercial broadcasters were given more freedom to schedule programmes as they liked, they saw themselves required to continue to supply news and information, educational and local programming, and so forth. More significantly, the Act specified that Channel 4 should retain its special minorities and cultural mission (so too would the Welsh Fourth Channel S4C). Rather than be privatised as Thatcherites had intended, Channel 4 was to become a corporation governed by a board part composed of ITC appointees and part drawn from its management. It would have to earn its own keep through running its own advertising but the Act did provide for a financial 'safety net' in case its revenue, in operating commercially, should suffer a shortfall which would otherwise prevent it from fulfilling its special minority and cultural remit. The Act also gave a statutory basis to a Broadcasting Standards Council (originally set up in 1987) to monitor such matters as the portrayal of violence on television and to ensure the maintenance of standards of taste and decency. Last but not least, the Act retained the former IBA's rules against media concentration and cross-media ownership. The marketising impact of the 'auctioning' of broadcasting franchises and the lighter touch regulation of the ITV sector should not be underestimated. Nevertheless, the fact remained that the parliamentary process had taken the radical Thatcherite edge off the Bill. The principal moderating factors were the persistence of a strong vein of support for the public-service principle among British Conservatives in parliament; and the fact that the traditional broadcasting Establishment retained a very influential enclave of support within government, namely the Department of National Heritage, which actually drafted the legislation. (Previously the Home Office had also been sympathetic to the public-service broadcasters.) Also, Britain's broadcasters enjoyed comparatively high public esteem. This undoubtedly further limited the government's freedom to act.

For all this, though, the franchise auction would have been inconceivable before the days of Thatcherite majoritarianism.

As for the BBC, under Thatcher's premiership, the corporation came under much more direct pressure. Dependent upon the government for its licence fee, it was compelled to engage upon a stringent 'efficiency' drive. The introduction of an 'internal market' within the corporation, through Director General John Birt's controversial 'producer choice' system, symbolised the coming to the BBC of a new managerial ethos. 'Producer choice' encouraged producers to shop around within the BBC for the cheapest production facilities and even gave them the right to go outside the corporation if need be. Its implementation elevated internal accounting mechanisms and values to a new importance; ironically, it also entailed a measure of increased bureaucratisation. As far as programme production was concerned, it bore a close resemblance to the pattern of rationalisation (introduction of cost centres, etc.) that had been introduced into the ITV sector throughout the period surrounding the 1990 Act to make them 'lean and fit' for the more marketised and competitive era approaching.

To the Italian or French observer, the changes made to the British broadcasting system during the 1980s and early 1990s might reasonably have appeared quite incremental. Given the slow take off of the new media – apart from BSkyB – the duopoly continued to dominate the scene. Nevertheless, Thatcherism's legacy to the 1990s was very much a duopoly that now found itself operating in a more competitive climate. The duopoly itself had been marketised in subtle as well as not so subtle (the auction) ways. Moreover, the successful (re)advertisement of the Channel 5 franchise in 1994 attracted bids in 1995 from no fewer than four consortia backed by British and international investors. North American capital had meanwhile poured into British cable development and combined with BSkyB to provide programme services for cable systems. BSkyB itself was making large operating profits and being taken very seriously as a competitor by the traditional duopoly broadcasters. By 1995 one-fifth of British households were receiving BSkyB and other satellite and cable services. Finally, London had become a base for a number of 'off-shore' satellite television services aimed at European markets.

Germany: the 'dual system'. A new public/private balance?

In Germany, the new media were adopted and diffused very rapidly
and extensively. Indeed, they were crucial to the success of German
policies of marketisation. At the same time, the German policy process was characterised by complex political trade-offs. The policy
process was complicated by the division of competences between the
country's constituent *Länder*, which were constitutionally responsible for broadcasting policy, and the central federation, the *Bund*,
which was responsible for telecommunications policy. During the
1980s the conservative CDU/CSU *Länder* and the CDU-controlled
Bundespost (the national PTT) together promoted deregulation.
However, the SPD controlled *Länder* initially resisted deregulation
and obstructed any inter-*Land* progress towards new national policies for commercial broadcasting regulation (e.g. programme and
ownership rules for national cable and satellite television channels).
This is where the Bundespost's control of technical resources came
into play. Under the direction of a CDU minister, the Bundespost
simply ignored the inter-*Land* stalemate and proceeded with a highly
voluntaristic programme of providing cable systems, satellite capacity and new terrestrial frequencies so that the new commercial
broadcasters – which had been franchised and given operating bases
in CDU/CSU controlled *Länder* – might access a national audience.
Faced with this new reality, the SPD *Länder* resorted to another
tactic: they appealed to the Federal Constitutional Court to safeguard the traditional public-service principles of German broadcasting regulation. In a major ruling of 1986 the court provided the basis
for a subsequent inter-*Land* treaty providing for new national broadcasting rules. The outcome was the introduction of a dual system of
broadcasting regulation, one that provided guarantees for the existing public-service broadcasters whilst opening up a new commercial
sector. Following the court's ruling, it was accepted that the very precondition for the introduction of private commercial broadcasting
was a commitment to the 'existence and further development' of the
public sector. The private commercial pillar of the dual system
would be allowed to benefit from a significant, but still controlled,
measure of deregulation. The private sector broadcasters were
required to su₁ ply diverse and balanced programming, although now
this might be achieved *across* the range of new services ('external
pluralism') rather than, as traditionally had been the case, *within*

them ('internal pluralism'). Within these broad parameters, it fell to the individual *Länder* to make their own detailed regulatory provisions; a point that was confirmed by subsequent court rulings. Generally, the private sector broadcasters in Germany saw themselves subjected to a fairly 'dense regulatory code of conduct' even though the rules were laxer than those placed on the public-service broadcasters (Ruck, 1992, p. 228). The commercial broadcasters were policed by a whole range of new regulatory bodies, established in the *Länder*. Responsible for franchising and overseeing the new private commercial sector, these regulatory bodies (*Landesmedienanstalten*) were endowed with the ultimate sanction of revoking licences. Thus German deregulation was qualified by certain unmistakable re-regulatory features. Certainly, the outcome stood in conspicuous contrast to the French case; there was no question of privatising the leading public-service broadcasting channel and reducing the others to a marginal role. Unlike in Italy, immobilism was avoided through the re-establishment of a basic consensus and as the result the market actors were not given an entirely free run. As in the British case, the German reform continued to value proven public-service traditions and institutions. Indeed, in the German case public-service values received special constitutional-legal protection. This was definitely not the case in Britain where the duopoly was left facing some uncertainty about the future.

Patterns of deregulation in Europe's smaller states

Most of Europe's small states had maintained historically a very strong commitment to the public-service model of broadcasting. Typically, they had long regulated their broadcasters most strictly. Luxembourg's commercial system was the notable exception. Elsewhere, if advertising was allowed, it was only supposed to supplement the licence fee as a source of revenue for the public service broadcasters. Here the only exceptions were Luxembourg, without any licence fee, and Spain (not a small state), where the public broadcasters became more or less entirely reliant on advertising during the 1980s. In many respects the European small states' broadcasting policies were rather conservative and non-innovative, giving clear priority to the serious cultural aims and duties of broadcasting. They were corporatist and consensual. They accorded an important role to 'socially relevant groups' in media policy-making. Decision-making, therefore, tended to be incrementalist, characterised by closely bargained outcomes.

Thus, in the Netherlands the various political and cultural 'pillars' had maintained a fairly tight grip on broadcasting. Belgium, too, had a politicised and strongly regulated public-service monopoly, differentiated linguistically. In Austria the two main political parties together had an armlock on the system. In each case, there was much resistance to commercialisation. The important role of consumer associations, too, reflected the potential for social forces to shape policy in consensus orientated systems. The Norwegian Consumer Council (*Forbrukerradet*) helped block the introduction of a national commercial television channel in the 1980s. When finally allowed in 1990 such a channel was given a monopoly of domestic advertising and subjected to strong regulation (e.g. like ITV until recently). Similarly, the Danish Consumer Council (*Dansk Forbrugerrad*) obstructed the introduction of advertising both for the second national television channel and for local radio and television (Sánchez-Tabernero, 1993, p. 57). Moreover, the smaller states had particularly strong economic grounds for commitment to the public service paradigm (Trappel, 1991; Meier and Trappel, 1992). With small home markets, and consequently small indigenous media industries, they could be expected to reap far fewer advantages than their larger neighbours from market liberalisation. With relatively small national production bases, they were already dependent on foreign programme imports. Conscious of their vulnerability to increased economic and cultural penetration, they naturally inclined towards protectionist and regulationist media policies. However, during the 1980s, the small states found themselves caught up in the slipstream of the deregulatory initiatives of their neighbours. They were exposed to the same imperatives of technology and international markets. At the same time, domestic lobbies and public pressure called for reform of their traditional structures.

In 1993, Austria had still not abolished its public-service monopoly despite a 1989 plebiscite in favour of such a course. The Swiss too had only allowed a couple of small pay-TV channels as well as some private investment in public channels. In Denmark's case the public service monopoly was abridged in 1988 with the introduction of a commercial second channel, but it remained public-service by regulation and identity and could hardly be counted as commercial. The

Netherlands had maintained a domestic public-service monopoly, although this had come to include some quite commercial services and the country had become very penetrated by foreign commercial stations (see pp. 142–143). The small states could not wish away satellite overspill nor effectively police cable systems. In fact, both Belgium and the Netherlands did try to bar certain foreign commercial programmes from their cable systems (virtually all television being transmitted this way in these countries), but the European Court ruled against such a prohibition. As a policy strategy, adherence to the public service-monopoly of domestic services meant limiting or denying to their indigenous commercial interests opportunities that satellite broadcasting was any how making widely available to foreign broadcasters. It was, as such, a leaky defensive ploy designed only to minimise the extent of marketisation. In the case of Austria and Switzerland, countries sharing languages with larger neighbours, the degree of protectionism afforded was very limited. Indeed, converted to a new strategy, the Swiss parliament at last gave its approval in 1993 to the launch of an entirely private channel, aimed at the Germanophone population (i.e. three quarters of the country). Nevertheless, this new channel was to supply information as well as entertainment; and it was predominantly owned by Swiss business interests.

Victims of wide scale 'imported deregulation', in fact, most small countries, bowed during the 1980s to the inevitable and introduced their own deregulation and liberalisation designed to encourage a response from indigenous commercial interests. The aim, as far as possible, was to make sure that domestic interests were the main winners from commercialisation. Thus, in strictly regulated Belgium, where France's privatised TF1, broadcasting terrestrially, had made inroads into the domestic advertising market, a new commercial television channel called RTL TVi was licensed to broadcast in the Walloon French speaking community in 1987. The new channel was a joint venture between nearly all the Wallonian newspaper publishers – organised in a group called Audiopresse – and Luxembourg's CLT in which Belgian interests (notably the powerful Banque Bruxelles Lambert) also had a stake. In Flanders a commercial television channel called VTM was allowed to start operating in 1989. VTM was owned largely by the Flemish press; indeed, majority participation of the Flemish press was an actual condition of liberalisation.

Even the Scandinavian countries, more protected by their peripheral situation and the fact that they were not so linguistically vulnerable (though there was a sizeable audience for a number of English language satellite services), followed the new paradigm. During the 1980s, Sweden had actually developed its own broadcasting satellite, mainly for reasons of industrial/commercial policy. In 1990 it duly allowed the satellite to carry domestic private commercial broadcasting services, notably a new advertising based channel called 'TV4 Nordisk'. Norway, fearful that the new Swedish services would poach in their advertising markets and also entice away indigenous commercial investors, soon followed suit by introducing in 1992 its own new private commercial channel called 'TVN'. Even though this channel remained subject to fairly strict regulation, the Norwegian case exemplifies all the same the irresistible pressure towards a degree of 'competitive deregulation'. In fact, both these countries' public service monopolies had already been abridged for several years by two commercial satellite channels aimed at Scandinavian audiences, namely TV3 (nicknamed 'Scansat'), headquartered in London, and Filmnet based in the Netherlands, both operating in true 'off shore' fashion from Luxembourg's Astra satellite. Thus, even in the traditionally strictly regulated Scandinavian countries, 'imported deregulation', carried by satellite, led to the adoption of new commercial strategies to give domestic interests a share of the action.

By 1993, Austria (see above) and Ireland were the only countries with no domestic commercial television channels. In Ireland, though, private commercial radio and television had been legalised in 1990 and a new national commercial channel licensed (it had merely failed to start up by 1993). Moreover, Ireland, the main east coast population area of which had always been exposed to commercial services from Britain, was by now thoroughly inundated by English language satellite television, receivable directly and relayed on its fairly developed cable infrastructure. In fact, in all the small countries, cable and satellite television was an effectively deregulated domain and carried a whole range of new advertising-based or subscription-funded services, mostly imported, and in many languages. Responding to public pressure, even Austria legislated in 1991 for the free reception of satellite television. As for private commercial radio, its expansion was ubiquitous in large and small states alike. Again, even Austria introduced it, as the first cautious step towards dismantling the ORF's monopoly.

Deregulation or re-regulation?

A case might be made for arguing that what has occurred is not so much deregulation as 're-regulation'. This line of argument switches the focus from the market liberalising aspect of deregulation, to the proliferation of new laws and regulatory bodies in the sector. Some have emphasised that this 're-regulation' has even entailed an element of over-regulation. The United Kingdom, it has been suggested, provides a very good illustration. In the United Kingdom, until the Thatcher government's reforms, the regulation of broadcasting was simply shared by two bodies – the BBC Board of Governors and the Independent Broadcasting Authority (IBA) – with their own comprehensive codes of practice for programming and advertising, and extensive powers to intervene if necessary in programming matters. In 1981 the government then established the Broadcasting Complaints Commission. Next, in 1984 the Cable Authority was set up to oversee the new media. Later, the 1990 reform of the commercial broadcasting sector saw the IBA's functions split between the ITC (now subsuming the Cable Authority) and a new Radio Authority. In the meantime, the Broadcasting Standards Commission had also been established, to operate a new programme code on matters concerning sex, violence, taste and decency. As Prosser (1992, p. 181) has remarked: 'rather than replacing the existing regulatory functions of the BBC and IBA (ITC), the creation of the Council added a further level of regulatory control'. In addition, the Office of Fair Trading and Oftel were given responsibility for regulating the new element of competition which Conservative reforms had introduced into the communications industry at large; Oftel was co-responsible for cable systems first with the Cable Authority and later with the ITC. In other words, by the 1990s a confusing system of no fewer than five regulatory bodies with their own codes of practice was in operation where two regulators had previously been deemed sufficient in the past. The result, it has been argued, was a regulatory maze with many competing and overlapping jurisdictions and more, not fewer, rules.

France too, it has been observed (Lange and Renaud, 1989, p. 25), shows how the 'process of deregulation can sometimes, paradoxically, destroy the initial aim of achieving less regulation', at least on the face of it. Certainly, the 1980s had seen a feverish succession of new regulatory bodies and law making. First the Socialists enacted a comprehensive law 'liberating' audiovisual communication in 1982. This law established a High Authority for Audiovisual Communication (*Haute Autorité*) with powers and responsibilities new to the French broadcasting tradition. These included the de-politicisation of key appointments in the public-service broadcasting organisations, the franchising of new local radio and cable services, and for the first time ever supplying independent IBA-style oversight over programming generally. Then, when the Right came briefly to power in 1986, it enacted another weighty law and replaced the High Authority (HA) with a National Commission for Communication and Freedom (*Commission Nationale de la Communication et des Libertés*, CNCL). The new body had more powers than the High Authority. It was responsible for overseeing telecommunications as well as broadcasting; with regard to the latter, its authority now extended to the private commercial sector. The Right's 1986 legislation also included a complex set of rules against media concentration (see pp. 217–221). In the words of Lange and Renaud (1989, p. 40), it 'created a dense web of obligations for the broadcasters' who found themselves 'restrained by specifications which [were] far more complex than under the previous system'. These rules were more or less retained when the Socialists, returning to power in 1988, replaced the CNCL with yet another regulatory authority, the Higher Audiovisual Council (*Conseil Supérieur de l'Audiovisuel*, CSA). Although these successive authorities never shook off the taint of politicisation (their members were political appointees), they undoubtedly provided a new element of IBA-style regulation. Their formal powers, too, had been progressively extended. The CSA could fine broadcasters heavily for non-observance of the extensive catalogue of programme regulations. It could even suspend channels. By now, the French statutory framework for broadcasting regulation could be decribed as being 'on paper ... almost perfect' (Wolton, 1992, p. 151). The re-regulatory aspect of German broadcasting policy in the 1980s has already been mentioned. In Germany, the 1980s had witnessed a quite awesome amount of legislative rule making as well as the establishment of a whole new layer of *Länder* regulatory authorities for the private sector. Yet, without downplaying the unquestionably significant re-regulatory elements of policy-making, much of the 're-regulatory' activity simply reflected this federalised nature of regulatory competences in Germany (i.e. the need for multiple *Land* laws, regulatory authorities, etc.).

It is important not to confuse the number of rules with their scope and substance; and equally, the number of regulatory bodies with the degree of 'hands on' regulatory intervention that they supplied. What mattered most, in the British case, for instance, was that the Cable Authority had been established as a 'light touch' regulator. Later the ITC was also given a 'lighter touch' remit. Reduced to a more passive monitoring function, its relationship to the broadcasters was looser than the former IBA's had been. Similarly, although a 'quality threshold' had been introduced into the ITC's franchising criteria, its main consideration in allocating broadcasting franchises remained economic; this was necessarily so in an 'auction'. Moreover, in licensing new domestic television channels and satellite services, the quality threshold was much weaker. For 'off-shore' satellite channels (like BSkyB) it was non-existent. Nor was any such threshold specified for new radio services. The division of the technical aspects of cable regulation between ITC and Oftel certainly did not make cable and satellite television services any more regulated towards public-service values. The existence of overlapping authorities concerned with decency standards and the like, could be seen as unnecessary duplication. (The 1994 White Paper on broadcasting has since suggested that the Broadcasting Standards Council be fused with the Broadcasting Complaints Commission). Finally, as will be seen in the next chapter, ownership regulations were relaxed. Certainly, the legislative process had diminished the radical deregulatory edge of the 1990 Broadcasting Bill, but this is the most that could be said. The franchise auction had already gone a considerable way towards 'marketising' the ITV part of the duopoly. Moreover, the commercial competition that the ITV companies would face in the future would be largely unregulated, another incentive for them to weaken their former public-service identification.

In France, it has been commonly observed, there has been a failure to observe restrictive regulations, even those in favour of 'made-in-France' programme quotas (Dyson and Humphreys, 1989, p. 145; Kuhn, 1995, p. 197). The point should be made, too, that the Socialists placed only minimal public-service obligations on the new commercial channels they introduced – Canal Plus, La Cinq and M6. As for the Right, as Kuhn (1995, p. 188) observes, one of the principal aims of its 1986 broadcasting legislation was to 'make the system more competitive and less hidebound by regulation'. The complex barrage of anti-concentration rules were to please the Constitutional

Council. An important insight into the new regulatory situation has been provided by Dominique Wolton (1992, pp. 147, 160). Examining the realities of French re-regulation, he concludes: 'notwithstanding the "fierce" determination to "protect" public television, in fact over the last ten years everything has been done to the benefit of commercial television' (p. 159).

In this connection, Wolton makes a very useful general point about the deregulatory trend in Europe: 'While there are still regulations to uphold a certain conception of what television should be, it is less their content than their context of meaning that has changed' (p. 147). The latter, Wolton judges, has been profoundly affected by marketisation: 'a policy of supply' has given way to a 'policy of demand'. Values and judgements about quality in broadcasting are no longer measured by the old public-service yardstick, instead they are determined by consumer choice. Regulatory 'practice' now tends 'toward a system emptied of any normative constraints' (p. 150). A common development in Europe, is the 'adoption of the strict logic of the market' (p. 152). Wolton gives voice to a *cri de coeur* when he concludes: 'never have the values in need of protection been so fully defined in the texts of legislation … yet never has television been so bad!' (p. 153).

The latter remark is, of course, a highly subjective one. Nevertheless, Wolton makes an important point. Broadcasting regulation has never been simply about rules and regulations. Commitment to a 'public-service ethos' has always been far more important than any particular body of written laws, rules and regulations. Regulatory authorities have exercised considerable discretionary powers. They have performed their functions through the exercise of 'moral suasion' as much as by wielding any sanction. Further, the broadcasters themselves have practised a 'high degree of self-regulation'; they have 'functioned within a complex field of self-imposed constraints'. The recent changes in statute may have involved a frenzy of rule-making, but to focus on this alone and to ignore the changed context of regulation would be a grave error. Formal re-regulation may cloak far-reaching changes in the culture of regulation, in the values underpinning its interpretation, and generally in its relationship to the new marketised realities (Dyson and Humphreys, 1989, p. 139–140).

An end to politicisation?

Liberalisation has diluted the effects of politicisation, it has not rendered it entirely a thing of the past. The public channels continued to remain vulnerable to external political pressure and to internal colonisation. The new private commercial channels were bound to be freer from these kinds of direct manipulation. They were also more likely to be generally apolitical and predominantly entertainment-orientated. All the same, the political neutrality of private commercial broadcasters could only be assured if they were subject to genuinely independent regulatory institutions and practices. The French case showed that 'liberation' from politicisation had its distinct limits. Old traditions die hard. One of the explicit goals of the French Socialists when they abolished the state monopoly in 1982 had indeed been to liberate the broadcasters; state control of broadcasting had worked to their disadvantage during over twenty years of the Right's incumbency in government. The Socialists' establishment of the High Authority was supposed to remove the state's powers of routine interference in the public channels and also to depoliticise appointments to key positions within them. However, despite the exercise of greater restraint than had been customary in the past, Giscardian appointees in the public sector had already been eased out of their posts prior to the reform and a number of clearly partisan appointments had been made before the High Authority had even been set up. The High Authority itself was given a reasonably balanced membership, albeit one that was tilted towards the centre left, and the new regulatory body certainly seemed to inject a whole new quality of impartiality into French broadcasting regulation. Nevertheless, the Right was able to point out that the new body both confirmed the politically partisan appointments that had preceded the reform and made some very important ones after it. Moreover, despite the High Authority's best efforts, television output continued to be biased towards the government, though not so crudely as before (Kuhn, 1995, pp. 170–177).

As for the new commercial sector, the process of allocating franchises had produced some controversies. While the French Socialists' broadcasting legislation had given the High Authority powers to franchise new local radio and cable services, it had reserved to the government the business both of franchising and drawing up the regulatory codes of any new national channels. Canal Plus was deliv-

ered into the hands of a close presidential associate, Andre Rousselet. Even more controversially, the High Authority was not even consulted about the launch of La Cinq and M6 in 1985 (Kuhn, 1995, pp.
177–178). The government allocated La Cinq to businessmen widely
judged to be political sympathisers, and Berlusconi (see above).
Berlusconi was a strong player in the field of commercial television.
He also had close relations to Italy's Socialist former PM, Bettino
Craxi. The whole exercise seemed designed to deliver the commercial broadcasting sector into safe hands before the Right returned to
power as the opinion polls suggested they certainly would (for details
see Dyson and Humphreys, 1986, pp. 111–112). Returned to office in
1986, true to form, the Right then replaced the Socialists' High
Authority with their own National Commission for Communication
and Freedom. The commercial channel franchises were promptly re-
allocated. Berlusconi was allowed to retain his stake in La Cinq, but
now alongside Robert Hersant, the Right-wing Gaullist press baron.
The M6 franchise was handed over to a consortium led by the water
utilities company Lyonnaise des Eaux; the latter's chairman, Jerome
Monod, was a former general secretary of the Gaullist party. However, TF1 did not go to the government's favoured candidate
Hachette (Dyson and Humphreys, 1988, p. 30; Kuhn, 1995, pp.
188–191).

Predictably, the pattern was different in Germany where a whole
system of new *Land* media authorities had been created to oversee
commercial broadcasting. German law laid great stress on their supposed independence. However, like the public-service broadcasting
corporations, there were distinct limits to their practical freedom
from political influence. Porter and Hasselbach (1991, p. 62) point
out that although generally they reflected party political and governmental interests less than the broadcasting councils of the public-service corporations, 'political representation [was] still substantial'. At
least, in clear contrast to majoritarian France, the principle of *Proporz* assured that a balance was maintained between the main
parties. Also, the principle of representation of 'socially significant
groups' made for an important degree of pluralism. Nevertheless, the
new regulators were still widely felt to be close to their respective
Land governments (Humphreys, 1994, pp. 282–283; also see Dyson,
1992, pp. 95–97).

Italy was a very special case, as seen. Marketisation had occurred
in an uncontrolled manner. One feature was that for many years,

American-style, the parties had been allowed freely to buy air-time for political advertising (this was actually tightened up by a 1993 law) whereas everywhere else in Europe the new private sector was subjected to the same strict controls over political advertising as the public broadcasters (Kaid and Holtz-Bacha, 1995). However, it was not so much this exceptionalism that made Italian commercial broadcasting so very controversial. Rather, it was the way that Italian commercial television was deployed so blatantly as an instrument of the political ambitions of one man: Silvio Berlusconi. Berlusconi simply did not need to buy any political advertising. He owned three channels – Rette 4, Canale 5 and Italia 1. In 1994 Berlusconi's virtual monopoly of private commercial broadcasting in Italy served as the main electioneering instrument of his hastily contrived Forza Italia movement. Indeed, the movement was virtually a media creation. With the help of his television empire, Berlusconi became Italian Prime Minister (briefly as it turned out).

Even in Britain's case – where the broadcasters have been able to boast a strong record of independence – marketisation could paradoxically be said to have increased their exposure to political pressures in two key respects. Firstly, a prominent feature of the rather subtle marketisation that has so far occurred has been the 'casualisation' of employment conditions and the increased reliance of both BBC and ITV on short-term contracts. This development, it has been argued (Etzioni-Halevy, 1987), is hardly conducive to journalistic independence. Freelances and contract employees are likely to be much more sensitive than permanent staff to any political pressures that may filter down via management. Secondly, a more direct source of external pressure – on the BBC itself – has been the threat to its funding base and the general weakening of its self-confidence that has accompanied marketisation.

Guide to further reading

J.G. Blumler (ed.), *Television and the Public Interest: Vulnerable Values in West European Broadcasting*, London: Sage, 1992.

R. Collins, *Satellite Television in Western Europe*, London: John Libbey, 1992.

K. Dyson and P. Humphreys with R. Negrine and J.-P. Simon, *Broadcasting and New Media Policies in Western Europe: A Comparative Study of*

Technological Change and Public Policy, London/New York: Routledge, 1988.

K. Dyson and P. Humphreys, 'Deregulating Broadcasting: the West European Experience', *European Journal of Political Research*, Vol. 17, 1989, pp. 137–154.

W. Hoffmann-Riem (ed.), *Media and the Law: The Changing Landscape of Western Europe*, A Special Issue of *European Journal of Communication*, Vol. 7, No. 2, June 1992.

P. Humphreys, *Media and Media Policy in Germany*, Oxford/Providence, RI, Berg, 1994, Chapters 5 and 6.

R. Kuhn, *The Media in France*, London/New York: Routledge, 1995, Chapters 6 and 7.

D. McQuail and K. Siune (eds), *New Media Politics: Comparative Perspectives in Western Europe*, London: Sage, 1986.

R. Negrine (ed.), *Satellite Broadcasting: The Politics and Implications of the New Media*, London/New York: Routledge, 1988.

B. Østergaard (ed.), *The Media in Western Europe. The Euromedia Handbook*, London: Sage.

M. Palmer and J. Tunstall, *Liberating Communications: Policy Making in France and Britain*, Oxford: Blackwell, 1990.

V. Porter and S. Hasselbach, *Pluralism, Politics and the Marketplace: the Regulation of German Broadcasting*, London and New York: Routledge, 1991.

K. Siune and W. Truetzschler (eds), *Dynamics of Media Politics: Broadcast and Electronic Media in Western Europe*, London: Sage, 1992.

6

Market trends: internationalisation, media concentration and cross-media ownership

In 1983 West European television was still completely dominated by public-service broadcasters. A study by the European Institute for the Media (*the Bulletin*, No. 4, 1993, p.1) counted thirty-six publicly funded channels in 1983, spread over seventeen countries. Really ITV and C4, public-service by regulation, should be added as well. The only assertively commercial channels could be found in Luxembourg where CLT was the sole service and in Italy where Berlusconi's private networks had recently formed. In 1983 there were just three pan-European channels and, of these, only the infant Sky TV was commercially orientated. The same study, however, showed that an astounding transformation had occurred by 1993. During the 1980s a striking range of new television channels had become available (see Table 6.1).

While there had occurred little increase in the number of public-service channels, Western Europe was now positively teeming with new advertising- and/or subscription-funded commercial services operating at the national level. Moreover, the number of pan-European services had leapt to seventeen; many of these were commercial operations. Alongside new general entertainment services were a host of special interest or 'thematic' channels (e.g. sports, news, music channels). There was also a large amount of DBS 'overspill', from a wide range of new services, as well as the deliberate 'relay' of numerous foreign channels. In a number of cases, commercial channels were being broadcast on newly released terrestrial frequencies; sometimes commercial services were offered terrestrially as well as via cable and satellite. The leading channels were reaching large and fast-growing audiences.

Table 6.1   Europe's changing television landscape

	1983	1993
AT	ORF(2)	ORF(2) 3SAT
BE fl	BRT(2)	BRT(2) VTM, *Filmnet*
BE fr[a]	RTBF(2)	RTBF(1) ARTE/Sport TV 21 RTL-TVi, *Canal Plus*
CH	SRG/SSR/TSI (1x3)	SRG/SSR/TSI (1x3) S-tv, *Teleclub, Telecine*
DE	ARD(2), ZDF	ARD(2) ZDF ARTE 3SAT DSF, Euronews, Eurosport, Kabelkanal, n-tv, PRO7, RTL, RTL2, SAT1, Viva, VOX, *Premiere*
DK	DR	DR TV2 TV3
ES	TVE(2)	TVE (2) Antena 3, *Canal Plus*, Canal 5, *Cinemania, Documania*, Galavision
FR	TF1/Antenne 2/FR3	FRANCE 2 FRANCE 3 ARTE TF1, *Canal Plus*, M6, Canal J/Jimmy, *Cine Cinema, Ciné Cinéfil, Euronews, Tv Sport, MCM*, Serie Club, Paris Première, Planete, RTL, TMC, TNT/cartoon
FI	YLE + Mainos Sharing two channels	YLE(2) Mainos MTV
GB	BBC(2) ITV, CHANNEL 4	BBC(2) ITV, Channel 4, *Sky1*, Sky News, *Sky Movie, Sky Movie Gold, Movie Channel, Sky Sports, Adult, Bravo*, Children's, *CMT*, CNNI, *Discovery*, Euronews, *Family*, Landscape, *Learning*, MTV, *Nickelodeon*, Parliamentary, Quantum, *QVC*, Super Channel, TNT/cartoon, *UK Gold, UK Living, Wire Tv*
GR	ERT(2) YENED	ERT(3) Megachannel, Antenna, New Tv
IR	RTE	RTE Sky 1, Sky News, *Sky Movie, Sky Movie Gold, Movie Channel, Sky Sports, Bravo, Children's, Discovery, Family, UK Gold, Uk Living, Wire Tv*, Euronews, Eurosport, *QVC*, Super Channel, *Nickelodeon*, CNNI, TNT/Cartoon

IT	**RAI(3)** Italia 1, Rete 4, Canale 5, TMC, Odeon	**RAI(3)** Italia 1, Rete 4, Canale 5, TMC, Odeon, *Tele Piu*, Elefante, Videomusica, Rete A, Italia 9, Junior, Euronews
LU	CLT	CLT, RTL-4
NL	**NED 1/2** (NOS + 8 societies)	**NED 1/2/3** (NOS+8 societies), *RTL 4*, RTL 5, Eurosport, Kindernet, *Filmnet*
NO[b]	**NRK**	**NRK** *CNNI, Eurosport, Discovery, MTV, Tele-Tv FilmNet, TV3 TVN*
PT	**RTP(2)**	RTP (2), SIC3, TV-1
SE	**SVT(2)**	**SVT(2)** *TV3*, TV4 Nordisk, *TV 5 Nordic*, TV 1000 Filmnet
EU	Pan-European channels, SKY tv, EUROPA, TV5	3SAT, Asia Tv, Avraysa, *BBC World*, CNNI, Deutsche Welle, Euronews, Eurosport, MBC, *Red Hot tv*, Super Channel, TV5, TVEi, Tv Asia, JSTV, MTV, Worldnet
	Relays of national channels	ARD, B3, France 2, MDR3, M6, N3, *NRK, RAI 1, RAI 2*, RTPI, RTL France *SVT1, SVT2,* SWF 3, TF1, TV Monte Carlo, WDR 3, ZDF

Notes:

AT–Austria; BE fl=Belgium (Flemish); BE fr=Belgium (Francophone); CH=Switzerland; DE=Germany; DK=Denmark; ES=Spain; FR=France; FI=Finland; GB=Great Britain; IR=Ireland; IT=Italy; LU=Luxembourg; NL=Netherlands; NO=Norway; PT=Portugal; SE=Sweden; EU=European Union.

Services supported by the licence fee are printed white on black, services requiring subscriptions or purchase of a decoder are printed in italics, etc.

[a] There is substantial viewing of TF1 and France 2 and 3. TV5 has a terrestrial transmitter covering the Brussels area.

[b] Five services for Norway are broadcast from the Thor (ex-Marcopolo) satellite.

Source: the Bulletin, Vol. 10, No. 4, December 1993, p. 1. Reproduced with the kind permission of the European Institute for the Media.

The removal of technical and regulatory barriers to market entry had encouraged a whole range of new investors to enter the broadcasting sector. They were attracted by the prospect of making profits in what was perceived to be an exciting new sphere of commercial operation. As will be seen, some investors and entrepreneurs were new entrants to the media. Others were media players seeking to diversify into other fields of activity in the pursuit of different markets, economies of scale, the exploitation of synergies between media sectors, the spreading of business risk, and so on. Whether new to the media field or not, most backers of commercial broadcasting were sizeable – sometimes giant, international – companies.

Across Europe, then, the picture was one of obvious market expansion. This could easily be interpreted as a manifest pluralisation of the kind promised by the free market radicals (see previous chapter). However, to look simply at the impressive multiplication of television channels could easily deceive about the extent of pluralism. In fact, Europe's emergent commercial broadcasting sector was characterised by conspicuous cases of multiple ownership, or significant cross-holdings, of commercial broadcasting channels. This kind of horizontal integration of the industry was also apparent in chains of cable television companies and radio stations in the ownership of, or heavily backed by, the same parent company or media entrepreneur. There were also some striking cases of cross-media ownership where the same interests owned more than one type of media operation. Such interests were in a position to control the information process through a number of different media. In addition, the commercial broadcasting sector was becoming vertically integrated as the same companies sought to control different stages of the production and distribution processes. The economic benefits of the latter strategy were essentially twofold: it secured access to production resources and distribution networks; and it kept transactions and profits within the same business. Finally, conglomerate growth was much in evidence. Often combining all three of the aforementioned corporate strategies, media conglomerates were necessarily very large businesses. Indeed, there were signs of the emergence of a potential European oligopoly of multinational, multimedia enterprises. All these developments were leading, paradoxically despite technical diversification, towards increased economic concentration in the European media. A relatively small number of concerns were assuming a commanding presence in the national and even the international markets for information and entertainment. Moreover, strategic alliances were being made between these large media concerns. Behind these strategies was the fact that there were economies of scale and potentially rich profits to be made from exploiting Europe's newly liberalised commercial broadcasting and multi-media markets (for useful overviews see Lorimer, 1994, pp. 85–88, and Negrine and Papathanassopoulos, 1990, Chapter 7, pp. 129–149. For a very detailed study, see A. Sánchez-Tabernero *et al.*, 1993).

There were numerous other reasons why concentration tendencies became quickly evident in the new commercial broadcasting sector. Lorimer (1994, pp. 89–93) helpfully lists a whole range of factors and the most important ones will be examined in more detail in the pages that follow. Generally, the sector attracted existing media interests keen to re-invest profits which, for 'winners' at least, had typically been high during the post-war period in the media field. Giant press companies were keen to re-invest their monopoly (or oligopoly) profits. Moreover, their borrowing to finance expansion was welcomed by financial institutions, themselves persuaded of the media's growing potential for profit-making. Media companies had a 'defensive–offensive' motivation: they anticipated fierce competition for their staple revenue (advertising) from the opening of new media markets. Therefore, they sought to pre-empt the competition by investing early in these very markets. Further, media markets – witness the press – had shown themselves to be not easily amenable to regulation along competition policy lines. Large media companies and conglomerates, therefore, sensed that the new markets were likely to be free.

The trends identified so far, of course, hardly augured any imminent market dominance at the European level. However, they could be said to contribute to media concentration tendencies at the national level. Most obviously, the potential profits and economies of scale from international diversification would translate back into competitive advantage for these large companies within their home markets. In some countries, as will be seen, the new commercial broadcasting sectors were already effectively in the control of a few giant companies or alliances. In Germany, the new commercial broadcasting sector was dominated by a few key players. In Italy, the sector was (near) completely monopolised by a single entrepreneur. In both cases, concentration assumed disturbing proportions. This stimulated a lively debate about what kind of countervailing policies might be introduced. However, governments were under pressure to promote the expansion of their large domestic players. Government were torn, therefore, between a regulatory rationale premised on the need to ensure media pluralism at home and a deregulatory rationale based on the need for domestic economic interests to be allowed to compete with other European media interests not so encumbered by such rules. As we shall see, some countries gave their home companies a distinct competitive advantage in the pursuit of their international expansion strategies through having lax anti-concentration rules. Other governments were careful that such rules should not be too strict. Unsurprisingly, this only served to encourage commercial media interests in the more strictly regulated countries to weigh upon their own policy makers to enact 'competitive deregulation'. The failure to do so, it was argued, would result in their failing to exploit the new market opportunities and even becoming easy targets for foreign marauders from the less regulated states. In short, there were dynamic aspects pointing towards increased concentration at the European level; and also to the need for European-level action. This latter matter will be explored in Chapter 8. First, we need to examine the main players and the national regulatory frameworks in which they are operating.

The business backers of commercial broadcasting: new concentrations of media power

Multi-media diversification of the press

Some striking cases of large-scale cross-media ownership emerged. Publishers of the press, and especially very large press groups, were important diversifiers into the new European commercial broadcasting sector. Indeed, during the 1980s (earlier in Germany) press interests had actively pressured governments to introduce the new media and to open up new investment opportunities in commercial broadcasting. There were several key reasons for this development. Firstly, by the 1980s 'mono-media' enterprise was fast losing its attraction. In most European press markets the scope for further empire building had become limited; and competition for readers and advertisers between big players had become a cut-throat business. Diversification offered a way out of the *impasse*. It also brought the press companies the advantage of spreading the risks attendant upon reliance on mono-media activity. Secondly, following the introduction of new press technologies some publishers had achieved high levels of profitability. This was notably the case in Britain and Germany where publishers were especially active diversifiers into the audiovisual media. Moreover, the 1980s had seen a boom in advertising expenditure in Europe. The press companies had been important beneficiaries. This had increased their financial capacity for internally financed expansion; or at least it had increased their creditworthiness with the banks, making possible their diversification into the fast expanding audiovisual sector. During the advertising boom, such a strategy was an attractive one to them (though in the 1990s an advertising recession in press markets occurred and some burnt their fingers). Thirdly, press interests shared a compelling 'defensive–offensive' motivation. They feared a future negative impact on their staple advertising revenues from the spread of new electronic media (cable, satellite, etc.). Ever since the public-service broadcasters had been allowed to supplement the licence fee with advertising revenue, the press had seen its share of the overall advertising cake decline. Public broadcasters had been nibbling into more and more of it. The threat the press now faced, though, was of a wholly new order of magnitude. An obvious response for the press companies was to diversify into broadcasting operations and to pre-empt thereby the challenge before it became much more grave. Fourthly, there were obvious synergies to be exploited in pursuing such a course of action. Editorial, journalistic and news-gathering tasks, expertise and resources, and other media-specific activities, could be shared. Not least of all, multi-media diversification promised to strengthen media companies' commercial bargaining position *vis-à-vis* the advertisers (Dyson and Humphreys, 1988, pp. 21–23, for a more detailed discussion, see Sánchez-Tabernero *et al.*, 1993, Chapter 3).

It was entirely unsurprising, therefore, that press interests played a leading role in launching a number of commercial television channels (see Table 6.2). The best examples were German publishers like Springer (with a key stake in the SAT 1 satellite channel), the French press baron Hersant (La Cinq – until he pulled out in 1990) and Rupert Murdoch (Sky TV – now BSkyB). In some cases, they associated themselves with established broadcasters. Thus, the giant German multinational publishing conglomerate Bertelsmann (Gruner and Jahr) and the giant regional WAZ press group both joined CLT

(Luxembourg's commercial broadcasting colossus) to launch RTL
Plus (later simply called RTL). Rupert Murdoch joined forces with
Granada TV in BSkyB. In Belgium, newspaper companies were the
principal investors in that country's new commercial television
sector. After more than two decades during which they had opposed
the introduction of commercial television, precisely because of the
threat it posed to their advertising revenues, the small country's francophone publishers joined forces with the CLT in a new commercial
channel called RTLTVi. Similarly, the majority of Flemish newspaper publishers became the main shareholders in *Vlaamse Televisie
Maatschappij* (VTM). The Flemish publishers were attracted by the
fact that VTM was granted an effective regional monopoly of commercial broadcasting in 1989. In the field of commercial radio, the
large German publishers dominated that country's new commercial
radio sector. Moreover, locally dominant publishers were involved in
a number of regional networks; this created a web of 'double
monopolies'. In France, the press baron Robert Hersant acquired in
1987 a private commercial radio network called 'Fun', made up of a
string of local radio stations. The Mondadori-Expresso publishing
group had a large slice of Italy's commercial radio business.

Table 6.2   Cross-media involvement in new commercial TU channels, 1990

Press company	Country	Channel	Country	% stake
Hersant	France	La Cinq	France	25.0a
Hachette	France	La Cinq	France	25.0[a]
Springer	Germany	SAT 1	Germany	27.0[b]
Springer	Germany	Tele 5(DSF)	Germany	29.0[c]
Bertelsmann	Germany	RTL Plus	Germany	39.0
Bertelsmann	Germany	Canal+(G)	Germany	50.0
Bertelsmann	Germany	Premiere	Germany	25.0
WAZ group	Germany	RTL Plus	Germany	10.0
Holtzbrinck	Germany	SAT 1	Germany	15.0
Murdoch[d]	UK	BSkyB	UK	50.0
Pearson (*FT*)	UK	BSkyB	UK	17.5
MGN[e]	UK	MTV	Europe	50.0
MGN	UK	Cable[f]	UK	Various
Ringier (major Swiss publisher)	Switzerland	Tele 5(DSF)	Germany	17.0
Consortium of all Flemish publishers	Belgium	VTM	B (fl)	50.0

Audiopresse (consortium of francophone press cos)	Belgium	RTLTVi	B (W.)	34.0
VNU	Holland	RTL 4	Holland	19.0
Elsevier	Holland	RTL 4	Holland	19.0

Non-press media company	Country	Channel	Country	% state
Kirch (film wholesaler)[g]	Germany	SAT 1	Germany	43.0
Kirch		Premiere		25.0
Kirch jnr (son)		Pro 7		48.0
CLT (TV co.)	Luxembourg	Tele 5	Germany	24.0[h]
CLT		RTL PLus	Germany	46.0
CLT		M6	France	25.0
CLT		RTL 4	Holland	35.0
CLT		RTL TVi	Belgium	66.0
Granada	UK	BSkyB	UK	12.0
Havas (advertising)	France	Canal+(F)	France	25.0

Notes:

[a] La Cinq was liquidated in 1992. Before this, first Hersant and then Hachette had reduced their stakes.

[b] Springer's direct stake was 20%, but it also had a 35% stake in a consortium of publishers with a 20% share in SAT 1.

[c] In 1992 this was reduced to 25%.

[d] Of course, Murdoch was Australian born and an American citizen. His News International company is a multinational company. Here 'UK' is to signify the large presence his newspapers have in the country where BSkyB had its main audience. News International also had an important stake in Spain's main new commercial TV channel, Antenna 3. It has since acquired a 50% controlling interest in a German channel called 'Vox'.

[e] MGN belonged to Robert Maxwell until his death in 1991. MTV has since been taken over by the US media company Viacom.

[f] MGN was an important investor in a number of UK cable franchises.

[g] Leo Kirch has a major stake in the Springer press. Obviously this fact contributes to the conspicuous pattern of media concentration in Germany; and cross media concentration at that!

[h] In 1992 the CLT pulled out and Tele 5 became the sports channel DSF, controlled by Kirch (24.5% stake).

Non-media diversifiers

Market entry into the broadcasting sector by a number of non-media financial interests and businesses from, at first sight, unrelated sectors, could be explained by several factors. In the first place, quite obviously, the 1980s deregulation of the public-service monopoly actually facilitated the entry of 'cash rich' new players into the pre-viously closely guarded sector. The expectation that deregulation would deliver new opportunities for profit-making had been a pow-erful inducement. The 1980s advertising boom, backed by the rosy predictions of the advertising industry, served to sharpen this expec-tation. Generally, international market developments and the hype about imminent technological possibilities (e.g. 'information super-highways'), suggested that multi-media interests were fast becoming a most attractive activity for big business and financial consortia to become involved in. Secondly, the internationalisation of broadcast-ing markets, combined with the very large investment required to actually launch operations in an increasingly 'high-tech' sector, required financial backing on a scale beyond the means normally available to all but the strong media players.Technical systems for the encryption (encoding) and distribution of pay-TV services did not come cheap. Nor indeed did the rental of satellite capacity. Nor did the sheer amount of programming that would be needed to feed the new services. Established media players had to be very profitable and creditworthy to be able to take the risks involved. Not all coun-tries had media groups confident enough to meet this challenge with-out strong support. Thirdly, even for non-media diversifiers there were still possible synergies to be exploited. Hence, for example, the interest of public utilities companies like the large French water com-panies in the cable television sector (cabling as ducting). Telecoms companies had an obvious interest in cable and satellite operations. BT became involved in British cable and also in marketing the Lux-embourg Astra satellite operation. Deutsche Telekom (soon to be privatised) acquired a direct stake in Astra, a rival provider of satel-lite services. The British leisure company Virgin joined with the Ital-ian music company BETA to operate the pan-European general entertainment channel 'Superchannel' (before it was taken over by the American company NBC). Finally, big business pursues political interests as well as commercial ones. Press barons are by no means the only businessmen with political axes to grind. The attraction for industrialists of acquiring a stake in the main media of ideological communication had long been very obvious in Italy. Witness the role of industrialists like Agnelli, De Benedetti and Gardini in the Italian press (see Chapter 3). Above all, Silvio Berlusconi personified the powerful entrepreneur with a keen eye for political opportunity. Having originally made in his fortune in construction and real estate he soon turned his attention to the media field. His acquisition of a virtual monopoly of Italy's private commercial television sector was a factor – arguably the crucial factor – in his election to the post of Italy's prime minister in 1994.

As a rule, non-media diversifiers (see Table 6.3) were to be found most thickly on the ground in countries where established media interests were weaker and where they were therefore presented with a relatively open field. Accordingly, non-media investors were thin on the ground in Germany where the major publishers of the press – together with Leo Kirch, the country's leading film distributer – virtually cornered the market in the new commercial broadcasting sector. Similarly, in Britain the commercial satellite television channel BSkyB was owned by established media interests: News International (Rupert Murdoch), Granada TV and Pearson (owner of the *Financial Times* among other media interests). France presented a mixed picture. Important media interests in the shape of the publishing groups of Hersant and Hachette, and the large advertising agency Havas, were certainly involved in developing commercial broadcasting. Havas actually held an important interest in Luxembourg's CLT and was the parent company of the highly successful pay-television company Canal Plus. However, the French media groups were weaker than their Anglo-Saxon or German counterparts. Their involvement in launching new television channels was more dependent upon their receiving state support (as with the launch of Canal Plus) or making alliances with strong foreign partners (La Cinq) (Guillou, 1984, esp. p. 139). Indeed, both Hachette and Hersant overstretched themselves through their involvement in La Cinq. The channel rapidly failed (see Chapter 7). Hersant had to content himself instead with running a commercial radio network, an altogether safer and cheaper investment. In France, an important role was played by powerful indigenous financial investors like the *Caisse de Dépôts et Consignation* (in cable television) and large industrial concerns like the construction giant Bouygues, the controlling interest in TF1, the main commercial channel (following its privatisation in 1987). Other important non-media investors were giant public utilities companies like *Compagnie Lyonnaise des Eaux*, which was an important backer of the commercial channel M6 and of a number of cable projects. In Italy, Berlusconi had built up his monopoly of Italian commercial broadcasting virtually entirely on the back of his huge real estate and construction business. Moreover he was very heavily dependent on bank finance (see next chapter, pp. 233–234).

Table 6.3   Big business involvement in main new commercial TV channels, 1990

Company	Sector	Country	Channel	Country	% stake
Bouygues	Construction	France	TF1	France	25.0a
Lyonnaise des Eaux	Water co.	France	M6	France	15.0[b]
Générale des Eaux	Water co.	France	Canal+	France	21.0
Berlusconi's Fininvest	Holding co.	Italy	Canal 5	Italy	100.0
			Italia 1		100.0
			Rete 4		100.0
			La Cinq	France	25.0[c]
			Tele 5 (DSF)	Germany	21.0
			Telecinco	Spain	25.0
BT	Telecoms.	UK	MTV	Europe	25.0
Virgin	Music/leisure	UK	Super-	Europe	46.0[d]
BETA	Music	Italy	channel	Europe	53.0[d]

Note:

[a] This is the figure for Bouygues alone. The Bouygues-led consortium had 50%.

[b] Originally 25%.

[c] La Cinq was liquidated in 1992.

[d] Now owned by NBC.

The internationalisation strategies of commercial broadcasting concerns

The involvement of international business corporations – whether in the shape of leading press companies like Bertelsmann and News International, other media interests like CLT, or the powerful European financial institutions that were aligned behind Luxembourg's Astra satellites – brought a new dynamism to the European broadcasting sector. The promise of stable investment by large commercial companies helped to offset the fact that media revenues were notoriously vulnerable to the periodic ups and downs of the advertising market. There were bound to be casualties but, generally speaking, short-term disappointments were unlikely to weaken the commitment of the powerful international companies which were now clearly being attracted by calculations of long-term profitability in a sector now seen as a key element of the global 'information revolution'. Backed by profits generated elsewhere, these investors were in a position to see the emergent new media ventures survive the long haul to profitability (see Sánchez-Tabernero, 1993, pp. 91–93).

From the above account, it will have become clear that foreign investment and international strategic alliance building were a striking characteristic of Europe's emerging commercial broadcasting markets. International diversification had several attractions. The most obvious one was the simple attraction of international market access. Also, the large costs of embarking upon new media operations could be amortised most quickly, and profitability thresholds most speedily surmounted, by maximising the geographic scope of media operations. There were obviously economies of scale to be gained. Further, strategic alliances presented scope to spread the risks of new ventures and to gain access to new technologies, production resources, distribution outlets, and so forth. Companies calculated, too, that international expansion by competitors would present them with fierce competition; therefore they had incentive to pre-empt and even co-opt the competition. In any case, it made strategic good sense to commit significant loss-leading investment in order to stake out an important share of the emerging pan-European broadcasting market and to foreclose future competition at the outset. Since markets could only sustain a finite number of players, to own 'one more channel [wa]s one channel fewer in direct competition for advertising revenue ... the larger the empire, the more limited the competition for revenues and audiences' (Negrine and Papathanassopoulos, 1990, p. 132).

Sánchez-Tabernero *et al.* (1993, pp. 123–133) have highlighted the key role played by developments in European advertising markets. Media companies, they suggested, sought to expand internationally because of the prospect of national market saturation for advertising and subscription revenues in Europe's more 'mature' media markets. More generally, they pointed out, media companies had to respond to a 'Europeanisation' of the advertising industry itself. The ability to offer advertisers international audiences would help to re-balance the bargaining power of the sellers *vis-à-vis* the increasingly multinational buyers of media air-time. Europeanised companies could offer the prospect of Europe-wide advertising campaigns. Yet another factor, they point to, will be discussed in detail in Chapter

8, namely the deliberate dismantlement by the EC of national legal barriers to transfrontier investment in and establishment of broadcasting operations across Europe. The attraction presented by the exploitation of a huge EC 'internal market' was an important inducement to investors. Of course, foreign investment might not even be necessary. Satellite broadcasting precluded the need to buy into a neighbouring country's media industries. Even terrestrial broadcasting allowed the privatised French channel TF1 to make major inroads into neighbouring Belgium's advertising markets. However, Luxembourg's CLT, more sensitively, saw advantages in combining with indigenous capital in Germany and France; it also set up Belgian and Dutch subsidiaries in order to supply these small countries' dense network of cable systems. All the same, EC deregulation of national 'cultural protectionism' in Europe confirmed the substantial economic scope for the exploitation of new market opportunities.

Vertical diversification

So far, the focus has been mainly on the television channels themselves, the horizontal integration of broadcasting operations and cross-media ownership. In addition, as an important Booz.Allen and Hamilton report (1989) has described, there occurred a rash of joint ventures, mergers and acquisitions as companies sought to diversify vertically. New broadcasters diversified 'upstream' in order to acquire or to secure access to production units, film stocks and the like. Other commercial media interests diversified 'downstream' in order to gain access to, or control of, transmission companies. The new private commercial operators typically had few in-house production facilities; they were therefore faced with an urgent requirement to gain access 'upstream' to production facilities, to secure rights to programmes and to acquire their own programme libraries. The Booz.Allen and Hamilton report (1989, p. 15) noted that a quarter of mergers and acquisitions in its data-base represented upstream investments into programme production by broadcasters concerned to guarantee their supply of programmes. Thus Bertelsmann's broadcasting subsidiary Ufa acquired film and video production companies. The CLT expanded its network of European production centres. Berlusconi's holding company Fininvest acquired production companies. Canal Plus was a major investor in cinematic film pro-

Table 6.4 The largest (by turnover) private commercial multi-media concerns in Europe in 1989 and their scope of activities

Company	Turnover ECU billions	International scope	Sectoral activity	Radio	TV	Film/ video	Press	Advert ising
Bertelsmann	6.0	US, Europe,	Finance	+	+	+	+	
		S. America	Prod'n	+	+	+	+	
			Dist'n	+	+	+	+	
News Corp.	3.6	US, Europe,	Finance		+	+	+	+
(Murdoch)		Australia	Prod'n		+	+	+	
Hachette	3.3	US, Canada,	Finance	+	+	+	+	+
		Europe,	Prod'n	+	+	+	+	
		Japan, Asia	Dist'n	+	+	+	+	
Fininvest	2.45	Europe	Finance		+	+	+	+
(Berlusconi)			Prod'n		+	+	+	
			Dist'n		+	+	+	
Havas	1.8	Europe	Finance	+	+	+	+	+
			Prod'n		+	+	+	
			Dist'n		+	+	+	
Springer/	1.3	Europe	Finance	+	+	+	+	
Kirch			Prod'n	+	+	+	+	+
			Dist'n	+	+	+	+	
Maxwell	1.25	Europe	Finance		+		+	
Communications			Prod'n		+		+	
			Dist'n		+		+	
Pearson	1.2	N. America,	Finance	+	+	+		
		Europe,	Prod'n	+	+	+		
		Japan, Asia,	Dist'n	+		+		
		Australia						
Hersant	1.1ᵃ	Europe	Finance	+	+		+	+
			Prod'n	+			+	
			Dist'n	+	+		+	

Note:
ᵃ 1988 turnover figure from R. Cayrol, *Les Média: Presse écrite, radio, télévision*, Paris: PUF, 1991, p. 149. Cayrol gives this figure as ffr. 7.2 billion; I have converted it into ECU.
Source: Adapted from a table by G. M. Luyken, 'Das Medienwirtschaftsgefüge der 90er Jahre. Horizontale und vertikale Unternehmensverflechtungen – Neue strategische Allianzen – öffentliches Interesse', *Media Perspektiven*, 10/1990, pp. 621–641, p. 625.

duction in France. The Booz.Allen and Hamilton report detected a general trend towards the takeover of production companies by large media conglomerates. The most striking case of acquisition of a film production company was, without question, Rupert Murdoch's acquisition of the Hollywood studio, Twentieth Century Fox. This secured him a source of movies for his European BSkyB operation and for his US 'Fox Broadcasting' network.

'Downstream' acquisitions were fewer. However, a striking example was provided by the Kirch group in Germany. Starting off as the country's dominant private sector trading company in programme rights, and an established supplier of popular (mainly American) film and series 'packages' to the country's public-service networks, the Kirch concern became a major multiple owner of private television channels in Germany; these included two national commercial TV channels and the country's leading pay-TV operation. Kirch also had a significant stake in Germany's dominant newspaper concern, the Springer group, itself a major player in commercial broadcasting. Not content with this scale of media influence, in 1994 Kirch joined together with Bertelsmann, his leading rival in the field of commercial television, to launch a joint venture called Media Services GmbH (MSG). The joint venture's purpose was to deliver pay-television and other multi-media services such as teleshopping and video-on-demand through decoders and smart cards. It represented a classic case of downstream diversification by both parties since the other partner in the planned enterprise was Deutsche Telekom, the monopoly owner of the country's cable networks. On this occasion, the European Commission blocked the venture on the grounds that it constituted a clear case of market dominance (see Chapter 8, p. 285).

Media concentration and counter-measures

Chapter 3 has already described how concern about media concentration is hardly new. However, while broadcasting had remained a function of the public-service monopoly, this particular source of potential threat to media pluralism had obviously not been an issue. (Nor was it in Britain's unique duopoly due to the strict regulatory controls placed on the commercial ITV companies – see below.) Of course, as seen, pluralism was still jeopardised in European broadcasting systems, but by the degree of the public broadcasters' exposure to political/bureaucratic control and interference (see Chapter 4). Clearly, this state of affairs changed with the opening up of a major private commercial sector. Commercial broadcasters were more likely to be free from state control. However, they were not necessarily so from political bias. Berlusconi's channels, for instance, were deployed very blatantly indeed in support of his *Forza Italia* movement's successful bid for political power in 1994. The danger existed of a more widespread translation of proprietorial power into the kind of editorial power that had undoubtedly marked the private commercial press sector. Moreover, not a few of Europe's new commercial broadcasting conglomerates were either wholly or largely owned, or controlled, by single individuals or families, a state of affairs very reminiscent of Europe's press 'barony'. Berlusconi's Fininvest has been mentioned. The powerful German Kirch media group might be adduced. So too the Springer group (since Axel Springer's death his family's influence had diminished, but Kirch had been quick to step in here too with a significant share). The giant Bertelsmann multinational was 90 per cent owned by the Mohn family. Rupert Murdoch deserves an obvious mention, too. This ownership pattern 'reduce(d) the easy transferability of control to others' through share deals (Negrine and Papathanassopoulos, 1990, p. 137). It also raised obvious questions about 'media power'.

No 'demonisation' of media entrepreneurs is intended here. Rather than engage in Berlusconi-style political campaigns, the other new commercial channels were manifestly concerned with the far more prosaic business of providing entertainment in order to deliver audiences to advertisers. Indeed, the new channels provided comparatively little news and information (see Chapter 7). Moreover, the satellite news channels operated by Ted Turner (CNN) and Rupert Murdoch (Sky News) appeared to be maintaining credible standards and were providing serious international news coverage. All the same, the press sector was testimony to the scope that the private accumulation of media power presented for the exercise of political bias. Nor could the possibility be overlooked that more impersonal media corporations, largely owned by complex webs of institutional investors, might still be tempted to trade support for governments in return for regulatory favours, business opportunities, and so on. Above all, the potential threat to pluralism and diversity of opinion could not be ignored. To do so, would be to neglect a long established axiom of West European broadcasting policy. Because of broadcasting's special nature, as a very powerful medium of mass communication, a strong case could be made for special ownership controls. Broadcasting had manifestly not yet become analogous to the press sector as radical free marketeers were predicting. The rationale for regulation based on the 'scarcity of frequencies' might no longer hold, it was true, but the 'electronic publishing' line of argument had yet to be confirmed by developments in the real world. The number of new mainstream broadcasters in national markets remained limited for various reasons, most obviously the costs and risks of market entry. Policy makers and regulators therefore found themselves compelled to confront the issue of how to ensure that the new private commercial broadcasting sector would be adequately pluralistic in terms of ownership.

The British duopoly, introduced as long ago as the mid-1950s, presented an exemplary model of how commercial broadcasting could be regulated for pluralism. The British case showed how a range of specific measures might be taken. Limits might be placed on the number of new commercial operations that might be owned by an individual person or company. A ceiling might be placed on the extent of individual shareholdings in single companies. Limitations might be set on cross-media ownership. In the 1980s measures had also been introduced in Britain to protect and to promote smaller independent producers against the market power of the large programme contracting companies (including the BBC). In fact, in all those European countries where the liberalization of broadcasting had gone the furthest, regulatory agencies – very much along the lines of the British IBA (now ITC) – were established, with explicit powers to grant and revoke the new commercial broadcasting licences. Through their franchising and supervisory functions, such bodies could ensure that concentration did not proceed too far. The laws and rules varied considerably between countries, but their common rationale was to prevent a single legal individual person or company from accumulating too much media power; and to protect media pluralism and diversity.

Restrictions of ownership of private broadcasting organisations

In Britain, as averred, there had always existed very strict ownership rules for the private broadcasters. Under the traditional duopoly, no company had been permitted to hold more than one regional ITV franchise. In fact, the deregulatory Broadcasting Act of 1990 relaxed this constraint so that a single company might hold two such franchises so long as they were not for adjacent regions or for two of the 'majors' (i.e. the larger franchises). Admittedly, this hardly amounted to a radical deregulation. However, the Broadcasting Act had provided an incentive for a further deregulatory step. The Act's continued restrictions on their expansion, so the larger franchise-holders complained, was a handicap on the ability of potentially very competitive British media companies to face up to the growing international competition. The Act's provision opening up the ITV companies to external takeover, previously something that had to be sanctioned by the IBA, might quickly lead to their falling into the hands of powerful foreign media interests. Alerted to the risk of such possible unintended consequences of its actions, the government (swayed by the Department of Trade and Industry) duly further relaxed the rules in 1993. From now on, large regional franchisees were also allowed to combine. There immediately followed a wave of mergers of ITV companies: Carlton took over Central; MAI Meridian took over Anglia; Granada took over LWT. Between them, the three resultant companies accounted for over two-thirds of ITV advertising revenues. Moreover, the government announced that it would consider relaxing cross-media ownership restrictions as well (see later, pp. 221–224).

Elsewhere in Europe the provisions were laxer (see Table 6.5). In Germany, the 1986 'dual system' ruling of the country's Constitutional Court had pointed very explicitly to the danger of' monopolistic control over the expression of opinion'. As a result, the 1987 inter-*Land* treaty, providing the national rules for broadcasting as agreed collectively by the *Länder*, restricted single legal entities to ownership of one generalist national private commercial service plus one specialised radio or television service. In each case the holding had to be less than 50 per cent. The same shareholder was allowed to hold up to 24.9 per cent of the shares in two other services. (The *Länder* set their own rules for regional and local services). However, these rulings failed to prevent the domination of the commercial broadcasting sector by the major alliances that have been described above. There also remained considerable scope for multiple ownership of local radio services (Porter and Hasselbach, 1991, p. 117–127; and Humphreys, 1994, Chapter 6).

In France, the rules were very complex indeed. The 1986 communications law (see Chapter 5) specified that no individual person or

Table 6.5 Restrictions on ownership of private television broadcasting in Western Europe (where relevant)

Country	Nature of restriction, if any
Belgium (fr)	Company holding more than 24% of capital in private TV station cannot hold more than 24% in another. Public broadcasters similarly limited to 24% in a private channel.
Belgium (fl)	Only one private TV company allowed to serve the entire Flemish community. Cable operators restricted to less than 20% of its capital.
Denmark	Business barred from majority ownership of the one new commercial channel.
France	One franchise only for national level terrestrial TV, participation limited to 25% (note: several allowed for local TV). For satellite TV two franchises allowed. If participation in one is less than 50 per cent, then up to 33% permitted in a second.
Germany	No more than 49.9% allowed in only one national generalist channel and one specialised thematic channel. Other stakes in nationally available broadcasting services must be less than 25%.
Greece	No more than 25% in one channel only.
Italy	Maximum of three channels allowed.
Portugal	No more than 25% in one channel only.
Spain	No more than 25% in one channel only.
UK	Ownership restricted to either two regional franchises; or one national Channel 3 licence (e.g. Breakfast TV; or ITN); or one Channel 5 licence (not yet launched). Franchisees in one of these categories limited to 20% interest in either of the others.

Sources: Commission of the European Communities, *Pluralism and Media Concentration in the Internal Market*, COM (92) 480 final, Commission Green Paper, Brussels, 23 December 1992, pp. 40 52; also see A. Sánchez-Tabernero *et al.*, *Media Concentration in Europe*, Media Monograph No. 16. Dusseldorf: European Institute for the Media, 1993, pp. 220–221.

enterprise might have a holding of more than 25 per cent in a company granted an authorisation to operate a national terrestrial service. If a person or enterprise already held a share of 15 per cent, then s/he or it might not own more than 15 per cent of the shares in another such company holding a similar authorisation. This share was reduced to 5 per cent if the same person already had a 5 per cent stake in two other broadcasting companies. No person or enterprise might exceed a 50 per cent share in a company authorised to provide a satellite broadcasting service. If the share was lower than half but above a third, the same person or enterprise was entitled to take up to a 33.3 per cent stake in another company granted a satellite broadcasting authorisation. No company was allowed to hold more than a single authorisation to operate a national terrestrial service, defined as a station serving more than six million people. No company with an authorisation to provide a radio service to more than 30 million people could hold an additional radio licence to provide a similar service to more than 15 million listeners. No satellite, terrestrial television or radio company could operate more than one other service of the same type. However, given the dominance of French private commercial broadcasting by the privatised TF1, there was hardly any scope for multiple television channel ownership in any case. Also, the law did not touch Hersant's radio network: his stations' combined audience fell way below the threshold. Moreover, as will be seen, cross-media ownership rules were fairly lax in key respects (CEC, 1992a, p. 43; also Sánchez-Tabernero *et al.*, 1993, p. 233).

The situation in Italy, too, was complex on paper but in practice it was very liberal indeed. Multiple channel ownership was set by a new 1990 law at no less than three national television services. As seen, since 1976 there had existed a more or less complete media policy vacuum. In the end the constitutional court succeeded in having a law enacted. In the interim, however, business interests had enjoyed a free run of the field. In particular, Berlusconi had acquired his control over the commercial half of the Italian television market, coming to own all three of the country's major private networks. When finally enacted, the legislation clearly followed market *faits accomplis*; it allowed Berlusconi to retain his private sector monopoly. For this reason, it was dubbed the 'Lex Berlusconi' (Wagner, 1994, p. 71).

Restrictions on cross-media ownership

As for cross-media ownership rules, there are indications, once again, that regulations have followed the market. It is interesting to note that much of the variation between the rules reflected closely

the pattern of investment already being established in the new commercial sector. Cross-media regulation appeared to have been conspicuously sensitive to the concern not to deter investment. Thus, at
first sight perhaps rather surprisingly, in the German case there were
no federal rules on cross-media ownership whatsoever. A few *Länder*
had fairly strict cross-media restrictions against 'double monopolies'
(locally important publishers controlling local broadcast services).
Other *Länder* were notably lax, keen as they were to attract media
investment. Ingeniously, SPD North Rhine Westphalia's law allowed
extensive local press investment but safeguarded against 'monopolistic control over expression of opinion', by detaching editorial control
from ownership. In Germany, as seen, achievement of a federal
agreement between the *Länder* had been a slow and difficult business.
By the time that agreement eventually materialised, certain market
faits accomplis had been generally accepted. The most obvious of
these was the fact that the press sector – especially the powerful press
groups, most notably Springer and Bertelsmann – was the main
source of investment in nation-wide commercial television broadcasting, and also in numerous local radio services. Thus in Germany
a central principle of the post-war media system was overturned:
namely, that of a very strict separation of the press and broadcasting
sectors. The erstwhile very central principle of a 'balance of powers'
between the different branches of the mass media, was allowed to fall
by the wayside (see Humphreys, 1994, Chapter 6).

Similarly Italy's cross-ownership rules were not very restrictive
and represented very little threat to market *faits accomplis*. The 1990
law, mentioned above, specified: (1) that the owner of three television networks (i.e. 'Berlusconi') should not own a daily newspaper;
(2) that the owner of two television networks could not control more
than 8 per cent of the total circulation of daily newspapers; (3) that
a proprietor who controlled more than 8 per cent of the daily newspaper market was debarred from owning a television network; and
(4) that no one might control more than 20 per cent of all media
(Mazzolini, 1991, p. 183). The salient point here is that the monopoly
owner of commercial broadcasting channels in Italy, Silvio Berlusconi, was not a press baron. The original source of Berlusconi's
wealth had been the real estate field. The interests that he had meanwhile acquired in the press sector certainly did not place him in the
category of a Murdoch, Hersant, Springer, Bertelsmann, and the rest.
His press interests could be painlessly divested (*Il Giornale* was actu-

ally bought by his brother). Moreover, his other main media interest was his advertising sales giant *Publitalia*, about which the law was silent. Berlusconi's ownership of no fewer than three television channels was not put in question.

In France, very complex restrictions had been placed on cross-media ownership by the 1986 Law on Freedom of Communication. However, Tunstall and Palmer (1991, p. 161) note that at the national level a single 'group [could] own terrestrial television, radio and cable interests as well as daily newspapers'. That is, so long as the radio audience did not exceed 30 million inhabitants; the terrestrial TV audience was no greater than 4 million; that for the cable service no more than 6 million inhabitants; and the press interests did not exceed a combined circulation of more than 20 per cent of total circulation of the daily press. The rules left satellite services out of consideration. Tunstall and Palmer go on to note how these restrictions did 'not appear to have hindered the media diversification strategies' of a number of media groups. Certainly, Hersant was able to diversify extensively beyond his press empire into radio broadcasting. Moreover, there were no provisions against cross-ownership with advertising interests. Nothing debarred advertisers from part-owning television services. Havas was able to own the pay-TV company Canal Plus and Publicis was able to become a leading investor in M6. The Hersant empire too had its own advertising agency, Publiprint. Significantly, one of the main reasons that French policy makers gave for the fairly liberal nature of these provisions was their concern not to penalise French media groups in competition with their European counterparts (Tunstall and Palmer, 1991, p. 160–161).

By contrast, the British 1990 Broadcasting Act retained some exceedingly strict cross-media ownership provisions. These were largely inherited from the previous duopoly model and might well be taken as a mark of the acknowledged success and worthiness of this model. All the same, it is worth noting that there already existed in Britain a thriving and diverse commercial broadcasting sector. There was no need to nurse one into life. Existing ITV companies were very keen to retain their commercial broadcasting franchises. Other commercial media interests (like Carlton TV) were equally keen to displace them. A cynic might say, there was no need to fashion legislation so as to facilitate more diversification into broadcasting. It was relatively easy to be virtuous.

Table 6.6 Restrictions on cross-ownership of press and broadcasting in Western Europe

Country	Nature of restriction
Austria	None (but legislation being considered).
Belgium (fr)	None (francophone press actually encouraged to become involved in private commercial broadcasting).
Belgium (fl)	A cross-media requirement! The new private TV company had to have minimum of 51% of its shares held by Flemish publishers.
Denmark	None.
France	Complex, but not restrictive enough to prevent Hersant gaining extensive broadcasting holdings (25% of La Cinq; a network of local radio stations).
Germany	No nationwide restrictions. Some *Länder* have fairly strict rules regarding local 'double monopolies'; others are notably lax. Publishers are the major backers of German private broadcasting.
Greece	None.
Ireland	Publishers restricted to 30% stake in TV or radio operation.
Italy	Publisher with more than 8% of press market restricted to ownership of one national TV channel; if less than 8%, ownership of two channels allowed.
Luxembourg	None.
Netherlands	Publisher with more than 25% of press market cannot hold broadcasting licence.
Norway	None.
Portugal	None.
Spain	Very restrictive. Shares in TV company restricted to 15% if applicant has 15% interest in the press.
Sweden	None.
Switzerland	None.
UK	Very restrictive. Maximum 20% holding (for any kind of cross ownership). However, Rupert Murdoch has escaped this regulation so far (by dint of BSkyB's being broadcast 'offshore' from Luxembourg's Astra satellite).

Sources: A. Sánchez-Tabernero *et al.*., *Media Concentration in Europe*, Media Monograph No. 16. Dusseldorf: European Institute for the Media, 1993, pp. 220 221; and Commission of the European Communities, Pluralism and Media Concentration in the Internal Market, *COM (92) 480 final, Commission Green Paper, Brussels, 23 December 1992, pp. 40–52.*

The main cross media provisions of the legislation were as follows: (1) advertising agencies and associates of advertising agencies, including any body controlled by these, continued to be disqualified from holding broadcasting franchises; (2) also disqualified was any body in which a person falling within these categories was a participant with more than a 5 per cent interest; (3) no owner of a national or local newspaper could have more than a 20 per cent stake in any body holding a broadcasting franchise, and vice versa; (4) newspaper owners were prohibited from having a significant financial interest in more than one franchise; to be precise, this meant that no owner of a national newspaper who already had more than a 5 per cent stake (up to the permitted 20 per cent) in a franchise-holding body could have a holding of more than 5 per cent in any other such body, and vice versa; and (5) owners of a local newspaper were debarred from holding above 20% of a body holding a local broadcasting franchise, and vice versa. These regulations were slightly more relaxed than those previously in operation under the IBA guidelines, but the 1990 Broadcasting Act actually now entrenched them in statute. However, as already averred, in early 1994 the National Heritage Secretary announced a review of these restrictions. He had meanwhile come under very intense business pressure, and also been leaned on by the Department of Trade and Industry, to relax the rules which were seen as an obstacle to the development of indigenous media interests as internationally competitive players. This was, of course, a classic argument in favour of 'competitive deregulation'!

However, the British case illustrated a fundamental problem, of a very practical nature, with national-level regulations of this kind in the age of trans-national broadcasting by satellite. Ever since the launch of Rupert Murdoch's Sky TV – now BSkyB – the commercial satellite broadcasting service had been able to circumvent British cross-media ownership restrictions by virtue of being broadcast from the Luxembourg based Astra satellite. Rupert Murdoch, remember, already owned a substantial portion of the British national press. Now he was also proprietor of one of Europe's largest commercial broadcasting companies, beaming a whole range of channels into Britain from an offshore operation. Even after the 1990 merger of Sky TV with British Satellite Broadcasting (BSB) (the latter having been franchised originally by the IBA as a British-based company) the resultant company BSkyB, half-owned and effectively controlled by Murdoch, counted as a non-domestic broadcaster for the purposes of the Act; this was the case despite the fact that overwhelmingly the channel's audience was British (and Irish). Other British commercial media interests complained bitterly about Murdoch's 'circumvention' of Britain's domestic ownership restrictions. However, this did not prevent them from using this precedent as an argument in favour of relaxing existing cross-ownership rules!

Against cross-ownership provisions, it has been widely argued that they impede the development of internationally competitive media companies in Europe. This view, increasingly assuming the character of conventional wisdom, stresses the economic irrationality of discouraging willing investors from a new field of activity that already carries formidable entry costs and commercial risks. Quite clearly, official policy makers, increasingly guided by the national economic stakes of encouraging commercial broadcasting, have been receptive to this kind of calculation. This is shown by the German, Italian and French cases described above. Britain, too, seemed poised to relax its much stricter ownership provisions that had been inherited from an earlier era. Certainly, the government was under pressure to produce a measure of 'competitive deregulation'.

In the case of small countries, specifically, it was even possible to detect a cultural policy dimension to the argument against having such provisions: the need to protect very vulnerable indigenous media interests. The Belgian case provided a good illustration of this apparent paradox. A small country, its media industries were further weakened, and its markets rendered even smaller, by its fragmentation into two linguistic communities. It was, therefore, entirely understandable that policy makers in the Flemish part of the country should have enacted a Cable Decree (virtually all broadcasting in Belgium being conducted by cable) designed to afford protection to endangered Flemish press interests. It did this simply by making a majority shareholding by the Flemish press a positive requirement for all new commercial broadcasting services licensed in that part of the country. On the other hand, this example shows how small countries found themselves in an impossible dilemma. The measure of external cultural protection gained had, of course, to be weighed against the loss of internal media pluralism it entailed.

Promotion of the 'independents'

The British case, again, provided a good example of how pluralism in the producer field might be encouraged by legislation aimed at reducing concentration, this time in the form of the vertical integration of large broadcasting organisations. However, this type of measure was aimed less at the new commercial broadcasters who were likely to operate more as 'publisher/contractors' buying in the large part of their programmes. Rather it was a measure aimed directly at loosening up the vertical integration of their competitors: the existing ITV companies and the BBC with their large in-house production capacities. In fact, this kind of vertical integration was typical of Europe's public-service broadcasters. In practice, therefore, the adoption of this kind of measure was part of the Europe-wide liberalisation of the industry. It was designed to free up the market and, in the British case certainly, to undermine the alleged 'restrictive' practices of established producer interests.

In Britain, the IBA had always been required to ensure that there was adequate competition in the supply of programmes within the ITV network. In practice, though, it was undeniable that the larger companies within the network (e.g. Granada, Central, etc.) had tended to dominate the sector. The BBC, too, had been virtually a monopoly producer. The 1990 Broadcasting Act, therefore, introduced a stipulation that a minimum of 25 per cent of production should come from the United Kingdom's very dynamic independent production sector, previously a supplier mainly of Channel 4. On the one hand, this measure could rightly be evaluated as potentially a very positive step for the industry as a whole (the BBC, too, was bound by it) despite the negative effects experienced by the workforces of the larger broadcasters forced to compete in this way. On the other hand, within the wider context of a deregulated commercialised system, some negative effects could be expected as well. Increased commercial competition inevitably produces a powerful incentive to minimise costs of production. This element of vertical disintegration of the public-service broadcasters could, therefore, easily produce a general production environment less conducive to creativity than before. A deterioration of working conditions might afflict both the in-house studios of the established broadcasters and those of the independent sector. Certainly, there was evidence of a 'casualisation' of the British broadcasting workforce in the early

1990s. Finally, particular care has to be taken to prevent large commercial companies and international conglomerates from exploiting this kind of quota at the expense of genuinely independent small producers. Moreover, independents were vulnerable to merger and acquisition activity in the industry. Lastly, it was questionable how independent they were of the large programme contractors.

How should we measure media concentration?

To conclude this discussion of the emerging structure of the European commercial broadcasting market, it is important to make the following points. Firstly, it could be argued that internationalisation positively decreased media concentration. It could be argued that both viewer choice and international cultural exchange were increased by the additional programme service provision arising simply from the establishment of new channels. Secondly, the new commercial broadcasting markets were still in their early days; corporate developments were still fluid. Some enterprises failed spectacularly (e.g. La Cinq – see next chapter), new ones were still being founded. Entering the market, as has been emphasised in the above discussion, was a high risk venture. Competition for audiences and revenue was very fierce. Moreover, the market was becoming more fragmented and could expect to become far more so, with the arrival of digital broadcasting (see the Conclusion). It could be argued that if the new commercial sector was to thrive, then new sources of investment would need positive encouragement, not regulatory discouragement. Thirdly, from a democratic pluralist perspective, the crucial test of the corporate strategies that have been described, is whether or not they increased the variety of information, and other media fare, presented to the public. To suggest that the expansion of powerful multinational multi-media corporations necessarily constituted a threat to pluralism, was arguably to make an ideological point rather than a statement of fact. Much more empirical monitoring of media performance was required. Finally, there was an undeniably difficult problem of defining markets in the new media environment; this raised real problems for the actual measurement of concentration. As Lensen (1992, p. 13) has put it: 'failure to recognise intermedia competition overestimates concentration ... [and yet] there is no consensus regarding the extent to which intermedia competition should be considered in defining the relevant market'.

The issue of market definition was crucial to the debate about whether there should be more cross-media flexibility in Britain. In this connection, it is interesting to conclude with a brief word about the case for de-regulating Britain's rather strict ownership rules. The British Media Industry Group – a lobbying group made of a number of leading British press concerns – produced a report in 1995 that made the point that media influence should be measured by share of 'voice' in the media at large. Newspaper circulation, television viewing and radio listening figures should all be taken into account. Given that much of radio fare was music, which did not impact on people's views, it might count for less and be correspondingly 'down-weighted' against newspaper circulation and TV viewing. The results were designed to reassure government that current levels of media concentration did not justify the present rules (which hampered these media interests in international competition). According to share of national media 'voice' the report found the BBC to have about 20 per cent, followed by News International with just over 10 per cent. A number of groups keen to expand their media operations had very modest shares by this measure. The Granada group had only 2.5 per cent; Pearson, 2.3 per cent; and the Guardian Media Group, 2.0 per cent. Beside the BBC, even News International's share of national media 'voice' looked distinctly modest (the *Guardian*, 22 March 1995, p. 8).

The BBC, of course, was not owned by a global media baron. Also, its output was strictly regulated to provide impartiality, balance, pluralism and diversity. Yet, a case could still be made for arguing that Britain's very strict cross-media rules were a carry-over from another era. They plainly did not affect all players equally. Notably, BSkyB was allowed to escape the restrictions. There was a strong case for restricting News International's (Rupert Murdoch's) expansion in British media markets, but the existing restrictions on other – British owned – media interests served merely to entrench News International's dominance. Furthermore, the distinctions between the press and the broadcast media were becoming far less significant than in the days when there were fewer sources of information available. In the multi-channel future, when many individual television stations could be expected to serve a diminishing share of the overall audience, was it fair to want to restrict cross-media ownership and the development of internationally viable multi-media companies at this early stage in the development of the market? A case could be made for actively encouraging commercial media interests across Europe. After all, the latter's common refrain was that they promised to build up the European broadcasting industry and to allow it to compete more competitively in international media markets. The new private sector players, it was certainly the sanguine hope of many, might provide an important stimulus to Europe's indigenous film industry as well as to its independent television and video production sector. The growth of 'Euromedia' conglomerates, accordingly, might be seen as a way for Europe to compete on better terms (mainly) with US media firms. However, others voiced caution. As we shall now see, there was good reason to proceed carefully.

Guide to further reading

Commission of the European Communities, *Pluralism and Media Concentration in the Internal Market*, COM (92) 480 final, Brussels, 1992.

K. Dyson and P. Humphreys with R. Negrine and J.-P. Simon, *Broadcasting and New Media Policies in Western Europe*, London/New York, Routledge, 1988.

R. Lorimer, *Mass Communications: A Comparative Introduction*, Manchester/New York: Manchester University Press, 1994. Chapter 4.

R. Negrine and S. Papathanassopoulos, *The Internationalisation of Television*, London/New York: Pinter, 1990, especially Chapter 7.

A. Sánchez-Tabernero *et al.*, *Media Concentration in Europe: Commercial Enterprise and the Public Interest*, Düsseldorf: European Institute for the Media, 1993.

J. Tunstall and M. Palmer, *Media Moguls*, London/New York: Routledge, 1991.

7

The impact of deregulation on programme services and the policy implications

Chapter 4 has already explained how there is a link between the financial structures of the broadcasting system, and the maintenance of programme range and quality. During the period of public monopoly programming regulations were only ever part of the explanation for the fulfilment of public-service programme requirements (diversity, quality, a balance between popular and serious programmes, etc.). The other pillar of the system was the fact that there had been little or no competition for the same source of financing. Competition for viewers, therefore, had not been of 'existential' importance to the broadcasters. Broadcasters even competed to produce quality programmes; there was no need simply to chase mass audiences in order to maximise revenue. This chapter focuses on how this state of affairs has been affected by marketisation. The first thing to say is that it is still early days in the development of the new paradigm; yet there are already clear signs of how it is shaping up.

Chapter 5 presented some reasons why the European viewer might reasonably have expected the expansion of channels to increase the range and variety of programmes on offer, above that offered by the public service monopoly paradigm. It showed how the promise of greatly increased consumer choice was the ideological battering ram deployed by the commercial broadcasting lobby during the fierce media policy debates of the 1980s. The removal of technical and regulatory constraints on market entry and operation, it was argued, would result in a medium increasingly resembling the press, supposedly characterised by multiple and diverse products and the rule of consumer sovereignty. New broadcasting markets were now expected to experience much the same pluralisation as a result of the abolition of bureaucratic public-service monopoly structures. After all, did not sheer expansion of the sector imply greater variety? Would there not now also be a greater specialisation of channels? Not only would there be more choice of entertainment channels, would not the public-service channels now be able to concentrate their resources on producing more minority interest programmes?

Automatic benefits from competition?

Expectations of automatic benefits were, in fact, rather idealistic. The new broadcasters had had to lay out huge sums to set up their new services. Long after operating profitability was achieved, the original start up investment still had to be amortised. In a deregulated market, it was reasonable to expect that – for a period at least – spending on programming would feature rather low down the new operators' scale of priorities. This could easily result in a drift 'down market' that would be difficult to reverse, not least because it encouraged imitation.

The plethora of new channels were now all competing for a limited and ultimately finite source of revenue; advertising was still the main source. Advertising might have experienced a long boom in the 1980s, but now more channels depended upon it. Under such circumstances competition became fiercer. In addition, audience fragmentation – another logical consequence of channel multiplication – made the competition to attract advertisers even more remorseless. Faced with these economic realities, the new commercial broadcasters had every reason to rely upon the kind of programming that was most likely to maximise audiences and that was at the same time relatively inexpensive. Such programming typically comprised light entertainment programmes, game-shows, cheap drama series and popular 'soaps'. Repeats and US imports were particularly attractive. Actually to produce programmes was more costly than to buy them in packages, or to run repeats: therefore there was unlikely to be much innovation. In the absence of countervailing regulatory intervention, programming schedules based on commercial criteria were likely to reflect this kind of imbalance towards inexpensive entertainment fare.

Further, the new marketised scenario brought the serious risk of a crisis of public-service broadcasting as well. By the 1980s most public-service broadcasters in Europe were supplementing their licence revenue by carrying advertising, sometimes considerable amounts (see Table 4.3). Therefore, very directly the public-service broadcasters were now caught up in the competitive scramble for audiences – to maintain their share of a distinctly finite source of income that was now in much greater demand. This meant that they too had to pay attention to economic as well as cultural and social criteria in the determination of their programme schedules. They faced a growing temptation to follow their commercial competitors 'down market'.

No longer able to rely upon captive audiences, they feared a desertion of viewers to the new private channels on a scale that would undermine their status. Worse still, they worried that they would find it increasingly difficult to justify the television licence fee, and its continuance. How long could politicians – even if they were very favourably disposed to the concept of public-service broadcasting – be expected to support a licence fee high enough to meet their requirements, when viewers were watching fewer and fewer of their programmes? If licence fee income fell in real terms then they would have little choice but either to lower the quality of their programming or else to reduce the range of quality programming. Their ability to provide a fully comprehensive service was at stake. If instead they rationalised the scope of their output to maintain its quality, they faced the prospect of being relegated to a public-service 'ghetto' (like PBS in the United States). Either way, they faced a crisis.

Their quandary was exacerbated by their loss of exclusive rights to, and the inflation of prices for, certain key categories of programme. Sports programming was an obvious example. Private commercial broadcasters, in particular those funded by subscription like BSkyB, had judged major sporting events to be a key populariser of their services and had been prepared to invest large sums in order to outbid their public sector competitors for key sporting events. Much the same applied to feature films and popular drama series. In the long term, the loss to the public sector or the reduction of such programmes could have a damaging effect on the general public's support for its continued funding by the universal television licence fee. On the other hand, forced to pay inflated prices for strategic programme rights, the public broadcasters' ability to concentrate resources on in-house quality production would suffer. Again, either way they faced a problem; that is, unless governments could be persuaded to intervene on their behalf and grant them licence fee increases that took account of this inflationary effect. Governments, though, were reluctant to incur the unpopularity that this entailed. (A more popular measure would certainly be to retain key sports fixtures as 'listed events').

Negative effects of too much competition: the French and Italian examples

France provided an interesting case study of a very ill-judged and mismanaged marketisation of the sector. By the end of the 1980s it was one of the most deregulated and commercialised systems in Western Europe. Most notably, the main public-service channel, TF1, had been privatised. Even from a purely commercial point of view, the result was disastrous. TF1's main commercial competitor, La Cinq, could not withstand the unequal competition unleashed thereby. La Cinq was liquidated in 1992, before which the channel had accumulated losses of nearly Ffr. 4 billion. TF1 quickly came to dominate the mainstream broadcasting market in France. So much for the promised pluralism! The two remaining terrestrial public-service channels, Antenne 2 and FR3 (now renamed France 2 and 3), suffered badly. Both were losing money and audience share. Falling advertising revenues without any compensatory increase in their licence fee income were resulting in cuts in their budgets. This further inhibited their competitiveness and, in a vicious spiral, contributed to their increasing marginalisation. It is true, the French did launch a number of cultural satellite channels, TV5, La Sept and Arte (which replaced La Sept – see later), all of them interesting collaborative ventures with other European public service broadcasters. However, none of them amounted to mainstream television; they were limited to cable and satellite delivery until Arte took over La Cinq's transmission network in 1992. The one great success story of French broadcasting policy was Canal Plus (which broadcast off-air); this had become one of Europe's most successful pay TV services with joint ventures in Belgium, Spain and Germany. But it ranked as a distinctly 'specialist' commercial service. In the mid 1990s it had around five million French subscribers.

The French experience would seem to suggest the need for regulating markets if they are to prosper. It offered headstrong free marketeers and privatisers several important lessons. Firstly, even if total amount of television adspend (ie. spending on advertising) increases, it is still a finite quantity. Ultimately, the more channels that depend upon it, *ceteris paribus* the less there will be for each. Of course, television advertising may increase and individual channels may 'win' in this new situation. TF1 had seen its share of total TV advertising revenue increase from around 40 per cent to well over 50 per cent. Moreover, television advertising in France more than doubled between 1986 and 1992. However, broadcasting costs also escalated. In the event, advertising revenues did not increase sufficiently to support La Cinq as well as TF1 under these circumstances. Secondly, under conditions of unregulated competition the overmighty (such as privatised public-service giants) drive out the weak. Freed from its former public-service regulatory ceiling on advertising, TF1 had deployed all its inherited resource advantages (expertise, programme stocks, etc.) to capture the market. Most importantly, it was in a position to offer lower advertising rates than its fledgling competitors. The swift demise of La Cinq showed how, rather than open up the market, unregulated competition could serve very quickly to close it down.

Thirdly, fierce competition for programmes (eg. sports events, popular films, etc.) and media stars, in a free market, can actually be expected to drive up certain strategic costs. In France, this reached excessive dimensions. Not least for this reason, the frequently mooted cost and efficiency gains of liberalisation have to be seen in a qualified light. Fourthly, these kinds of increased costs, combined with squeezed profit margins or as yet unattained profitablity thresholds, lead companies to search for compensatory cost savings. These can be made by divesting production resources and relying more on buying in cheaper programmes (low quality series, game shows, etc.). This trend was much in evidence in France. Broadcasters succumbed to the temptation to drive 'down market' in order to maximise the audience they might deliver to the advertisers. When re-elected in 1988, it is true, the French Socialists attempted to salvage something from the mess. However, reversal of the Right's privatisation of TF1 was not attempted. Instead, characteristically, the reflex was protectionist (see below).

Italy, too, testifies to a similar kind of development. This country was another leading example of deregulation in Western Europe. In Italy's case, as suggested, there was a long period of virtual non-regulation of the private commercial sector. Right from the start, Berlusconi's three commercial channels had relied heavily on American or American-style entertainment programmes. The reaction of the public-service broadcasters was predictable: RAI massively increased its supply of popular entertainment programmes and ran more and more American imports bought in packages direct from Hollywood (Dyson and Humphreys, 1988, p. 24–25). An empirical survey (of a two week period in 1991) found that just under half of the movies shown by RAI were of American origin (48 per cent) while the proportion was well over half (56 per cent) for the private commercial channels. Much more surprising was the finding that the American proportion of series run on the Italian public-service channels, at no less than 90 per cent, actually exceeded that of Berlusconi's private commercial channels, at 67 per cent (De Bens *et al.*, 1992, pp. 90–93). Tunstall and Palmer (1991, p. 32) noted that in the late 1980s 'Berlusconi's initial near total reliance on Hollywood programming was somewhat reduced [as] Berlusconi made more of his own programming.' However, this anomaly had a simple explanation: 'much of the home-made or in-house programming was based on local versions of American game shows'.

By the early 1990s, both RAI and the private broadcasters in Italy were facing a financial crisis as a result of the escalating costs produced by unbridled competition. By September 1993 the RAI had run up a deficit of ITL 281.6 billion or £115 million (ECU 150 million). As in France, the RAI's problems stemmed from the 'savage struggle for audiences with the Berlusconi group'. RAI's difficulties, meanwhile were greatly exacerbated by the crisis of the political system upon which its channels had come to depend so much. By the end of 1992, Berlusconi's Fininvest group, too, had accumulated a massive debt of ITL 3,333 billion or £1.4 billion (ECU 1.7 billion). The interest charges on this debt amounted to about ITL half a billion or £204 million (ECU 261 million), 'almost double the [then] current losses of RAI'. Since these exceeded the group's profits, Berlusconi now found himself having 'to give careful attention to the opinion of his bankers' (Altichieri, 1993, pp. 28–29).

A general lesson from these two cases was that there were real risks involved in backing new commercial broadcasting operations (unless they were privatised public channels like TF1) particularly if to do so meant relying on external sources of finance. A recession in press advertising that set in at the end of the 1980s exposed the vulnerability of the French press companies that backed the ill-fated La Cinq venture: Robert Hersant's group and Hachette. In their eagerness to diversify and expand into broadcasting both had became heavily indebted to financial institutions and subsequently found themselves in considerable financial difficulties. Berlusconi's difficulties were a similar case. Even Rupert Murdoch's global media empire narrowly escaped a crisis of overextension of the beginning of the 1990s (Belfield *et al.*, 1994).

Britain: how blunted was Thatcherite deregulation?

In Britain's case, both the commercial and the public-service aspects of the sector suffered less than in France and Italy. As suggested, deregulation turned out to be less dramatic than had seemed likely at the height of Thatcherism. Enough Conservatives had been reluctant to deregulate too much what had undoubtedly been a quality broadcasting system that combined commercial enterprise with public-service provision. An energetic, and quite successful, lobbying exercise had been conducted by the traditional broadcasting policy community to secure some damage-limitation. Moreover, this lobby had friends in government (not least the minister who played a lead role in drafting the Bill). During the legislative process, a series of key public-service safeguards had been inserted into the 1990 Broadcasting Act. A 'quality threshold' was added and the ITV companies saw themselves bound to continue to fulfil a number of public-service obligations: to supply news and information, local programming, and the like. Rather than be privatised as Thatcher had intended, Channel 4 too kept its special public-service remit. In fact, an arrangement was put in place especially to provide insurance against a shortfall of revenue for the culture- and minorities-orientated channel that had become so much a valued part of the British public-service model. In return for a commitment that the ITV companies would bail it out if it fell into difficulties, they were to receive from it an 'insurance premium' in good years. As a disincentive against the channel's self-commercialisation this was set at half the revenue it made over and above an allocated 14 per cent share of total television adspend on terrestrial television. On the face of it, this measure seemed to be well conceived. Channel 4's identity and future was secured.

However, the Act still went a certain distance down the road of deregulation. In the first place, the ITV companies (strictly speaking now called Channel 3) were granted freedom to schedule more entertainment during prime-time. Secondly, despite the safeguards mentioned, Channel 4 was still allowed to compete for advertising directly with the ITV companies. In fact, so commercially successful did it prove to be, that controversy soon erupted because the channel was paying so much in seemingly unnecessary 'insurance' to the ITV companies. Above all, though, it was the 'franchise auction', widely seen as an ill advised piece of doctrinaire extravagance, that destabilised ITV. In the event, the ITC chose to award no fewer than eight of the franchises to applicants who had not bid the higher sum but whom it judged to be capable of offering a better service. In this way, some famous names in British broadcasting were saved, among them Granada TV. However, other famous names were unsuccessful, notably Thames TV which lost its lucrative London week-day franchise to Carlton TV, a company which though no newcomer to the audiovisual field had still made little secret of its intention to act as a 'programme publisher' rather than a traditional ITV-type company with extensive in-house production facilities.

Probably the worst effect of the 'auction', though, had been to extract bids from the broadcasters which some would spend years recuperating (this in addition to paying the normal levy). To the benefit of the Treasury alone, certain ITV companies – notably Yorkshire TV – were saddled with a financial burden. This could not help but divert resources away from programming. Moreover, in the run up to the 'auction', the ITV companies had been compelled to re-prioritise their operations towards simple profitability. This had involved rationalising their workforces and in-house production centres, creating a marked worsening of industrial relations in the process. Indeed, the BBC had suffered a very similar fate; in this case the pressure came even more directly from the government. The changes made to the British broadcasting system may not have been nearly as dramatic as in certain other European countries. Nor had multi-channel television yet emerged as strongly; both cable and BSkyB were still limited in their audience reach. The duopoly's finances remained secure (especially in light of the 1994 White Paper's commitment to continue to underpin the BBC's licence funding). There had occurred a subtle marketisation all the same. As a result, the extent of the ITV companies' future commitment to public-service type programming policies was at least a matter of question. This was unsurprising: resources that might have been expected to flow to quality programmes, had been diverted to the Treasury. Concern was expressed by a 1994 ITC report singling out two ITV companies, for disappointing programming and requiring improvements (duly noted in its 1995 report). One thing was very clear. The IBA ethos survived within the ITC!

Germany: public service and the challenge of multi-channel television

Germany provided the best premonition of what the multi-channel future might look like. Rapidly becoming one the more densely cabled countries in Europe, the new media sector had grown very much faster than in Britain and France. The country entered the 1990s with no fewer than four substantial private commercial broadcasting channels, two of them very large operations indeed. It also had a range of smaller services on its extensive and still fast expanding cable infrastructure. Moreover, the leading channels were broadcasting terrestrially in much of the country as well as by cable. They were also available via an overabundance of satellite delivery systems (including Astra). The country had a host of local cable services, thematic or 'special interest' channels, foreign channels, and so on. Furthermore, regional 'third' channels were being broadcast nationwide by satellite channels and some new public-service satellite channels had been introduced in joint ventures with other European public broadcasters. Although one or two ventures failed, new ones replaced them; unlike in France and Italy, the economics of the sector had not neared collapse.

Though there were serious problems of inflating costs, both the public-service and the private broadcasters could be reasonably confident. There was a strong commitment to the public-service licence fee. Behind the impressive range of new private commercial channels stood an oligopoly of some of the strongest, largely internally financed, private commercial media companies in Europe (indeed Bertelsmann was a world class multi-media giant). Germany's was, in short, a competitive 'dual system'. On the other hand, as suggested, broadcasting reform had also been a more careful, measured, business. In particular, the Federal Constitutional Court had confirmed, unequivocally, in several crucial rulings over the period 1986 to 1994, that the very *sine qua non* for the establishment of a private commercial broadcasting sector was a requirement that public-service broadcasting should continue to provide a dynamic and comprehensive kind of 'basic provision' (*Grundversorgung*) according to time worn constitutional principles of balanced and diverse public-service programming. Moreover, there should be a commitment to the future development of the public-service pillar of the dual system. As seen, the court had originally established this principle when its 1986 Ruling laid the legal basis for the 'dual' broadcasting system.

With the widespread expansion of a commercial sector in Germany during the latter half of the 1980s and early 1990s, two trends became quickly apparent. Firstly, the public-service broadcasters' share of the viewing audience declined appreciably. This trend was all the more marked in Germany because of the rapid progress made in cabling the country and the fact that maximum use was made of local terrestrial spectrum to relay the new commercial channels. In 1988 the three public-service channels (ARD, ZDF and the 'Third' regional Channel) accounted between them for an audience share of no less than 89.4 per cent. However, by 1990 this had fallen to 68.7 per cent, and by 1992 to 52.3 per cent, barely half of the audience. Moreover, in cabled homes, one-third of the country by 1992, their share was by now reduced to well under half, 41.7 per cent. The main beneficiaries of this decline were the two main commercial channels, SAT 1 owned by the Springer/Kirch multi-media group and RTL owned by the Bertelsmann/WAZ/CLT multi-media alliance (Darschin and Frank, 1993, pp. 114–126).

Secondly, as well as eroding the audience shares of the public service broadcasters, the new private commercial broadcasters had registered a negative impact on their advertising revenues. In 1989 the ARD drew DM 935 million and the ZDF DM 679 million in advertising revenue. However, by 1993 the ARD's advertising revenue had fallen to DM 445 million and the ZDF's had plunged to DM 370 million. During the same period the private commercial broadcasters' advertising revenue had grown from DM 642 million to DM 4,114 million (*Medien Perspektiven Basisdaten 1994*, pp. 10 and 21). This predictable state of affairs, then, was a very good test both of the commitment laid on the German public-service broadcasters and of the regulators' ability to avoid a dash 'down-market'.

Moreover, the challenge was all the more serious given that in Germany the private commercial sector was – for the most part – dynamic and strong.

The German public-service broadcasters very soon found themselves accused by a number of pro-commercial interests, most notably by the private broadcasters' own industry association, of having gone 'down market'. At the same time, it was claimed that the new private broadcasters had themselves contributed positively to programme diversity and the country's 'culture industries'. A 'convergence', it was argued, was occurring. The pro-commercial lobby saw this as justification to call for the eventual abolition of advertising by the public-service broadcasters; they had, of course, a blatantly self-interested motive. However, independent empirical research conducted since 1985 suggested that there had occurred no self-commercialisation of the German public-service broadcasters. Rather the latter continued to adhere to the principles of providing a careful balance of information, culture, and entertainment and respect for socio-cultural diversity. The private commercial broadcasters, on the other hand, were shown to have relied heavily on the entertainment function. What masqueraded as 'convergence' was in fact 'infotainment'. They had also demonstrably relied on imported programmes, mainly from the US (Krüger, 1993, pp. 246–266; and Kiefer, 1992, pp. 614–623; for an overview in English, Humphreys, 1994, pp. 271–276).

The enduring commitment by Germany's public-service broadcasters to their special public-service remit could be explained by the ethos of the broadcasters themselves, by the regulatory culture in which they operated, and by the interventions of the Constitutional Court, which as seen helped determine it. An important reason was the political support the public broadcasters continued to receive; this was manifest in the periodic upward revisions of the licence fee (though the public broadcasters claimed they were inadequate). The amounts invariably involved some political tussle, but there was little serious questioning so far of the licence-fee's future. There were some controversial calls for dramatic cuts in the public-service broadcasting service but everyone was well aware that the Constitutional Court would throw out any such suggestion. Also, national re-unification in 1990 had served to bolster political support for the public broadcasters' important role in integrating the citizens of the former GDR (see Humphreys, 1994; Dyson, 1992).

Cross-national research into broadcasting finance and programme quality

The findings from the national case-studies reported above have been confirmed by several cross-national studies. In the mid-1980s Blumler *et al.* (1986, pp. 343–364) conducted a cross-national study into the impact of changing structures of broadcasting finance on programme quality* It included a content analysis of the range of programmes available to prime-time (ie. peak viewing period) audiences in seven countries with different broadcasting structures. Five of them were European countries at different stages of marketisation; these were Britain, France, Germany, Italy and Sweden. The other two were Australia and the US, the latter's system being the only throughly commercial one. Blumler *et al.* admitted that cross-national comparison was difficult: the countries varied considerably according to population size and resources, broadcasting traditions and structures, and so on. They were able, however, to detect 'signs of a drift across most systems towards more avid competition for large audiences (even among public-service broadcasters) and the provision of more mass-appeal programming' (p. 347). Furthermore, they concluded that the 'evidence suggest[ed] that broadcasting systems which [were] most dependent on advertising also schedule[d] the narrowest range of programming' (p. 351).

That public-service regulation and the absence of commercial competition mattered for programme quality, seemed to be confirmed by their finding that Britain – which remained dominated by the duopoly and at that time had very little new media – stood up 'very well to international comparison' (p. 351). Moreover, the ITV companies, which had not yet been subjected to the marketising rigours of the 1990 Broadcasting Act, offered a 'programme range ... superior to most ... other purely commercial channels' (p. 351). By contrast, Italy's Canale 5, one of three private channels owned by Silvio Berlusconi's Fininvest company scheduled largely light entertainment and foreign series; it also ran 'far and away the largest amount of advertising' (p. 351), higher even than the US commercial networks. The study by Blumler *et al.* also drew upon a

---

* The findings were originally reported to the Peacock Committee on financing the BBC, which in the event came down against the BBC being alloweed the option of advertising.

number of reports from national experts. Worryingly, all of the European commentators commented upon a trend towards the increasing adoption of marketing criteria in the programme decisions of their respective national public-service broadcasters.

Sepstrup (1989, pp. 29–54) has made much of the distinction between different categories of broadcaster. As explained in Chapter Four, Sepstrup distinguished between what he called 'non-commercial' and 'commercial' public broadcasters, the former being solely dependent on licence fee income and the latter drawing supplementary revenue from advertising. Both categories of public-service broadcaster, though, were to be distinguished from private commercial channels. In his study Sepstrup produced aggregate data showing that in one week in 1986 Europe's 'non-commercial' public broadcasters had scheduled the least entertainment programming in prime-time (on average 46 per cent). They were closely followed by the 'commercial' public broadcasters (52 per cent). The private commercial broadcasters, unsurprisingly, ran mainly entertainment programmes (86–88 per cent). On the basis of this information Sepstrup hypothesised, echoing Blumler *et al.* (see above), that 'the role of entertainment programming [wa]s strongly correlated with profit goals and probably with public service channels being advertising financed or not'. Moreover, Septrup's overall conclusion was a grim one: that pressures towards commercialisation – encouraged by the European Community's liberalising policies (see Chapter 8) – were likely to lead, over time, to the decline of public-service, broadcasting.

This prediction has been given some substance by a more recent survey, conducted by members of the Euromedia Research Group (De Bens *et al.* in Siune and Truetzschler, 1992, pp. 75–100). They examined the programmes transmitted by fifty-three European stations, both private commercial and public service, during a two week period in January 1991 and came to the following broad conclusions. Predictably, the survey revealed that 'the new commercial TV stations programme mainly entertainment and fiction' (p. 95). More disturbingly, they found that the reliance of Europe's public-service broadcasters on 'popular' as distinct from 'serious' programming was significantly higher than they had expected. Considered alongside the findings of a similar study they had conducted in 1988, the 1991 data led de Bens *et al.* to suggest 'that the proportion of serious programmes on European public stations [was] decreasing (p. 83).

They concluded that 'the process of commercialization ha[d] had a downmarket effect on the overall TV supply'. The public-service broadcasters ran 'the risk of abandoning their *raison d'être* (p. 95).

All the same, some public broadcasters appeared to be more at risk than others. De Bens *et al.* found that the German and Norwegian public broadcasters, closely followed by the Belgians, British, Swiss and the Swedish, all ran a balanced service overall, although they noted, too, that only the Germans, the Norwegians and the Swiss maintained this performance in prime-time. It is interesting to observe, linking back to Blumler *et al.* and Sepstrup (see above), that all these better performing public broadcasters were either 'non-commercial' (i.e. wholly licence-fee funded) or else they ranked among the most strictly regulated 'commercial' public broadcasters in Europe. De Bens *et al.* noted that individual public stations – notably, FR3 (France), WDR (Germany), NOS3 (Netherlands) and, exceptionally, the commercially funded Channel 4 (Britain) – carried more serious programming than the national average. This had a simple explanation: FR3, NOS3 and Channel 4 all had special remits to do so (see Chapter 4); WDR was one of Germany's most progressive public-service corporations. De Bens *et al.*'s data revealed, too, that among those public broadcasters most heavily reliant on popular programmes, especially in prime-time, were those of Spain where advertising was their principal source of funding and those of Italy where the broadcasting system was, as seen earlier in this and the last chapter, the most deregulated and commercialised in Western Europe. Furthermore, Antenne 2, the main public channel in France following TF1's privatisation, had the distinction of carrying a conspicuously heavier freight of fiction and entertainment than any other public broadcaster in Western Europe, around two-thirds of its schedule, more even than the privatised TF1 with which it was now competing. Was it a coincidence that Antenne 2 depended on advertising for around two thirds of its income? (Mattelart and Palmer, 1991, p. 544).

Kleinsteuber *et al.* (1991, pp. 33–54) have produced an important comparative analysis of' specific dualisation processes' in Europe. Like the earlier study by Blumler *et al.* they drew two non-European countries into the frame, this time Australia and Canada. Both of the latter countries had had long experience of dual broadcasting systems. Both the Australian and the Canadian experiences demonstrated that marketisation led to the increasing marginalisation of public-service broadcasting. Kleinsteuber *et al.* warned that the public broadcasters in these two countries had 'continuously lost range, finance and political support'. However, they also noted that European public broadcasters could draw on important reserves of strength. They were embedded in a very different culture; public broadcasting was very much part of the European identity. It still enjoyed considerable political and social support. Privileged in their sole claim to public funding and their superior production capacity, European broadcasters were proving themselves capable of withstanding the commercial challenge so far. In a number of countries – notably Scandinavia, Austria and Switzerland – the public-service broadcasters were still dominant (see Chapter 5). In Germany, the political mood had swung against deregulation. The British duopoly had experienced rather little change, at least so far. The French and Italian cases were exceptional. No other country in Europe had imitated France's privatisation of its major public-service broadcasting channel, a step which had clearly incurred damaging unintended consequences. No country in Europe other than Italy had left the commercial broadcasting sector virtually unregulated for well over a decade. Nevertheless, Kleinsteuber *et al.* spelt out the danger; most 'dualised' European systems produced sufficient data to suggest grounds for concern. Commercial broadcasters devoted few resources to in-house production, relied on entertainment programming and were conspicuously more dependent upon US imports. They certainly placed public broadcasters under competitive pressures. The future challenge for the public broadcasters, Kleinsteuber *et al.* concluded, was to withstand the commercial challenge without relinquishing their own distinctive goals and duties. Much depended, on the one hand, on the 'reactions and strategies' of the public broadcasters and, on the other hand, on the 'political will to maintain them' (p. 41).

The dilemma facing Europe's public-service broadcasters

Public-service broadcasting in Europe stands at a crossroads. The scale of the challenge it faces has become clear in the course of this chapter. So far, it would appear, much has depended on the manner by which the new 'marketised' paradigm has been introduced. In some countries the process of marketisation has been mismanaged.

In France both public-service and private broadcasters have paid the price for deregulation and privatisation. In Italy the broadcasting sector, both public and private, has found itself in a crisis that has been exacerbated by the political turbulence in that country. Yet in Germany, and indeed in a number of other northern European countries, the picture was very different. In Germany, the very precondition for introducing a commercial sector was a constitutional–legal guarantee for the public-service broadcasters, not simply assuring them a future but also stipulating their further development, including a full share in the opportunities presented by the new media. At the same time, the court showed itself sympathetic to the needs of the new private operators. In the court's view, the future possibilites for both the public and private parts of the 'dual system' were connected.

Without any question, the key factor for the future prospects of the public sector is the continuation of its basic public resource base: the licence fee. The point here is not that advertising *per se* is bad for public-service broadcasting, as Chapter 4 has already made very clear. Rather, it is competition for commercial sources of revenue that is pernicious on the quality of service provision. However, many disinterested observers (as well as free marketeers) have questioned seriously the long term future of the licence fee. The willingness of the public to pay it in the multi-channel future, it is often suggested, is bound to diminish progressively as audiences fragment and the share taken by the public channels decreases. Whether this developent will attain such consequential proportions, remains to be seen. What is often forgotten, is that television funded by the licence fee offers very good value for money. Quite patently, it is very cheap television. Compare it with the price of subscription services! On the other hand, we are still in the early days of multi-channel television and the pressure for abolition of the licence fee and a move to voluntary subscription may well become overwhelming.

For the moment, at least, the licence fee appears to be safe. Only free market radicals argue against it. Interestingly, few private commercial broadcasters want to see the public-service broadcasters competing with them more for commercial sources of revenue. In Britain, the 1986 Peacock report advised against advertising on the BBC, but did envisage broadcasting moving towards a consumer-based market system. In the multi-channel future promised by new technologies the licence fee could be replaced by subscription, pay-per-view and grants for public-service programmes. While the 1994 White Paper on the BBC still saw the licence-fee as the BBC's most appropriate primary funding mechanism until at least 2001, Peacock's vision may yet be realised (helped by digital broadcasting). Finally, in a thoroughly marketised paradigm the licence fee could be deemed one day to be an unfair subsidy for privileged broadcasters. Indeed, if the public-service broadcasters become too identified as commercial players in the new markets, they may be conniving in the removal of their privileged funding mechanism!

The public broadcasters certainly face compelling pressures to become more aggressive and 'internationally competitive' operations. The British White Paper on the BBC's future was quite explicit about this (Department of National Heritage, 1994). For a number of years, particularly under the entrepreneurial leadership of director-general John Birt, the BBC had already been commercialising its activities. Shortly before the publication of the 1994 White Paper the corporation had announced a deal with the leading British media group, Pearson, an internationally ambitious private sector multi-media player, to launch two European news and entertainment satellite channels. The White Paper gave this commercial orientation of the BBC further official encouragement. The government clearly saw no contradiction between the BBC retaining its domestic public-service character while becoming an internationally competitive commercial 'national champion'. Critics were not so confident about the compatibility of these twin identities. Yet, it is clear, Europe's public-service broadcasters cannot remain backward-looking. They cannot afford to remain wedded to cultural paternalism, nor can they afford to remain over-bureaucratic (although critics of 'Birtism' pointed – with apparent justification – to how his introduction of an 'internal market' within the BBC had actually increased the organisation's bureaucratisation). The public broadcasters have to respond to the new marketised realities. A strategy of embracing competition over-enthusiastically may be self-defeating but a strategy of ignoring the commercial challenge, would be equally harmful. In any case, it would be quite unrealistic to expect public-service broadcasters to remain unchanged by the marketisation of their environment. All the same, a strong case could be made for saying that they should 'compete complementarily' with the private broadcasters. In other words, they should continue to provide a comprehensive range of programming, mixing 'thoughtful and involvement-worthy mass appeal programmes with programmes targeted at the more defined tastes of smaller but more committed audiences' (Blumler and Hoffmann-Riem, 1992, p. 207). Yet, one thing was certain. Only if the public broadcasters continued to be granted adequate public support, would they be able to compete in this way. If not, then the possibilities were limited: they would *either* be compelled through financial constraint to retreat into a public-service 'ghetto' or they would be encouraged – if policy makers allowed – to increasingly commercialise their identity and scope of operation.

An Americanisation of European broadcasting?

So far, we have only touched – in passing – upon one of the most controversial issues that has been raised by the marketisation of West European broadcasting systems: namely that it would appear to have entailed an increased dependence by Western European broadcasters on American programme imports. Several studies – including two already mentioned above – have pointed to the strong correlation between the increased share of US-produced programme supply and the commercialisation of European broadcasting systems. In the words of Sepstrup (1989, p. 46): 'the more commercialisation, the more (US) imports and concentration of this import in prime time'.

In 1983, 73 per cent of total national supply of television programmes was domestically produced. Only 13 per cent came from the US. The rest was mainly accounted for by imports from other West European countries or co-productions. The American share of imports may have been impressive, but this share as a percentage of total national supply could hardly be counted as domineering (Sepstrup, 1989, p. 40; based on figures from Varis, 1985). In 1983, it is important to note, the West European broadcasting scene was still dominated by public-service channels; and the public-service broadcasters did not seem to be over reliant upon American imports. By 1986, however, over twenty new commercial channels had appeared. Drawing on commercial research data, Sepstrup (p. 47) found that the public broadcasters' reliance on US programmes as a share of their total programme supply varied between 10–15 per cent depending upon whether they were 'non-commercial' (solely reliant on public funding) or 'commercial' (part advertising funded). By contrast, in the case of the commercial broadcasters, the figure varied between 22 and 47 per cent. The statistical accuracy of these 1986 data, Sepstrup warned, was uncertain, but Sonnenberg (1990, p. 109) – drawing on a different source – has produced corroborating data. According to Sonnenberg's data, in 1986 the public service broadcasters in Western Europe were still showing around 12 per cent US imports (and, interestingly, Britain's ITV companies less than this average). By contrast, the new commercial sector relied on US imports for one-third of its programmes. Further, two thirds of the programmes on Berlusconi's three Italian commercial channels were US imports according to this source. This bore out Sepstrup's link between profit goals, reliance on entertainment, and US imports.

A number of years later, the 1991 Euromedia study by De Bens *et al.* (1992) found the European broadcasters to be heavily reliant on American imports for their supply of films and television series. The commercial channels were still more more dependent than public channels on imports. Averaged across Europe, the commercial sector drew two-thirds of its total supply of movies from the USA while the public sector drew only 45 per cent (and the figure would have been 42 per cent were it not for Ireland's public broadcasters' extraordinarily high reliance on the US for four-fifths of all films broadcast). French and Italian commercial channels were singled out as being strikingly reliant on American imports for around three quarters of their movies. De Bens *et al.* (p. 89–91) deemed the French case to be especially surprising given that France had the strongest film industry in Europe; it was even more surprising, they might also have mentioned, in view of France's – clearly nominal – protectionist quotas (see later). Commercial broadcasters in small states were found to rely heavily on US movies, a finding that was much less surprising.

The data provided by De Bens *et al.* (p. 92) suggest a more nuanced pattern for television series. On average, Europe's commercial channels drew just under two-thirds of this category of programme from the US whereas the average figure for the public sector was around 50 per cent. However, the dependence of Europe's large public broadcasters on imported US series was much lower than this European average: the figure for France was 44 per cent; for Germany, 34 per cent; and for Britain, 32 per cent. These large countries' public-service broadcasters, of course, had more impressive in-house production capacities than those of the smaller countries. Sweden's home production was also quite impressive, however the rest of Europe's small – or smaller – states were very dependent on foreign imports. It was interesting, all the same, that the public broadcasters in the other Scandinavian countries and Netherlands drew heavily on the rest of Europe for their imported series. The same could not be said of any of Europe's commercial channels which were overwhelmingly reliant upon US imports. Nor could it be said of movies; the latter programme category was manifestly Europe's Achilles' heel when it came to audiovisual production. De Bens *et al.* (1992, p. 96) estimated 'the outflow of revenue from Western Europe to the USA for programmes ... to be in the region of at least $800 million annually' and this already staggering figure could 'be trebled to include film and video rights'. Moreover, this was a one way traffic: 'only 2 per cent of programmes on US screens [came] from Europe' and these were overwhelmingly British.

In fact, Britain's programme industry was uniquely strong in European comparison. Britain was the world's second exporter of television programmes after the USA and maintained a positive trade balance in programmes throughout the 1980s. (Of course, English-language producers benefited from a tremendous competitive advantage in world markets). By contrast, France may have been the world's second largest exporter of cinema films, but by 1989 it was also Europe's biggest purchaser of US television programmes (Collins, 1994, p. 90). This was largely explained by the hunger of French commercial channels – including the privatised TF1 – for US programmes (as explained above). Overall, the extent to which the Europeans – and especially the French – had come to rely on US imports by the end of the decade was illustrated by 1988 figures produced by the 1989 *Assises de l'audiovisuel* (cited in Collins, 1994, p. 43). In 1988, the Europeans bought $700 million of US programmes. France accounted for $228 million of this sum, Germany $151 million, Italy $85 million, Britain $86 million and the others, $93 million. Such figures help explain French concern about an Americanisation of European culture!

Policy implications

Protectionism:

One possible policy response to the threat of 'Americanisation' was to embrace protectionism. From the outset of the broadcasting revolution, in the early 1980s, the French Socialists had inclined

towards such a course of action. The party's original enthusiasm
about cable television flowed partly from the rather idealistic hope
that it would offer a possible line of defence against foreign satellite
television and provide a vehicle for a flowering of French cultural
output. However, until the Right effectively privatised the cable programme and introduced a more liberal regulatory regime in 1986,
cable development made very slow progress in France. One reason,
ironically, had been the Socialists' 'stringent programme regulations
regarding the amount of local and national programming to be
shown on the networks' (Kuhn, 1995, p. 215). In the mid-1980s the
Socialist government tried to obstruct Luxembourg's satellite television ambitions on the grounds that the practically unregulated
Duchy would constitute a Trojan Horse for an invasion of 'Coca-
Cola' (ie. American) television. As seen, despite French interference,
the Luxembourgers went ahead with their own satellite plans and in
1988 the first Astra satellite beat its French – and German – competitors to the market (Dyson, 1990; Kuhn, 1988). Returned to power
in 1988 – and by now confronted with a thoroughly marketised
domestic broadcasting system – Socialist Culture Minister Jack Lang
emphasised the importance of observing national quotas of 60 per
cent of programmes made in Europe, 40 per cent of these having to
be of French origin. In fact, an attempt was made in 1990 to raise
the latter quota to 50 per cent. This bid failed in the face of the combined resistance of the European Commission and the French private
commercial lobby. The latter was by now a strong force in domestic politics and it was anyway inclined to ignore the quotas. Not so
easily disheartened, the French government concentrated instead on
championing the adoption by the European Union of protectionist
'Euro-quotas' (see Chapter 8). Thanks to French insistence, the EU
trade commissioner defended, within the GATT negotiations of
1994, the right of Europeans to subsidise their audiovisual industry.
Finally, the French government lent its weight to several pan-European initiatives designed to provide support to the industry. However, these defensive measures also had a certain 'symbolic' quality.
They could not disguise the fact that since the early 1980s French
domestic policies had themselves contributed to the 'Americanisation' of the country's broadcasting system (Fraser 1993, pp. 35–37).

Industrial support, co-productions and co-financing:

One of the more positive features of French thinking about how to defend Europe's audiovisual industries, was the stress that the Socialists laid on the need for increased industrial support for the audiovisual industries, particularly in the shape of more European co-production and co-financing of programmes. Co-productions are ventures where the various partners are involved both in sharing costs and in cooperating on the production of programmes. Co-financing deals are either where the producer interest looks for investors to share the production costs alone or else where buyers of the production are lined up in advance of production (Negrine and Papathanassopoulos, 1990, p. 99; Pragnell, 1985, p. 53). There are obvious advantages to be gained from this approach: notably, cross-border economies of scale. Indeed, there is some evidence to suggest that the internationalisation of European broadcasting has led broadcasting interests to engage in greater activity of this sort. Thus, the European public-service broadcasters have launched a European Production Group, the new commercial broadcasters have formed the European Consortium and the independent production sector has formed the European Producers Corporation (Sonnenberg, 1990, p. 113). As will be seen (in Chapter 8), during the 1980s the French Socialist government lent its weight to a number of pan-European government–industry initiatives to encourage precisely these kinds of cooperation. However, there are problems attached to co-production and co-financing ventures. As Sonnenberg (1990, pp. 112–114) has pointed out, the striking differences in production capacity between Europe's larger countries and its smaller ones, means that the latter would very often have to content themselves with a junior role. Another drawback was the probability, in Sonnenberg's view, that – overall – the production of only specific programme categories would be internationalised: primarily entertainment programmes. In this connection, Negrine and Papathanassopoulos (1990, p. 101) have observed a possible contradiction in, for instance, the French engaging in more joint-ventures with English-language partners – in order to break into world markets – if their programmes embrace North American production values as a result.

Support for the European film industry

As seen, American movies dominated this particular programme category of European broadcasting. Only France had managed to sustain a fairly successful domestic film industry. About one-third of the films shown in the country in 1993 were made in France; by European comparision this was an impressive market share. The French cinema had achieved this performance mainly thanks to governmental nurture and protection. For years the French had levied a special 13 per cent tax on cinema tickets, the proceeds of which were ploughed directly into production subsidies for the country's film industry. Public-service broadcasting, too, had always been – and furthermore continued to be – a protected market for the French cinema. The above-mentioned cross-national study by de Bens *et al.* (1992, p. 90) found that in 1991 a high 62 per cent of movies shown on the French public-service channels were still of home origin. The figure may have been a very low 20 per cent for the private commercial channels – which explained France's voracious appetite for US imports – but the 62 per cent share of the public channels represented a higher share of home-origin movies than was the case anywhere else in Europe. In Germany, the public broadcasters carried 41 per cent home-origin films; in Britain, 38 per cent. However, after TF1's privatisation in 1987, the public sector in France was rather more marginal than it was in either Britain or Germany. Lastly, Canal Plus – the terrestrial pay-TV channel launched with impressive state backing by the Socialists in 1984 – had become a major source of support to the French film industry. Not only did it provide a captive market for French films, it also financed them directly and, through a web of subsidiaries, played a role in production itself. A major investor in French cable, with off-shoots in Belgium, Spain and Germany, Canal Plus had considerably energised the market for French films (Kuhn, 1995, pp. 202–203). Post-war German cinema, too, has had its high spots. This could be partly explained by the support supplied by the public-service broadcasters in cooperation with a special Institute for Film Sponsorship (*Filmförderungsanstalt*); the latter was funded, as in France, by a levy on cinema tickets. The 1970s success of the 'New German Cinema' depended largely upon this indirect kind of public support (Porter and Hasselbach, 1991, p. 165). Under the so-called 'film/TV agreement' (*Film/Fernseh-Abkommen*) the public-service broadcasters themselves have contin-

ued to make a very substantial financial contribution to the production of works suitable for both television and cinema and, under
political pressure, the German private commercial broadcasters have
also begun to make a modest contribution (Porter and Hasselbach,
1991, p. 163). In Britain, in the 1980s, Channel 4 had helped to reviv-
ify the domestic film industry. Interestingly, BSkyB – mainly owned
by Rupert Murdoch's News International, as well as Granada and
Pearson – also claimed to have begun to make a significant contribution. BSkyB invested £13 million in the British film industry in
1994 through licensing films for pay-television distribution
(*Guardian*, 24 March 1995, p. 13).

Support for the independent production sector:

A potential source of dynamism in European programme production
was the 'independent sector'. As seen, public policy in Britain during
the 1980s was geared explicitly towards stimulating this sector. As
Chapter 8 will show, action was also taken at the level of the European Union to stimulate its growth. The sector was actually diverse.
It embraced a growing number of large industrial producers; among
these were well known names like Hachette Television in France,
Bavaria Atelier in Germany and Goldcrest in Britain. It also consisted of a far greater number of much smaller companies with low
capitalisation. Large and small alike, though, were beneficiaries of
the expansion of broadcasting markets in Europe. Although a few
European public-service channels had long been accustomed to commission from the independent sector – notably Britain's ITV companies and Germany's ZDF – the sector did not really amount to much
in Europe until the founding of Channel 4 in Britain which from 1985
onwards took much of its programming from the independents and
gave an important boost to the British film industry by commission-
ing a number of highly successful low budget films and drama series.
Before long, with the expansion of commercial broadcasting, independent production was taking off on the continent as well. However, it was questionable to what extent the 'Channel 4 equation' –
whereby the independents stimulated creativity – would be emulated.
There were some signs that a market logic would produce increased
conformity; also it was unclear how genuinely independent these
companies were of the broadcasters (Lange and Renaud, 1989, pp.
239–246).

Expanding public-service provision

Another positive initiative of the French Socialists, to counterbalance the commercialisation of French broadcasting, was to establish a number of new public sector services. Their first step in this direction was the launch in the early 1980s of a francophone cultural channel called TV 5. The channel, a cooperative venture of the public broadcasters in France, Belgium and Switzerland, used a Eutelsat telecommunications satellite to feed European cable systems. In the late 1980s, the French Socialists established another cultural channel called La Sept, and allocated it a channel on France's DBS satellite. La Sept's launch was partly a response to the need to provide the satellite (widely felt to be a white elephant) with programme services and partly a retort to the Right's privatisation of TF1 (many Socialists felt that a reversal of the privatisation would have been more appropriate). The principal concept behind La Sept, however, was to stimulate European cultural exchange and promote French culture: the channel was replaced in 1992 by a Franco-German cultural channel called ARTE. Until ARTE inherited the defunct La Cinq's transmission network, these channels were limited to cable and satellite homes. Cable penetration was higher than in Britain, but still very low by European comparison; satellite homes were very thin indeed on the ground (see Chapter 5). In Germany the public-service broadcasters, under their own initiative, launched two new channels of this kind. In 1984 they launched a satellite channel called 3 SAT in cooperation with the public broadcasters of Austria and Switzerland. This channel started off using a Eutelsat telecommunications satellite to feed cable systems. Later it was also relayed on a relatively large scale direct-to-home (DTH) via a number of satellites. The second public-service satellite German channel was called Eins Plus. Launched on Intelsat communications satellite in 1986, it too was later relayed DTH by several satellites. These channels benefited from wider domestic availability than their French counterparts because by the end of the decade Germany was very well supplied with new media (again, see Chapter 5). An addition to these public-service channels has been Euronews, a pan-European news channel launched in 1993, sponsored by the European Broadcasting Union (EBU) and drawing on the support of a whole range of European public-service broadcasters. The establishment of such channels represented a strategic alternative for public-service broadcasters, to that of engaging upon their own commercial operations in Europe. As a response to internationalisation, it was certainly more in tune with the philosophy of public-service.

The scale of the future challenge

As chapter 6 has described, in a little more than a decade the number of television channels available in Europe had risen from around forty in 1980 to well over a hundred in 1993. Admittedly, many of these new services were confined to cable and satellite systems and still had fairly limited audiences. Nevertheless, this massive increase in channels had led to a voracious demand for programmes. According to one study, within a decade the number of programme hours broadcast per year had risen from 120,000 in 1980 to 400,000 hours in 1990 (Lensen, 1992, p. 8). The latter figure was probably an underestimate. The EC Commission (1992, p. 2) produced data that put the 1989 figure at 480,000 hours. This figure broke down into: 30 per cent 'redistribution' (repeats, networking, European programme exchanges, etc.), 30 per cent broadcasters' own production, and 35 per cent programme purchases (the remaining 5 per cent accounted for by independent productions and coproductions). Moreover, it was estimated that the demand for television programmes would increase by 32 per cent to 635,000 hours by 1999. Somewhat disturbingly, this enormous increased demand was projected to be met by even greater reliance on the external purchase of programmes, expected to grow by 51 per cent. Indeed, it would fulfil no less than 40 per cent of the total 1999 demand. By contrast, broadcasters' own production would grow by a mere 7 per cent and meet a reduced 25 per cent of demand. These forecast trends – precipitously downward for European production as a share of total programming and upward for the share accounted for by purchases – were extremely worrying. Admittedly, the study predicted an 84 per cent growth in the number of independent and co-productions in Europe. Yet, this sector was still very undeveloped in Europe; this was manifest in the fact that it accounted for a mere 19,000 hours of programmes in 1989 and an expected 35,000 hours in 1999 (still only 5 per cent of total demand). The simple problem, therefore, was that projected growth in European productive capacity was not anywhere near equal to the huge leap in demand. In fact, a marked deterioration was in prospect; a vortex threatened to suck in even more imports.

It should, in fairness, be pointed out that much depends on the future strategy of Europe's new commercial broadcasters. At present Europe's new commercial broadcasters – struggling to amortise market entrance costs and become profitable – are responding to an immediate requirement for the bulk purchase of low cost programmes, hence their large reliance on cheap US imports. However, as Negrine and Papathanassopoulos (1990, p. 80) have pointed out, 'once established, their priorities may change to include investment in productions'. After all, in its early days, ITV in Britain relied heavily on low budget programmes, yet before long a significant share of the sector's huge profits were being ploughed back into quality programming. However, it should be pointed out that the ITV companies were both *required* to produce a quality service by the public-service regulation of the IBA and *able* to do so by dint of their monopoly profits (their advertising monopoly had been described as a licence to make money!). The ITV/IBA pattern is unlikely to be repeated in a more competitive and de-regulated market.

Guide to further reading

J.G. Blumler (ed.), *Television and the Public Interest: Vulnerable Values in West European Broadcasting*, London: Sage, 1992.

E. De Bens *et al.*, 'Television Content: Dallasification of Culture?', in K. Siune & W. Truetzschler (eds), *Dynamics of Media Politics: Broadcast and Electronic Media in Western Europe*, London: Sage.

H. Kleinsteuber *et al.*, 'Public Broadcasting im internationalen Vergleich', *Rundfunk und Fernsehen*, Vol 39, No. 1, pp. 33–54.

A. Lange and J.-L. Renaud, *The Future of the European Audiovisual Industry*, Manchester: European Institute for the Media, 1989, Media Monograph No. 10.

R. Negrine and S. Papathanassopoulos, *The Internationalisation of Television*, London/New York: Pinter, 1990, Chapters 5,6 and 8.

8

The European Community and pan-European broadcasting

Until the 1980s, regulation of the European mass media had been principally a matter of national policy-making. Certainly the International Telecommunications Union had always had to approve national decisions about frequency allocations and make recommendations about technical standards. Nevertheless, the latter were mainly the product of national strategies. Other technical matters remained largely the preserve of national telecommunications authorities together with competent agencies specific to broadcasting like the IBA (Britain) or *Télédiffusion de France* (France). Regulations governing programmes and their providers – including rules for advertising – were entirely determined by statute and codes of conduct at the national level. These reflected decisions made by national parliaments, courts and regulatory bodies (or by regional ones as in the German and Belgian cases). State frontiers circumscribed the spheres of application of press and broadcasting laws alike. Equally, the main policy actors were national ones: governments, parliaments, courts, political parties, and 'socially relevant groups'. Business lobbies, professional associations, consumer organisations, trade unions, cultural communities, and the press and broadcasters themselves, all were accustomed to lobby at the national level to promote their sectional media interests. As for European integration, the European Broadcasting Union (EBU), the pan-European organisation of public broadcasters, had fostered a measure of professional cooperation between broadcasters and promoted international programme exchanges. The Council of Europe (CofE), too, had long occupied itself with the cultural purposes of the medium. Important though they were, these organisations' achievements were limited.

Transfrontier satellite broadcasting changed all this. In the first place, an important contribution to the development of satellite services was made by international bodies. Two international satellite organisations, Intelsat and Eutelsat, played a key role in providing satellite capacity for satellite-to-cable television transmission. An important role in the development of broadcasting satellites was played by the European Space Agency (ESA). Its Orbital Test Satellite (OTS), launched in 1978, carried the original Sky Channel before it transferred first to an ECS satellite (of Eutelsat) and then to the Luxembourg-based 'medium-powered' Astra satellite. The role of the ITU's World Adminstrative Radio Conference (WARC '77) has also been mentioned; it allocated DBS frequencies and orbital slots to each European country for 'high-powered' DBS satellites (for detail see McQuail and Siune, 1986, Chapter 6, and Collins, 1992). Secondly, satellite broadcasting represented an obvious threat to national media sovereignty; it provided scope for the circumvention of national regulations. This worried national media policy makers but at first many were inclined to bury their heads in the sand. Yet, as seen in the preceding chapters, governments committed themselves to the development of the new media technologies. Enthusiastically in some cases, less so in others, policy makers embraced policies to open up new commercial broadcasting markets. The coincidental coming to power of governments committed to the new technologies and markets in the EC's three largest states was an important factor for change. The deregulatory policies now vigorously pursued at the domestic level across Europe led inevitably towards the internationalisation of the new commercial market. As a result of their own decisions, therefore, national policy makers were now compelled to accept that important aspects of broadcasting policy would have to be handled at the supranational level (Wagner, 1994, pp. 25ff). This chapter examines, in detail, exactly how the European Community (EC),* acquired an important role in broadcasting policy. Given the decline in the regulatory capacity of its member states, the European Community was an obvious institutional focus for re-regulation. The question whether 're-regulation' is an appropriate term to describe EC policy, we will now examine.

---

* Now called the European Union (EU).

Why have a European audiovisual policy?

At the European level, the initial impulse for a European-level media policy was the optimistic expectation – shared by members of the European Parliament (EP), officials of the Commission of the European Communities (CEC), and other forces in favour of closer European union – that transfrontier broadcasting might give a welcome fillip to the process of European cultural and political integration. Quickly, however, the main thinking behind European media policy began to prioritise economic aims. These various factors, and the shift in priorities, will now be examined.

The cultural factor

The hopes of many originally centred on the contribution that pan-European television channels and companies, and broadcasting satellites, might make to European cultural and political integration. The need to exploit this potential through regulation and positive interventionism was a theme developed in the Hahn report and subsequent Hahn resolution of the European Parliament (EP 1982a and 1982b). In this resolution, the EP positively urged the European Commission and Council of Ministers to help establish a European satellite broadcasting channel. In response, the Commission announced its support for an initiative already under way within the European Broadcasting Union (EBU) to develop pan-European channels and to increase cultural exchange in both the production and viewing of programmes (CEC, 1983). However, the early EBU's attempts to launch a European channel failed conspicuously (later EBU-sponsored channels – Eurosport launched in 1989 and Euronews, in 1993 – were more successful). In 1982 a limited experiment called Eurikon was launched, followed in 1985 by the launch of Europa TV, a fully fledged satellite channel operated by a consortium of European public-service broadcasters – from the Netherlands, Germany, Ireland, Italy and Portugal – and headquartered in Geneva, the base of the EBU. Europa TV collapsed after only one year's operation. The commitment of Germany's ARD and Italy's RAI was weak; the German public broadcasters were more interested in launching their own satellite channels (see Chapter 7). Britain's public broadcasters remained aloof. Neither viewers nor advertisers were attracted by the channel.

As the decade wore on, many began to fear, pessimistically, that to be successful pan-European channels would have to be altogether brasher commercial operations with modest cultural aspirations (or else, as Eurosport and Euronews later proved felicitously, thematic channels). In particular, they worried: (1) that commercial channels would standardise programming along popular commercial lines; (2) that the internationalisation of commercial broadcasting would diminish cultural diversity and expose Europe's smaller countries to increased 'media colonisation' by their larger neighbours; and (3) that European cultural diversity would be further exposed to 'cultural' invasion by the United States. As the 1980s wore on, the second and third concerns led many policy makers away from a (perhaps naive) optimism about creating a unified 'European culture' towards a much more realistic concern about how to preserve Europe's existing rich cultural diversity (Collins, 1994). At the same time, cultural policy concerns very soon became interwoven with, and subordinated, to the leitmotiv: 'competitiveness in world markets' (Kleinsteuber *et al.*, 1990, p. 3).

The economic stakes

Commission officials were well aware of Europe's substantial trade deficit in television programmes, notably films and series, with the United States. They were aware that Europe's vulnerability was increasing due to the imbalance between the growing demand for programmes and Europe's own productive capacity (CEC, 1983, p. 9). One of the main attractions of imported US programmes was the fact that they were relatively cheap; to buy in such programmes was cheaper than to produce them domestically. The main reason they were so cheap were the economies of scale that a huge, homogeneous and integrated domestic market provided US producers. This advantage enabled the latter to offer already amortised products on world markets at 'bargain basement' prices. Europe, by contrast, was disadvantaged by the fragmented character of its audiovisual markets. It had numerous different systems of production and distribution and it was divided by linguistic and cultural heterogeneity. Yet, the arrival of transfrontier broadcasting appeared to hold out a welcome opportunity to re-balance these historically unfavourable terms of competition between European and US producers. Provided that the market barriers within Europe were lowered, Commission officials thought, European commercial interests would benefit from expanded markets and the economies of scale they brought. Therefore the European Commission – more precisely DG III, the Directorate-General responsible for the internal market – staked much on the promise that, legal barriers once removed, European countries would satisfy their escalating demand for programmes from increases in European production and intra-European exchanges, rather than by gravely increased dependence on US imports.

The Commission also came to accept the need for a measure of cultural protectionism and for some interventionism to support the European film and television programme industry; these matters were pushed by DG X, responsible for information, communication and culture. In addition, DG XIII – responsible for telecommunications, information industries and innovation – was in favour of industrial interventionism to boost Europe's electronics and telecommunications industries. Indeed, Collins (1994, pp. 18–19) identifies DG III (and the competition policy DG IV) as having a 'markedly more liberal, market orientation' whereas DG X and DG XIII 'advocated political intervention in the market'. Collins's very detailed study of the emergence of a Community audiovisual policy shows that it was marked by a struggle between 'liberals' and '*dirigistes*' – a struggle which was conducted both within and beyond the Commission, as will be seen.

The Commission as a whole leaned towards market liberalisation. This was not merely because the '1992' Single European Market (SEM) programme lent special weight to DG III although of course it did. So long as it was accompanied by appropriate cultural policies, DG X also welcomed the single market as a factor for increased European cultural integration. For its part, DG XIII saw great opportunities in the single market for the European telecoms and electronics sectors. From the early 1980s, television was seen increasingly as a key element in a grand European high technology strategy. Before long DG XIII had become a driving force behind the development of a European satellite broadcasting standard for 'High Definition Television' (HDTV) (Niblock, 1991). This HDTV strategy proved, in the end, to be abortive (see Dai, Cawson and Holmes, 1994). Nevertheless, during the 1980s the creation of a liberalised market for broadcast programmes came to be seen as a vital ingredient of an ambitious industrial strategy for the European electronics sector (see Table 8.1).

Table 8.1   *The supranational actors and their interests*

Actors	Their interests
DG III	To create internal market. To stimulate audiovisual industry through market liberalisation.
DG X	To provide some external protection and some industrial support to programme industry.
DG XIII	To promote new technologies (eg. high definition TV).
The EP	To promote European integration with emphasis on cultural as well as the market aspects.
The Court of Justice	To safeguard the EC Treaty's commitment to free exchange of goods and services.

As suggested, Europe-wide liberalisation of broadcasting markets was entirely in line with the '1992' Single European Market (SEM) goals developed from mid-decade onwards. Transfrontier broadcasting's special role would be to promote, through advertising, the free trade in products across the SEM.

EC case law and European broadcasting: the key role of the European Court of Justice

The EC's involvement in the sector appeared to be more than reasonably justified by the tangle of regulatory obstacles within Europe that impeded a free flow of programmes. These obstacles were exposed, sometimes quite dramatically, by the 1980s increase in transfrontier commercial broadcasting. There had always been some transfrontier broadcasting, of course, caused by terrestrial 'overspill', particularly affecting frontier regions and smaller countries. All the same, European countries had by and large found it relatively easy to accommodate the reception by their population of neighbouring countries' public-service channels. However, the advancing paradigmatic transformation of broadcasting structures and regulations across Europe – from a nearly universal public-service model towards a commercialised one – served to sharpen the tensions between European media systems.

In the absence of EC action to harmonise or to promote mutual recognition of national regulations, a member state appeared to be quite free to prevent the retransmission within its national territory of foreign programmes if the latter infringed its broadcasting laws. Since much of Europe's broadcasting was provided by cable there was considerable practical scope for obstructing foreign broadcasts in this way (particularly in the Benelux countries – see Table 5.1). Commercial broadcasting was obviously a very contentious issue: some countries had much stricter laws relating to programmes carrying advertisements than others. Some set very low limits on the quantity of advertising, others had strict rules regarding how programmes might be interrupted, or the content of adverts. Others, still, sought to ban the practice altogether on some services. Copyright law was yet another potential legal barrier to the free circulation of programmes. However, although EC member states may have enjoyed cultural sovereignty, Article 59 of the Treaty of Rome clearly demanded the free exchange of goods and services among them.

While broadcasting in Europe had remained predominantly a public-service business, there had been little call to invoke this latter principle. Broadcasting, it was generally accepted, was primarily a cultural activity, rather than an economic good or service. Nevertheless, as early as 1974, the European Court of Justice (ECJ) had been called into play to settle a commercial dispute that hinged upon whether broadcasting did indeed fall under the Treaty of Rome or not. The Court was the highest legal authority in the Community with the task of interpreting and ensuring adherence to Community laws. Member states had to accept its rulings. In the 1974 Sacchi case, it ruled that broadcasting was so covered. In the early 1980s, the court was now called upon to adjudicate a series of disputes arising from the new commercial tensions attendant upon the structural changes in European broadcasting. In doing so, the court effectively confirmed its Sacchi ruling and established a body of European case law treating broadcasting as a tradeable service (notably the 1980 Debauve ruling). The development of this body of case law cleared a path for the Commission's involvement in broadcasting policy-making by establishing its regulatory competence. The sector had been legally defined as of economic interest in terms of the Treaty of Rome (Lange and Renaud, 1989, p. 66; Negrine and Papathanassopoulos, 1990, pp. 63–64).

The Council of Europe and the free flow of information

From 1982 onwards the Council of Europe (CofE), too, played an important role in initiating new principles for pan-European broadcasting regulation. Its relationship to the EC was ambiguous. As Tunstall and Palmer (1991, p. 15) suggest, there were elements of 'rivalry and cooperation' between them. The differences were, in the main, caused by: (1) their different membership composition, the wider CofE membership giving more voice to the concerns of Europe's smaller countries; and (2) their different policy preoccupations, the CofE being expected to give greater voice to cultural policy concerns, whereas the European Commission focused on economic priorities. Much hope was invested in the CofE by those interests favouring a cautious approach. These included the European public-service broadcasters, the German *Länder* (as distinct from the CDU-led federal government), and many of Europe's small states, which were keen to see established in a European convention some regulatory protection for their cultural sovereignty. Belgium, Denmark and Netherlands, all EC member states unhappy with the Commission's deregulatory thrust (see below), saw the CofE as an attractive alternative forum for prosecuting their interests. They were joined in the CofE by other small states (eg. Austria and Switzerland) which were not (in Austria's case 'not yet') members of the EC and which feared being swept up in the latter's deregulatory slipstream.

The CofE had, after all, long busied itself with the field of the media and in particular with the promotion of cultural diversity in Europe. These hopes, though, proved to be largely misplaced. The CofE was an intergovernmental forum: it presented plenty of opportunity for the liberalisers to obstruct any upward regulatory harmonisation. Moreover, in accordance with the CofE's own organisational culture, its deliberations were guided above all else by Article 10 of the European Convention on Human Rights* which provided for the freedom 'to hold opinions and to receive and impart information and ideas without interference by public authority and regardless of frontiers'. In the past it had certainly been recognised that several factors justified state broadcasting monopolies, most

---

* The European Convention on Human Rights was signed by the (then) twenty-one member states of the Council of Europe on 4 November 1950. It entered into force in 1953. It was ratified by all the states that later became EC/EU members.

notably the historical 'scarcity of frequencies' and the right of states to pursue certain fundamental goals (for example, safeguarding national security and protecting health and morality, cultural values, and so forth). Accordingly, Article 10 had added that states should not be prevented 'from requiring the licensing of broadcasting, television or cinema enterprises'.

Cable and satellite broadcasting, however, plainly removed the 'scarcity of frequencies'. The CofE's 'particular political philosophy' (Gavin, 1991, pp. 26–27) meant that it was bound to be keenly sensitive to the social and cultural risks of the deregulation being pursued in its member states, yet its main concern was to prevent a protectionist backlash and to 'limit the international grounds on which freedom to impart and receive information and ideas might legitimately be impinged upon'. This meant that throughout the 1980s the CofE members – including those which were member states of the EC – worked towards the enactment of a convention to establish certain *minimum* regulatory standards to govern, thereby to ensure, the free flow of programmes in Europe. Unsurprisingly, therefore, the CofE's 1989 convention proved to be in virtually all respects compatible with the liberal thrust of EC policy making. However, it did advocate that broadcasters, where practicable, should present a majority of European works; it also contained an understanding that the member states should support the development of the European audiovisual industry and, in particular, those of countries with a low audiovisual output and limited linguistic area (Gavin, 1991, p. 29). As will be seen, the EC too was compelled to address these matters. The CofE, however, was a much weaker legislative organisation than the EC. Its convention was only politically binding upon its signatories and not 'directly applicable' in national law. The EC, by contrast, could enact legislation in the form of Directives and Regulations that were ultimately enforceable by the European Court of Justice.

The EC Commission's Green Paper: 'Television Without Frontiers'

As seen, the first steps towards elaboration of an EC policy on transfrontier broadcasting were actually taken by the European Parliament whose various committees – most notably the one responsible for culture, but also those concerned with political and legal affairs

– had been concerned since 1980 with the opportunities, risks and legal implications of satellite broadcasting. The 1982 Hahn report and resolution of the EP (see above) invited the European Commission – the Community institution responsible for initiating policy – to explore these issues. DG X duly prepared an Interim Report (CEC, 1983) which recommended the EC's involvement in helping to establish a European channel (see above). A year later, the Commission produced a 1984 Green Paper on the *Establishment of the Common Market for Broadcasting, Especially by Satellite and Cable* (CEC, 1984). Entitled 'Television Without Frontiers' in short, this Green Paper was intended to provide the basis for the drafting of an EC Directive which in due course should become binding EC law. The Green Paper was produced by DG III – the 'liberal' internal market directorate general of the Commission. Cultural policy was dealt with in general terms, but clearly now the Commission's main substantive preoccupation was with seeing broadcasting as a tradeable sector falling within the EC Treaty's provisions for a common market in goods and services. The Green Paper stated explicitly that its aim was the 'opening up of intra-Community frontiers for national television programmes' (p. 4). It also noted that 'the [EC] Treaty [did] not exclude any sphere of activity. As a matter of principle, therefore, it grant[ed] the right of establishment to broadcasting organisations' (p. 6). To underpin its argument, the Green Paper referred back to the European Court's earlier rulings.

The central idea of the Green Paper was the need to create a single European market for broadcasting. Moreover, in order to achieve this single market, the Commission advocated the principle of regulatory 'tolerance'. Member states would be able to lay down more demanding rules on broadcasters within their jurisdiction, but crossfrontier broadcasts would only have to abide by the Community's minimum standards. Without question, the most important issue in this regard was advertising. On the one hand, it would be the motor of the commercial sector, the main source of revenue for the new channels. On the other hand, the persistence of different advertising rules among the member states presented the main barrier to the establishment of a common market in broadcasting. The Green Paper stressed the contribution that a free flow of advertising would make to the achievement of the internal market and economic activity within it. The Green Paper favoured a lowest European denominator of regulation. A liberal daily maximum of 20 per cent of total output was proposed. This approximated closely to the actual situation in the EC's most liberal regimes in this regard, Luxembourg and Italy, and was clearly to the advantage of the advertising industry (which had a very active Eurolobby – see below). A liberal ceiling was justified, in the Commission's view, not least in order to give private commercial broadcasters a sufficient chance to compete with channels that received public support. The ceiling also took into account the steadily increasing demand for advertising airtime. All advertising adhering to this lowest denominator should be permissible, even in the territory of member states with stricter national advertising regulations. The Commission favoured allowing sponsoring as another source of income so long as it did not interfere with the programme's content. The advertising of tobacco was to be banned and that of alcohol strictly regulated. The Green Paper also invited discussion by the member states about the harmonisation of other laws that might impede the common market: notably, laws protecting children and young people (eg. from violence and hard pornography), right of reply laws, and copyright laws.

Following the publication in 1985 of an EP resolution pressing for an EC regulatory framework, and having prepared its path by consulting with COREPER working groups that had meanwhile been set up to consider the issues raised by the Green Paper, the Commission gave the policy process a further thrust forward by publishing in April 1986 a draft Directive and passing it on to both the Council of Ministers and the European Parliament for further discussion and comment. The draft Directive had lowered the advertising ceiling to 15 per cent. Concern had been expressed in the EP that a 20 per cent ceiling would make broadcasting too commercialised. Also in response to calls from EP parliamentarians and also pressure from the French Culture Minister, the draft Directive introduced some protectionist programme quotas and seemed to endorse the idea of establishing a Community aid scheme for film and television co-productions (which, however, was never realised within the aegis of the EC – see below). Yet, the principal objective still did not differ from that defined in 'Television Without Frontiers': it was to 'sweep away the entangled underwood of national regulatory obstacles' to the free market for the circulation of television services within the EC (Papathanassopoulos, 1990, p. 108; Negrine and Papathanassopoulos, 1990, p. 66). Its economistic line of argumentation furnished the European Commission with a legally defensible claim to legitimate regulatory jurisdiction in the field of media policy. A large number of EP parliamentarians were concerned about the lack of an expressly culture-orientated component to the Green Paper and also about the absence of any anti-concentration measures (Wagner, 1994, pp. 114–115). Cultural policy, however, still fell beyond the scope of the EC Treaty (until incorporated by Article 128 in the Maastricht Treaty). In the words of Hoffmann Riem (1987, p. 66): 'it [was] almost inevitable that when the European Commission [took] a look at the subject of broadcasting, it (would) have an economic bias … [and was] likely to favour something close to the marketplace model'. This was certainly so, yet a case could still be made that the Commission had now entered cultural matters into its sphere of jurisdiction, 'albeit via an economic back door' (Collins, 1994, p. 63).

Eurolobbies and national interests

Unsurprisingly, the period between publication of 'Television Without Frontiers' and the eventual enactment of a Directive, five whole years later in 1989, was characterised by considerable tugging and hauling between various interest groups and governments. As Hirsch and Petersen (1992, p. 45) have noted, 'regional authorities, opposition parties, commercial interests, multinational broadcasters and professional organisations all put pressure on their governments to minimise the damage to their own interests'. The Commission's role, of course, was to propose and to draft legislation; it could not dispose. The EC's ultimate locus of decision making was intergovernmental, namely the Council of Ministers. The Commission, therefore, was bound to take cognisance of the various conflicting viewpoints and interests, not least when these were articulated by national governments. Moreover, lobbying was not just directed towards the Commission. Between the Commission's production of the Green Paper (1984) and the Council of Ministers' enactment of the final Directive on 'Television Without Frontiers' (1989), EC decision-making shifted away from the 'functionalist inspired' Commission towards the 'intergovernmental bargaining' of the Council of Ministers (Fraser, 1993, p. 30).

The policy alliances and oppositions were complex but there existed a clear-cut polarisation between two different sets of concerns regarding the regulation of broadcasting. On the one hand, there was a European-level coalition in favour of deregulation and liberalisation (Collins' 'liberals' – see above). One of the most influential members of this coalition was the European advertising industry, which was represented in Brussels by several bodies, most notably by the European Advertising Tripartite (EAT). Naturally, the advertisers sought to ensure the most liberal Europe-wide limits on the percentage time per day and per hour that could be devoted to advertising. They also opposed proposals to confine advertising largely to blocks and limit it in 'natural breaks'. In seeking these objectives, the advertising lobby was well placed to influence the Commission. The number of Eurolobbies in the media field was distinctly limited because media had always been a national concern, but the advertising lobby was already internationalised; being already established as a Eurolobby was undoubtedly advantageous. The lobby's most potent political resource was its ability to produce persuasive quantitative estimates of the commercial costs of 'over-restrictive' regulations. As Tunstall and Palmer (1991, p. 95) suggest, the Commission lawyers who drafted the 1984 Green Paper and the subsequent Directive 'used industry supplied data to document their case'. They note, in particular, that an EAAA study of 'New Communication Developments' provided six of the Green Paper's seventeen statistical appendices (see also Fraser, 1993, p. 27). Alongside the advertisers, increasingly influential during the latter half of the 1980s were the new commercial broadcasters themselves. During this period, as seen in the Chapter 6, a number of important corporate actors, often from the adjacent press sector, together with an array of powerful financial backers, began to invest heavily in the broadcasting sector. At first, their lobbying focus was the national level; this is where most deregulation was occurring in the early and mid-1980s. At the European level they contented themselves at first with expressing their views individually or through their national governments. By and large, they welcomed the Green Paper's liberal advertising proposals. By 1989, the commercial broadcasters had formed a Eurolobby in the shape of the Association for Commercial Television (ACT). The ACT's membership was dominated by major commercial organisations like Luxembourg's CLT, Murdoch's Sky Television, the German satellite broadcasters SAT 1 (Springer) and RTL Plus (Bertelsmann/CLT) and Berlusconi's Fininvest; Italy's Silvio Berlusconi was the ACT's first chairman.

European-level market liberalisation naturally drew considerable support from certain national governments. Liberalisation was in line with the policies of domestic deregulation being pursued by Europe's larger countries (see Chapters 5 and 6). It was entirely consistent with the realities of Italian broadcasting. The German federal government was in favour of a single broadcasting market, seeing exciting opportunities in it for Germany's electronics industry. However, it was gravely constrained by the negative position of the German *Länder* (see below). The Thatcherite British government, although nominally against any extension of the Commission's jurisdiction, a position widely shared by the British broadcasting policy community, was a most vigorous champion of the free market principle and soon became a driving force behind the EC's '1992' programme for the Single Market; this translated into support for the Commission's efforts to create a free broadcasting market and opposition to attempts to encumber it with restrictions (see later). Britain's strong trade balance in the sector testified to its comparative advantage over other EC states in broadcasting. It was felt that Britain only stood to gain even further from a liberalised European market. Also highly enthusiastic about European market liberalisation was Luxembourg; a lax European regulatory framework would greatly advantage its domestic commercial broadcasting interests – CLT/RTL and SES/Astra (Wagner, 1994, p. 77; see also Table 8.2).

However, the Green Paper provoked a widespread hostile response. It upset an array of established broadcaster interests. As Fraser (1993, p. 27) notes, because the key role in drafting it had been played by DG III (the internal market Directorate General), many broadcasting professionals had felt excluded from the policy process. Their customary connections were to DG X (responsible for cultural policy) but this branch of the Commission had played little role in the production of the Green Paper. Many established broadcasters complained – with some reason – that DG III had been captured by the advertising lobby. Their own European lobby, the European Broadcasting Union (EBU), was an influential organisation. Committed steadfastly to uphold public service values and interests, it was critical of the Commission's Green Paper. This was unsurprising since the Green Paper 'challenged the EBU's very *raison d'être* as a programme consortium for public networks … commercial competition [threatening] to undermine the EBU's main function as a cartel that buys sports and information programming on behalf of its members' (Fraser, 1993, pp. 27–28; also see Collins, 1994, p. 62). The EBU accepted the desirability of an integrated European broadcasting zone but argued strongly that it should be regulated in such a way as to protect public-service broadcasting. The EBU argued that it was capable of serving this aim itself in cooperation with the CofE and it questioned the community's competence in the field (Wagner, 1994, p. 73, p. 116 and p. 136; also see Collins, 1994, p. 56).

Table 8.2   *National interests in market liberalisation*

Belgium, Denmark, Ireland, German *Länder* and Netherlands[a]	No advantage in free market. Very sensitive to the threat to broadcasting sovereignty.
Britain, German federal government and Luxembourg	Enthusiastic about market liberalisation. Advantageous for national interests.
France and Italy	In favour of European market but a protected one, which subsidises European industry.
Greece, Spain and Portugal	Not notably interested.

Note:
[a] The Netherlands government, however, was ambivalent. It was keen that its electronics industry (Philips) should benefit from the new commercial opportunities.
Source: Simplified from overview provided by J. Wagner, *Policy-Analyse: Grenzenlos Fernsehen in der EG*, Frankfurt/Main: Peter Lang, 1994, pp. 76–79).

Broadly speaking, European Social Democratic parties, broadcasting professionals' associations, and trade unions, remained committed to the public-service model. The left in the European Parliament was concerned that deregulation would have harmful cultural consequences; it also worried that media-concentration would increase in a liberalised market. The European Trade Union Confederation (ETUC) feared that Community policy was far too deregulatory and market-orientated. The unions felt that not nearly enough consideration had been given to protecting public-service broadcasting and employment in the sector, and they were also concerned about media concentration. As mentioned, the smaller countries in Europe (Luxembourg excepted) were apprehensive about liberalisation because they feared it would both damage their relatively weak broadcasting industries and expose them to 'cultural colonisation'. Belgium, a country that was particularly open to French language broadcasts, remained negative about EC market liberalisation throughout the whole process. Belgium had very restrictive rules regarding foreign ownership of broadcasting channels, the licensing of foreign cable and satellite programmes, foreign programme quotas and the prohibition of foreign advertising. The Netherlands had similar regulations. Indeed, Dutch attempts to prohibit foreign advertising 'targeted' at their viewers were soon to bring the state into conflict with the European Court (see p. 278). At the same time, though, the Dutch were mindful of the benefit to the Dutch electronics industry (Philips) that an expanded broadcasting market would bring. The Danes simply objected to the EC's disregard for their 'cultural sovereignty'. The situation in Germany was complicated. The federal German government (CDU/CSU/FDP) was a strong partisan of commercialisation, and of the '1992' programme more broadly. However, the West German *Länder* (and not just those governed by the Social Democrats), had always held the CofE to be the proper forum for discussing a pan-European regulatory framework. They objected that EC discussion of broadcasting regulation was based on a primarily economic understanding of the medium. They also resented unanimously the way the EC discussions circumvented their own cultural sovereignty – which included jurisdiction over broadcasting – because the federal government was responsible for EC affairs. Nevertheless, the federal government had to remain sensitive to *Länder* views. To the last, Germany's position was uncertain.

The Green Paper and draft Directive also prompted a critical response from Collins' *dirigistes*, in the EP and in DG X, but most notably the French government. During the formulation stage of the Directive, the French position became pivotally important. As seen in Chapter 7, the French broadcasting system – through radical domestic policies of liberalisation – had become very reliant on popular entertainment programmes imported from the USA. Under pressure from a very powerful domestic film and television lobby, the French Socialists, returned to government in 1988, were strongly committed to seeing the EC adopt a policy of external protectionism along the lines of its own domestic broadcasting laws. These, in theory at least, prescribed quotas of 60 per cent 'European' programmes on television. Moreover, if the quotas were not as effective as hoped, French government subsidies to indigenous audiovisual producers were comparatively generous: financed by a 13 per cent levy on cinema box office receipts and video tapes. The French position, although enthusiastic about the Green Paper's proposals for the creation of an internal audiovisual market, was at the same time in favour of the adoption of protectionist quotas. As seen, these were duly incorporated into the 1986 draft Directive. The French also pushed for some EC financial support for the European audiovisual industry. This idea too was adopted though not within the Directive (see later).

The controversies: protectionist European programme quotas and advertising and copyright regulations

The issue of quotas nearly deadlocked the policy process entirely. The French government's demand for the incorporation of 60 per cent European-produced programme quotas as a defensive measure to limit non-European (i.e. US) imports had first been aired by French Culture Minister Jack Lang within the Council of (Culture) Ministers in June 1984 where it had already engendered controversy. Largely due to the initiative of French MEPs, the idea was embraced by the European Parliament. Then, in its 1986 draft Directive the Commission introduced a specific recommendation that an immediate quota of 30 per cent of transmission time, rising to 60 per cent after three years, be devoted to productions of EC origin. It was added that at least 20 per cent of these should be first viewings. Moreover, it was suggested that 5–10 per cent of a broadcaster's production budget should be devoted to purchases from the European independent production sector. Although the quotas would not include news, sports, game shows and advertising, the proposal still marked a significant policy shift from the originally liberal position, expressed in the Green Paper, towards a more protectionist one. If such a protective measure were not adopted, its supporters argued, the free market would act as a vortex sucking in a flood of non-European programme imports. Sepstrup (1989), however, pointed out that, for this very reason, the EC's liberalising measures would be counterproductive. Hoffmann-Riem (1987, p. 69) drew attention to the evident contradiction in 'abandoning broadcasting to market forces on the one hand and calling for national quotas or subsidies on the other'.

The French inspired proposal was supported unreservedly by Belgium, Italy and Spain, but it encountered the stubborn resistance of certain other member states. The British government objected on principle to any such interference with the free market; doubtless it was also mindful of the impact such restrictions would have on the future role of Anglophone programmes in Europe. The British principled objection to protectionism was shared by Denmark and Germany. In Germany by now the new commercial broadcasters were very influential within the domestic policy community. That the commercial broadcasters were firmly set against quotas almost goes without saying. It was to their advantage to rely on relatively inexpensive US programming (already amortised in the huge US markets and therefore saleable to European commercial operators at 'bargain basement' prices). Yet many European public-service broadcasters, including both BBC and ITV, also disagreed with the proposal. They viewed it as an invasion of their discretion in the matter of programming decisions. Perhaps more pertinently, the quota measure was seen as an unwelcome competitive handicap in the new context of deregulated markets. Broadcasters in the smaller countries in particular worried about the cost implications. In fact, the European broadcasting community at large was very divided by the issue. Many ancillary industrial interests feared that quotas would increase costs of broadcasting and therefore hold back the sector's expansion. This was, for instance, the view expressed by UNICE (the *Union des Industries de la Communauté européenne*). On the other hand, numerous practitioner lobbies – European artists, actors, producers – were positively in favour of the quotas. Unsurprisingly, the American producer lobby, notably the Motion Pictures Association of America (MPAA), pressured the US government to apply strong diplomatic pressure and even threaten trade reprisals against the EC to compel it to drop the quota proposal. The US government argued that quotas would be highly damaging to US economic interests and that they would infringe the principles of the Uruguay Round of the General Agreement on Tariffs and Trade (GATT). The latter international body was in the throes of discussing how to expand its agreements to include services such as television not yet formally covered. The issue of European audiovisual protectionism became a central controversy in the GATT negotiations (Hirsch and Petersen,

1992, pp. 46–47). Right up to the last, the quota issue looked capable of wrecking the Directive. The French culture minister insisted on including strict quotas and against watering them down significantly. He was supported by the Left in the EP.

The quota issue was the most contentious, yet far more hinged upon advertising. As suggested, it was the motor of an expansion of the broadcasting sector. The myriad different advertising regulations operated by the member states amounted to the main obstacle to the free movement of broadcasting services in the Community, and they were a major potential source of market distortions. This had been recognised from the start, in the Green Paper. There were a number of issues relating to advertising which could be ironed out relatively easily: such as the proposal for a Europe-wide ban on broadcasting the advertising of tobacco and tobacco products (already banned in most member states); and special rules for the advertisement of alcoholic drinks. Much more difficult, however, were the crucial questions of how much air-time should be permitted to be devoted to advertising and within what limits and constraints sponsorship might be condoned. The European advertising lobby and the new commercial broadcasters organised in the ACT, argued hard and furiously in favour of leaving the matter to the discretion of the broadcasters. This position was supported by the British, German and Luxembourg governments. Against this, some political lobbies pushed for a much more restrictive limit. The EC's Economic and Social Committee argued for a 10 per cent ceiling and the Dutch government even argued for a 5 per cent advertising ceiling. Importantly, though, the draft Directive's proposal of a 15 per cent ceiling for advertising was acceptable to nearly all member state governments (Wagner, 1994, p. 132). However, a very bitter wrangle over advertising occurred because some lobbies and governments, most vocally the British, were especially concerned to protect the freedom to continue to practise spot advertising (interrupting programmes) while others, led by the Germans, advocated obligatory block advertising (which did not). The British position was strongly supported by the European advertising lobby which mounted a vigorous lobbying campaign over the issue that undoubtedly helped in the end to swing the balance of the argument in favour of the British (see Tunstall and Palmer, 1991, p. 96ff.).

Another issue that caused considerable disagreement was copyright regulation. The Green Paper and subsequent draft Directive had suggested what effectively amounted to a dramatic liberalisation of the practice of copyright protection. For reasons of practicability – and the smooth creation of the internal market – it had first of all been proposed effectively to remove the ability of the owners of intellectual property to prohibit the distribution of a work across national frontiers (enshrined in the right of the owners to negotiate national deals). The Commission also proposed to by-pass the complex tangle of different national approaches to the issue. To promote intra-Community trade, the Commission recommended the granting by member states of a compulsory licence allowing transfrontier distribution within Europe but at the same time ensuring that the owner of intellectual property would be adequately remunerated. However, this compulsory measure was widely criticised as an infraction of the owner's rights. So, at the EP's suggestion, the Commission retreated from the idea of granting a statutory licence and instead suggested the establishment of an arbitration body to sort out copyright problems. In the end, the controversial issue proved so difficult to resolve that it was simply dropped from the Directive, to allow its enactment, and thenceforth pursued by the Commission as a separate policy (for a detailed account of this 'missing chapter' of the Directive see Collins, 1994, pp. 73–80).

The EC Directive 'Television Without Frontiers'

By 1989, the momentum towards the '1992' Single European Market (SEM) was giving a powerful stimulus to the policy process. The year before, Jacques Delors had singled out 'Television Without Frontiers' as a priority task for the Community. Further, the Council of Ministers, meeting at Rhodes in 1988, officially adopted audiovisual policy as a Community competence. Meanwhile, negotiations over the CofE's convention had almost reached their conclusion; the controversy over advertising had actually been settled between culture ministers during these discussions. To push matters through, the European Commission now gave warning of its preparedness to seek confirmation for the Directive's specific contents via a whole series of European Court of Justice cases if the member states themselves could not reach agreement among themselves (Wagner, 1994, p. 163; also see Collins, 1994, pp. 68–69). Finally, it was important that the draft television Directive was one of around three hundred SEM measures which the Council of Ministers could decide by qualified majority voting.*

In October 1989, the Twelve adopted the television Directive 'Television Without Frontiers' by qualified majority. There had been a last minute eruption of dissent within the Council of Ministers. France, it had briefly appeared, might join the 'anti' camp and sink the Directive because the quotas had been watered down too much. Germany's position had remained highly uncertain to the last. In the event, only Denmark and Belgium voted against it. Inevitably, the Directive reflected compromises struck between the member states. Above all, though, the Directive represented a classic example of the EC's '1992' strategy of reliance largely on the essentially de-regulatory principle of mutual recognition, rather than on re-regulatory harmonisation. So long as its minimal regulatory provisions were met by the rules of the originating member state, it removed the legal grounds for another member state to impede the reception or re-transmission of broadcasts from it. Having established the principle of regulatory tolerance (mutual recognition) in this way, it still left scope for stricter regulations to be applied to a country's own national services. (This was very much in tune with the CofE's Convention signed a few months earlier). Yet, the EC member states' broadcasting sovereignty was now a thing of the past.

The advertising rules reflected a compromise between the British and Germans over their wrangle; the British had accepted that there should be fewer advertising breaks in films while the Germans had dropped their demand for no advertising breaks whatsoever and their insistence upon block advertising. Far more significantly, though, the Directive prescribed in favour of the Commission's long-standing liberal principle of an unrestricted free flow, in transfrontier broadcasting, of all programmes carrying advertising. For the latter, the Directive established generous limits which amounted to an important victory for the powerful European advertising lobby and provided great encouragement to the new commercial broadcasting operators. The Directive settled on a maximum daily advertising limit of 15 per cent of air-time but with a maximum of 20 per

---

* 54 out of 76 votes. Luxembourg had 2 votes; Denmark and Ireland each had 3 votes; Belgium, Greece, the Netherlands and Portugal each had 5, Spain 8 and Britain, France, Germany and Italy each had 10 votes.

cent in any one hour during prime time periods. It should be pointed out that these thresholds were seldom reached even in the United States. To exceed these limits would be counter-productive for the commercial interests anyway, since the viewer would be likely to discriminate against any such programmes by simply switching channels. As for sponsorship, the Directive banned it for news and current affairs programmes and, beyond this, merely suggested that sponsors should not exert any editorial influence on the content of programmes. Judgement in this matter rested entirely with the broadcaster, again another advantageous outcome for the commercial interests.

As regards protectionist quotas, the EC had certainly watered down the original proposals. To be precise, the Directive stated that a majority share of broadcasting time should be reserved for European productions (Article 4). It went on to add that broadcasters should reserve at least 10 per cent of their programming budget or transmission time to 'European works created by producers who are independent of the broadcasters' (Article 5). However, the meaning of 'European' was defined very loosely and both articles contained the get-out words 'where practicable' (echoing the CofE Convention) and added that these aims 'should be achieved progressively'. (In each case, the quotas would not count for news, sports, games, advertising and teletext). This dilution of the original quota proposal marked a retreat by the French government and a disappointment for many European parliamentarians, notably those on the Left. However, there was a trade-off for the French preparedness to compromise. As we will shortly see, the Commission lent its weight to several French-inspired projects to provide financial support to the European audiovisual sector. Also, several years later within GATT, at French insistence, Community Trade Commissioner Leon Brittan had stubbornly to defend EC member states' right to deploy programme quotas and to subsidise programme production.

Nevertheless, as Negrine and Papathanassopoulos (1990, p. 76) concluded: 'the final version of the Directive [was] clearly a victory for commercial forces and those who favoured anti-protectionist policies'. They continued, 'it could also emerge as a clear victory for US interests and other commercial broadcasters who will now attempt to extend their powers across Europe'. Kleinsteuber (1990, p. 44) described the outcome even more succinctly, 'the EC Directive ha[d] plumped for lightly regulated commercial television ... In the future we can expect to see a further watering down of national media regulation, [a development] which will lend itself to be interpreted as a harmonisation through liberalisation in accordance with EC law'. Indeed, unlike the Council of Europe's Convention, the television Directive constituted binding European law in all community member states. Within a transition period of two years, it was to be translated into member states' national laws and regulations. Compliance with its provisions could therefore be enforced by the European Court of Justice. Already in 1988 the Court of Justice had ruled against Dutch cable regulations that banned Dutch-subtitled programmes with advertising aimed at the Netherlands. Again, in 1989 the Court ruled against Dutch attempts to impose their own strict advertising rules on foreign advertising-based services (Nieuwenhuis, 1992, pp. 208–209). These decisions confirmed the Directive's most liberal and effective element: namely, its definitive removal of national sovereignty over transfrontier broadcasts. Ironically, the Directive did rather less to achieve its goal of creating a single market: European markets continued to be defined along largely domestic, or more accurately, along linguistic lines. Nor were European producers necessarily the best-placed to exploit the market opening that had occurred (Negrine and Papathanassopoulos, 1990, pp. 160–163).

European initiatives to promote the programme production industry

Simply to de-regulate the European market for the distribution of broadcast programmes was a risky – and potentially counterproductive – strategy (for an excellent critique of EC policy leading up to the Directive, see Sepstrup, 1989). As in other sectors, there were bound to be winners and losers of the single market. The principal beneficiaries, at least in the first instance, were likely to be those producers who already had a dominant worldwide market position and who were therefore able to sell or distribute programmes at a competitively low price – in other words, American producers. On the basis of its past performance, the growth of the European audiovisual sector's productive capacity was most unlikely to keep up with the future expansion of demand for programmes. Many feared that, in the absence of countervailing action, the single market in broadcasting would actually increase Europe's exposure to US cultural penetration (see Chapter 7). Nor was the threat to diversity just American: countries with small media industries were unlikely to benefit from the single European market as much as European neighbours with large and competitive ones. Indeed, Belgium's exposure to private commercial French broadcasts (notably TF1) and the Netherlands' exposure to Luxembourg's (RTL) illustrated the phenomenon of small country vulnerability to neighbouring 'media powers' very clearly already. Such countries could reasonably expect the EC at least to take compensatory action to help maintain their cultural industries. The rationale for EC cultural policy interventionism was compelling (Burgelman and Pauwels, 1992).

The call for an active interventionist cultural policy for the audiovisual sector had long been led by France and supported by DG X within the Commission. As explained, Collins (1994) refers to these interventionists as the '*dirigiste*' (as opposed to 'liberal') influences on EC policy-making. Further, ever since the Hahn report and resolution (1982), the European Parliament – in a series of resolutions and reports – had continued to advocate cultural policy interventionism by the Community. The EP's committee responsible for culture and media was also '*dirigiste*' in Collins' terms and, he notes, 'allied to DG X'. However, the development of an interventionist policy was made problematic by the Community's lack of competence for cultural affairs until Article 128 of the Maastricht Treaty gave it one in 1991. To be adopted, any cultural policy measure required unanimity within the Council of Ministers. However, Denmark resisted the EC trespassing over its 'cultural sovereignty'. At first, Germany was not very positively disposed to the EC committing expenditure to this field. British media policy in the 1980s was liberal, 'free market' orientated, and a 'peculiarly domestic concern' (Negrine, 1990). The Thatcher government, whilst a supporter of the single market, was unenthusiastic about active interventionism in the audiovisual field of the kind advocated by the *dirigistes*. The latter's view of Britain as a Trojan horse for the feared US cultural penetration of Europe did little to bring Britain 'on board' (for a clear analysis of Britain's 'detached-ness' see Collins, 1994, esp. pp. 89–92). As a result of this dissension, no agreement was reached on a proposal to establish an EC programme of direct support for film and television co-productions. The French, not to be thwarted, simply went outside the aegis of the EC to pursue this particular goal (see below). Nevertheless, by the end of the 1980s DG X was able to introduce at least a modest interventionist policy to support European audiovisual production and distribution. It was called the MEDIA programme (*Mesures pour Encourager le Dévelopement de l'Industrie Audiovisuelle*). It was agreed because the British and German governments, under pressure from domestic film lobbies, had dropped their opposition to EC expenditure in this field; and because the Danish, still opposed in principle to the pursuit of EC culture policy, did not see the matter as worthy of the exercise of their national veto (Wagner, 1994, pp. 42–43).

The EC's MEDIA programme

An experimental phase was actually launched under the acronym 'MEDIA 92' in 1988. It was financed from the Commission's own discretionary resources and therefore did not require the assent of the Council of Ministers. Subsequently, in December 1990, the Council of Ministers was able to adopt it as a fully fledged five year programme. Renamed 'MEDIA 1995', it was now given an EC budgetary appropriation of ECU 200 million. Its aims were: (1) to remove the barriers from national markets and to initiate cross-frontier cooperation' in order to promote economies of scale;(2) to give 'priority to small and medium sized operators'; and (3) to 'maintain proper regard for national differences and cultural identities, avoiding any cultural uniformization and paying particular attention to the needs of smaller countries and less widely spoken languages' (CEC, *European File*, 6/92, p. 7). Its interventions were mainly 'upstream' and 'downstream' of production. Its activities included support for the distribution of European films, particularly low budget ones, through the establishment of a European Film Distribution Office (EFDO). Other activities were: guaranteeing bank loans; supporting training; encouraging networking; the improvement of facilities for production; the promotion of the application of advanced technologies; support for joint initiatives between small countries; the promotion of language transfer (through financial help towards dubbing, subtitling); and so on. Worthy in the aims and breadth of its vision, its one obvious problem was that it was exceedingly modestly financed. The MEDIA programme's five-year budget of ECU 200 million was one-tenth of the Commission's spending on information technology research (Burgelman and Pauwels, 1992, p.

180) and considerably less than the ECU 268 million that France allocated in support of the French programme industry in 1990 alone (CEC, 1994b, p. 31). Therefore, it promised little 'compensatory benefit' to small countries and small businesses confronted by the fierce competition that would undoubtedly be unleashed by the single market. This limitation reflected both the continued reluctance of the British and the Germans to allow higher expenditure and the fact that DG X – its sponsoring directorate general – was not a notably strong voice in the Commission's bureaucratic hierarchy. Given these constraints within the EC, the French resorted to a strategy of 'variable geometry': the pursuit of interventionist policies beyond the EC arena (Collins, 1994).

'Audio-visual Eureka'

To this end, the French Socialist government (re-elected in 1988, in power until March 1993) conceived of an inter-governmental complement to the Commission's supranational MEDIA programme. Called 'Audio-visual Eureka', it was first presented to the Rhodes European Council of December 1988 during the sensitive final stage of inter-governmental negotiation of the 1989 broadcasting Directive. The initiative's name reflected the intention that it should become the cultural policy equivalent to the wider inter-governmental 'Eureka' initiative promoting European technological collaboration that had been instigated by President Mitterrand in 1985. Eureka already included an audiovisual component, which the European Commission strongly supported, namely commitment to development of a 'European High Definition Television' (HDTV) standard (see Peterson, 1993; also Dai *et al.*, 1994). Collaborative support for programme production was seen as an entirely logical addition to Eureka's activities. To launch 'Audio-visual Eureka', the French government, then holding the EC presidency and enthusiastically supported by the European Commission and its interventionist president Jacques Delors, organised a major conference in Paris in October 1989. Called the *Assises de l'audiovisuel*, the conference assembled a range of actors from the European media policy community at large. With much hyperbole, a 'Common Declaration on Audio-visual Eureka' was signed at the close of the conference by twenty-one European states and Jacques Delors on behalf of the EC Commission. This signalled the official launch of the French-inspired, EC

Commission-backed, but pan-European initiative. Hirsch and Petersen (1992, p. 52) found it significant that 'the following day the French government made official its acceptance of the Directive on Television Without Frontiers'. Similarly Fraser (1993, pp. 31–33) saw the creation of Eureka-Audiovisuel as a trade-off for the French, for voting 'Television Without Frontiers' through in the EC's Council of Ministers despite the Directive's diluted quota regulation.

The Common Declaration established an inter-governmental coordination committee that gave representation to the EC Commission. According to Gavin (1991, pp. 101–106), this committee was to function as the key 'intermediary between the broadcasting community and member governments'. Concerned with strategic policy making, it was given a secretariat and plans were also laid for the establishment of an 'audiovisual observatory' which would serve as an information centre for legal, economic and other relevant data pertaining to the European audiovisual industry. In 1993 this latter body was-established with a small team in Strasbourg. Audio-visual Eureka aimed explicitly to give a boost to the supply of European-made programmes in order to counter the trade imbalance with the United States. Not reserved to EC member states alone, its aim was to stimulate the production, co-production and co-distribution of programmes across the wider Europe. It was also intended to do more than compensate for the negative effects of the EC's single market. It was to be the 'ultimate link in the chain of a grand industrial strategy for the European audiovisual market of the 1990s'. Its function was to stimulate the production of the programmes needed to feed the envisioned European HDTV system and thereby help the latter become a market success (on the European HDTV policy failure, see Dai, Cawson and Holmes, 1994). In its conception, therefore, Eureka audiovisuel 'merged' cultural and industrial policy (Gavin, 1991, pp. 101–106, p. 101).

Collins (1994, p. 136) sees the 'consistently reiterated support' that Audio-visual Eureka received from both the EC Commission and the Council of Ministers, despite its not being an official EC programme, as a sign of 'the strength of the commitment of major sections of the European Community to a '*dirigiste* policy and programme for the European audio-visual sector'. It certainly showed that there was sizeable support within the EC for a much more active European audiovisual policy. It was also politically a very astute initiative. Audio-visual Eureka was open to a wider Europe than the EC, it therefore overcame the reservations that some member states had about the EC's involvement in cultural affairs, yet at the same time it gave the EC Commission a 'platform for new initiatives' (Hirsch and Petersen, 1992, p. 52). On the other hand, participation in Audio-visual Eureka was entirely voluntary and it had no more resources than its members were prepared to produce for its individual initiatives. Gavin (1991, p. 106) notes that its design was 'to facilitate the functioning of the market and not to protect the audio-visual sector in the form of quotas, subsidies and other forms of state aids'. Therefore, it certainly fell short of what the *dirigistes* would have preferred ideally. It was essentially a Europe-wide policy network with the special remit to stimulate cooperation between market actors. Nevertheless, as a supply side agency of this kind, it had considerable promise. One important interventionist measure was the setting up in 1991 of *Euro Media Garanties* (EMG), a guarantee fund designed to encourage European co-production projects involving producers from EC and CofE states. Loans could be guaranteed by *Euro Media Garanties* up to 70 per cent. The fund was co-financed by the EC's MEDIA programme and the French government (ECU half a million each), and by a number of shareholding banks (ECU one million). Headquartered in Paris, EMG was located in the French *Institut pour le Financement du Cinéma et des Industries Culturelles*, a public body which had operated such a loan-guarantee system in France since the Socialists' advent to power in the early 1980s. This symbolised, somewhat, the French inspiration behind Audiovisual Eureka (*MEDIA Newsletter*, 04/1991, pp. 23–24).

The Council of Europe's 'Eurimages' programme

As seen, the CofE's broadcasting policy has developed in parallel to that of the EC. A good example was the CofE's establishment in 1988 of a support fund of its own, called 'Eurimages', designed to stimulate European film and television production. The fund's cumbersome full title suggests its direction of intervention: the European Support Fund for the Co-production and Distribution of Creative Cinematographic and Audiovisual Works. Eurimages worked by granting aid to co-productions between three or more member states. Again, France was the principal driving force behind Eurimages, the most active participant in its projects, the principal contributor of funds, and the main beneficiary therefrom. Collins (1994, pp.

132–133) evaluates Eurimages as an 'exemplary instance ... of "European variable geometry"': that is, an EC member state resorting to a pan-European institution to achieve goals unachievable within the EC. The problem for *dirigistes*, again, was the fact that Eurimages had a very modest budget, in fact less than the EC's MEDIA scheme. Indeed, Collins (1994, p. 155) concludes his in-depth account of EC audiovisual policy-making with the observation that the *dirigistes'* successes were of 'lesser consequence than those of the liberals'. By this, he was not only referring to the successful creation of the Single European Market in broadcasting, but also to the role that the Commission's competition directorate – DG IV – seemed to be playing in defining the new market framework.

European competition law and the single market

In Collins's view, DG IV was the 'paradigm of liberalism' in the Commission; this was reflected in its 'implacable pursuit of the public service broadcasters' (pp. 155–156). This evaluation of DG IV's role is based largely on two noteworthy competition policy interventions designed to open up the market and to lower market entry barriers by tackling what were seen as abuses by public broadcasters of their 'dominant market position'. The particular market in question was that for the purchase of programme rights for sports events and popular entertainment films. As already mentioned in Chapter 7, in the highly competitive market of the late 1980s and 1990s, these programme categories were of strategic importance to public and private broadcasters alike. In the two cases in question, DG IV considered that public-service broadcasters were exploiting unfair advantages in order to acquire such programme rights. In the first case, in 1989, DG IV reversed a deal that gave the German public-service ARD organisation exclusive rights to German-language transmission of a very large 'package' of popular American entertainment programmes over a lengthy period of time. This deal was deemed to foreclose the market and therefore to be essentially anti-competitive. Certainly, the way DG IV targeted the public-service ARD without examining the market power of the giant private sector Kirch film merchandising group, could be seen as rather prejudiced. As seen, the Kirch concern had become a key player in Germany's new private commercial broadcasting sector (see Chapter 6).

The concern already held what might have been seen as a dominant market position for US film rights in Germany. Porter and Hasselbach (1991, p. 161) note that the Commission was well aware that the Kirch group held 'the German-language rights in some 15,000 feature films and 50,000 hours of television products, including the most lucrative parts of the libraries of the American majors'.

Next, in 1991 the Commission upheld a complaint by W.H. Smith, the main backer of a commercial satellite sports channel called Screensport, against the Eurosport channel which was a joint-venture (launched in 1989) between the private satellite broadcaster Sky Channel (owned by News International) and the Eurosport Consortium, a group of EBU members. This joint-venture, too, was deemed to be anti-competitive and market-distorting. The deal disarmed the competitive threat posed to Europe's public broadcasters by Sky Channel which benefited from access to the EBU's wide programme-acquisition and -sharing network. In DG IV's view, 'the long-established EBU programme acquisition and sharing arrangements ... [were] abuses of dominant market positions by a public broadcasting cartel' (Collins, 1994, p. 150). In both cases, DG IV could be said to have been acting to free up the market entirely in the spirit of the 1989 Television Directive. These rulings could be seen as an attempt to remove some of the unjustified privileges enjoyed by the European public-sector broadcasters. Action of this kind was needed, it could be argued, in order to remove barriers to market entry and to ensure that newcomers to the market became quickly competitive. Nevertheless, the interventions created the impression that DG IV's liberalism was hostile to Europe's public-service broadcasters.

However, a third important intervention by DG IV in 1994 concerned market dominance by the private sector. The issue was a proposed joint-venture between Bertelsmann, Kirch and Deutsche Telekom, Germany's public telecommunications operation. The joint-venture, called MSG Media Service, was intended to provide pay-TV services, including video-on-demand and a number of other advanced 'interactive' services. It attracted DG IV's interest because of the threat that the alliance of these giant companies posed to an open market for pay-TV – and indeed also for future digital communication services – in Germany. The reasoning was straightforward. Deutsche Telekom was Germany's leading cable television operator and had recently acquired an important stake in Luxembourg's 'Astra' satellite operation. As seen, Bertelsmann and Kirch were already giant media companies. Moreover, they co-owned Premiere, Germany's only existing pay-TV company. DG IV argued that dominance of the German market for pay-TV by such a powerful strategic alliance would impede market access by companies from other EU member states. On these grounds DG IV blocked the deal.

The MSG Media Services case fore-shadowed DG IV's growing interest in the whole question of ownership by large companies of 'proprietory systems' for the encryption (encoding) of subscription services. As things stood, those services that reached the market first were very likely to monopolise the pay-TV market; this appeared to be the lesson of BSkyB in Britain, Canal Plus in France and Premiere (Bertelsmann/Kirch) in Germany. The competition issue that was now becoming apparent was that ownership of the encryption technology gave such companies the potential for 'gate-keeping' – and even monopolistic control – of all pay-TV channels carried by the system regardless of their ownership. Companies were already positioning themselves to provide the next generation of encryption technology for digital television (see Conclusion). Therefore, if DG IV's activity may have appeared to be discriminatory *vis-à-vis* the public-service broadcasters in order to establish the ground rules for the new market, private sector companies as well soon found themselves to be the object of its scrutiny. Future decisions like the MSG Media Services one could certainly not be ruled out. Indeed, the issue of proprietory conditional access systems for pay-TV (and similar services) was becoming one of the hottest controversies in the media policy community at large by the mid-1990s. Yet it still remains true to say that DG IV's concerns were largely reflective of its economic liberalism. It was – hardly surprisingly in view of its remit – primarily interested in the efficient functioning of the market.

EC regulation and media concentration

But what about media concentration and its implications for media pluralism? Pressure for European-level action had long been exerted by the European media unions and journalists associations through their European umbrella organisations and the European Trade Union Confederation (ETUC). The CofE, too, had monitored the problem. Characteristically, the first EC institution to become concerned with the issue was the European Parliament. The EP expressed disappointment that the 1984 Green Paper and subsequently the Directive 'Television Without Frontiers' contained no anti-monopoly measures. The Economic and Social Committee echoed this concern.

The 1989 Directive said little indeed about the problem of media concentration. Certainly, it aspired to a number of worthy ideals. Thus, in its opening preamble it stated: its aim to institute 'a system ensuring that competition in the common market is not distorted'; its aim 'to establish conditions of fair competition without prejudice to the public interest role to be discharged by the television broadcasting services'; and, its concern for the 'member states to ensure the prevention of any acts ... which may promote the creation of dominant positions which lead to restrictions on pluralism' (originally inserted into the draft Directive after pressure from the EP). Also, Article 5 of the Directive did specify that: 'broadcasters reserve at least 10 per cent of their transmission time, excluding the time appointed for news, sports events, games, advertising and teletext services, or alternatively, at the discretion of the member state, at least 10 per cent of their programming budget, for European works created by producers who are independent of broadcasters'. This measure was intended 'to stimulate new sources of television production, especially the creation of small and medium sized enterprises'. The Article was designed both to introduce more competition into the sector and to 'offer new opportunities and outlets to the marketing of creative talents of employment of cultural professions and employees in the cultural field' (as explained in the Directive's preamble). However, Article 5 was the only binding concrete provision that dealt, in any conceivable sense, with the important issue of media concentration. Its economic liberal accent was clear.

Of course, as just seen, DG IV already had authority to act independently (subject only to judicial review by the Court of Justice) to enforce the Treaty of Rome's generic competition laws (Articles 85 and 86), which banned anti-competitive practices and the abuse of dominant market position. Moreover, the Community's merger control regulation (based on Article 87) had been enhanced in the run up to the 1992 Single European Market. To be precise, a Council Regulation of December 1989 (which came into effect in September 1990) required DG IV to examine all mergers and acquisitions where:

1   the companies concerned have a combined aggregate worldwide

turnover value of ECU 5 billion; and/or
2   at least two of the companies concerned produce an aggregate
    turnover value totalling ECU 250 million.

The second threshold had an important qualification. It did not
apply where each company derived more than two thirds of its
aggregate EC turnover within one and the same state. This meant
that mergers of mainly national impact would remain a national
affair. Previously, though, without explicit financial thresholds, EC
merger control had been weak. These new thresholds were, however,
not very relevant to the media field. The inadequacies of generic rules
governing industrial concentration in the media sector, have already
been remarked upon in the case of national level anti-trust legislation (see pp. 94–102). The main problem is, simply, that media companies do not customarily achieve turnover approaching such levels.
An additional problem with the EC's generic rules was, just like most
national anti-trust laws, they allowed for a large measure of regulatory discretion. In particular, special dispensation could be made in
the cause of promotion of the Common Market. Given that the
Commission's primary objective was the 'creation of an internal
market for media products and services, *not the preservation of
pluralism and diversity*' (my emphasis), this scope for discretionary
exemption would appear to be quite pertinent (Lensen, 1992, p. 19).

The Commission's 1992 Green Paper: pluralism and media concentration in the internal market

The Commission had always dodged the issue of media pluralism
and diversity by arguing that it was a matter for national authorities
to decide upon. However, the Commission was compelled to give
attention to the threat posed to pluralism by media concentration
because of the build-up of irresistible pressure from the European
Parliament (EP) where concern about media concentration had been
expressed throughout the 1980s. In February 1990 the EP adopted a
resolution on media takeovers and mergers (EP, 1990). This took the
view that 'unlimited and unchecked concentration in the media
threaten[ed] the right to information, editorial independence and
journalists' freedom'. It called upon the Commission in Brussels to
produce 'proposals for establishing a special legislative framework

on media mergers and takeovers' and called for anti-trust laws 'to ensure that: minimum professional standards [were] guaranteed; journalistic ethics [were] protected; the risk of subordination of small companies [was] eliminated; [and] freedom of expression for all those working in the media [was] safeguarded'. The resolution also suggested that those member states that did not have anti-concentration laws should be required to introduce them forthwith. Over the course of the following two years, the EP's 'Committee on Youth, Culture, Education, the Media and Sport' drew up and considered a special report on media concentration (EP, 1992a). It contained a whole range of suggested measures by which diversity might be safeguarded. It also called upon the Commission to prepare a 'proposal for a Directive or another equally effective instrument to combat concentration in the media'. In September, the European Parliament voted yet another resolution urging Community action. Entitled 'Resolution on Media Concentration and Diversity of Opinion', its call for action was explicit (EP, 1992b).

In December 1992 the Commission at last produced a Green Paper entitled *Pluralism and Media Concentration in the Internal Market: An Assessment of the Need for Community Action* (CEC 1992). This document was prefaced by an invitation from DG III for all interested parties, in addition to the European Parliament and competent national authorities, to volunteer their opinions. It addressed itself 'particularly [to] the European organisations representing television broadcasters, radio broadcasters, publishers, journalists, audio-visual creative artists, audio-visual producers, satellite distributors, cable distributors and advertisers'; in other words, the European media policy community at large. The Green Paper itemised a number of questions: Had the Community scale of media activity rendered ineffective any national restrictions on media ownership? Was Community action required? What should be the content of a possible harmonisation measure? Was it desirable to set up an independent regulatory body? It also asked for comment on three broad alternative directions of action (see below).

The Green Paper's overview of the economic aspects of media concentration was based on a comprehensive cross-national study commissioned by DG III from Booz.Allen Hamilton (1992).* On the basis

---

* Rich in data on media consumption and concentration.

of this economic study's evidence, the Green Paper accepted that the media sector exhibited a 'fairly high level of concentration compared to other sectors'. This was especially the case in the press sector. With respect to broadcasting, though, its findings were ambiguous. On the one hand, the Green Paper noted the corporate strategy of cross-media ownership, mainly from the press into broadcasting. It also documented the broadcasters' strategies of vertical integration and international expansion. It pointed to the 'complex web of shareholdings and media ownership networks centred around a few national operators' (p. 27), remarking that often even minority inter-ests could control companies through 'alliances with sleeping part-ners'. Therefore it seemed alert to the fact that the problem of control was a larger matter than one simply of ownership. All this seemed to suggest that the Commission saw cause for concern. Against this, though, it stated that if state broadcasters were included in the analysis, then broadcasting had experienced increased plural-ism through the expansion of the private sector.

The Commission's view of the potential role of the Community, too, seemed rather ambiguous. On the one hand, it made clear that it saw protection of media pluralism as being primarily a matter for national law. Member states were quite entitled, it accepted, to restrict broadcasters from other member states if they circumvented their national pluralism and competition requirements. In fact, the point was explicitly made that national laws restricting maximum holdings, or cross holdings, in companies were permissible and to be distinguished from illegal discriminatory restrictions on foreign own-ership. Moreover, the Green Paper made very clear that member states were entitled to prevent mergers in order to protect pluralism even in cases where the mergers did not affect competition under the Community's Merger Control Regulation (pp. 8–9). However, in some contradiction to the thrust of these points, and clearly getting to the nub of its concerns, the Commission expressed anxiety that there might be problems of compatibility between such laws and the concept of broadcasting without frontiers. Differences between national pluralism regulations – and the Green Paper documented their wide variance – might lead to interference with the operation of the Single Market. National regulations might distort or restrict competition. They might restrict the free movement of services or free establishment of companies. Legal uncertainty might harm the competitiveness of companies. For example, there might be divergence of views as to what constituted circumvention. Moreover, the scope for misapplication of these national rules was strongly hinted at: national laws might actually limit access to the media 'when access should be facilitated so as to permit the establishment of the single market and secure the competitiveness of media companies which pluralism requires' (p. 9).

The Green Paper presented three alternative courses of Community action:

1 *No specific Community action.* This course would leave it to member states to deal with the matter. There may be no real need for Community involvement: national rules may be sufficient. This would allow for member states to impose restrictions 'in keeping with the national situation'. Against this, though, it would disregard the wishes of the European Parliament. It would make it impossible to manage any future problems arising from media concentration and the 'malfunctioning of the internal market'; and equally it would allow the possibility of increased national restrictions interfering with the latter's development and placing 'more and more obstacles ... in the way of media companies'. Such a course might render difficult implementation of the 1989 Directive 'Television Without Frontiers'. This could be seen as a reason for rapid action.

2 *Action to improve transparency.* The Community could propose cooperation between the member states to increase transparency of media ownership and control. A recommendation – and, that failing, a legal instrument – might aim to achieve greater disclosure and exchange of information relating to media ownership. This would both facilitate the task of national authorities in managing the problem and provide information that would be useful in the event of further Community action. On the other hand, there was no evidence that the lack of such a community instrument has impeded the exchange of information between national authorities. More revealing of the Commission's main concern is the argument that 'this type of action would not solve the problems created by the effect which restrictions have on the functioning of the internal market'.

3 *Community action to harmonise laws.* This raised three possibilities: (a) A Council Directive to harmonise national laws on media ownership and to produce common rules striking a bal-

ance between guaranteeing diversity of ownership and the easing of access to media activities. This would ensure the removal of obstacles to the internal market, but it might allow member states too much flexibility in implementation. (b) A Council Regulation. This would be more 'directly applicable' and would not require translation into member state law. It would also have to be more precise than a Directive; the resultant inflexibility might prove to be problematic. (c) A Directive or Regulation plus an independent committee, consisting of independent authorities from member states, to assist in implementing the harmonisation instrument. However, this would entail the risk that matters best handled at the national level would be centralised at Community level.

Useful though it was in presenting the options, the Green Paper had obvious faults. In the first place its overall line of argumentation could be criticised for a lack of clarity. Above all, it could be said to have suffered from having a contradictory quality at its core. While it gives considerable attention to the question of pluralism, the Green Paper makes clear that the Commission's primary interest is in the operation of the single broadcasting market set in place by the 1989 Directive 'Television Without Frontiers'. This, it has been pointed out, 'produces a tension which pervades the whole of the Green Paper and ultimately limits the scope of its proposals' (Hitchens, 1994, p. 587). The Green Paper stresses the need for a competitive media industry and the contribution this might make towards pluralism. It suggests that this competitiveness may be harmed (it says 'affected' or 'interfered with') by national regulations brought in to safeguard pluralism. This concern may well be justified. Equally, though, as Chapter 6 has suggested, the real problem may well turn out to be the 'competitive deregulation' by governments of their existing concentration regulations. Moreover, the Green Paper comes close to making the simplistic assumption that competition will necessarily foster diversity (Hitchens, 1994, p. 587).

The Green Paper provoked a considerable response. Despite its liberal undercurrent, a range of private commercial interests argued that there was no call for Community action against media concentration. Among these were the European Publishers' Council (EPC), Berlusconi's Fininvest, BSkyB and Rupert Murdoch's News International. By contrast, European trade union federations connected with the media were in favour of Community action. Prominent among these was the European Group of the International Federation of Journalists (EGIFJ). In between these polar positions there were a number of interests that plainly felt unjustly disadvantaged by instances of circumvention – by their rivals – of national regulations that they themselves were compelled to abide by. Thus, Channel 4 and the ITV Association both complained about BSkyB's circumvention of Britain's cross-media ownership restrictions. Those arguing for no action tended to be those benefiting from liberal national laws, whilst those pressing for regulation were those who felt disadvantaged (Hitchens, 1994, p. 596–597).

In the autumn of 1994, the Commission, reporting on its first round of consultation, noted that the positions of the various interests remained divided and recommended that a further round of consultation be conducted before any firm decision were made on the need for and the parameters of any EC action. The Commission noted that the European Parliament and the Economic and Social Committee were both in favour of Option III to harmonise national media ownership laws (CEC, 1994c, p. 4). The debate had meanwhile been influenced towards Option III by the publication, in May 1994, of the highly influential 'Bangemann Report' entitled *Europe and the Global Information Society; Recommendations to the EC* (CEC, 1994a). Regarding the impact of media ownership rules on the Single Market, 'especially in multimedia', and on the 'global competitiveness of Europe's media industry', this technocratic report was explicit that 'rules at the European level [were] going to be crucial … [and that] the Union [would] have to lead the way in heading off deeper regulatory disparity' (CEC, 1994a, p. 21).

The EU's evolving strategy for the European programme industry

In December 1993 Jacques Delors, the outgoing president of the European Commission, published a very important White Paper, entitled *Growth, Competitiveness and Employment: The Challenges and Ways Forward into the Twenty First Century* (CEC, 1993). This White Paper, adopted by the European Council of December 1993, was concerned with the future prospects for growth, competitiveness and employment in the European Union (as the EC was now known). Significantly, it singled out the information society and, in particular, the audiovisual sector as the area of greatest potential for growth and job creation. This White Paper was followed, in 1994, by the above-mentioned 'Bangemann Report' (CEC, 1994a) which developed the theme. With regard to audiovisual markets, the Bangemann report stated unequivocally that 'the biggest structural problem [was] the financial and organisational weakness of the European programme industry' (p. 11). The Commission, meanwhile, had conducted a wide-ranging consultation of the European media policy community and also established an 'audiovisual Think Tank' to explore the problem and make recommendations. The Think Tank published a detailed report in March 1994 (Vasconcelos *et al.*, 1994). Thus informed, the Commission produced a 1994 Green Paper called *Strategy Options to Strengthen the European Programme Industry in the Context of the Audiovisual Policy of the European Union* (CEC, 1994b). This latter document noted the 'strategic role' played by films and television programmes within the context of a high growth sector undergoing major technological change, and stressed the need for Europe's programme industry to 'compete on world markets, to help European culture to flourish and create jobs in Europe' (p. 53). The Green Paper identified the main trends in the European programme industry, noting the explosion of demand, rising prices and Europe's propensity to import (mainly from the US). It highlighted Europe's 'atomistic local market structures', the poor intra-European distribution of programmes, and the industry's 'chronic loss-making situation'. It deplored the European programme industry's failure to 'attract significant flows of European and foreign investment' (p. 54). The Green Paper raised numerous questions and floated ideas about policy options (after all, this was a key function of a Green Paper). It also displayed a very keen awareness of what was at stake.

One of the striking features of the Green Paper was its preoccupation with the 'digital revolution' and with the information society more generally. Digital compression technology could be expected to multiply the number of channels and services even further than cable and satellite had so far done (see the Conclusion, pp. 301–303). The continuing convergence of broadcasting and advanced telecommunications was making possible a range of new 'multimedia' services. The Green Paper recommended that the 'EU press ahead with the introduction of technologically advanced infrastructure', stressing that this should be combined with a mobilisation of resources 'to invest in the development of a programme industry capable of competing at home and on the world market' (p. 55). Otherwise, Europe would just be allowing others to exploit the opportunities promised by new technologies. It pointed out that the new technologies raised questions about the future definition of 'programmes', and underlined the need for strategy to take account of the more diversified range of programme services that would be possible in the future. The Green Paper discussed a whole range of issues and questions concerning what might be done to improve support for the programme industries. It concluded by presenting three 'options' for the future. Regarding 'options for the rules of the game', the Commission held that existing rules provided a 'sound framework for the cross-border development of the industry that should be retained for the time being'. In the Commission's view, 'the development of the market for the establishment of infrastructure, the liberalisation of services and the removal of obstacles to the single market [was] the first objective'. Beyond this, the Commission invited comment on 'how the application of Community law and its monitoring [might] be made more effective'. A number of more technical questions were also raised: for example, whether 'preference should be given to incentives to *invest* in the production of programmes and the acquisition of rights rather than mechanisms based on *broadcasting* time' (i.e. the programme quotas). As for 'options for financial incentives', the Green Paper did not suggest any kind of figure for the level of future financial support that would be necessary, settling instead for discussion of the principles that should govern it and the mechanisms for providing it. Nevertheless, the need to cater for 'countries with low production capacity or restricted language areas' was highlighted. Finally, the Green Paper asked whether the option of 'convergence of national support systems' might be 'appropriate or feasible' (CEC, 1994b, esp. pp. 53–58).

Meanwhile, there had occurred a new round of the battle over the European programme quotas that had originally been introduced by the 1989 Directive 'Television Without Frontiers' (Article 4). The French had continued to press for the quotas to be more strongly worded and to be more strictly implemented. Indeed, European cultural policy was now highlighted as one of the main policies of the French presidency of the European Union during the first half of 1995. However, in their endeavour to see the quota rule strengthened, they found themselves increasingly marginalised. They were supported by Belgium and Austria (which joined the EU in 1985), both small countries which felt themselves to be particularly vulnerable to 'cultural penetration', but most other member states opposed strengthening the quota rule; 'liberal' Britain and Luxembourg were notably fierce in their opposition. By now the commercial broadcasting lobby was very strong in many countries. Dependent on imported entertainment programmes, commercial broadcasters were resolutely opposed to quotas. Also, by now the composition of the European Commission had changed: Jacques Delors, a supporter of quotas, had retired and the new president of the Commission, Jacques Santer (a former Prime Minister of Luxembourg) was openly critical of the quotas (for a full account of this struggle see Panis, 1995). In June 1995, the French presidency's cultural policy received a cruel blow when European culture ministers voted both to limit increases in funding for EU film production and rejected any strengthening of the programme quota article. The Germans, Dutch and British blocked French and European Commission ambitions to double the modest budget for the next 5-year stage of the MEDIA programme from £200 million to £400 million, and limited it instead to £310 million (*Financial Times*, 22 June 1995, p. 2). Again, the 'liberals' appeared to have prevailed over the *dirigistes*.

Guide to further reading

R. Collins, *Broadcasting and Audio-visual Policy in the European Single Market*, London: John Libbey, 1994.

B. Gavin (ed.), *European Broadcasting Standards in the 1990s*, Manchester/Oxford: NCC Blackwell, 1991.

M. Hirsch and V.G. Petersen, 'Regulation of Media at the European Level', Chapter 4 in K. Siune and W. Truetzschler (eds), *Dynamics of Media Politics: Broadcast and Electronic Media in Western Europe*, London: Sage, 1992, pp.42–56.

P. Humphreys, 'The European Community and Pan-European Broadcasting', *Journal of Area Studies*, Vol. 1, No. 1, 1992, pp. 97–114.

H.J. Kleinsteuber, V. Wiesner and P. Wilke (eds), *EG-Medienpolitik. Fernsehen in Europa zwischen Kultur und Kommerz*, Berlin: Vistas, 1990.

R. Negrine and S. Papathanassopoulos, *The Internationalisation of Television*, London/New York: Pinter, 1990, Chapter 4.

J. Wagner, *Policy-Analyse: Grenzenlos Fernsehen in der EG*, Frankfurt/Main: Peter Lang, 1994.

Conclusion

In the end the central issue in the relationship between the media and political institutions revolves around the *media's relative degree of autonomy* and to what extent and by what means this is allowed to be constrained (Gurevitch and Blumler, 1977, p. 263).

The maximum feasible *decommodification* and 're-embedding' of communications media in the social life of civil society is a vital condition of freedom from state and market censorship (Keane, 1992, p. 119).

Has 'politics' mattered?

Throughout this book our focus has been on the complex relationship between technological, economic and political determinants of media systems. Our main postulate was that, in societies at comparable stages of technological and economic development, 'politics' – variation in public policy – would help to explain much of the difference in media systems. To put it very simply, the power of technology and markets would tend to lead towards the broadly convergent development of media systems. Public policy, in the round sense, would help explain divergence. We also proceeded from the understanding that European media systems were configured according to a mix of two rationales: the libertarian/free market one and the social responsibility one which in the field of European broadcasting had, for a long time, the public-service monopoly as its core feature. It was the role of public policy to determine the mix between market freedom and public control. Political decisions constrained the application of technologies and the freedom of markets.

What conclusions can we now draw?

Our survey has revealed that the press has been allowed to function everywhere, in the main, according to the 'free market'. Nevertheless, political factors have made a difference. The extent of state influence on the press has varied according to the state tradition and the political system. Censorship, it seems, varied according to the 'opportunity to censor' presented by different political structures. The degree of freedom of information and journalistic immunities varied according to political culture. The character and extent of 'social responsibility' regulation also varied. State economic support for the press assumed different dimensions. Some governments supported weaker papers to promote political diversity among publications. This was the case in small consensual, corporatist countries with vulnerable press markets and especially so where Social Democracy was influential, notably Scandinavia. In France, press subsidies could also be explained by the post-war interventionism that characterised many sectors of the post-war economy. Press subsidies reflected France's traditional *étatisme*. Where the press industry was not strong − as in France, Italy and Spain − press subsidies were indiscriminate and comparatively generous. In Italy the main beneficiaries of these state subsidies during the 1970s were the big business press concerns. This, too, reflected the country's politics and political culture. Nevertheless, the main findings of our study are firstly, that apart from certain protections − of the individual, officialdom, or state secrets − the West European press has been conspicuously free from restrictive regulation. Secondly, our study would seem to suggest that the 'free market' is a myth, it is not free, and it is certainly not self-regulating. Instead press markets have been prone to striking imperfection and trends towards 'dominance'. Some might add that this situation results, partly, from regulatory weakness: the laxity of anti-trust law and practice.

'Politics' has clearly mattered much more when we look at broadcasting. Certainly, there were technical and economic reasons why Western Europe produced its fairly distinct model of 'public-service' broadcasting. Yet, quite clearly, there was no *a priori* reason why they required publicly owned broadcasting monopolies. After all, Luxembourg departed from the model. Its governments favoured a commercial monopoly. The United States adopted a competitive commercial system. Japan, comparable in terms of population density to Western European countries, opted for a mixed system with a strong commercial ingredient. Italy, after all, went down this road before the 'new media revolution'. Britain's ITV sector was part of a public-service duopoly; but this too reflected political choice. Clearly, the fact that generations of West Europeans have been limited to a public-service broadcasting monopoly reflected a widely shared politico-philosophical agreement that it was necessary. It was such a powerful medium of political persuasion that from the beginning state control was regarded as desirable. Media abuse by Fascists and Communists later led to a new stress on the broadcasters' relative autonomy and their democratic accountability structures. The commercialism of much American broadcasting long deterred most West European countries from introducing even a strictly regulated private sector. Cultural concerns led policy makers to prevent its 'commodification'. Above all, though, West European elites saw public-service broadcasting as an essential feature of their systems of pluralist democracy. It was to reflect, and promote, pluralism and diversity of opinion. Strengths and weaknesses flowed from its 'closeness to the political realm'.

'Politics' also made for significant differences between versions of public-service broadcasting. Notwithstanding the near universal public-service nature of the evolution of broadcasting in Western Europe, quite clearly there were important differences between countries in the way they organised their broadcasting systems. The political environments in which broadcasting systems were embedded were highly significant. Political factors were highly relevant for explaining why some broadcasting systems were prone to executive dominance (e.g. France), while in others influence over broadcasting was shared between parties and 'socially significant groups' (e.g. Germany, the Netherlands), and in yet others the broadcasters enjoyed relative autonomy (Britain). They helped explain, too, why certain countries had very strict and legalistic regulation (Germany) while in others regulatory implementation was very lax (e.g. Italy). The extent of 'majoritarianism' or 'consensus' in countries' political profiles was found to be important. All in all, there appeared to be a marked congruence between political systems and their respective media systems. The kind of political system made for a difference as to how much the publicly owned media enjoyed relative autonomy or were subject to traits of dominance in their relations to the 'political realm'.

Media policies also reflected trends in political ideology. For sev-

eral post-war decades in Western Europe there prevailed an ideological consensus that was highly supportive of the public-service
model. For one thing, public-service broadcasting was a feature of a
much larger socio-economic paradigm in which public intervention
in economy and society was widely regarded as virtuous. For another
thing, Western Europe's pre-war ideological polarisation had, in
many countries, ceded place to a post-war 'cartelised' system of
moderate parties of government (following Katz and Mair, 1995). In
many countries it was normal practice for these parties to share
influence on the broadcast media, consequently they each had a continuous stake in the system. In more adversarial systems, as in
France, there was always the promise of governmental alternance.
Another alternative, as in Britain, was the exercise of restraint with
regard to media control. Whatever the case, the post-Second World
War 'end of ideology' was conducive to the entrenchment of the
public-service model.

To a degree, as well, the public-service model was flexible enough
to accommodate the ideological rejuvenation that began in the 1960s.
In various ways the broadcasters responded to censure of their elitist
paternalism, their unrepresentativeness of minorities, their conser-
vatism. They introduced more differentiated and exciting programming, new television channels, new radio services. On the one hand
they became more sensitive to modern mass culture, on the other
hand they ensured that this did not predominate over their provision
for a diversity of public tastes. These efforts were enough to assuage
all but their more radical critics; those on the Right who demanded
a return to moral paternalism and those on the libertarian Left who
demanded still more minority representativeness and grass-roots participation. In the 1980s, however, this all changed profoundly. The
'libertarian' theme was hijacked by the neo-liberal Right. The call
now was not so much for reform of the model as for its displacement. This ideological sea-change drew much, for the force of its
argument, upon new technological and market realities.

By now, it seemed that technological and market imperatives were
becoming the crucial determinants of broadcasting structures. Not
all countries had neo-liberal inclined governments, yet they were
caught up willy-nilly in the paradigmatic change. The general,
Europe-wide 'deregulatory' trend was the more or less direct result
of powerful technological changes and international market developments which presented far-reaching and unavoidable challenges to

existing policies. Technological change, in the shape of cable and especially satellite, undermined the rationale for the public-service monopoly. It brought the prospect of regulatory circumvention. Everywhere traditional patterns of broadcasting regulatory policy were confronted with the prospect, increasingly the reality, of decreased national autonomy for media systems. In this context, industrial and international market considerations to an increasing extent determined policy as much as traditional cultural concerns. The collapse of the precarious boundaries between the broadcasting, telecommunications and computing sectors, coupled with governments' concern to promote domestic information technology industries, led to irresistible pressures to establish a new, looser and more flexible regulatory framework for the 'electronic media'. Increasingly, 'politics' appeared to be at the service of markets. Nevertheless, as this study has shown, there remained considerable scope for 'politics' mattering. There was a marked difference between those countries which embraced radical marketisation either through 'majoritarian' political voluntarism (France) or political 'immobilism' (Italy); and countries where a 'consensual' style of government and even constitutional/legal intervention constrained its direction (Germany). The British case, too, showed that political and media traditions and culture continued to count for something.

Digital TV and the telecoms revolution

It is important to point out, in concluding, that a further technological leap is imminent. Most of the cable links to the home so far laid in Western Europe have used traditional copper-coaxial cable. Though very capable of providing multi-channel television its bandwidth (i.e. channel capacity) is still extremely limited compared to that of modern fibre-optic cable. Moreover, the latter has an 'interactive' capacity. It allows two-way communication making possible advanced home-shopping, home-banking and video-on-demand services, among other things. Telecommunications operators like British Telecom have been very busy during the decade laying nationwide fibre-optic 'trunk lines'. All that is now required for the creation of the 'information superhighways', now engaging very serious government interest in the USA and Western Europe, is the fibre-optic link to the home. Yet this is not the only technological factor for a much greater multiplication of broadcast services than we have so far witnessed – and, remember, there are well over one hundred television channels in Europe at the moment. The most important technical change is signal digitalisation. Since its development during the 1930s television has been supplied by means of analogue signals. Essentially, these are continuous electrical waves, carrying a signal; they are converted into a pattern of electrons, discharged onto the picture tube, to reproduce the signal in the form of moving pictures. By contrast, digitalisation stores and transmits information in the binary 'bits' of the world of computers. Digital signals are capable of being broadcast by satellite, cable and terrestrially. Moreover, they can even be carried on telephonic cable, raising the possibility that BT, for instance, might soon supply commercial video-on-demand services (it has proven its technical capability so to do already). 'Intelligent' television sets, to receive digital signals, are in principle as easy to manufacture as CD players (already using digital technology). The final technical punch is that digital signals can be compressed. Digital compression, currently being developed in the USA, Britain and Germany, means that countless more channels still will be capable of supply via fibre-optic cable (one day, several hundred!). Satellite channel capacity, too, will leap. Even terrestrial television will be transformed; several channels will be capable of supply for every channel now available.

There has been much technological 'hype' about all this. There are real problems of financing the new technological developments. Private interests will be naturally wary about making a strong commitment to the new technologies without the probability of an economic reward. Currently, the corporate sector still faces all kinds of uncertainty about markets. What will consumers be prepared to pay for? How much fragmentation will the market bear? Also, business uncertainty surrounds the future regulatory environment. What regulatory barriers will governments place in the way? Will the British government, for instance, waive the ban of BT's supplying broadcast services? Nevertheless, in the United States there has already occurred an impressive wave of merger and acquisition activity between telecoms, computer, broadcasting and cable interests (including some 'mega-mergers'). The US government has begun to relax regulatory barriers, notably competition regulations limiting the scope for multi-media diversification, in order to encourage giant corporations to develop the much vaunted new 'information superhighways'. There is every likelihood that, in Europe too, regulatory barriers will be removed to encourage investment. Certainly, this is the message of this book's examination of new media developments to date. Increasingly, public policies have tended to follow techno-logical and market developments.

A new age of media pluralism?

One thing is clear. As broadcasting converges with computing and advanced telecommunications, it will become increasingly 'multi-media' in nature. Moreover, although technology development costs are enormous and the new media economics will be complex, in the long run entrance costs can be expected to plummet. In the fullness of time, digitalisation, fibre-optics, and so forth, can be expected very significantly to reduce the costs of media access. Some broad-casting, at least, will resemble 'electronic publishing'. More new ser-vices will be of the 'video-on-demand' kind. There will be scope, too, for grass-roots 'citizen channels'. There has already occurred an expansion of specialist 'narrowcast' (as opposed to 'broadcast' ser-vices). In Western Europe, there are children's channels, sports chan-nels, news channels, and so on. Cable operators have provided for experimental open access channels and channels for ethnic minori-ties. The choice among services, in this sense, is increasing. Also, spe-cialist thematic channels – like sports channels, music channels, and news channels – have being launched in international markets. On this basis, optimists predict a significant 'de-massification' of the mass media. In the future, it has been suggested, the media will bear the hallmarks of the general socio-economic shift away from 'Fordist' standardised mass production, aimed primarily at the domestic level, towards flexible, differentiated production for global markets.

On the other hand, our study also contains some cause for a less optimistic evaluation. Commercial competition can have a perni-cious effect on a medium like broadcasting. Access costs might be set to diminish in the long run, but programme costs for 'mainstream' media fare have already inflated because of increased competition for scarce programme resources. There is alarming evidence that multi-channel distribution possibilities are already running ahead of pro-gramme production capacity. There is little sign that audience fragmentation leads most broadcasters to be less concerned about audience maximisation. There is every sign that oligopolistic developments in the mainstream European industry are the price to be paid for the sector's growth and for the development of the new technologies which Schumpeterians might argue actually require a period of oligopolistic profits. In the field of broadcasting, therefore, the possibility exists that on balance what we are witnessing – at least in the main – might rather be a shift away from the relatively differentiated production that in the past has been required to meet the standards of highly regulated domestic public-service systems, and a drift towards the more standardised lowest-common denominator commercial kind of television associated with less differentiated, increasingly homogenised international markets.

Is 'electronic publishing' even an attractive analogy? The answer, of course, depends much on the distinction between ideal and praxis. The history of the press sector certainly does not suggest that the sheer technological potential for very diverse media has been realised. In fact, for the most part, the reverse has been the case. Technical innovations have certainly lowered certain costs of production. However, labour costs, editorial costs, newsprint costs and distribution costs, have not fallen. Moreover, even if the new computerised technologies have cut running costs and lowered market entry barriers, the competitive position of weaker newspapers has not been improved in relative terms *vis-à-vis* their stronger rivals. The market share of the large press concerns has not diminished, nor has there occurred the promised multiplication of titles. The twentieth century, as a whole, has seen a steady diminution of titles (albeit occurring in concentration waves). Admittedly, there are exceptions to this rule, notably free-sheets and specialist magazines. All the same, there has been a decline in the political pluralism of the press. Though partly explicable by the 'de-ideologisation' of politics during the 1950s and most of the 1960s, it is more reflective of the way diversity has fallen victim to unrestrained market forces in imperfect markets. Quite evidently, over the course of time, the press sector has witnessed fierce struggles for 'dominance' leading to a remarkable concentration of ownership and media power in a restricted number of hands. Local monopoly and national oligopoly is now the rule.

The new media revolution may, we have to recognise, be developing in a similarly oligopolistic direction. As this study has made clear, the media are currently caught up in dynamic processes of integration and diversification. Large multi-media groups are expanding internationally and across media sectors. What is more, these media giants are forging strategic alliances with each other. Thus Berlusconi's Fininvest company has allied in Germany with the Kirch/Springer group and acquired stakes in French and Spanish private commercial broadcasting as well. The CLT was allied with Bertelsmann in German commercial television and it was the mainstay of the French commercial channel M6 (the privatised TF1's principal rival). The CLT also set up joint ventures in the Netherlands and Belgium. Germany's public telecoms operator, Deutsche Telekom, took a stake in the highly successful Astra satellite television company, an erstwhile rival provider of satellite services. Moreover, the planned pay-TV joint venture between Deutsche Telekom, Bertelsmann and Kirch (prohibited by the European Commission) showed how oligopolistic competition between rivals was no obstacle to the pursuit of monopolistic alliance strategies in key European markets. Finally, the BBC's tie-up with Pearson in a pan-European satellite television joint venture showed that even public/private strategic alliances were conceivable. The giant players' intent, it seemed, was to 'carve up' the 'European mediascape' (Burgelman and Pauwels, 1992, p. 171)

Re-regulation, de-regulation or "liberalising re-regulation"?

There has occurred some discussion about the use of the terms 'de-regulation' and 're-regulation'. Siune *et al.* (1992, pp. 4–5), in the Introduction to an important study of the *Dynamics of Media Politics*, see 're-regulation' as the more appropriate term, yet note in almost the same breath that 'throughout Europe the national regulatory environments are becoming weaker'. They prefer to speak about the re-regulatory activity of the EC and the Council of Europe, yet remark that it was 'undertaken in a spirit of liberalisation'. In the Conclusion of *Dynamics of Media Politics*, a volume that shows how the balance between the role of markets and regulation in shaping the new order has swung towards the former, Siune and McQuail (1992, p. 192), employ the term 'liberalising re-regulation'. Most will probably be happy to settle for this.

That there has been an element of re-regulation cannot be denied.

These days media laws are more numerous, more specific, and made at more levels – in that we now have the European one. As this study has shown, new regulations have been manufactured on an impressive scale in order to respond to the new technical and market developments. Marketisation has required the construction of new regulatory authorities and a whole tranche of new rules – just as, it might be suggested, in the mid-1950s the introduction of ITV in Britain necessitated the establishment of the IBA (ITA as it then was known), heavily equipped with rules and regulations, the whole ITV/IBA edifice being governed by statute. In the 1980s, as seen, additional regulatory bodies were added to the British duopoly, new laws were constantly being discussed and enacted. The state was far from inactive in the broadcasting policy field. Similarly, both the French and the German cases testified to a furious amount of re-regulatory activity during the 1980s. This included the establishment by the state of commissions of inquiry, the production of official reports, the discussion of legislative proposals, and so forth. In the end, even 'immobilist' Italy managed to produce what looked on paper to be a complex regulatory framework. In all these cases, the introduction of commercial broadcasting meant that the state had to define new ownership and cross-media ownership rules. Similarly, rules governing the programming obligations of the private broadcasters were required. All this was certainly, in a sense, 're-regulation'. The state had not withdrawn from the sector, it had become – in a sense – an active 're-regulator'.

However, this study has argued that de-regulation could most definitely be seen at work in the way that marketisation has profoundly altered the overall regulatory context. The private sector may have been formally subjected to new regulations, but it certainly saw itself released from the kind of public-service obligations that had previously been universal in Western Europe (except for Luxembourg). The extent of exemption, of course, varied according to the country in question. In Scandinavia new commercial channels were fairly strictly regulated. In Britain, ITV still had to respect some key public-service obligations and perform above the famous 'quality threshold'. Even so, the rules were less strict than they had been previously and the ITC's authority to intervene was less than that of the IBA. Everywhere, the public broadcasters continued to remain legally obligated to provide a balanced mix of quality programmes, but the context in which they now functioned was a transformed one. They found themselves under pressure to adapt to the marketised new realities. In Italy and in France, the public broadcasters' performance would appear to have been negatively affected by the new competition. The fact that their public-service duties were protected by formal regulation, seemed to be rather inconsequential. In Germany, on the other hand, a commitment to re-regulation could certainly be seen in the Constitutional Court's 1986 crucial judgment (and subsequent rulings) that explicitly underlined the central importance of public-service broadcasting and the future development of the public broadcasters. This, the court made clear, was the *sine qua non* for the introduction of commercial broadcasting. All the same, despite this variation, the fact remains that where broadcasting services were once solely reserved to public operators and governed by strict rules, the situation now is that they can be owned privately and the rules governing them are more relaxed. Some might feel that this is de-regulation.

The argument has also been developed in previous pages that, although national regulatory frameworks still vary considerably at present, there exist significant pressures towards 'competitive de-regulation'. These pressures place the traditional cultural goals of broadcasting in some jeopardy, to the extent that they may even be perceived to be a competitive handicap according to the increasingly economic criteria of broadcasting policy-making. This is reflected very clearly in policies governing the ownership of commercial media. In a simple sense, again, the very production of ownership rules where generally none existed before, might be seen as 're-regulation'. However, the real test should be the extent to which these rules provide constraint on new concentrations of private media power. In some cases, clearly, the rules would appear to have been tailored to market requirements. It is hard to evaluate the regulatory framework in Italy – allowing a single media entrepreneur to retain a monopoly of private commercial broadcasting – as 're-regulatory'. Equally, it is difficult indeed to judge the conspicuous weakness of cross-media ownership rules in Germany as anything other than a departure from – in effect a deregulation of – that country's historical attachment to a 'separation-of-media-powers' between press and broadcasting (see Humphreys, 1994). Finally, in Britain, the fierce industry lobbying of government to relax comparatively strict ownership rules was testament to the pressures towards competitive deregulation. In fact, the very purposes of broadcasting regulation were being tested. Was it to guarantee pluralism and diversity in the media? Or was it to 'provide a minimum level of control in order to facilitate trade and competitive activity?' (Hitchens, 1994, p. 587).

Future re-regulatory possibilities

In the future, the European Union is an obvious agency for promoting the kind of supranational re-regulatory initiatives that will be required to counter the forces of national 'competitive deregulation' and 'regulatory circumvention' that clearly have arisen. The involvement of EU institutions in the debate about media concentration holds out some promise in this regard. The European Commission has already started to bare its teeth in defence of competition. This was clearly illustrated by its intervention to block the proposed vertically integrated pay-TV joint venture between the giant German media interests, Bertelsmann, Kirch and Deutsche Telekom. The Commission's 1992 Green Paper *Pluralism and Media Concentration in the Internal Market* also raised the possibility of future EU legislative action to counter media concentration. Certainly, the European Parliament has pushed hard for action. However, the Green Paper's content arguably betrayed a primary economic policy motivation: the Commission was concerned that disparate national anti-concentration rules might constitute an obstacle to the functioning of the single European broadcasting market. Also, the Green Paper was not exactly enthusiastically received. As far as other regulatory matters were concerned, it could be argued that the 1989 Directive *Television Without Frontiers* was only nominally 're-regulatory'. In key respects, it was clearly deregulatory in that it established the 'lowest common denominator' principle of mutual recognition for transfrontier broadcasting. Even the controversial made-in-Europe quota rule was a political commitment, without any legal force. Arguably, the main beneficiaries of the EC's regulatory policies thus far would be the larger multi-media groups with ambitions to operate widely across the Community. Driven by an industrial and commercial logic, the Community's policy was unlikely to benefit small players or countries (Burgelman and Pauwels, 1992).

What kinds of regulation and public intervention are desirable and, importantly, feasible? For a start, there is no reason whatsoever why new concentration regulations, catering to the new multi-media realities, should not be designed. There may be problems in defining markets, but this is surely a technical task not beyond the wit of policy makers. The fact of numerically increased inter-media competition hardly disguises the fact that giant corporations are taking control of more and more media outlets. The pluralism that underpins the Western European understanding of democracy, demands no less than diverse and independent mass media. Yet at the local, national and even European levels, there are tendencies towards 'dominance' of media markets. Therefore, one of the main challenges for the future will be to keep the media diverse and pluralistic in the face of powerful pressures towards economic concentration. This will become especially important wherever control of technologies – cable television networks, encryption systems for pay-TV, or future 'smart card' conditional access systems for digital television – presents scope for monopolistic control over media content. The issue of 'proprietory' high technology systems raises the important matter of regulating for open media access and against the potential that large corporations may have for 'gate-keeping' – and monopolistic control – through ownership of such systems. Beyond this, there is an argument for requiring large 'mainstream' channels or operations to provide reasonably diverse programming. They need not, of course, be subject to strict 'public-service' requirements so long as a healthy public broadcasting sector co-exists with them. A case can be made, though, for at least some regulatory oversight of their programme schedules and content. Here, the German approach to multi-channel broadcasting is very interesting. In the first place, the legal requirement of a dynamic public-service sector is axiomatic. In the second place, the law requires an overall 'pluralism' of private media offerings; if this state of affairs is not attained 'externally' (i.e. across services) then a measure of 'internal pluralism' (within services) is called for. Further, private media in Germany are supervised by 'external' supervisory bodies, very much in the model of the British IBA/ITC with the important qualification that they are more socially representative.

Another radical measure would be to direct public support towards improving public access to the media, to encourage the development of 'non-market, non-state' media. Accordingly, a 'revised public-service model', seeking to democratise established practices and institutions, might disburse support to 'non-profit and legally guaranteed media institutions of civil society'. These might

take various forms: for instance, local recording studios, media cooperatives, community radio, and in the future information society,
numerous other kinds of grass-roots multi-media services for the citizenry. The new media's potential might be enlisted, in this way, in
order to 'socialise' aspects of communication, rather than simply to
'marketise' it (Keane, 1992, pp. 121–2). This kind of thinking needs
to be taken more seriously at the European level as well. Certainly,
the kind of cultural policy measures supported by the French and
developed by programmes like the EC's MEDIA and the Council of
Europe's 'Eurimages' initiatives are very important (if also modestly
funded). The need for greater public support for the media – and the
'culture industries' at large – might be given more sympathetic attention in some countries. Our study suggests that, while electronic
media delivery systems are multiplying, there is developing a crisis of
European programme production. Some of the growing demand will
be met, within Europe, by the increased inter-European programme
flows facilitated by the EC's liberalising measures. However, much
of this demand will continue to be met by imports from the United
States. Much of the rest will come from Europe's larger countries
with stronger production capacities. Moreover, it will mainly be
popular entertainment fare. There is arguably a reasonable need,
therefore, to take cultural policy more – not less – seriously. Despite
the objections of the US government, under pressure from its own
film industry, a strong case can be made for more vigorous public
interventionism to support what are, after all, Europe's 'culture
industries'. Both at the national and the European level, cautious
supply-side measures, within the context of deregulated markets, are
unlikely to be sufficient. In sum, a 'revised public-service' paradigm
may be a very apt and entirely characteristic West European policy
response, at national and European levels, with public support following the kind of programming as well as the kind of broadcaster.

Finally, radical perhaps, but arguably the best practical way to
protect freedom and pluralism in the media, given the direction of
new technological developments, would be to extend further the
legal rights and protections of journalists, media workers and consumers. So far, technological and market forces have been an excuse
to diminish the independence of journalists. Especially in the press
sector, this 'independence' was, in any case, arguably in a state of
underdevelopment. The recent tendency has been towards a 'casualisation' of media workers' conditions of employment in the cause of

'efficiency' and 'competitiveness'. Yet one of the reasons why public broadcasters had often been confident enough to offer significant resistance to the political pressures to which they were exposed in the past, was precisely because they enjoyed relative security of employment. In Germany, for example, the broadcasters' comparative employment security served to counteract the debilitating influence of the parties. In Britain, on the other hand, it has been suggested, the reduction of job security in recent years has gone hand in hand with a certain diminution of their independence (this rather iconoclastic but nonetheless very interesting comparison is from Etziony-Halevy, 1987). On the threshold of a new era of mass communication, there are now the strongest of grounds for establishing a new regulatory paradigm for workers in all areas of media activity, to guarantee their free creativity, investigative powers, access to information and freedom of opinion; and above all, their security both *vis-à-vis* state and their employers. In this regard, it might be felt that French law provides a model in the *clause de conscience*.

As far as the consumer is concerned, some radical theorists have gone so far as to advocate that large corporations even be treated as 'common carriers', legally required to grant access to a range of 'citizens' messages' (Keane, 1992, p. 120). This latter option may seem radical, but it deserves to be given serious consideration wherever markets are monopolised: local newspapers, cable television networks, pay-tv distribution systems, etc. Citizen access and media representativeness may end up being greatly improved by modern technical developments, but to make sure that this is the case may well call for imaginative legislative action. Certainly, one obvious area where public access might be improved right away is by tightening up – or implementing more rigorously – the legal Right of Reply. The incorporation of the Right of Reply in the 1989 'Television Without Frontiers' Directive (Article 23), a measure pressed by the European Parliament, might be seen as an important step in this direction. Like much else, however, the test will be in the implementation.

The spectre of an 'Americanisation' of the European media?

Historically, European media systems have shared some things in common and some very marked differences with the American one;

the greatest similarities were to be found in the press sector, the differences in the field of broadcasting. As in the United States, the press was organised largely according to the libertarian/free market rationale, with some social responsibility refinements. As in America, there occurred an early period of press diversity; indeed in Europe ideological pluralism was greater than in the United States, although polarisation was certainly more destabilising. However, in both the United States and Europe the twentieth century has witnessed a diminution of this press pluralism. As will be seen, part of this loss could be explained by a post-war de-ideologisation of traditional politics on both sides of the Atlantic. Yet many new ideological issues have become very salient without any corresponding flowering of press diversity, apart from the appearance of a small 'alternative' press. Much of this loss of diversity could be explained by the commercial standardisation of the press. There might be more specialist periodicals nowadays but by and large newspapers and magazines now follow standardised patterns of format, design and content. Above all, as will be seen, the loss in press pluralism has followed from a decline in the number of titles and a rise in the extent to which markets have become dominated by national oligopolies and local monopolies.

For all their shortcomings, the European public-service broadcasters have provided a balance to these developments. They have provided for a range and diversity of programming that the private commercial US networks have always been quite unable to match. Though regulated to a degree, the latter have in the past far more resembled the press in their orientation to mass markets. The US public-service channel has always been overshadowed by commercial giants. Moreover in the United States the traditional commercial networks themselves have been under challenge for some time now. Increasingly since the 1970s the United States has provided a developed model of a multi-channel commercial broadcasting system. This new scenario has been subject to even fewer regulatory controls than existed before. The United States experience, therefore, makes for an interesting reference point for the future of European broadcasting. There can be very little question but that the US experience points towards the marginalisation of public-service provision and values. More than ever, it would therefore appear, the future of the European public-service concept depends upon political resources of support that have never existed in the US. Further, the American media system is sustained by an enormous unified market, while the European market is still very fragmented. 'Americanisation', therefore, takes on another meaning as well; any expansion of European demand for programmes without a concomitant increase in European production capacity and in intra-European programmes exchange carries the risk of greater dependence on American imports. Policy makers in Europe therefore bear responsibility for structuring the emerging media markets, intervening in them when necessary, in such a way as to sustain the European 'culture industries'. In this latter regard, 'deregulation' – or if it is preferred, 'liberalising re-regulation' – is unlikely to prove an adequate response.

Bibliography

Albert, P. (1990), *La Presse Française*, Paris: La Documentation Française; third edition.

Allaun, F. (1988), *Spreading the News: A Guide to Media Reform*, Nottingham: Spokesman.

Altichieri, A. (1993), 'Italy: Broadcasting in Crisis', the Bulletin of the European Institute for the Media, Vol. 10, No. 4, pp. 28–29.

Article 19 (1993), *Press Law and Practice*, London: Article 19.

Axberger, H.-G. (1993), 'Sweden', in Article 19, *Press Law and Practice*, London: Article 19, pp. 150–166.

Barile, P. & Rao, G. (1992), 'Trends in the Italian Mass Media and Media Law', *European Journal of Communication*, Vol. 7, pp. 261–281.

Belfield, R., Hird, C. & Kelly, S. (1994), *Murdoch: The Great Escape*, London: Warner Books.

Berka, W. (1993), 'Austria', in Article 19, *Press Law and Practice*, London: Article 19, pp. 22–37.

Blumler, J. (ed.), (1992), *Television and the Public Interest: Vulnerable Values in West European Broadcasting*, London/Newbury Park/New Delhi: Sage, in association with the Broadcasting Standards Council.

Blumler, J., Brynin, M. and Nossiter, T. (1986), 'Broadcasting Finance and Programme Quality: An International Review', *European Journal of Communication*, Vol. 1, No. 3, September 1986, pp. 343–364.

Blumler, J. & Hoffmann-Riem, W. (1992), 'New Roles for Public Service Television', in J. Blumler (ed.), *Television and the Public Interest: Vulnerable Values in West European Broadcasting*, London: Sage, pp. 202–217.

Böckelmann, F. (1984), *Italien: Selbstregulierung eines 'freien' Rundfunkmarktes*, Volume 2 in the series edited by AfK (Arbeitsgemeinschaft für Kommunikationsforschung e.V.) *Kommerzielles Fernsehen in der Medienkonkurrenz*, Berlin: Wissenschaftsverlag Volker Spiess.

Booz.Allen & Hamilton (1988), *Funding European Television: The Challenge of the 1990s*, London: Booz.Allen & Hamilton.

Booz.Allen & Hamilton (1989), a study by J. Hughes, A. Mierzwa and C. Morgan, *Strategic Partnerships as a Way Forward in European Broadcasting*, London: Booz.Allen & Hamilton Inc.

Booz.Allen & Hamilton (1992), *Study on Pluralism and Concentration in Media – Economic Evaluation*, Brussels: Commission of the European Communities/Directorate-General III/F-5.

Brants, K. & Jankowski, N (1985), 'Cable Television in the Low Countries', in R. Negrine (ed.), *Cable Television and the Future of Broadcasting*, London: Croom Helm, pp. 74–101.

Brants, K. & McQuail, D. (1992), 'The Netherlands', in B. Østergaard (ed.), *The Media in Western Europe: The Euromedia Handbook*, London/Newbury Park/New Delhi: Sage, pp. 152–166.

Brants, K. & Siune, K. (1992), 'Public Broadcasting in a State of Flux', Chapter 7 in K. Siune & W. Truetzschler (eds), *Dynamics of Media Politics: Broadcast and Electronic Media in Western Europe*, the Euromedia Research Group, London: Sage, pp. 101–115.

Brants, K. & Slaa, P. (1994), 'The Netherlands', in J. Mitchell and J. Blumler (eds), *Television and the Viewer Interest: Explorations in the Responsiveness of European Broadcasters*, London: John Libbey/European Institute for the Media, Media Monograph No. 18, pp. 11–23.

Briggs, A. & Spicer, J. (1986), *The Franchise Affair*, London: Century.

Brittan, S. (1989), 'The Case for the Consumer Market', in C. Veljanovski (ed.), *Freedom in Broadcasting*, London: News International.

Broadcasting Research Unit (1986), *The Public Service Idea in British Broadcasting*, London: BRU.

Burgelman, J.-C. (1986), 'The Future of Public-Service Broadcasting: A Case-Study of "New" Communications Policy', *European Journal of Communication*, Vol. 1, pp. 173–201.

Burgelmann, J.-C. (1989), 'Political Parties and Their Impact on Public-service Broadcasting in Belgium: Elements from a Political Sociological Approach', *Media, Culture and Society*, Vol. 11, No. 2, pp. 167–193.

Burgelman, J.-C. & Pauwels, C. (1992), 'Audiovisual Policy and Cultural Indentity in Small European States: The Challenge of a Unified Market', *Media, Culture and Society*, Vol. 14, No. 2, pp. 169–184.

Burns, T. (1977), *The BBC. Public Institution and Private World*, London: Macmillan.

Calcutt, D. (1990), *Report of the Committee on Privacy and Related Matters*, London: HMSO, Cm. 1102.

Calcutt, D. (1993), *Review of Press Self-regulation*, London: HMSO, Cm 2135.

Cayrol, R. (1991), *Les Médias: Presse écrite, radio, télévision*, Paris: Presses Universitaires de France.

Coliver, S. (1993), 'Comparative Analysis of Press Law in European and Other Democracies', in Article 19, *Press Law and Practice*, London: Article 19, pp. 255–290.

Collins, R. (1992), *Satellite Television in Western Europe*, London: John Libbey.

Collins, R. (1994), *Broadcasting and Audio-Visual Policy in the European Single Market*, London: John Libbey.

Commission of the European Communities (1983), *Realities and Tendencies in European Television: Perspectives and Options*. Brussels: COM (83) 229 final.

Commission of the European Communities (1984), *Television without Frontiers. Green Paper on the Establishment of the Common Market for Broadcasting Especially by Satellite and Cable*, Brussels: COM (84) 300 final.

Commission of the European Communities (1990), *Communication by the Commission to the Council and to the European Parliament on Audiovisual Policy*: COM (90) 78.

Commission of the European Communities (1992a), *Pluralism and Media Concentration in the Internal Market*, Brussels: COM (92) 480 final.

Commission of the European Communities (1992b), 'European Community Audiovisual Policy', *European File*, No. 6.

Commission of the European Communities (1993), *Growth, Competitiveness and Employment: The Challenges and Ways Forward into the Twenty First Century*: COM (93) 700 final, 5 December 1993.

Commission of the European Communities (1994a), *Europe and the Global Information Society; Recommendations to the EC*, (The Bangemann Report), Brussels: European Commission, 25 May 1995.

Commission of the European Communities (1994b), *Strategy Options to Strengthen the European Programme Industry in the Context of the Audiovisual Policy of the European Union – Green Paper*: COM (94) 96 final.

Commission of the European Communities (1994c), *Communication from the Commission to the Council and the European Parliament: Follow-up to the Consultation Process Relating to the Green Paper on 'Pluralism and Media Concentration in the Internal Market – An Assessment of the Need for Community Action'*, Brussels: COM (94) 353 final.

Council of the European Communities (1989), *Directive on the Coordination of Certain Provisions Laid Down by Law, Regulation or Administrative Action in Member States Concerning the Pursuit of Television Broadcasting Activities*, 89/552/EEC, *Official Journal of the European Communities*, L 298/23, 17/10/89.

Council of Europe (1988), *European Ministerial Conference on Mass Media Policy. Vienna 9–10 December 1986. Proceedings of the Conference*, Strasbourg: Council of Europe.

Curran, J. & Seaton, J. (1991), *Power Without Responsibility: the Press and*

Broadcasting in Britain, London/New York: Routledge (fourth edition).

Dai, X., Cawson, A. & Holmes, P. (1994), 'Competition, Collaboration and Public Policy: A Case Study of the European HDTV Strategy', *Working Papers in Contemporary European Studies*, No. 3, Sussex European Institute, University of Sussex.

Darschin, W. & Frank, B. (1993), 'Tendenzen im Zuschauerverhalten', *Media Perspektiven*, 3/93, pp. 114–126.

De Bens, E. (1992), 'Belgium', in B. Østergaard (ed.), *The Media in Western Europe: The Euromedia Handbook*, London/Newbury Park/New Delhi: Sage, pp. 16–32.

De Bens, E., Kelly, M. and Bakke, M. (1992), 'Television Content: Dallasification of Culture?', in K. Siune & W. Truetzschler (eds), *Dynamics of Media Politics: Broadcast and Electronic Media in Western Europe*, London: Sage.

de Mateo, R. and Corbella, J. (1992), 'Spain', in B. Østergaard (ed.), *The Media in Western Europe: The Euromedia Handbook*, London/Newbury Park/New Delhi: Sage, pp. 192–206.

Department of National Heritage (1994), *The Future of the BBC: Serving the Nation, Competing Worldwide*, London: HMSO.

Desmond, R. (1978), *The Information Process: World News Reporting to the Twentieth Century*, Iowa City: University of Iowa Press.

Dimitras, P. (1992), 'Radio und Fernsehen in Griechenland', in Hans-Bredow-Institut (ed.), *Internationales Handbuch für Rundfunk und Fernsehen 1992/93*, Baden-Baden/Hamburg: NomosVerlagsgesellschaft, pp. D106–114.

Dunnett, P. (1988), *The World Newspaper Industry*, London/New York/Sydney: Croom Helm.

Dunnett, P. (1990), *The World Television Industry: An Economic Analysis*, London/New York: Routledge.

Dyson, K. (1977), *Party, State and Bureaucracy in West Germany*, London: Sage.

Dyson, K. (1980), *The State Tradition in Western Europe*, Oxford: Martin Robertson.

Dyson, K. (1990), 'Luxembourg: Changing Anatomy of an International Broadcasting Power', in K. Dyson & P. Humphreys (eds), *The Political Economy of Communications: International and European Dimensions*, London/New York: Routledge, pp. 125–147.

Dyson, K. (1992), 'Regulatory Culture and Regulatory Change in German Broadcasting', in K. Dyson (ed.), *The Politics of German Regulation*, Aldershot: Dartmouth, pp. 79–104.

Dyson, K. & Humphreys, P. (1986), 'Policies for New Media in Western Europe: Deregulation of Broadcasting and Multimedia Diversification', in K. Dyson & P. Humphreys (eds), *The Politics of the Communications*

Revolution in Western Europe, London: Frank Cass, pp. 98–124.

Dyson, K. & Humphreys, P. with Negrine, R. and Simon, J.-P. (1988), Broadcasting and New Media Policies in Western Europe, London/New York: Routledge.

Dyson, K. & Humphreys, P. (1989), 'Deregulating Broadcasting: the West European experience', European Journal of Political Research, Vol. 17, No. 2., pp. 137–154.

Dyson K. & Humphreys, P. (eds), (1990), The Political Economy of Communications: International and European Dimensions, London/New York: Routledge.

Eisendrath, C. (1982), 'Press Freedom in France: Private Ownership and State Controls', Chapter 3 in J.L. Curry & J.R. Dassin (eds), Press Control Around the World, New York: Praeger, pp. 62–84.

Errera, R. (1993), 'France', in Article 19, Press Law and Practice, London: Article 19, pp. 57–77.

Etzioni-Halevy, E. (1987), National Broadcasting Under Siege. A Comparative Study of Australia, Britain, Israel and West Germany, Basingstoke: Macmillan.

European Institute for the Media (1988), Europe 2000: What Kind of Television?, Report of the European Television Task Force, Media Monograph No. 11, Manchester: EIM.

European Parliament (1982a), Report on Radio and Television Broadcasting in the European Community on Behalf of the Committee on Youth, Culture, Education, Information and Sport (The Hahn Report). PE Document – 1–1013/81.

European Parliament (1982b), Resolution on Radio and Television Broadcasting in the European Community (The Hahn Resolution), OJ. 87 5.4.82., pp. 110–112.

European Parliament, (1990), Resolution on Media Takeovers and Mergers, OJ. C 68/137–138.

European Parliament, (1992a), Report by the Committee on Culture, Youth, Education and the Media: Media Concentration and the Diversity of Opinion, DOC EN/RR/207249, Strasbourg: European Parliament.

European Parliament, (1992b), Resolution of 16 September 1992 on Media Concentration and Diversity of Opinions, OJ. C 2.84, 2.11.92, p. 44.2.

Flichy, P. (1984), 'Media Control in France: Conflict between Political and Economic Rationale', in V. Mosco and J. Wasko (eds), Critical Communications Review, Vol. 2: 'Changing Patterns of Communication Control', Norwood New Jersey: Ablex Pub. Corp.

Franklin, B. & Murphy, D. (1991), What News? The Market, Politics and the Local Press, London/New York: Routledge.

Franklin, B. (1994), Packaging Politics: Political Communications in Britain's Media Democracy, London/New York/Melbourne/Auckland: Edward

Arnold.

Fraser, M. (1993), 'Television without Frontiers: Decoding European Broadcasting Policy'. Paper presented at the conference: 'The Impact of EU Action on National Policy and Policy-Making in the Industrial, Financial and Service Sectors', Centre for European Politics, Economics and Society, University of Oxford, 10–11 December 1993.

Friedman, A. (1988), *Agnelli and the Network of Italian Power*, London: Harrap.

Gavin, B. (ed.) (1991), *European Broadcasting Standards in the 1990s*, Oxford: NCC Blackwell.

Gross, H.-W. (1982), *Die Deutsche Presse-Agentur*, Frankfurt (Main): Haag & Herchen Verlag.

Guillou, B. (1984), *Les Stratégies Multimédias des Groupes de Communication*, Paris: La Documentation Française, Notes et Études Documentaires, No. 4763.

Gurevitch, M. & Blumler, J. (1977), 'Mass Media and Political Institutions: the Systems Approach', in S. Gerbner (ed.), *Mass Media Policies in Changing Cultures*, New York: John Wiley & Sons, pp. 251–268.

Gustafsson, K. & Hadenius, S (1976), *Swedish Press Policy*, Stockholm: Sweden Books.

Gustafsson, K. (1992), 'Sweden', in B. Østergaard (ed.), *The Media in Western Europe: The Euromedia Handbook*, London/Newbury Park/New Delhi: Sage Publications.

Hanley, D., Kerr, A., & Waites, N. (1984) *Contemporary France: Politics and Society since 1945*, London/New York: Routledge & Kegan Paul (revised edition).

Hardt, H. (1983), 'Press Freedom in Western Societies' in L.J. Martin & A.G. Chaudhary (eds), *Comparative Mass Media Systems*, New York: Longman, pp. 291–308.

Harris, R. (1990), *Good and Faithful Servant*, London: Faber & Faber.

Hayward, J. (1983), *Governing France*, London: Weidenfeld & Nicolson (second edition).

Hirsch, M. (1986), 'Belgium', in H.J. Kleinsteuber *et al.* (eds), *Electronic Media and Politics in Western Europe*, Frankfurt/New York: Campus, pp. 17–28.

Hirsch, M. (1992), 'Luxembourg', Chapter 10 in B. Østergaard (ed.), *The Media in Western Europe: the Euromedia Handbook*, London: Sage, pp. 143–151.

Hirsch, M. & Petersen, V. (1992), 'Regulation of media at the European Level', Chapter 4 in K. Siune & W. Truetzschler (eds), *Dynamics of Media Politics: Broadcast and Electronic Media in Western Europe*, London: Sage, pp. 42–56.

Hitchens, L. (1994), 'Media Ownership and Control: A European

Approach', *Modern Law Review*, Vol. 57, pp. 585–601.

Hoffmann-Riem, W. (1984), 'Tendenzen der Kommerzialisierung im Rund-funksystem', *Rundfunk und Fernsehen*, Vol. 32, 1.

Hoffmann-Riem, W. (1986), 'Law, Politics and the New Media: Trends in Broadcasting Regulation', in Kenneth Dyson and Peter Humphreys (eds), *The Politics of the Communications Revolution in Western Europe*, London: Frank Cass, pp. 125–146.

Hoffmann-Riem, W. (1987), 'National Identity and Cultural Values: Broad-casting standards', *Journal of Broadcasting and Electronic Media*, Vol. 31, No. 1, pp. 55–72.

Hoffmann-Riem, W. (1989), 'Medienstädte im Wettbewerb', *Medien Jour-nal*, 2/1989, pp. 66–76.

Hoffmann-Riem, W. (ed.), (1992), *Media and the Law: the Changing Land-scape of Western Europe*, Special Issue of *European Journal of Communi-cation*, Vol. 7, No. 2, June 1992.

Hollstein, M. (1983), 'Media Economics in Western Europe', in L.J. Martin & A.G. Chaudhary (eds), *Comparative Mass Media Systems*, New York: Longman, pp. 241–264.

Hood, S. (1983), *On Television*, London: Pluto Press.

Hultén, O. (1984), *Mass Media & State Support in Sweden*, Stockholm: The Swedish Institute.

Humphreys, P. (1991), 'Political Structures and Broadcasting Marketisation: A Comparison of Britain and West Germany', in M. Moran & M. Wright (eds), *The Market and the State: Studies in Interdependence*, Houndmills, Basingstoke: Macmillan.

Humphreys, P. (1992), 'The European Community and Pan-European Broadcasting', *Journal of Area Studies*, Vol. 1, No. 1, pp. 97–114.

Humphreys, P. (1994), *Media and Media Policy in Germany: The Press and Broadcasting since 1945*, Oxford/Providence, RI: Berg.

Jones, B. (1991), 'The Mass Media and Politics', Chapter 12 in B. Jones *et al.*, *Politics UK*, New York/Toronto/Sydney/Tokyo/Singapore: Philip Allan, pp. 200–223.

Kaid, L. & Holtz-Bacha, C. (1995), *Political Advertising in Western Democ-racies: Parties and Candidates on Television*, London: Sage.

Karpen, U. (1993), 'Germany', in Article 19, *Press Law and Practice*, London: Article 19, pp. 78–97.

Katsoudas, D. (1985), 'Greece: A Politically Controlled State Monopoly Broadcasting System', in R. Kuhn (ed.), *Broadcasting and Politics in West-ern Europe*, London: Frank Cass, pp. 137–151.

Katz, R. & Mair, P. (1995), 'Changing Models of Party Organization and Party Democracy: The Emergence of the Cartel Party', *Party Politics*, Vol. 1, No. 1, pp. 5–28.

Katzenstein, P. (1985), *Small States in World Markets: Industrial Policy in*

Europe, Ithaca, NY: Cornell University Press.

Keane, J. (1991), *The Media and Democracy*, Cambridge: Polity.

Keane, J. (1992), 'Democracy and the Media: Without Foundations', *Political Studies*, Vol. 40, Special Issue on 'Prospects for Democracy', pp. 116–129.

Keeler, J. & Stone, A. (1987), 'Judicial–Political Confrontation in Mitterrand's France', Chapter 9, in George Ross, Stanley. Hoffmann & Sylvia Malzacher (eds), *The Mitterrand Experiment*, Cambridge: Polity, pp. 161–181.

Kellas, J. (1989), *The Scottish Political System*, Cambridge: Cambridge University Press.

Kepplinger, H.-M. (1982), *Massenkommunikation*, Stuttgart: Teubner Studienskripten.

Kiefer, M.-L. (1992), 'Partikularinteressen als Leitlinie: zu den rundfunkpolitischen Vorstellungen des VPRT', *Media Perspektiven*, 10/92, pp. 614–623.

Kleinsteuber, H. (1982), *Rundfunkpolitik in der Bundesrepublik*, Opladen: Leske Verlag & Budrich GmbH.

Kleinsteuber, H. (1986), 'Federal Republic of Germany' in H.-J. Kleinsteuber, D. McQuail and K. Siune (eds), *Electronic Media and Politics in Western Europe*, Frankfurt/New York: Campus Verlag.

Kleinsteuber, H. (1990), 'Europäische Medienpolitik am Beispiel der EG-Fernsehrichtlinie', in H.J. Kleinsteuber, V. Wiesner & P. Wilke (eds), *EG-Medienpolitik: Fernsehen in Europa zwischen Kultur und Kommerz*, Berlin: Vistas Verlag, pp. 35–54.

Kleinsteuber, H. (1993), 'Mediensysteme in vergleichender Perspektive: zur Anwendung komparativer Ansätze in der Medienwissenschaft: Probleme und Beispiele', *Rundfunk und Fernsehen*, Vol. 41, No. 3, pp. 317–338.

Kleinsteuber, H., McQuail, D. and Sinne, K. (eds), (1986), *Electronic Media and Politics in Western Europe*, Frankfurt/New York: Campus.

Kleinsteuber, H., Wiesner V. & Wilke, P. (1990), (eds), *EG-Medienpolitik: Fernsehen in Europa zwischen Kultur und Kommerz*, Berlin: Vistas Verlag.

Kleinsteuber, H., Wiesner, V. & Wilke, P. (1991), 'Public Broadcasting im internationalen Vergleich', *Rundfunk und Fernsehen*, Vol. 39, No. 1, pp. 33–54.

Kleinsteuber, H. & Wilke, P. (1992), 'Germany', in B. Østergaard (ed.), *The Media in Western Europe: The Euromedia Handbook*, London/Newbury Park/New Delhi: Sage, pp. 75–94.

Krüger, U. (1992), 'Kontinuität und Wandel im Programmangebot', *Media Perspektiven*, 6/93, pp. 246–266.

Krüger, U. (1993), 'Kontinuität und Wandel im Programmangebot', *Media Perspektiven*, 6/93, pp. 246–266.

Kuhn, R. (1985a), (ed.), *The Politics of Broadcasting*, London: Croom Helm.

Kuhn, R. (1985b), 'France and the New Media', West European Politics, Vol. 8, No. 2, pp. 50–66.

Kuhn, R. (1988), 'Satellite Broadcasting in France', in R. Negrine (ed.), Satellite Broadcasting: The Politics and Implications of the New Media, London/New York: Routledge, pp. 176–195.

Kuhn, R. (1995), The Media in France, London/New York: Routledge.

Lange, A. & Renaud, J.-L. (1989), The Future of the European Audiovisual Industry, Manchester: European Institute for the Media, Media Monograph No. 10.

Lensen, A. (1992), Concentration in the Media Industry: The European Community and Mass Media Regulation, Washington DC:The Annenburg Washington Program, Northwestern University.

Les dossiers du Canard (1984), La Presse en Revue, Paris. No. 10, March–April, (Special Issue on the French Press).

Lindblom, C. (1977), Politics and Markets, New York: Basic Books.

Lijphart, A. (1984), Democracies: Patterns of Majoritarian and Consensus Government in Twenty-one Countries, New Haven: Yale University Press.

Lopez-Escobar, E. (1992), 'Spanish Media Law: Changes in the Landscape', in W. Hoffmann-Riem, (ed.), Media and the Law: The Changing Landscape of Western Europe, Special Issue of European Journal of Communication, Vol. 7, No. 2, pp. 241–260.

Lopez-Escobar, E. & Faus-Belau, A. (1985), 'Broadcasting in Spain: A History of Heavy-handed State Control', in R. Kuhn (ed.), Broadcasting and Politics in Western Europe, London: Frank Cass, pp. 122–136.

Lorimer, R. (1994), with Scannell, P., Mass Communications, Manchester/New York: Manchester University Press.

Manschot, B. & Rodenburg, M. (1990), 'Broadcasting in the Netherlands', Medien Journal, No. 3, pp. 133–141.

Marsh, D. (1993), 'The Media and Politics', in P. Dunleavy et al. (eds), Developments in British Politics, Basingstoke: Macmillan (fourth edition), pp. 332–352.

Mathes, R. & Pfetsch, B. (1991), 'The Role of the Alternative Press in the Agenda-building Process: Spill-over Effects and Media Opinion Leadership', European Journal of Communication, Vol. 6, pp. 32–62.

Mattelart, A. & Palmer, M. (1991), 'Advertising in Europe: Promises, Pressures and Pitfalls', Media, Culture and Society, Vol. 13, No. 4, pp. 535–556.

Mayer, W. (1993), 'The Rights and Responsibilities of Journalists and the Means of Upholding Them in the West', International Affairs, Moscow: No. 9, pp. 13–18. (Proceedings of an International Colloquium, into 'Conditions for the Economic and Political Independence of the Media', Moscow: 19–22 June 1993.)

Mazzoleni, G. (1991), 'Media Moguls in Italy', Chapter 6 in J. Tunstall &

M. Palmer, *Media Moguls*, London/New York: Routledge, pp. 162–183.

Mazzoleni, G. (1992a), 'Is There a Question of Vulnerable Values in Italy?,' in J. Blumler (ed.), *Television and the Public Interest*, London: Sage.

Mazzoleni, G. (1992b), 'Italy' in B. Østergaard (ed.), *The Media in Western Europe: the Euromedia Handbook*, London: Sage, pp. 123–142.

Mazzoleni, G. (1994), 'Italy', in J. Mitchell & J. Blumler (eds), *Television and the Viewer Interest: Explorations in the Responsiveness of European Broadcasters*, London: John Libbey/European Institute for the Media, Media Monograph No.18, pp. 123–134.

McQuail, D. (1987), *Mass Communication Theory: An Introduction*, London/Newbury Park. Beverley Hills/New Delhi: Sage (second edition).

McQuail, D. (1992a), 'The Netherlands: Safeguarding Freedom and Diversity under Multichannel Conditions', Chapter 7 in J. Blumler (ed.), *Television and the Public Interest: Vulnerable Values in West European Broadcasting*, London/Newbury Park/New Delhi: Sage.

McQuail, D. (1992b), *Media Performance: Mass Communication and the Public Interest*, London: Sage.

McQuail, D. & Siune, K. (eds) (1986), *New Media Politics: Comparative Perspectives in Western Europe*, London: Sage.

Media Perspektiven. Basisdaten (1993). These are regular booklets of data on the German media published by the journal *Media Perspektiven*.

Meier, W. & Trappel, J. (1992), 'Small States in the Shadow of Giants', Chapter 9 in K. Siune & W. Truetzschler (eds), *Dynamics of Media Politics: Broadcast and Electronic Media in Western Europe*, London: Sage, pp. 129–142.

Miliband, R. (1969), *The State in Capitalist Society*, London: Quartet.

Milne, A. (1988), *DG: Memoirs of a British Broadcaster*, London: Hodder & Stoughton.

Minc, A. (1993), *Le Média Choc*, Paris: Grasset.

Mitchell, J. & Blumler, J. (eds), (1994), *Television and the Viewer Interest: Explorations in the Responsiveness of European Broadcasters*, London: John Libbey/European Institute for the Media, Media Monograph No. 18.

Negrine, R. (ed.), (1985), *Cable Television and the Future of Broadcasting*, London: Croom Helm.

Negrine, R. (1988), (ed.), *Satellite Broadcasting: The Politics and Implications of the New Media*, London/New York: Routledge.

Negrine, R. (1990), 'British Television in an Age of Change', in K. Dyson & P. Humphreys (eds), *The Political Economy of Communications: International and European Dimensions*, London/New York: Routledge, pp. 148–170.

Negrine, R. (1994), *Politics and the Mass Media in Britain*, London/New York: Routledge.

Negrine, R. & Papathanassopoulos, S. (1990), *The Internationalisation of*

Television, London/New York: Pinter Publishers.

Newton, K. & Artingstall, N. (1994), 'Government and Private Censorship in Nine Western Democracies in the 1970s and 1980s', Chapter 18 in Ian Budge and David McKay (eds), *Developing Democracy*, London: Sage, pp. 297–321.

Niblock, M. (1991), *The Future for HDTV in Europe*, Manchester: European Institute of the Media, Media Monograph No. 14.

Nicol, A. & Bowman, C. (1993), 'United Kingdom', in Article 19, *Press Law and Practice*, London: Article 19, pp. 167–191.

Nieuwenhuis, J. (1992), 'Media Policy in the Netherlands: Beyond the Market?', in W. Hoffmann-Riem (ed.), *Media and the Law: the Changing Landscape of Western Europe*, Special Issue of *European Journal of Communication*, Vol. 7, No. 2, pp. 195–218.

Østbye, H. (1986), 'Norway', in H. Kleinsteuber, D. McQuail & K. Siune (eds), *Electronic Media and Politics in Western Europe*, Frankfurt/New York: Campus.

Østbye, H. (1992), 'Norway' in B. Østergaard (ed.), *The Media in Western Europe: The Euromedia Handbook*, London/Newbury Park/New Delhi: Sage, pp. 167–182.

Østergaard, B. (1992), (ed.), *The Media in Western Europe: The Euromedia Handbook*, London/Newbury Park/New Delhi: Sage.

Palmer, M. and Tunstall, J. (1990), *Liberating Communications: Policy-making in France and Britain*, Oxford: Blackwell.

Panis, V. (1995), *Politique Audiovisuelle de l'Union et Identité Culturelle Européenne: La Position des Principaux Acteurs Institutionels face aux Quotas de Diffusion d'Oeuvres Européenes dans La Directive "Télévision Sans Frontières"*, Bruges: College of Europe, Department of Admistration and Politics, Thesis.

Papathanassopoulos, S. (1990a), 'Broadcasting, Politics and the State in Socialist Greece', *Media, Culture and Society*, Vol. 12, pp. 387–397.

Papathanassopoulos, S. (1990b), 'Broadcasting and the European Community: The Commission's audiovisual policy', in K. Dyson & P. Humphreys (eds), *The Political Economy of Communications: International and European Dimensions*, London/New York: Routledge, pp. 107–124.

Peak, S. (1993), *The Media Guide 1994*, London: Fourth Estate. A *Guardian* Book.

Peterson, J. (1993), *High Technology and the Competition State. An Analysis of the Eureka Initiative*, London/New York: Routledge.

Petersen, V. & Siune, K. (1992), 'Denmark' in B. Østergaard, (ed.), *The Media in Western Europe: The Euromedia Handbook*, London/Newbury Park/New Delhi: Sage, pp. 33–46.

Porter, V. & Hasselbach, S. (1991), *Pluralism, Politics and the Marketplace: The Regulation of German Broadcasting*, London/New York, Routledge.

Pragnell, A. (1985), *Television in Europe. Quality and Values in a Time of Change*, Manchester: European Institute for the Media, Media Monograph No. 5.

Prosser, T. (1992), 'Public Service Broadcasting and Deregulation in the UK', in W. Hoffmann-Riem, (ed.), *Media and the Law: The Changing Landscape of Western Europe*, Special Issue of *European Journal of Communication*, Vol. 7, No. 2, pp. 173–194.

Quatrepoint J.-M., Le Boucher, E., Arnaud, D. and Mauduit, L. (1987), *Histoire Secrète des Dossiers Noirs de la Gauche*, Paris: éditions moreau.

Read, D. (1992), *The Power of News: The History of Reuters*, Oxford: Oxford University Press.

Ruck, S. (1992), 'Development of Broadcasting Law in the Federal Republic of Germany', in W. Hoffmann-Riem (ed.), *Media and the Law: The Changing Landscape of Western Europe*, Special Issue of *European Journal of Communication*, Vol. 7, No. 2, pp. 219–240.

Safran, W. (1985), *The French Polity*, New York/London: Longman.

Sánchez-Tabernero, A. with Denton, A., Lochon, P.-Y., Mounier, P. and Woldt, R. (1993), *Media Concentration in Europe: Commercial Enterprise and the Public Interest*, Düsseldorf: European Institute for the Media, Media Monograph No. 16.

Sandford, J. (1976), *The Mass Media of the German-Speaking Countries*, London: Oswald Wolff.

Sassoon, D. (1986), *Contemporary Italy: Politics, Economy and Society since 1945*, London/New York: Longman.

Schenk, U. (1985), *Nachrichtenagenturen*, Berlin: Vistas Verlag.

Schoenbaum, D. (1968), *The Spiegel Affair*, Garden City, New York: Doubleday.

Schütz, W. (1985), 'Zeitungen in der Bundesrepublik Deutschland', in *Die Presse in der deutschen Medienlandschaft*, Bonn: Bundeszentrale für politische Bildung, Themenheft 6, pp. 13–24.

Schütz, W. (1991), 'Deutsche Tagespresse 1991', *Media Perspektiven*, 2/92, pp. 72–107.

Schütz, W. (1994), 'Deutsche Tagespresse 1993', *Media Perspektiven*, 4/94, pp. 168–198.

Sepstrup, P. (1989), 'Implications of Current Developments in West European Broadcasting', *Media, Culture and Society*, Vol. 11, pp. 29–54.

Servaes, J. (1988), 'Neue Trends in der belgischen Presse', *Media Perspektiven*, 6/88, pp. 338–346.

Seymour-Ure, C. (1974), *The Political Impact of the Mass Media*, London: Constable.

Seymour-Ure, C. (1991), *The British Press and Broadcasting Since 1945*, Oxford: Basil Blackwell.

Siebert, F., Peterson, T. & Schramm, W. (1956), *Four Theories of the Press*,

Urbana/Chicago/London: University of Illinois Press (eleventh paperback printing, 1978).

Siune, K. & McQuail, D. (1992), 'Conclusion', in K. Siune & W. Truetzschler, (eds), *Dynamics of Media Politics: Broadcast and Electronic Media in Western Europe*, the Euromedia Research Group, London: Sage, pp. 190–199.

Siune, K. & Truetzschler, W. (eds), (1992), *Dynamics of Media Politics: Broadcast and Electronic Media in Western Europe*, the Euromedia Research Group, London: Sage.

Siune, K., McQuail, D. & Truetzchler, W. (1992), 'Setting the Scene', Chapter 1 in K. Siune & W. Truetzschler (eds), *Dynamics of Media Politics: Broadcast and Electronic Media in Western Europe*, the Euromedia Research Group, London: Sage, pp. 1–7.

Smith, A. (1978), *The Politics of Information: Problems of Policy in Modern Media*, London & Basingstoke: Macmillan.

Sonnenberg, U. (1990), 'Programmangebote und Programmproduktion in den Ländern der Europäischen Gemeinschaft', in H.J. Kleinsteuber *et al..*, *EG-Medienpolitik: Fernsehen in Europa zwischen Kultur und Kommerz*, Berlin: Vistas.

Sorbets, C. & Palmer, M. (1986), 'France', in H.J. Kleinsteuber *et al.* (eds), *Electronic Media and Politics in Western Europe*, Frankfurt/New York: Campus, pp. 87–109.

Stenholm, O. (1993), 'Protecting Society from Abuse of Freedom of the Press, *International Affairs*, Moscow: No. 9, pp. 13–18. (Proceedings of an International Colloquium, into 'Conditions for the Economic and Political Independence of the Media', Moscow: 19–22 June 1993.)

Tapper, H. (1992), 'Finland', in B. Østergaard (ed.), *The Media in Western Europe: The Euromedia Handbook*, London/Newbury Park/New Delhi: Sage, pp. 47–56.

Todorov, P. (1990), *La Presse Française à l'Heure de l'Europe*, Paris: Documentation Française.

Trappel, J. (1991), *Medien – Macht – Markt: Medienpolitik westeuropäischer Kleinstaaten*, Vienna: Österreichischer Kunst-und Kulturverlag.

Trappel, J. (1992), 'Austria', in B. Østergaard (ed.), *The Media in Western Europe: The Euromedia Handbook*, London/Newbury Park/New Delhi: Sage.

Tunstall, J. (1984), 'Media Policy Dilemmas and Indecisions', *Parliamentary Affairs*, Vol. 37, No. 3, pp. 310–326.

Tunstall, J. & Palmer, M. (1991), *Media Moguls*, London/New York: Routledge.

van Lenthe, F. & Boerefijn, I. (1993), 'Netherlands', in Article 19, *Press Law and Practice*, London: Article 19, pp. 98–115.

Varis, T. (1984), 'The International Flow of Television Programmes', *Jour-*

nal of Communication, Vol. 34, No. 1, pp. 143–152.

Varis, T. (1985), *International Flow of Television Programmes*, Reports and Papers on Mass Communication, No. 100. Paris: UNESCO.

Vasconcelos, A.-P., Cotta, M., Fleischmann, P., Balmaseda, E., Puttnam, D. and Stuchi, G. (1994), *Report of the Think-Tank on the Audiovisual Policy in the European Union*, Luxembourg: Office for the Official Publications of the European Communities.

Vaughan, M. (1985), 'In Search of Pluralism: The Broadcasting Media in France', *Journal of Area Studies*, No. 12, Double Issue Part II, pp. 20–23.

Veljanovski, C. (ed.), (1989), *Freedom in Broadcasting*, London: Institute of Economic Affairs.

Veljanovski, C. (1990), *The Media in Britain Today: The Facts, the Figures*, London: News International.

Wagner, J. (1994), *Policy-Analyse: Grenzenlos Fernsehen in der EG*, Frankfurt/Main: Peter Lang.

Williams, P. (1972), *Crisis and Compromise: Politics of the Fourth Republic*, London Longman.

Williams, A. (1976), *Broadcasting and Democracy in West Germany*, London: Bradford University Press/Crosby Lockwood Staples.

Wilson, H.H. (1961), *Pressure Group: The Campaign for Commercial TV*, London: Secker & Warburg.

Wimmer, K. (1992), 'Struktur und Einfluss der Medien', in W. Mantl (ed.), *Politik in Österreich*, Vienna: Bohlen, pp. 479–499.

Wolland, S. (1993), 'Norway', in Article 19, *Press Law and Practice*, London: Article 19, pp. 116–130.

Wolton, D. (1992), 'Values and Normative Choices in French Television', Chapter 10 in Jay Blumler (ed.), *Television and the Public Interest: Vulnerable Values in West European Broadcasting*, London: Sage, pp. 147–160.

Index